LIBRARY LIT. 7 - The Best of 1976

edited by

BILL KATZ

The Scarecrow Press, Inc.

Metuchen, N.J.   1977

R-f.
Z
671
.L702
1976

CONTENTS

INTRODUCTION

Once more--the 30 best articles published between November 1975 and November 1976. In this seventh consecutive gathering there is a good representation of information and persuasion to neutralize "the incredible stream of garbage."

There is, it is true, a considerable amount of less than readable library material published each year. If it is the antithesis of what we have come to expect from our daily reading of the press, it is at least an honest effort to proctor the world of libraries and librarians, and having rambled through about 120 library periodicals over the past year, I don't think things are quite as bad as some believe. The yoke of boredom isn't that obvious and much comes close to being added to the group of articles for consideration.

Eventually one must get down to the final 60 or 70 pieces, where it becomes increasingly difficult to separate the best from the better. At this point the judges gather and decide which of the group is to be included. It is a fairly frustrating experience, particularly when one's favorite piece is gently nudged out of further consideration.

A glance back through other introductions for other years will tell the curious how the choices are made, although briefly it is a matter of weighing style with content, new, imaginative ideas with what the judges consider to be the interests of the readers. The present writer aside, a glance at the names of the judges should convince even the most skeptical that those judges know something about libraries and librarians. Still, the match is not always perfect, and anyone who thinks an area has been skipped over is invited to submit nominations for next year's effort. This, by the way, is an open invitation to one and to all--send citations of suitable articles. We need all the help we can get from you, the reader.

Lacking any particular fascination with statistics, I can't necessarily claim this to be true, but it does seem to me that the articles are getting shorter, certainly less and less trying to mimic War and Peace. The writers may have discovered the diminutive. It is a sometimes pleasant change, and one which is followed in the present introduction.

Bill Katz
Library School
SUNY-Albany
Albany, N.Y.

ACKNOWLEDGMENTS

The 1976 Jury

The jurors who selected the 30 best articles this year were: Janet Klaessig, Director, Guilderland Public Library; Patricia Glass Schuman, President of Neal Schuman Associates; John N. Berry III, Editor of Library Journal; Eric Moon, President, Scarecrow Press and President-elect of the American Library Association; and the perennial juror, Bill Katz.

Thank you, Ms. Andrea Tarr

As usual, the real work of putting this volume together is due to a graduate assistant--in this case the capable, equally blessed with a sense of humor, Ms. Andrea Tarr.

PART I

LIBRARIES AND LIBRARIANS

THE OPINIONATED LIBRARIAN*

Aristides

A bookish person, I live, naturally enough, surrounded by books. Bookcases are in my living room, in my hallways, in my dining room; in my bedroom stand five unmatched bookcases, not only jammed full but spilling over, with books and magazines lined up atop them. Books do furnish a room, as the saying goes, but at my place they bid fair to take over the joint. The mailman groans under the load of my purchases from Marboro, Blackwells, Strand, and various publishers. One morning I expect to wake up, walk into my bathroom, and find written in shaving cream on the mirror, in the style of the old maniac-killer movies, "Stop Me Before I Buy More Books." To prevent this happening, I made what for me is a radical decision: to trim down my personal library. Although I did not know it when I first set out to do this, I was engaged in a task of the most intimate literary criticism.

I recall a conversation I had some years ago with a man who has a reputation for living simply. He is an engineer by training, a photographer by interest, and, though not bookish, very intelligent about the books he does read. We talked about a book he had just read. I do not remember its title, but the book had recently come out, so he could only have read it in a cloth edition. He made it sound most interesting, and so I asked him if he would let me have a look at it. "Oh," he said, "I am afraid that after finishing it I threw it in the garbage." Stunned does not begin to describe my reaction to this act. For days afterward I rolled it around in my head, trying to get it straight. He had bought a new book in a cloth edition, read it--actually rather liked it in the bargain--and, when finished, slipped it into the garbage as if it were an empty wine bottle. Was

*Reprinted by permission of the author and publisher from American Scholar, Vol. 45, No. 1, Winter 1975, pp. 709-171. Copyright © 1975 by the United Chapters of Phi Beta Kappa.

4

the man a barbarian? Or merely sensibly efficient? Was I contemptuous of such an act? Or secretly envious?

Put aside those questions for a bit while I attempt to draw the reader's tears. As a boy, I did not grow up in a bookish home. But through one of those accidents that go by the name of Fate, I caught the fever in college and soon became irrevocably bookish. When I read a book, I kept it, rather like a Boy Scout badge to display achievement earned. An habitué of secondhand bookstores on Fourth Avenue and University Place in New York, I also bought a goodly number of books--desert-island specials, as I thought of them-- that I hoped one day to get around to reading. In this way I compiled a library of, roughly, three or four hundred books. Nothing fancy, but a literary man's library containing the modernist writers, the great nineteenth-century Russian, French, and English novelists, Americans of the 1920s, some history, the standard philosophers--small, as personal collections of books go, but mine own. Then I found myself having to make a move, at my own expense, across the country. Because I was a young married man with small children, economy measures were forced upon me. Moving books is expensive, so I decided to make the supreme sacrifice and sell my library. A man from the Argosy Bookstore on University Place was called in, and for the price of $135 he carried several loads in a laundry cart from my apartment to his station wagon. A pitiable sight I must have made--a child watching the Christmas tree being taken down on December 23. Of all the books I had acquired I saved only six or seven thin volumes of Max Beerbohm's essays, Macaulay's four-volume History of England (which I have yet to read all the way through), and a luscious green cloth-covered Bodley Head edition of James Joyce's Ulysses.

The story has what I suppose is a happy ending. I now sit in an apartment with approximately twelve or thirteen hundred books around me. I have reacquired all my Edmund Wilson volumes, my magnificent Russians, my Americans, my Frenchmen and Englishmen, and added a great deal besides. The character of my library, though still chiefly literary, has changed somewhat to match my changing interests: more history, more autobiography and memoir, a bit more philosophy, less drama, and (a new item) many volumes on language and usage. It is a reader's library, though, more than a scholar's. There is little in it that cannot be found even in a mediocre university library or purchased in paperback. Often I find it useful to have these books on hand--

when preparing a lecture or writing a piece--but not too often.
Like a diamond stickpin, or for that matter a Phi Beta Kappa
key, my personal library is not altogether functional.

Let me now go on to a bloodcurdling story, though one
that can only curdle the blood of the bookish. I see fairly
frequently a writer of international celebrity. He gets heavy
mail, much of it of a bookish kind. Bound galleys and review copies flood into his home, propelled by the dreams of
publishers and writers that he will read these books, be
swept up by them to the point of championing them in a public way: by supplying a blurb or perhaps writing a review.
An intellectual to the bone, he is a wide-ranging and vora-
cious reader, but a man has his limits even if publishers,
apparently, do not. On occasion he has asked me if I cared
to have any of the books recently sent to him. I too have
my limits, and once, when I chose not to take any from a
small pile he offered, he picked up the pile, walked over to
the incinerator in his kitchen, and dropped them down. I
gulped. Book-burning, for God's sake! He laughed, announcing, "I am the Torquemada of the thirteenth floor." My immediate impulse was to run down fourteen flights of stairs to
the basement and pull the books from the flames.

Obviously, I have not developed the degree of resistance of my friend--who is a virtual black belt, a monk
of the highest contemplative order when it comes to discrimination in such matters. I still cannot pass a secondhand
bookstore without going in. In England, I head straight for
Charing Cross Road--street of Foyles, of other used and
new bookstores, of a store filled to the ceiling with sleek
new Penguins. I read all catalogs, browse in all bins.

Books, like money, tend to bring out the neurotic
strain in the bookish. Some months ago, I was interested
to read in Walter Lacquer's memoir of his friend George
Leichtheim, the political writer, that Leichtheim was, in his
writing, unable to quote from any book he did not own. Others will not lay hand on a paperback. Still others will read
only books in British or foreign editions. I myself cannot
bear to read a book in which someone else has underlined
passages. I can read the books of V. S. Naipaul only in
Penguin editions, those of Theodore Dreiser only in cloth.

But along with being a tale of tears and of terror,
this is also a tale of human reform--it has an element of
uplift. In this aspect of the tale, necessity turns out to be

the mother not only of invention but of virtue.   A problem
of space and demand was involved.   To retain the books now
in my possession--and I do not speak of backlogs of issues
of magazines and journals--and to accommodate those that
continue to stream in, would necessitate radical measures:
move to a larger place, remove some ample piece of furni-
ture or major appliance to make room for more bookcases,
sell a child.   The alternative, only slightly less painful, was
clear: trim down my library by a hundred or so books and
possibly more.   But which books?

        The job might have been a good bit easier if my li-
brary contained a great many fifth-rate books--an ample collection of detective stories, say, or of science fiction.   But
nothing of the sort exists to make the job easier; rather than
fifth-rate, I have a good many second- and third-rate books.
All of them, alas, are serious books, many of them, as I survey them now, a bit too serious for my taste.   Many of them,
too, are not books that I went out and purchased, but are books
that over the years I have been asked to review or that I have
acquired in order to fulfill one or another literary task.   A personal library often represents a man's character or, if it consists largely of unread books, his aspirations.   But my library,
while doing both these things, also represents what others, chiefly editors, have thought of me.   Only my tailor measures me
correctly, said Dr. Johnson, who usually went about ill dressed.

        Attrition might make a start in cutting back my li-
brary, and by attrition I mean not to bother calling in those
volumes that I have lent to others.   One such volume is the
Letters of Lord Chesterfield, whose advice I am now probably too old to make much use of, and the friend who borrowed it several years ago has apparently not learned much
from it either (see Lord Chesterfield on punctuality).   Another volume out on loan is Edith Sitwell's English Eccen-
trics; because it is at the home of a friend who keeps more
books in smaller quarters than I do, more likely than not
the book is unfindable anyway.   The two volumes of Malcolm
Muggeridge's autobiography, Chronicles of Wasted Time,
which I enjoyed greatly, have been lent to the Torquemada
of the thirteenth floor.   Have they by now, I wonder, met
the flame?   No matter.   The author of Chronicles of Wasted
Time would probably agree that I ought not to waste any
more time on his books.

        Trimming down a library in this way makes me wish
I owned certain books I do not in fact own--if only for the

delight of getting rid of them.   The novels of Harrison Salis-
bury, if I owned them in the first place, would, I should
imagine, be easily jettisoned.   Books about show business,
about politics in Latin America, about auto racing; books
with titles that begin The Death of ... or The Politics of
...; books on new forms of psychotherapy, on urban renewal, on arms control--shelves and shelves of these, if
only I owned them, could go without a quiver of hesitation
on my part.

          But I am stalling.   The problem is, I have come to
have an unhealthy respect for books, and this is not lightly
shaken off.   Part of it is a respect for books generally, but
an even greater part is for the books I have acquired.   Walter
Benjamin, in an essay entitled "Unpacking My Library" in his
book Illuminations, a book I intend to retain in my library,
notes with characteristic subtlety: "Every passion borders
on the chaotic, but the collector's passion borders on the
chaos of memories.   More than that: the chance, the fate,
that suffuse the past before my eyes are conspicuously present in the accustomed confusion of these books.   For what
else is this collection but a disorder to which habit has accommodated itself to such an extent that it can appear as
order?"   A book in one's own library is in a sense a brick
in the building of one's being, carrying with it memories, a
small block of one's personal intellectual history, associations unsortable in their profusion.   Yet this building from
time to time needs landscaping, tuckpointing, sandblasting.

          Books on social problems seem good ones to begin
chipping away.   Social problems in America in recent years
seem to be distinguished by two special qualities: they are
perpetually changing and they are never solved.   They do
not really go away; instead people merely grow bored with
them.   Take an excellent book from my library, Robert
Penn Warren's Who Speaks for the Negro?   Most of those
who deigned so to speak--the book was published in 1965--
are by now dead, superannuated, or have lapsed into obscuri-
ty.   The Negro, in many quarters, isn't any longer even
called Negro.   Time has done the book in; turned a lively
and passionate work into a historical document.   My copy
happens to be in paperback and hence does not take up much
shelf space, so I shall keep it.   Another paperback in the
social problems realm that I shall relieve my shelves of is
an item entitled A Manual for Direct Action, which appeared
in the early 1960s and offered advice about staging sit-ins
and other protest demonstrations.   One small piece of its

advice, I recall, was for a demonstrator to wear two or
three pairs of underpants when sitting-in, so that if the police dragged him off at least his bottom would not get unduly
scraped.

     Children of Crisis, Robert Coles's three-volume work,
will, I am afraid, have to go. A few years back, I read its
more than 1,700 pages, most of them interviews, and I can
remember almost nothing about them, except for an impoverished Appalachian woman's observation that, after losing
one's first tooth, losing the rest of one's teeth comes much
easier.   (Why we remember what we remember from books
is itself a splendid and mysterious subject.)   Chances are
great that I shall not return to Dr. Coles's three volumes,
and they do take up a good deal of space.   Out, then.

     I should like to accomplish the task of trimming down
my library with an even hand politically.   Because Dr. Coles
has come to have something of a leftish reputation, it would
be well if I could match his departure from my shelves with
that of a writer from the Right--to keep, so to say, a certain political balance.   The books of William F. Buckley,
Jr. , are my choice.   He is further to the Right than Dr.
Coles is to the Left, true enough, but, more important than
such political niceties, the seven or eight books of his that
I own take up much more space.   Besides, Mr. Buckley is
better on television than in his books anyway, and should I
ever grow hungry for him, he will be within easy reach.

     Fiction is my next big cut, especially contemporary
fiction of very recent years.   Borges, Beckett, and Nabokov,
though I do not adore their work, may stay.   The work of
their imitators, or workers in the same vineyards--Barth-
elme, Barth, Gardner, and the rest--I have come to consider English department teaching aids, and no longer read
them.   They go.   Along with them goes a category of fiction that might be termed Last Year's Novel of the Year--
fiction of purported seriousness with high commercial possibilities.   Among such works that I am able to weed from
my shelves are American Mischief by Alan Lelchuk, Julian
by Gore Vidal, and Something Happened (nothing, incidentally,
did) by Joseph Heller.   I could, I suppose, get a jump on
next year right now by throwing out E. L. Doctorow's Rag-
time, This Year's Novel of the Year, but I think I shall
wait.   Continuing on in the dispensable fiction category, the
great Gravity's Rainbow question arises.   I found myself unable to finish reading Mr. Pynchon's blockbuster novel.   I

read only enough to realize it was a book on which one might
write an essay or deliver a lecture, but surely not read.   If
I go to my grave without reading it, which I figure to do,
this will not be my chief regret.   (A reviewer in a recent
issue of the Times Literary Supplement wistfully remarked
that, for all the liveliness of American fiction, there were
still moments when he yearned for the fiction of J. D. Salin-
ger: "One [moment] might occur on reading page 235 of
Pynchon's Gravity's Rainbow where the girl is defecating into the open mouth of Brigadier Pudding and you realize there
are 500 pages still to go. ")   Still, it is harder to get rid of
an unread than a read book.   Gravity's Rainbow, then, will
stay, the rationale for this decision being, "Best let sleeping
dogs lie. "

      As I go through these books of mine, criteria emerge.
One category marked for elimination is that of books I have
read but do not expect ever to return to.   Another category
is books I have bought but have not yet got around to reading
for the first time.   How many unread books there are in my
library I do not know.   Usually these volumes represent
failed aspirations.   Consider some of their titles: a biography of Benjamin Jowett, another of Anatole France, The
Selected Writings of Sydney Smith (introduction by W. H.
Auden), The Emergence of the Steppes: A History of Central Asia by René Grousset, Essays and Portraits in Anglo-
Jewish History by Cecil Roth, Manners and Morals in the
Age of Optimism by James Laver, Saint-Simon's Historical
Memoirs, and a beautifully bound and handsomely boxed
three-volume Bollingen edition of The Muqaddimah by Ibn
Khaldûn.   (This last is a work I first learned about from
the writings of A. J. Liebling, who not only once made a
pass at reviewing it but used regularly to quote and para-
phrase Khaldûn, the fourteenth-century Arab scholar, in his
own pieces on boxing, food, and the press.   What books I
now have of Liebling's, by the way, will stay, and I shouldn't
mind acquiring more.)   All these unread books, too, must
be retained, if only to show that I have not yet given up all
hope of self-betterment.

      Retained as well will be all those books I have par-
tially read, sometimes only dipped into.   Justice Holmes,
in a letter to Harold Laski, once said that he had a puritanical streak in matters of reading: he could not, till well
into his seventies, begin a book, no matter how poor it
proved, without finishing it.   What Holmes was able to
manage only in his seventies, I have been able to bring off

in my thirties. Among the partially read books in my li-
brary are William James's Principles of Psychology, Scho-
penhauer's The World as Will and Representation, Leslie
Stephen's English Thought in the Eighteenth Century, Van
Wyck Brooks's five-volume Makers and Finders, and Steven
Runciman's three-volume A History of the Crusades. But
I seem able to put aside less monumental works as well.
Sitting on my shelves with bookmarks still in them are E.
M. Forster's Goldsworthy Lowes Dickinson, Evelyn Waugh's
Msg. Ronald Knox, Henry Mayhew's London Underground,
and Albert Jay Nock's Memoirs of a Superfluous Man. All
these volumes will remain; I have hopes of completing them.
(I plan a long life.)

     The books of scholarly and intellectual and artistic
friends must remain too, although their number grows larger
as I grow older. Walter Benjamin notes that "of all the
ways of acquiring books, writing them oneself is regarded
as the most praiseworthy method. " Having friends who
write them is next best. The Torquemada of the thirteenth
floor, who is my secretly wished-for alter id in bibliographical matters, deals in a rougher justice here than I could
ever hope to accomplish. In a secondhand bookstore, I once
saw a book autographed for him by its author. I chuckled,
then chilled. I have not the courage to do the same: I too
much fear someone might do it to me. Also, I have always
been touched by a story, told in P. P. Howe's Life of William Hazlitt, about Wordsworth's first visit to the home of
Leigh Hunt, during which Hunt pointed out to Wordsworth a
copy of the Lyrical Ballads on his shelf next to the works
of Milton. Wordsworth, normally severe, is said to have
melted.

     I see that I make little progress. Time for a radi-
cal move, a slashing away to make space. With teeth grit-
ted in determination, I remove the entire contents of a four-
foot high bookcase holding years and years of back issues
of Commentary, Dissent, the TLS, the New York Review
of Books, Hudson Review, Prose, Partisan Review, Encounter, and Modern Occasions. I love--loved in the cases
of those magazines that are now defunct--these magazines,
have myself at one time or another contributed to most of
them, but efficiency here subdues enthusiasm. Macaulay
once commented that he felt that the life of any piece of intellectual journalism, his own included, was roughly six
weeks. He was mistaken about his own, of course, but
otherwise probably not too far off. The back issues of these

Libraries and Librarians   **11**

magazines go--with love, but go they do.

        The cleared space allows for rearranging shelves.
Virtue not being sufficiently its own reward, I take time out
for a bit of low-grade comic relief in the juxtaposing of
books. Next to Christopher Lasch's The Agony of the
American Left I insert Woody Allen's Without Feathers; next
to Nietzsche's My Sister and I, Caffi's A Critique of Vio-
lence; next to Silone's Bread and Wine, Brillat-Savarin's The
Physiology of Taste; next to Norman O. Brown's Love's
Body, Santayana's The Last Puritan; and, finally, between
Susan Sontag's Against Interpretation and Styles of Radical
Will I insert A. Alvarez's Beyond All This Fiddle.

        Back to work. My next cut is a fine one--many fat
volumes. These are the books of what might be termed the
"agitational culture": works that appear on the scene, make
a great flap (and much money), and then merely lie there.
The Kingdom and the Power by Gay Talese is such a book,
and the same author's Honor Thy Father is another. Out!
David Halberstam's The Best and the Brightest is yet another. Out! Tom Wolfe's The Kandy-Kolored Tangerine-
Flake Streamline Baby also goes with this lot. (Wolfe's The
Pump-House Gang, which I have in paperback, and which
consequently takes up less space, stays.) If Gloria Steinem
had written a book, or if I owned one by Andy Warhol, they
would be gone in this batch as well. Philip Roth's Our
Gang, which I do own, goes. I remember that Roth's Our
Gang and Talese's Honor Thy Father were reviewed in the
same week in the daily press, one reviewer saying of the
first that as satire it was of the quality of Swift, and another reviewer saying of the second that it surpassed Balzac.
I reported these findings to a friend, who commented: "We
sleep tonight--criticism stands guard." I sleep tonight without these books in my room.

        I am getting the hang of this task. Because I am
now not quite so hard pressed for space, I begin to look
ahead to eye further possible deletions from my library for
next year. Books of movie criticism are prime candidates.
The same goes for all novels that assume no serious linkage
between cause and effect in the lives of their characters;
most French literature written after 1950; autobiographies
written by Americans who have not yet reached their fortieth
birthday; literary criticism that does not take a healthy interest in literary history or in the biography of writers;
philosophy that does not at least make the pretense of being

written with its readers' personal salvation in mind; and all
psychobiographies of men and women who have been dead
more than a century and hence whose backs never felt the
couch.   Books of this kind in my library, take warning:
prepare to meet, if not thy maker, then thy recycler.

Some books, however, I find I cannot dispose of for
sheerly sentimental reasons.   Two sports novels for boys
written by the late John R. Tunis, for example, which gave
me so much pleasure so many years ago.   I cannot imagine
getting rid of three volumes of Dwight Macdonald's essays,
which, though all are dated now, were written with marvelous verve and dash; until I came across them, at a most im-
pressionable age, I had no idea that prose could be written
with such panache.   The same goes for the books of A. J.
Liebling, who has always seemed to me the superior New
Yorker writer--with a more interesting mind and a more
fetching prose style than either James Thurber or E. B.
White.   Not all Edmund Wilson's books equally repay re-
visiting, but I find I cannot rid myself of any of them.   Although many have said he was an objectionable man, to me
his writing has always represented an ideal.   He stays, in
toto.

Apart from books kept out of sentiment, further criteria for retaining those in my library now present themselves.   First, all books I retain should be true.   If they
are not true, they should at least be well written.   If they
can be neither true nor well written, they should at a minimum be well made.   With these criteria in force, one might
think that a reasonably educated man could keep his library
down to roughly five hundred books.   A sensible number,
but I am not sure I can actually do this with my own library.
I ask myself, given my personal tastes, critical standards,
prejudices, acquisitive habits, what is irreducible in my library as it now stands?

W. H. Auden--most of whose books I have and all of
which I intend to keep--makes a distinction very much to the
point here.   "Critical Judgment and Personal Taste, " he
wrote, "are different kinds of evaluation which always overlap
but seldom coincide. "   It is personal taste, for example, that
makes me value Auden's work, both poetry and prose, more
than that of T. S. Eliot, who clearly had the more original
and powerful mind of the two men.   It is the warmth of
Auden that attracts me, the idiosyncrasies and commonsensi-
cality of his mind.   In selecting books that will stay in my

library, personal taste probably has a larger place than does critical judgment, but that is what makes it a personal library.

   Books that I find I cannot get rid of, that I hope to go down with, and that my children will have to dispose of afterward, are almost all those I have been able to lay hold of by and about Tolstoy, Henry James, Chekhov, and Joseph Conrad. I have a similar enthusiasm for a less great writer who was a very great man: George Orwell. I will not release the French aphoristic writers, from La Rochefoucauld through La Bruyère to Alain, men who have come by their truths less through power of argument than through refinement of formulation. I do not love but I keep the books of the dark writers, chief among them Dostoevsky, Melville, and Kafka. Perhaps I suffer blind spots, but I do not make any conscious effort to collect the fiction of Mark Twain, D. H. Lawrence, or Virginia Woolf. Apart from E. M. Forster and Leonard Woolf, I prefer to read books about Bloomsbury than to read the Bloomsbury writers. I keep the books of F. Scott Fitzgerald, though I do not think they are very profitable reading for anyone over twenty-five years old. I have come to feel much the same about Ernest Hemingway. I read Norman Mailer, but am unable to reread him, and thus do not keep his books. I would, in fact--to put it in terms of marble-swapping on the playground--trade four Mailers for a single nonfiction V. S. Pritchett any day of the week. I do save the novels of Saul Bellow, who, though a novelist, is to me the foremost historian of contemporary American life. I cherish the books of Isaac Bashevis Singer for their Jewish spirit, those of Max Beerbohm for their exquisite wit, and those of William Hazlitt for what they have to teach about English prose style. Of single works, I cannot let go of I. J. Singer's The Brothers Ashkenazi, Edward Dahlberg's Because I Was Flesh, Ford Madox Ford's The Good Soldier, and Alexander Herzen's My Past and Thoughts. Nor of Tocqueville's Democracy in America, C. M. Bowra's Memories, and Dwight Macdonald's marvelous anthology, Parodies.

   Looking over my books, I see that I keep a good deal of poetry around the house. Not all of it is of the first quality, though I find I can eliminate none of it--too much like putting a kitten on the doorstep in a snowstorm. Of the poetry I do have, I turn more often to Wallace Stevens and e. e. cummings than to Eliot or Frost or Yeats. (Another instance, I suspect, of personal taste winning out over criti-

cal judgment.) Among the next generation of poets, I turn
more often to Randall Jarrell than to Robert Lowell, and
(recently) to Philip Larkin more than to either.

Another shelf of books I cannot bring myself to purge
are those written by dissidents within the Soviet Union:
Pasternak's novel, books by Medeyev, Amalrik, and Sharkov,
Nadezhda Mandelstam's two valuable volumes of memoirs,
her husband Osip's poetry, all of Solzhenitsyn.   These are
books I do not so much love as find necessary.   (Excepting
only Hannah Arendt's The Origins of Totalitarianism and
Raul Hilberg's The Destruction of the European Jews, I do
not save books about the Nazi era.   Why I should keep the
chronicles of one segment of barbarian history and not of
another, I do not know.) I like to have these books around;
they are a useful reminder.

I seem to have loaded up on Roman history in recent
years, most of it in black-spined Penguin editions, which I
read for what it has to convey about human nature played
out on the grand scale.   It stays in my library as does the
two-volume Hobbes translation of Thucydides.   To be kept,
too, are the books of the lucid and nontechnical philosophers:
Hobbs, Hume, Mill, Bertrand Russell, and William James.
I shall keep Santayana, whom I do not always understand but
whom I appreciate for his serenity.   I have the five volumes
of Freud's Collected Papers, along with some of his separate
studies and his Letters.   Even though I do not believe in his
general system ("Sublimation, " writes Nadezhda Mandelstam,
"what gloomy German brooding in his study ever thought of
this one!"), I greatly admire his peripheral wisdom and his
sense of mission.   On the matter of great men, I have of
late become a pushover for books by and about Dr. Johnson.
John Wain's Samuel Johnson, one of my better recent acquisitions, stays.

In addition to all this are other standard and irreducible items: the English novelists and poets, Shakespeare (but
no Shakespeare criticism), Cervantes, Gibbon, Pascal,
Rousseau, Voltaire, Thomas Mann, Proust, Joyce, and a
Gideon Bible stolen from a hotel room.   Then there are the
tools of the trade: Webster's Dictionary, the two-volume
Oxford English Dictionary, an older edition of the Britannica,
the Fowler and Follett books on usage, Mencken's The American Language, and a fine slender book by Sir Ernest Gow-
ers entitled The Complete Plain Words.   There must be
other items I have missed enumerating.... But in all it is

enough to keep a fellow off the streets for a good while.

Having cleaned out these shelves, and disposed of
several of the superfluous books in my library, I feel a bit
like Henry James, who, having shaved off his beard and prepared to enter upon his major phase, remarked that he felt
"forty and clean and light." An illusory feeling for me, of
course, not only because I am most distinctly not Henry
James, but because the likelihood is great that in no time
at all I shall load up the shelves again. The current week's
TLS has nine previously unpublished drawings by Max Beerbohm; I have tried but I cannot throw that issue out. Looking over my library, I notice that I am two volumes short
of having the complete Collected Works of Walter Bagehot.
The novels of Evelyn Waugh have gotten away from me, too
--all I have is his autobiography, the book on Ronald Knox,
and a collection of travel writings. Neither do I have an
Aristotle. I am missing some of the more recent volumes
of Lewis Mumford. No copy can I find of Robert Penn Warren's All the King's Men. I would like to have all the novels
of Conrad in the uniform J. M. Dent edition. I should like
to acquire all these books--and countless others. Is there
no end to all this, short of death? Probably not.

But I am determined to institute a rule to keep the
size of my library within bounds. It is a rule taken from
Cyril Connolly's Enemies of Promise (I keep all the Connolly
I can find). That book, it may be recalled, was written in
1938 "as a didactic enquiry into the problem of how to write
a book which will last ten years." My adaptation of this
rule is to pledge myself not to keep any book in my library
that is unlikely to interest me ten years from now. As
rules go, it is quite sound. One problem it does present,
though, is that, strictly adhered to, it would not allow me to
keep my own books and other scribblings. The efficient life
is hard.

AMERICAN LIBRARIANSHIP*

Anne E. Brugh and Benjamin R. Beede

> In the United States we find [in librarianship] ...
> the elysium of women. [M. S. R. James, 1902][1]

> Librarianship is ... a dead end for women.
> [Phyllis Wetherby, 1970][2]

Relatively little has been written about women in American librarianship, [3] considering the numerical predominance of women in the field and the number of journals in which librarians may express themselves. The problem has not been to assist women to enter the field, since it has been long considered a women's preserve, but to ensure that women librarians receive equitable treatment. Salary discrimination is both a source of controversy and closely related to exclusion of women from major administrative posts. Another controversial issue is the degree to which women's predominance in the field has kept librarianship a "semiprofession."

The object of this paper is to review publications of the past five years which offer a new perspective on women in librarianship. Emphasis is given to work on salary discrimination, the socioeconomic and historical bases for discrimination in the structuring and development of the library profession, and the actions women are taking to change the patterns of inequality that have been uncovered.

Several federal reports document the basic problems facing women in the field. A general survey prepared in 1974 showed that 97,000 women made up 84 percent of all

---

*Reprinted by permission from Signs: Journal of Women in Culture and Society, Vol. 1, No. 4, 1976, pp. 943-955.
© The University of Chicago.

librarians in 1970.[4] The largest proportion of these women
worked in school libraries, where prestige is lowest; and
the smallest proportion worked in academic libraries, where
prestige is highest. An important factor affecting the prospects of women is the increasing number of men entering the
field. There were 18,000 men librarians in 1970, compared
with 10,000 in 1960.[5] Another study showed that men librarians earn more than women librarians, but that they earn
less in that profession than do men in other professions.
Women librarians, on the other hand, have salaries comparable to those of other professional women. Because the
feminine image of librarianship is said to exert a negative
influence on the profession, many administrators are actively
encouraging men to become librarians; consequently, men advance farther and faster than women.[6] Bureau of the Census
statistics indicate that, from the beginning, women in library
work received lower salaries than men for comparable work.
Men almost invariably held the highest-paid administrative
positions in large libraries.[7]

        As early as 1886, Melvil Dewey, one of the leading
American librarians of the nineteenth century, asserted that
men receive higher salaries than women because women have
poorer health than men, lack business and executive training, and do not plan to work permanently. Even if an individual woman did not have these disabilities, she would
have to accept lower pay "because of the consideration which
she exacts and deserves on account of her six."[8] He observed, however, that women's salaries should improve as
they obtained more education and experience. Dewey has
been assailed often by feminists for these sexist assumptions,
although he did much to open the profession to women. Much
less well known than this address is his speech at the Second International Library Conference in 1897. Dewey described what he regarded as the ideal qualifications for "a
great librarian." He then added, "When I look into the future, I am inclined to think that most of the men who will
achieve this greatness will be women."[9] Rather than attacking Dewey for his sexist beliefs in the 1880s, it might
be more fruitful to ascertain why his prediction of 1897 was
not fully realized during the next seventy years.

        An explanation lies in the ascription of roles in the
library profession on the basis of sex. Not only are occupations sex typed,[10] but categories of jobs within a field
can be and are assigned by sex. One way to describe this
situation is through the application of the theory of caste:

"The concept of caste conveys how social roles are determined by birth rather than by achievement. In a society not
conditioned by caste, work roles would be assigned or chosen
according to individual aptitudes. "[11] Perhaps the fact that
men and women came to have different career paths within
the field resulted in librarianship becoming a "semiprofession" in which women made up the vast majority of practitioners. One report speaks of the "four classic female pro-
fessions--education, library science, social work, and public
health. "[12] An excellent analysis of diverging career patterns
of women and men in librarianship is Wanda Auerbach's survey of the status of women in academic libraries. [13] Auerbach, a librarian and social worker, tried to determine what
progress women had made in fighting for their rights. She
found discrimination in academic libraries to be more serious than in public libraries. This was not a new finding. [14]
Nevertheless, Auerbach had much to contribute to the discussion of women in library service. She described a "ha-
rem" model to explain library staffing patterns. A division
of labor exists in which men hold leadership roles and wom-
en fill subordinate posts. The same model is applicable to
other fields where women predominate numerically, such as
nursing, teaching, and social work. [15] In these "semiprofessions, " little autonomy devolves on the individual practitioners; advancement, moreover, comes through the assumption of administrative duties, rather than through professional achievement.

Auerbach cited the common reasons offered for differentiating between men and women librarians in appoint-
ment, promotion, and salary determination:

1. Women are more tractable than men.
2. Women are less intellectually and educationally am-
    bitious than men.
3. Women are less committed to their professional
    careers than men.
4. Women do not like to work for other women and
    accept the cultural prescription that they should defer
    to men.

She argued that discrimination cannot be justified on such
grounds. Role expectations imposed by society have such a
powerful impact that "a mutually reenforcing relationship
then persists between the organization that discriminates
against women and the cultural norms which seem to give
such discrimination a valid foundation. "[16]

An intensive study by two sociologists confirmed the
accusations made by practitioners such as Auerbach. [17]
Pointing to the fact that studies of advancement by women
in the professions have usually dealt with occupations in
which women are very much in the minority, Carol Kronus
and James Grimm believed it would be valuable to study a
field in which there was a significant representation of both
sexes but in which women made up the majority. They found
men coming to dominate librarianship to an increasing degree. Using several criteria such as the sex of deans of library schools, of editors of major library periodicals, and
of presidents of state library associations, the researchers
determined that the percentage of women in each category
was falling. Only among school librarians were women
represented in leadership roles roughly proportionate to their
numbers. "One could almost posit a 'vacuum' concept of
female power, in which women get promoted to top positions
only in the complete, rather than relative, absence of male
alternatives."[18]

The authors discussed the reasons often given for
women not moving into leadership roles in librarianship.
They did not assess their accuracy, but they did evidence
surprise at the results. "Is it possible that one finds less
administrative talent and ambition among 75,000 women than
among 13,000 men?" The authors applied the concepts of
"employment queues" and "promotion queues" to the position
of women librarians. This approach led to a conclusion that,
"although they are not bypassed when it comes to filling routine library positions, they are clearly rejected in favor of
men as promotion candidates. In broader terms, we find
no necessary connection between a group's position on the
employment and promotion queues. This suggests that the
two queues are independent, possibly resulting from a different mix of objective and subjective criteria used to array
groups on the two continuums."[19] Changes can only occur
when there are shortages of individuals in the preferred
groups or when employers take a more favorable view of
groups that have been given second preference. The authors
asserted, "Neither of these conditions is present in librarianship today, so in this field where women predominate, men
dominate."[20]

One of the catalysts in prompting more intensive studies of women librarians has been the findings of various salary surveys within recent years. The first major survey of
the current decade was sponsored by the Special Libraries

Association, an organization consisting primarily of librarians employed by private firms.   When a special committee
reported the data for 1970, it was not reticent about stating,
"There is evidence for a real male-oriented bias in salaries
for all categories" of librarians.   Education, status as a director, and other factors had little effect; there was an overall differential of 25 percent between men and women, in
favor of male librarians. [21]

The American Library Association made a survey in
1970-71 which also showed salary gaps between the sexes.
The association's Library Administration Division reported
the data without comment.   "The principal salary determin-
ants are academic degree, type of employer, and sex. "[22]
No matter what their background, women on the average ran
$2,000-$3,000 behind their male counterparts.   The average
salary for full-time librarians was $14,471 for men and
$10,874 for women. [23]   This was an important survey, for
the association was making a distinction between the salaries
of men and women for the first time.

Carlyle Frarey and Carol Learmont of Columbia University made an inquiry into sex distinctions in salaries and
job opportunities in library science as part of a general survey in 1971. [24]   This was the first year in this series of
studies that the impact of sex was considered.   The compilers sent questionnaires to thirty-nine graduate schools of library science to learn whether deans believed discrimination
against women existed.   The vast majority either denied
there was any discrimination or stated they had insufficient
data to make a judgment.   The authors inferred, "Our simple question elicited a response and some suggestive statistics
that imply real inequities, at least in some places.   Obviously the time is here when we need to keep better statistical
information upon which to base our judgments and to rely
less upon what we suppose or feel to be true. "[25]   This brave
beginning was negated by the very conservative approach they
took in succeeding years.   Their next survey seemed to
"imply discrimination, " but they were unwilling to analyze
possible trends because of the lack of comparable data from
earlier years.   Frarey and Learmont suggested educational
and experience differences might explain some of the patterns in salary distribution.   They concluded that "time,
space, and the lack of comparable data preclude a full discussion of this issue in our 1972 report. "[26]   The 1973 survey continued comparisons between the sexes but did not exhibit much enthusiasm for the subject.   Although asserting

that "women generally fare somewhat less well in salaries
than do men," the compilers were unwilling to make gen-
eralizations. "Whether the salary differentials reflect real
discrimination is not clear since we have insufficient data
concerning such relevant variables as education, experience,
and mobility to make any assessment." As a result, they
threw up their hands. "It seems unlikely that we will ever
be able to make an in-depth analysis of the differences and
the reasons for them. "27 They did not recognize that there
could be discriminatory forces in library education and in
the availability of employment opportunities which helped to
determine the salary level of women librarians. Their latest
report says even less about sex differences than the previous
three. Figures are reported, but there is little analysis.
The current data "reinforce what we have long known: that
whether or not there is any real discrimination intended or
practiced, men, in general, fare better in their beginning
salaries than do women. "28

Fortunately, there have been library educators willing
to come to grips with the problem. Two library school professors, Raymond L. Carpenter and Kenneth D. Shearer, initiated a series of surveys in 1971 which dealt forthrightly
with sex discrimination. Although their data was limited to
major American and Canadian public libraries, it is of general interest. Public libraries are a pure type which facilitates comparisons between men and women. In academic and
special libraries, differences in education may exist which
can be used to explain away discriminatory patterns in salary
and promotion. This distinction cannot be maintained in public libraries, where both men and women rarely have more
than a master's degree in library science.

The first Carpenter-Shearer survey showed there was
a gap of approximately 30 percent between the median salaries
of men and women library directors. A disproportionate
number of men were directors, and the larger the library,
the more likely the director was to be a man. Libraries
headed by men tended to receive more support from their
communities. Salaries for new librarians, whether male or
female, were usually higher in libraries headed by men.
The average per capita budget (the amount of money allocated
to a library by a local government unit divided by the population of the unit) manifested the same pattern. The authors
asserted sex differences in salary and library support should
be eliminated: "We have a long way to go in attaining a
reasonable approximation of 'equal pay for equal work.' But

through our professional organizations and unions we can insist that differences in pay for equal work at least be independent with respect to the director's gender. "[29]

According to their next survey, published about a year
later, sex patterns had not changed much. The gap in per
capita support between libraries headed by men and women
had narrowed but was still substantial. The 30 percent salary advantage of men persisted.[30] Because of "the continuation of differences in salary and per capita statistics by sex
[the authors decided to make] an exploration of what may be
a result of sexism in a 'female' occupation. "[31] Carpenter and
Shearer asked rhetorically whether such differences were the
consequence of the superior fitness of men for administration
or the result of discrimination. They concluded that discriminatory patterns in American society were the root cause.
They discussed the reasons commonly given for appointing
men to directorships in preference to women--for example,
that women are oriented toward their families and not toward
their jobs.

The authors did not endorse these arguments, but they
believed opponents of sexism should examine and understand
sexist assumptions in order to combat them more effectively.
They stressed the need for continuing education opportunities
and encouraging women who might want to become administrators. Other recommendations included discussion groups
in libraries to consider sex attitudes and related topics, efforts by library directors and other librarians to improve
salaries, and attempts by directors to raise per capita support.

The professional association, as Carpenter and Shearer
pointed out, is one major means of effecting change in the library field. Nevertheless, the historical record suggests
that problems exist in exploiting this means. A recent study
of women's participation in state and local library associations between 1890 and 1923 concluded that women were more
active in these associations than at the national level.[32] At
neither level were women represented in proportion to their
numbers in the profession. Despite this, the record of
women seemed quite good, considering the sexist societal patterns prevalent in the years studied. Gradually, women began to outnumber men in holding leadership posts in the associations; they went over the 50 percent mark in 1908. The
trend was accelerated by World War I, when the numbers of
men both in the profession and active in library associations
declined.

More evidence on the role of women in the professional associations appeared in a report by Phyllis Wetherby
at a conference of professional women in 1970. Noting the
greater number of men now being attracted to library work
and their continued gravitation to administrative positions,
Wetherby scored the major library associations for having
failed to do anything about discrimination against women.
As late as 1969, although the American Library Association
and the Special Libraries Association "regularly gather[ed]
statistics on salaries ... neither has yet seen fit to analyze
the differences in salaries for men and women."[33] Other
areas of discrimination included membership on the faculties
of library schools and the holding of offices in professional
organizations. With respect to the associations, Wetherby
made the telling point that women help to select men in
preference to women "when they have the opportunity to elect
officers.... In the American Library Association's 100-
year history, only 14 of the 52 Presidents have been wom-
en."[34]

Another attack on sexism in the professional associations, especially the American Library Association, came
from Anita R. Schiller, probably the leading proponent of
sex equality in the library profession.[35] She contrasted librarianship with occupations in which there were efforts to
make up for past exclusion of women by a strong recruitment program. The library profession, particularly as embodied in the American Library Association, seemed content
with the status quo. Schiller believed that this inaction
might be attributed to the fear of many librarians that making an issue of discrimination would emphasize the predominance of women in the field and thereby degrade the
profession in the eyes of outsiders. Schiller asserted that,
instead of a badge of shame to be concealed, the large number of women in the occupation offers librarianship the opportunity to become the first profession to establish equality
for both sexes.

Within the American Library Association, women's
role in librarianship has become a matter of concern primarily to a task force of the Social Responsibilities Round
Table (SRRT).[36] While the Task Force on Women is keeping the issue alive, the status of women would probably be
improving more rapidly if there were more commitment at
higher levels of the association. Many librarians are skeptical about achieving change through the American Library
Association. As a result, Women Library Workers, an

organization outside the framework of the association, has
been formed.   This group will cooperate with the SRRT Task
Force on Women but will remain independent.   Its first newsletter was issued in September 1975.   Presumably, this publication will become an important medium for the discussion
of issues confronting women librarians. [37]

        Trade unionism is another path for women who wish
to increase their vocational opportunities and protect their
economic and social interests.   As the Twentieth Century
Fund recently observed, "Unions can and should play a key
role in the struggle to bring equal opportunity to women. "[38]
This principle has been applied to librarianship by Joan Dillon. [39]   She warned that the gap between the earnings of men
and women is widening and cited statistics that demonstrated
the need for women to look to unions in order to gain their
share of economic resources.   While approximately 10 percent of women workers belong to unions, their median income is 70 percent higher than that of nonunion women.   She
described changes in union organization and in union attitudes
which allow women more voice in the movement.   Dillon reminded readers that, while the majority of librarians are
women, men hold most of the significant positions in the
field.   Her advice to women was, " 'If you haven't got a
union, fight to get one!   If you have a union, fight to make
it fight. ' "[40]

        Another important form of activity is an affirmative-
action program.   Wendy De Fichy described the role an affirmative-action committee may play in enabling women to
overcome discrimination and advance to managerial posts.
The committee should first determine the existing status of
women employees and study current employment practices.
To do this, De Fichy stressed, the committee must have the
full support of top management.   The committee should then
map out plans to increase "the percentage of women in management, effect antidiscrimination policies and improve the
attitude of workers toward women managers. "[41]   To overcome past discrimination, libraries should fill managerial
vacancies with women whenever possible, until the percentage
of women in library management equals the percentage of
women employed as librarians.   Library schools can assist
affirmative action with courses encouraging women to become
administrators and programs which allow women to return to
work after rearing their children.

        Before attempting to change social conditions, one

needs to know precisely how they have arisen. Within the
past few years, several efforts have been made to examine
the early years of the American library profession to determine how sexist preconceptions took root. The development
of children's librarianship in the late nineteenth and early
twentieth centuries reflects some of the problems faced by
women. It was a women's field from the beginning. As
Margo Sasse pointed out, "American women ... originated
what has been called America's most valuable contribution to
the library world--library service to children."[42] Yet the
status of children's librarians was and is low in relation to
other groups of librarians. Sasse showed that children's librarians, who should be regarded as pioneers, have been excluded in the main from major biographical sources such as
Notable American Women, 1607-1950. Sasse concluded that
"a necessary reordering of priorities should both provide
tribute to the women founders of children's service and a
realignment of the status of those currently providing children's services."[43]

    One of the best studies directed to women in the early
history of the profession was prepared by Dee Garrison, a
historian at Rutgers University. Using her library experience and her training as a historian, Garrison traced the
process by which librarianship became a "woman's job" in
public libraries between 1876 and 1905. The moral halo that
surrounded women in the nineteenth century combined with
the cultural atmosphere of the public-library movement to
make the field a natural one for women. The assumed ability of women to perform jobs requiring great attention to detail suggested the availability of women for cataloging books,
a subspecialty which was and has remained among the lowest paid and least prestigious types of library work. There
were several negative effects of the feminization of public
libraries. Municipalities did not seem to support libraries
so vigorously as women came to predominate on their staffs.
The influx of women also lowered salaries. "The same
economic factors were at work in librarianship and teaching,
for educated women, with few other job opportunities flocked
into both fields, with a depressing effect on wages."[44]

    The second half of Garrison's article deals with the
professionalization of librarianship. The predominance of
women hampered this process because of the nature of nineteenth-century society and the role of women therein. Married women were discouraged by law and social custom from
working. This shortened the careers of women who married.

Those who did not marry were regarded with little respect,
since the goal of every woman was conceived to be to find a
husband. When she failed, she was regarded as an ineffective
human being with little to contribute. According to Garrison,
"The negative traits for which librarians indict themselves--
excessive cautiousness, avoidance of controversy, timidity,
a weak orientation toward autonomy, little business sense,
tractability, overcompliance, service to the point of self-
sacrifice, and willingness to submit to subordination by
trustee and public--are predominantly 'feminine' traits."[45]

Some recent articles explore in depth the validity of
the stereotypes of the female librarian and attempt to assess
their job satisfaction. David Lee and Janet Hall investigated
the stereotypes by comparing female college students and female library school students.[46] Using Cattell and Eber's
Sixteen Personality Factor Questionnaire, which scores subjects on a scale for self-assurance versus apprehensiveness,
and other traits, the authors found the occupational stereotype disproved. "[In] contrast to the occupational stereotype,
this group of library science students was not found to be
more rigid, conscientious, conventional, conservative, tense,
or less intelligent or less stable than the college female
norm group."[47] Three scores on the scales which revealed
significant differences between the two groups (more intelligent, experimenting, self-sufficient) reflected favorably on
the prospective librarians.

Susanne Wahba compared the sources of job satisfaction for women and men librarians in order to measure
the effects of the differential treatment women receive in libraries.[48] Porter's Need Satisfaction Questionnaire was used
to measure the individual's rating of his or her job. Such
a rating was based on the subject's perception of the fulfillment or nonfulfillment of the following needs: security, social esteem, autonomy, and self-actualization. The study
showed that women receive less satisfaction from their work
than do men. This conclusion points to the need for studying
the conditions under which women work to determine more
specifically where improvements should be made. By exposing the differential treatment given to men and women,
the investigators helped to disprove the assertions of sexists
that women are satisfied with their present role in the profession.

Besides action through professional organizations,
trade unions, and other structures such as affirmative-action

committees, the literature promotes consciousness raising
for the individual librarian as a remedy for some of the
problems women face in the profession. Many articles state
clearly that change will not occur until more women librarians rethink their attitudes. In "A Healthy Anger," Helen
Lowenthal suggested that women librarians have developed a
"nigger mentality," that is, a degree of conditioning to male
prejudices that teaches them not to strive above their "natural" station. Lowenthal was one of the few writers to criticize librarianship as a career for women. She argued that
a lack of options forced many women into the field. Once
within it, they overadapted: "[We] shuffle along and say,
'But I really don't want to be an administrator. I truly enjoy doing the less prestigious work.' This may ... be the
result of our nigger mentality or it may just be the absolute
truth, but in either case we must realize that we have not
had a choice."[49]

Perhaps Lowenthal's most significant contribution to
the discussion of women in librarianship was her consideration of the dual stereotype. Among nonlibrarians, members
of the profession are often regarded as pedantic old maids.
Within the field, women are viewed as conservative and un-
businesslike. Courses in library school which employ the
case method of teaching administration frequently reflect this
stereotyping. Lowenthal's remedies were more in the direction of consciousness raising than political and legal action.
She wanted women to recognize the narrow parameters which
govern their options. Like many others in the women's
movement, Lowenthal stressed the need for women to be
angry when faced with discrimination. "The most oppressive
force we face in liberating ourselves is not at home, nor at
work, but in our minds."[50]

Another plea for women to look honestly at their status in the library world came from Helen Tuttle. Like
Lowenthal, Tuttle firmly asserted, "Women must change
their own attitudes and activities before they can change the
attitudes of others."[51] It seemed to her that married wom-
en who are librarians should pursue their careers as seriously as do their husbands. Relocation decisions should take
into consideration the careers of both husband and wife, and
they should avoid any undue restrictions on the professional
advancement of either.

The fight for equality of the sexes in librarianship is
far from over, as can be seen from the publications dis-

cussed in this survey. To conclude, something should be
said about the importance of further research and writing to
the struggle. To at least one librarian writing in 1972,
many of the recent articles seemed sexist, whether or not
the authors professed sympathy with women's liberation.
Mary Wood also found the literature deficient. "The labor
of attacks and counterattacks has been redundant, weakened
by a lack of definitions, largely undocumented, sporadic in
data collection, and impaired by a reluctance to draw from
the bodies of anthropological, sociological or biological theory. Whether from the male or female viewpoint, a continuing polemic seems fruitless."[52] Over the past three
years, there seems to have been a definite improvement in
the quality of articles on women in librarianship. Scholarly
historical and sociological treatments have been made of
several facets of the problem. Moreover, there seems to
have been some movement away from rhetoric about women's
degradation in libraries and toward substantial proposals for
remedying existing problems.

Research on women in the "semiprofessions," including librarianship, can take several forms: "First, research could focus ... on the degree to which women in the
semi-professions are interested in responsibility and advancement. Second, research might focus on the degree to which
the semi-professions are bureaucratically oriented and structured, making them particularly vulnerable and sensitive to
female career interruption.... Third, research could ...
study the relationship between (changing) occupational structures and sex-typed employment in the semi-professions."[53]
Research of this kind can help to define goals and to collect
the data needed, if women in librarianship are to make the
profession something more than a dead end for the majority
of practitioners.

Notes

1. "Women Librarians and Their Future Prospects,"
   Public Libraries 7 (January 1902): 5.
2. Phyllis Wetherby, "Librarianship: Opportunity for
   Women?" in Sixteen Reports on the Status of Women
   in the Professions (New York: Professional Women's
   Caucus, 1970), p. 2.
3. The most useful bibliography consulted was "Women in
   Librarianship, 1920-1973," in Women in Librarianship: Melvil's Rib Symposium, ed. Margaret Myers

and Mayra Scarborough (New Brunswick, N.J.: Rutgers University Graduate School of Library Service, 1975). Additional citations were supplied by Lillian A. Hamrick, librarian, U.S. Department of Labor Library; Lelia Alexander, Women's Action Program, Office of the Secretary, U.S. Department of Health, Education, and Welfare; and Jenrose Felmley, librarian, Business and Professional Women's Foundation, Washington, D.C.

4. U.S. Department of Labor Bureau of Labor Statistics, Library Manpower: A Study of Supply and Demand, Bulletin no. 1852 (Washington, D.C.: Government Printing Office, 1975), p. 12.

5. Ann Kahl, "What's Happening to Jobs in the Library Field?" Occupational Outlook Quarterly 18 (Winter 1974): 21.

6. U.S. Department of Labor, p. 26.

7. Rudolph C. Blitz, "Women in the Professions, 1870-1970," Monthly Labor Review 9 (May 1974): 36.

8. Melvil Dewey, "Librarianship as a Profession for College-bred Women" (address delivered before the Association of Collegiate Alumnae, March 13, 1886), p. 20.

9. Melvil Dewey, "Relation of the State to the Public Library," in Transactions and Proceedings of the Second International Library Conference, Held in London, July 13-16, 1897 (London, 1898), p. 22.

10. See Cynthia Fuchs Epstein, Women's Place: Options and Limits in Professional Careers (Berkeley: University of California Press, 1970), pp. 151-66.

11. Carol Andreas, Sex and Caste in America (Englewood Cliffs, N.J.: Prentice-Hall, Inc., 1971), p. 48.

12. Eli Ginzberg et al., Life Styles of Educated Women (New York: Columbia University Press, 1966), p. 76.

13. Wanda Auerbach, "Discrimination against Women in the Academic Library," University of Wisconsin Library News 17 (February 1972): 1-11.

14. Anita R. Schiller, Characteristics of Professional Personnel in College and University Libraries, Research Series no. 16 (Springfield: Illinois State Library, 1969), p. 76.

15. Auerbach, pp. 1-2.

16. Ibid., pp. 5-6.

17. Carol L. Kronus and James W. Grimm, "Women in Librarianship: The Majority Rules?" Protean 1 (December 1971): 4-9.

18. Ibid., p. 7.
19. Ibid., p. 8.
20. Ibid., p. 9.
21. "SLA Salary Survey, 1970," Special Libraries 61 (July-August 1970): 348. There was no decrease in this differential through 1973. See "Equal Pay for Equal Work: Women in Special Libraries" (New York: Special Libraries Association, 1976), pp. 3, 7.
22. "ALA Salary Survey: Personal Members," American Libraries 2 (April 1971): 410.
23. Ibid., p. 411.
24. Carlyle J. Frarey and Carol L. Learmont, "Placement and Salaries, 1971: A Modest Employment Slowdown," Library Journal 97 (June 15, 1972): 2154-59.
25. Ibid., p. 2159.
26. Carlyle J. Frarey and Carol L. Learmont, "Placements and Salaries, 1972: We Hold Our Own," Library Journal 98 (June 15, 1973): 1886.
27. Carlyle J. Frarey and Carol L. Learmont, "Placements and Salaries, 1973: Not Much Change," Library Journal 99 (July 1974): 1774.
28. Carlyle J. Frarey and Carol L. Learmont, "Placements and Salaries, 1974: Promise or Illusion?" Library Journal 100 (October 1, 1975): 1767.
29. Raymond L. Carpenter and Kenneth D. Shearer, "Sex and Salary Survey," Library Journal 97 (November 15, 1972): 3685.
30. Raymond L. Carpenter and Kenneth D. Shearer, "Sex and Salary Update," Library Journal 99 (January 15, 1974): 103.
31. Ibid., p. 101.
32. Margaret Ann Corwin, "An Investigation of Female Leadership in Regional, State, and Local Library Associations, 1876-1923," Library Quarterly 44 (April 1974): 133-44.
33. Wetherby, p. 1.
34. Ibid., p. 2.
35. Anita R. Schiller, "The Disadvantaged Majority: Women Employed in Libraries," American Libraries 1 (April 1970): 345-49.
36. This organization grew out of the National Women's Liberation Front for Librarians, which was formed in 1969.
37. The next issue was planned for January 1976.
38. Exploitation from 9 to 5: Report of the Twentieth Century Fund Task Force on Women and Employment (Lexington, Mass.: Lexington Books, 1975), p. 17.

39. "Union Women," Booklegger 1 (March-May 1974): 21-
     24.
40. Ibid., p. 23.
41. Wendy De Fichy, "Affirmative Action: Equal Oppor-
     tunity for Women in Library Management," College
     and Research Libraries 34 (May 1973): 198.
42. "Invisible Women: The Children's Librarian in Ameri-
     ca," Library Journal 98 (January 15, 1973): 213.
43. Ibid., p. 217.
44. Dee Garrison, "The Tender Technicians: The Feminiza-
     tion of Public Librarianship, 1876-1905," Journal of
     Social History 6 (Winter 1972-73): 133.
45. Ibid., p. 146.
46. David L. Lee and Janet E. Hall, "Female Library Sci-
     ence Students and the Occupational Stereotype: Fact
     or Fiction?" College and Research Libraries 34
     (September 1973): 265-67.
47. Ibid., p. 267.
48. Susanne Patterson Wahba, "Job Satisfaction of Librari-
     ans: A Comparison between Men and Women," Col-
     lege and Research Libraries 36 (January 1975): 45-
     51.
49. Library Journal 96 (September 1, 1971): 2597.
50. Ibid., p. 2599.
51. Helen W. Tuttle, "Women in Academic Libraries,"
     Library Journal 96 (September 1, 1971): 2595.
52. Mary S. Wood, "Sex Discrimination: The Question of
     'Valid Grounds.'" Protean 1 (December 1971): 38.
53. James W. Grimm and Robert N. Stern, "Sex Roles and
     Internal Labor Market Structures: The 'Female'
     Semi-Professions," Social Problems 21 (June 1974):
     704.

LIBRARIES AND MASS COMMUNICATION
IN THE PEOPLE'S REPUBLIC OF CHINA*

Birgitte Goldberg

When it came into being in 1949, the People's Republic of China took over an education system and cultural
life that had been created by and appealed to a minority of
the population. It is true that various movements in the
'20s and '30s had worked to make education and culture less
exclusive--but in 1949 only 20 per cent of the population
could read.

During the war against the Japanese, and the civil
war, the Communist Party had developed and practised in
its base areas methods of adult education, and for the mediation of culture, that proved extremely fruitful, both in imparting various skills and from the standpoint of indoctrina-
tion. The same methods are in use today, and cultural
policy is based on the "Yanan forum on literature and art"
(1942).

The evaluation of Chinese achievements in these fields
presents a number of problems, one of which is the lack of
statistical material for recent years. Further problems for
the foreigner are the language barrier, and the difficulty of
"getting inside" a culture as alien as the Chinese.

The following account, therefore, does not pretend to
offer more than superficial observations, made during a hec-
tic journey through China in the autumn of 1974, in the
course of official visits with the services of an interpreter,
and independent excursions using very imperfect Chinese.
We travelled through China (we being a Danish friendship delegation) with the larger towns of Peking, Xian, Zhengzhou,

*Reprinted by permission from Scandinavian Public Library
Quarterly, Vol. 8, No. 2, 1975, pp. 62-71.

FACTS ON LIBRARIES IN CHINA

1955 Directive on libraries

Libraries are defined as cultural institutions using books and periodicals to educate the people to patriotism and socialism, and to make them capable of assisting the party and the government in propaganda and education.

The most important tasks of the libraries are:

To acquire, preserve and lend books, periodicals, newspapers and other publications making propaganda for Marxism-Leninism

To give people the opportunity to acquire a knowledge of culture and science

To provide professional assistance to smaller libraries in the area

To serve the area with books, material and bibliographies

To increase circulation, improve library techniques, collect bibliographies, and plan development.

1955 Conference of the central organisation of trade unions to establish library policy

The conference established policy, planning, a budget, and organisation in this field.

1956-57 Programme for rural development 1956-57

This programme contained plans for the establishment of a basic cultural network in the rural districts within the space of 7-12 years.

1957 Act on the Production and distribution of Books

This act provided inter alia for the following measures:

The creation of national and regional library centres

The compilation of joint catalogues on the national book collections

The responsibility of libraries to serve scientific research, to collect publications, and to compile joint catalogues and lists of new publications, the international exchange of publications, and the compulsory supply of library copies

The establishment of training in librarianship.

FACTS ON LIBRARIES IN CHINA (cont'd)

1959 Resolution by representatives from the provinces,
the village Communes, and
the autonomous areas

To develop study clubs for
the masses under the leadership of the Party, and in
collaboration with related
institutions

To increase book circulation

To assist counties, factories

and clubs to establish libraries and reading-rooms

To provide services for
the Production Brigades in
the People's Communes

To support collaboration
between libraries and re-
lated institutions

To develop library services
in a socialist direction.

Wuhan, Guilin and Guangzhou (Canton) as our bases, spending 2-3 days at each visiting institutions and activities, making excursions to People's Communes, residential districts,
and cultural "sights," and sampling opera, films, musical
concerts, and other entertainment.

The purpose of such a journey is to promote friendship between the two peoples, and both before and during the
visit our group had an opportunity to say what it would like
to see. Throughout, we were received with great hospitality
by the Chinese. One is on one's feet most hours of the day,
and overwhelmed with impressions by the time one is "let
out" in Hong Kong--but absolutely incapable of answering the
intelligent question everyone puts, namely "What was it like
in China?" As a librarian, I tried to devote some of my
time to collecting material on the libraries, mass communications, and the mediation of culture.

In Peking I had an opportunity to visit Peking Library,
which is the centre of all library activities in China, and
exchange experiences with two Chinese colleagues, Mr. Pao
Cheng-si and Mrs. Chen Hsing-chen.

Libraries in China

The library system taken over from the Kuomintang government in 1949 was very inadequate, and since that time the government has assigned great importance to the development of modern libraries; on the basis of a succession of directives published in the '50s, work has been devoted to promoting planning, centralisation, uniformity, and expansion. Here, as in other fields, the Chinese have pursued the policy of "walking on two legs," i.e., building large library centres, and at the same time establishing activities at grass-roots level in the People's Communes and at places of work.

Mr. Pao Cheng-si defined the objective of the Peking Library as follows: "To disseminate a knowledge of Marxist-Leninist-Mao Tse Tung thought, to serve the three great revolutionary movements, the class struggle, the struggle for production, and the struggle for scientific experiment"-- in practice, this wording means that the task of the library system in China is to make it possible for people to borrow Marxist literature and literature, particularly technical literature, that will assist in building up the country. One can also obtain classical literature, which was not available to the general public in the old days, being literally locked away in the Emperor's palace, "The Forbidden City," or in the hands of private collectors.

The methods used for purchasing, cataloguing and lending are, in themselves, familiar enough to a Scandinavian. China's public libraries, for which the Peking Library is the centre, are organised at all levels--the province, the county, the town, the place of work, the People's Commune--and co-operate in a system involving, for example, inter-urban lending. In addition, all places of education, scientific institutions, and government offices have their own libraries. My round tour of the Peking Library and conversation with my two colleagues were an encounter with very familiar procedures and problems. The libraries were regarded as playing an important role in the education system, and in the mediation of culture. The Peking Library had just concluded a succession of seminars on subjects relating to the campaign criticising Confucius (Kong futse). These had covered Confucianism, above all the reactionary view of the function and role of women reflected in this philosophy, the legalistic school (a school of philosophy arising as a reaction against Confucianism), Marx's criti-

cism of the Gotha programme, and Lenin's works on im-
perialism. During our journey through China, these subjects appeared in numerous contexts. They were the subjects dealt with by study circles in the People's Communes,
in residential districts, and at places of work. This, of
course, was no accident, they were all part of the mass
campaigns initiated by the Party. Whatever attitude one
may take to this steering of what people should discuss, it
made a fantastic impression to hear an old Brigade Leader
from a People's Commune, a young girl in the port of Canton, and the manager of a pig slaughter-house juggling easily
and elegantly with such theoretical and philosophical problems. I would add that the whole attitude of people at the
Peking Library was more open and outward-going that I had
expected.

It was considered important to help people to find
their way, and that any qualified criticism of Confucius
should be based on the original texts. Our visit concluded
with a quick course in the development of the written language, printing and illustration in China, a course which left
us feeling somewhat "barbarian" faced with this evidence of
an ancient culture. It is not without pride that the Chinese
confront foreigners with examples from their history, but
they emphasise that they were produced by the people and
are evidence of the people's skill; also, particularly in the
case of the scrolls and books we saw on this occasion, that
they are public property and available to all. Nor is this
meaningless talk, in that it was previously impossible to
gain access to the collections of the imperial libraries.
The concern now shown for classical works, their preservation and restoration, also confirms that the attitude prevailing during certain phases of the Cultural Revolution, when
old books were destroyed, has been succeeded by a desire to
preserve them, as a valuable treasure.

During my trip through China, I also had the opportunity to visit and hear about a number of other libraries--
including examples of a university library, the library at a
place of work, libraries in People's Communes and residential areas, a children's library, and a district library in
an autonomous area. The larger libraries have profession-
ally trained personnel, the smaller are looked after by
"amateurs," usually with assistance from the regional library, which sends stocks and provides general guidance.
One tends to remember what is unexpected, and unusual.
At the Xian University of Communications, special premises

had been reserved for classical works: it was thought important that the students, who were actually studying technology, should also read philosophy, history and poetry.

The library at a cotton factory in Zhengzhou was not particularly large--some 1,000 volumes--and was open only two hours a day in the evening, a fact that was regretted by one of the families we visited, which lived and worked at the factory. This library, like all those at Chinese places of work, came under the union and was operated by an amateur. Although these libraries are often small, they try to "meet the cultural, scientific and technological needs of the working masses."

The libraries in residential areas come under the local Revolutionary Committee, which is the area's administrative body, and they adjoin as a rule the local assembly building.

In the People's Communes, an enormous effort has been made to establish a basic cultural network. Eighty per cent of the Chinese population live in rural areas, and here in particular an effort has been necessary to eliminate illiteracy and raise the level of education.

The country libraries, which like those at places of work and in residential areas, are often "reading-rooms," play an active role in adult education. They can consist of some 100 volumes, up to several thousand. The stock comprises popular works on current subjects, general or scientific information, and picture-books. The country libraries are regarded as an essential tool of the public library system in increasing people's knowledge of farming techniques and socialism, and in eradicating illiteracy. Their purpose is "to increase knowledge of the peasants, to popularise cultural and technological knowledge, to excite enthusiasm for production, and promote production." As in the residential areas, it is the Production Brigade's Revolutionary Committee which is responsible for activities.

I found my way to a children's library in Wuhan (pop. 2 million), simply because I wondered what hundreds of children could be waiting for in a great queue. They were off school that day, and the Wuhan children's library had been forced by the rush to introduce entry tickets, and let the children in in groups. The building, in Soviet style, was in two storeys, the ground floor for smaller children,

and the first floor, for larger children, divided into a lending department and study room. The rooms were furnished
with tables and chairs, the walls were devoted to exhibitions,
with placards and sentences relating to the campaign criticising Confucius. Books--the majority of them popular cartoon series, in pocket-size--were supplied at a desk where
they were on show behind glass. Within a few minutes I
was buried in children who wanted to see the strange foreign-
er--a situation often encountered in China if you go about on
your own--and was duly rescued by two adults, who invited
me to tea and tried to explain about the library. They could
understand my questions, but unfortunately I could understand
their answers only to a limited extent. Children's libraries
are common in the larger towns, but such activities are often
organised in the context of the "Palace of Children's Culture. " I was unable to establish whether the limited admission was for reasons of discipline, or simply because there
was not enough material. In addition to the library's lending and reading-room functions, it showed films and organised
lectures, readings, and "talking about the old days, " when
old people come and speak about the "bitter past. " As a
traveller in China, one constantly speculates how the new
generations are to be kept not only to the political ideology,
but above all to the enormous moral demand on the individual
not to seek happiness in the satisfaction of personal needs.
One of the methods used to confirm the foundation for building
a socialist society is to get the old people who experienced
the period prior to 1949 to speak about their misery and
wretched conditions in those years.

        In Guilin in Southern China--surely one of the loveliest
towns in the country--I had the opportunity to visit the library in the area, which is an autonomous region. Here,
too, the building was in the Soviet style, witnessing to the
expert assistance provided by the Soviet in the '50s. The
entrance hall housed an exhibition of the then Danish Prime
Minister Mr. Hartling's visit to China--he was also in
Guilin. It was used at the same time as a parking area for
bicycles, which offset the pompous impression the building
gave from outside. I was shown upstairs, where there were
three departments, one devoted to newspapers and magazines,
one that was essentially a reading-room for study purposes,
and a lending department that had just opened. Here, too,
one went to the desk to borrow, the majority of books being
on display behind glass, as at the children's library in Wuhan.

I would sum up my impression of library activities in
China as follows.   The Chinese have built up an organisation
or network of libraries which are often small, but well integrated in the environment; everyone knows where the library is, because it is there they go to read the papers.
The furnishing and range of titles are Spartan, but the system is in process of being built up; the Cultural Revolution
involved a radical criticism of the stock, and the number of
new book titles produced since then is small in relation to
the size of the country.   If the organisation and methods re-
semble those with which we are familiar in our own societies, the object in China is definitely not to create neutral
or impartial institutions.   The libraries, like all other public
institutions, like the mass media, and like all cultural production, are the bearers of an ideology.

We visited a number of families during the journey,
and the first thing you see in a Chinese home is in fact not
books, but posters from operas and films, a radio on the
table beside a large thermos, and often a loudspeaker outside
the house.   When a Chinese family talk about what they have
achieved since 1949, they say first that now they have somewhere to live, that they have all the food they can eat, that
they have this or that many bicycles in the family, and that
they have a radio.   They put money in the bank every month,
partly to help the state, partly to save up for larger consumer goods, such as a television.

Radio and Television

The number one medium of mass communication in
China is the radio, by reason of both linguistic and geographical barriers.   Radio broadcasts now cover some 90
per cent of the country.   People listen collectively via the
loudspeaker, or individually via the family's own set; however, as one grandmother in a People's Commune remarked,
"We've got a radio of our own now, but I find it easier to
listen to the loudspeaker, it broadcasts automatically three
times a day. "

In the People's Commune of Xinxiang (with a population of 54,000 divided into 38 Production Brigades), we asked
about people's opportunities to watch television, listen to the
radio, and see professional performances, and we were given
the following information:

"The Commune has a section which deals with film
shows. Some of the Production Brigades have their own film
teams and propaganda groups, amateur groups which produce
their own performances. Professional artists visit the Commune at regular intervals, and give performances. Television is transmitted both from the province itself and from
Peking, and we see programmes about farming, industry and
mass criticism such as the campaign to criticise Confucius
and Lin Piao. We also see cultural programmes and trans-
missions from festivals and gala performances in Peking.
We can receive radio programmes at a number of levels--
nationally, at the provincial level, and also foreign programmes. The loudspeakers often transmit programmes
produced within the Commune. "

     Radio and television, like all other mediation of news
and culture, are built up at all levels--the national, provincial, and county levels and the Commune. Television, however, is still in its infancy. Even so, the entire country--
except Tibet--can be reached with television programmes.
It is not usual to see television sets in private homes, people watch in meeting-rooms at the place of work, in the
Commune, and in the residential area. But in the living
quarters of a cotton factory, where eight families lived, one
family had bought their own set, and a neighbouring family
was now saving up to do the same. Both families and the
interpreter, with whom we continued the discussion, had difficulty in understanding our arguments against two families
living door-to-door each acquiring their own television. The
Chinese considered that this was their own business, and
did not feel that any problems could arise such as a tendency to isolate the individual family, or a wrong investment of
resources. In China, people's opportunities to buy consumer
goods are to some extent steered by pricing, and a television
set is still an expensive item for a Chinese family. But it
makes a great difference to production planning whether the
aim is for people to be able to watch television in their own
homes, or whether the attitude taken is that television is
something to watch collectively in the local assembly building. There are no licence fees, and programmes are broadcast for 3-4 hours every week-day. According to Alan P.
Liu's Radio Broadcasting in Communist China (1964), programme titles give the following breakdown: 30 per cent
news, 35 per cent cultural and educational programmes, and
45 per cent music, primarily folk music, dance, and opera.
Although Liu's information is from 1964, it is in agreement
with that obtained by a group of Swedish journalists visiting
Shanghai in 1973.

Newspapers and Magazines

The Xin Hua News Agency plays a central role in the mediation of news: newspapers, magazines, the radio, and television, all obtain their information from this source. Xin Hua has branch offices throughout China, and foreign correspondents in more than fifty countries. It has three fields of operation: secret intelligence, foreign news, and publishing. Apart from services to the bodies mentioned, it produces a daily radio broadcast in English on Chinese affairs, designed for foreign consumption, and a news sheet which is published in a variety of languages.

The People's Daily (Renmin ribao) is the official Party newspaper, other papers being to some extent "local editions" of this; they can, however, contain "unofficial" items and views--this is one of the conclusions we can draw from the Chinese requesting us (politely) not to take out other papers than the People's Daily. Two Shanghai papers, Wenhuibao and the Liberation Army Daily (Jie fang ribao) occupy a position as more "leftist" papers. The number of papers has dropped sharply since the Cultural Revolution: on the other hand, great emphasis has been accorded to building up a provincial press characterised by "people's journalism." According to a proclamation in 1968, the press is to promote the transformation of Chinese society in accordance with the ideas of Chairman Mao. "It shall strongly and persistently criticise the reactionary and bourgeois line in journalism. It shall not only inform, but above all mobilise the people to make permanent revolution. It shall organise, encourage, enthuse, criticise, and show the way to liberation of the masses. Without a revolutionary public opinion, there is no revolution. Journalism shall fight, with the pen as its sword, continuously to assume power. Every journalist should make himself familiar with the thinking of the masses, and get to know their feelings, problems, and language." There is no intent to achieve an objective mediation of news, which is above class. All journalism has a class function.

People had not previously been accustomed to reading newspapers, so that the press has both linguistic and geographical barriers to overcome. In the Communist base areas, newspaper study circles were set up, in which those who could read read aloud to their comrades. Now that illiteracy has been eliminated among all those under 40, newspapers have become more general. Many of the people we met said they went to the library to read the daily paper.

Newspapers are distributed by post, but I also saw them being sold on the street.   Chinese newspapers are nothing like
the popular press in the west, but they are illustrated with
simple photographs.

The Cultural Revolution saw a violent cut-back in the
number of periodicals, but a succession of scientific and other specialised journals has now begun to re-appear, often
with a résumé in English.   The Red Flag (Hongqi), the official party organ, is the best known and most frequently
quoted periodical in China.   Periodicals in other languages
are also published, including Renmin huabao (The People's
Illustrated) in 16 languages, and with a total circulation of
a million.

Other Means of Communication

Apart from the means of mass communication with
which we are familiar in the west, such as newspapers,
radio and television, China has methods and ways of communication that are more specifically Chinese.   It is true
that we are familiar with mass campaigns in our own society, but a mass campaign in China is designed and implemented in a far more embracing and efficient manner.   Such
campaigns are initiated and managed by the Party's Central
Committee.   Party members at all levels are mobilised, and
they exploit the entire range of media available, from radio,
television and study circles to wallsheets.   A campaign is
carried out in stages: preparation, mobilisation, implementation and summary, with continual evaluation of effect.

There is no doubt that mass campaigns play a major
role in shaping Chinese society, and modern Western research in the field of organisational sociology confirms the
importance of mass campaigns in accordance with the "integration via conflict" model.   The Chinese also claim that
mass campaigns can perfectly well start "from below" with
items in newspapers, on the radio etc., and that they have
had negative experiences of campaigns on subjects which have
excited no interest among the population.   The first campaign on birth control was a failure, although great successes
have since been noted.   The campaign to criticise Confucius,
which to a foreigner who is unfamiliar with Chinese society
and has no points of reference can seem odd--why turn on
an old philosopher?--gave us the impression, at many levels,
of being an entirely necessary showdown with a philosophy

and line of thought that has permeated the everyday life of
all Chinese more than any religion.   We heard it mentioned
with particular frequency in discussions about the liberation
of women.   It can be added, as a curiosity, that one of the
other members of the group, who is now travelling around
East Asia, has mentioned in a letter that a big campaign is
now under way in Singapore to rehabilitate and strengthen
Confuciansim.

Wall-sheets

        Wall-sheets date back many years in China.   The
"winged" pillars one can see in many cultural monuments
were originally "pillars of criticism" on which the populace
could express criticism of the ruling power.   Nowadays
these pillars only serve a decorative purpose, but "official"
and "unofficial" wall-sheets are encountered everywhere.   In
Canton a whole square was plastered, all the way round,
with wall-sheets, which people stood studying and discussing
in groups.   This is a direct and concrete form of communication in which people are involved.

Slogans

        Another specifically Chinese form of communication
is provided by the "slogans" one encounters on boards in
the towns, on banners and posters in factories, in the residential districts, and, for example, in the ground in the
Communes--laid in stone, or painted on the earth.

        Wall-sheets and slogans affect the appearance of both
town and countryside in much the same way as advertising
in the west.   As in Hong Kong you see, wherever you turn,
advertising for Coca-Cola, Leica, Yashica, cars, watches,
sewing-machines etc. etc. , so in China you see such slogans
as "Rely on your own strength, " "Work hard, live simply, "
"Make revolution, promote production, " "Women carry half
the sky, " and "Peoples of the world unite. "

Study Circles

        To attend a meeting or a study circle is a very com-
mon leisure pursuit for the Chinese, whether at the place of
work, in a residential area, or in a Commune.   People meet

and discuss not only political matters, but also the concrete
problems arising in the immediate community. People meet
a lot in China, and use their leisure actively. This does not
mean that recreation is forbidden. People go a lot to the
cinema and the theatre, to the opera, and to acrobatic and
musical performances. It was difficult for us to get tickets
to these popular entertainments, but we fortunately succeeded
and it is a fantastic experience to go to a Chinese theatre,
where you meet people of all ages. The audience is far
from being uncritical, and follows the performance very actively. Walking in parks is very popular, and the Chinese
sense of harmony and aesthetics is very much reflected in
their construction. It was a rare experience to walk in a
park in Canton where "shadow boxing," in particular, was
practised--it put one in a strange, dreamlike state to see
between ten and fifteen people standing each on their little
area of grass, with the trees, bushes and pagodas round
about, practising this mixture of gymnastics and meditation,
in which each muscle of the body is brought into use in the
course of the "programme." It was extremely beautiful.

Books in China

          Any picture of Chinese book publishing and distribution
today is bound to be very incomplete owing to the lack of
statistics and a national bibliography. The latest figures are
from 1966, which means from the beginning of the Cultural
Revolution--and, as with news services, the Cultural Revolution involved great changes in this field.

          Xin Hua--which is the key to Chinese news services--
also plays a central role in book publishing. It is not the
only, but by far the biggest and most important publishing
house in China, and it is responsible for the bulk of distribution. Even in 1952 Xin Hua distributed 80 per cent of what
was published, and Xin Hua's bookshops are to be seen in
all the towns.

          The Marxist classics, in particular individual works
by Marx, Lenin, Stalin and Mao, scientific and other professional literature, philosophy (the legalistic school in particular), books on art and music, and--in fiction--the popular pocket-size cartoon series--these are what one sees in a
Chinese bookshop. The supply of titles is amazingly small
for a country the size of China: on the other hand, one
hears a great deal about books produced locally and at

places of work, on the basis of concrete experiences and
real conflicts. One sees very little foreign and translated
literature.   Guozi shudian is the central organisation responsible for the import of foreign books and the export of Chinese books, in the original and translated, to other countries.

As in other artistic fields, there is great emphasis
on involving amateurs in the production of books, and "3-in-
1" groups, in which amateurs work together with professional writers, have been introduced in several areas. R. G.
Nunn, in Publishing in Mainland China (1966), writes that
the supply in 1964 comprised 5,180 different titles, and it is
believed subsequently to have fallen.   In spite of the limited
number of titles, China is reckoned as one of the world's
largest producers of books, owing to the size of editions.
The normal edition of a book is 600,000, and in the case of
Marxist classics and the works of Mao the figure is many
millions.

There is a particular emphasis on publications for
children and minority books, i. e., publications in the minority languages.

Efforts are being made to build up an effective distribution network in the country districts, but I only saw
books in one of the three People's Communes we visited.

When reflecting on the limited supply of titles, it is
perhaps necessary to recall China's literary tradition.
"Spoken" and "sung" literature play an important role, and
are perhaps still the preferred literary form.

Considering the mediation of news, and book publishing and distribution, including the libraries, one comes--
not surprisingly--to the conclusion that mass communication
in China is centralised, controlled, and under the management of the Party.

By Western norms, we would expect such a system
to mean uniformity, to promote passivity and obedience;
one would assume that self-realisation, a critical attitude
and spontaneity cannot thrive under such conditions.

But the society one encounters as a tourist in China
is not characterised by uniformity and passivity.   On the
contrary one experiences a dynamism and self-realisation at
practically all levels, from the assembly buildings in the

People's Communes to the kindergarten children performing
for each other in a park; a fact which confirms, yet again,
that we cannot simply transfer our norms, and apply them to
a country like China.   For the Chinese it is seldom a question of either/or but of both/and.   They "walk on two legs."
Communications from the centre are effected in a constant
interplay with the people, and amateurism is greatly encouraged in all fields--at the same time, it is clear that the
situation involves a continual struggle to maintain power.
There is the class struggle, and the struggle between the
two lines, the "correct" and the "wrong" (=socialism versus
capitalism), and these are topical problems.

     By the Chinese way of thinking, an objectiveness that
is above the class struggle is impossible.

     When one comes to Hong Kong and sees the uses to
which the "objective" mediation of news, and "freedom of
speech," have been put, one is better able to understand the
Chinese model, and it is strikingly obvious that "impartiality"
is not necessarily a virtue.

RANGANATHAN THE MAN*

Girja Kumar

To re-paraphrase the famous saying, history is of people, made by and for them. Great men fall in the last category because they mould history for the people in directions preconceived by them. They, however, do not create history in a vacuum. It is because they have the feel of the times, strong convictions and tremendous desire that they leave their imprint on history. Great man are of heroic proportions. S. R. Ranganathan was also built in the heroic mould. Instead of talking of him as the doyen of librarians, let us view him as a human being with qualities of head and heart. It is time that an assessment be made of him, now that he has passed into history.

Father of Library Science

Dr. S. R. Ranganathan, father of library science, like Gandhi, had his strong likes and dislikes. Gandhi hardly tolerated any opposition to him in the Congress party. The whole Subhash Bose episode had been revealing to all concerned. More than Gandhi, Ranganathan brooked no opposition and believed in dividing the community into black and white. His involvement with the Indian Library Association was so complete until the Hyderabad session in 1953 that there was hardly any place for others who did not think along with him. His break with the Association was so total afterwards that he forsook all connections with the national body. He gave in without any fight, knowing full well that his successors were never serious about furthering the cause of the profession. He maintained the same stance until his death. No wonder that Valmiki's Ramayana was his favourite. Lord

*Reprinted by permission from Indian Library Association Bulletin, Vol. 10, Nos. 3-4, July-Dec. 1974, pp. 53-62.

Rama, its hero, had to be prodded into action. He is a contrast with Lord Krishna of <u>Bhagwat Gita</u>, always ready to go
into action but without caring for results.   Hindu ethos is
thus not achievement-oriented.

        In spite of his intense involvement with the library
profession, he became a helpless spectator, dying several
deaths before his actual demise last month.   In his last letter to me, dated Dec. 21, 1971, he wrote: "I have given
up all hopes about the university library.   Whenever I hear
reports about it my mind goes to Sir Maurice Gwyer.   I
wonder how he would take the present changes in the university library. " On going through the records of personal correspondence with him, ranging over a period of seven years,
I stumbled upon a prophetic letter from him about Sapru
House Library (a subject of red hot controversy in Parlia-
ment and the press) as late as July 16, 1968.   The insight
of the man is remarkable, considering the fact that those involved with the affairs of that library were unable to project
themselves into the future as he did.   Perhaps the maturity
of age proved stronger than the exuberance of young people
manning the Sapru House Library.   While showing his concern about its future, he viewed the problem in a much larger perspective: "I trust that the evil forces will be handled
without head-on collision.   They seem to specialize in pulling
down if not killing the best library service and library institutions in the country.   This reminds me of 'Riemann Integration' which begins with the topmost point and then goes
down.   The small pack of monkeys visit the little garden in
our house and pluck away all the new roots and apical buds.
Whenever I see this, I am reminded of the vandalism going
on against the library personality of India. " The story of
the Sapru House Library need not be recapitulated here but
it would suffice to say that here is a good example of a public institution being smothered under too much attention being
paid by its well-wishers.   The "monkeys" inside and outside
the profession who have been playing havoc with it are still
going scot free.

<u>Qualities of Great Men</u>

        Great men may be good judges of historical forces
but certainly not of men.   They are bound to possess certain authoritarian traits inherent in their very character.
They are empire builders, and like empire builders they can
be intolerant of others.   They seem to feel at home with the

docile, the submissive and the fanatics. Being in a hurry,
they are prepared to sacrifice the present for the future.
A number of such traits apply to Ranganathan as well. It
is the measure of the man that in his last remaining years of
life at Bangalore, he ruminated over his generosity towards
several undesirable characters. In our last meeting in February 1972, he confessed that the confidence reposed by him
in one of these "faithful" disciples, extending over a period
of more than two decades, had been belied. He regretted
the fact deeply because Mrs. Ranganathan had her reserva-
tions from the very early stages. This very gentleman and
others had made a fetish of the award of Padmashree by the
Government of India to Ranganathan, a third-level award
which was no recognition to the library profession by any
standards. The work done by Ranganathan deserved a greater recognition by the country. The cowardice of his former
self-proclaimed "chelas," being afraid of the authority of the
day, by calling upon him stealthily in the dark hours, amused
him to no end. Besides the selfless devotion of Mrs. Ranganathan, his ironic sense of humour carried him through the
years and helped to overcome impossible situations. Much
more light needs to be thrown on this aspect of his life.

The child is said to be the father of the man. This
adage has indeed a basis in science. It is essential to go
back into the past history of every individual to find out the
incidents and influences in the formative period of his life.
The pioneering work of Sigmund Freud has been carried forward by applying his techniques to the study of great men.
A considerable amount of biographical literature is now available which traces the man to his childhood. Erik Erikson
has very much refined the art of biography-writing by his
remarkable insight into the life of Martin Luther, the founder of the Protestant Church. He followed it up by living at
Ahmedabad to collect data for the remarkable biography of
Gandhi, by examining the early life of Gandhi which, in his
view, shed much light on his subsequent career. In his
view, childhood experiences largely determine the achievements and failure of adults. There is a large element of
truth in what Erikson says in his penetrating studies. He
repeatedly demonstrates in his two famous biographical studies that psychoanalytic insight can help us to understand how
a tormented adolescent can develop into a great man. Interesting results can follow by applying the same techniques
to the life of Ranganathan.

Formative Period

        Not much is known precisely about the early life of
Ranganthan on which to base definite conclusions about him.
There are two facts already known about him which can be
employed as the launching pad for further study. His phe-
nomenal memory and, surprising as it may seem, his considerable handicap of stammering are two distinctive features
of the man. A story narrated by him about his remarkable
feat of memorizing is worth recapitulation. His entry into
his school was banned by the headmaster because he was
suffering from chronic dysentery. The ban was in force for
several months just before the final examination for Matriculation was to take place. A boy living next door, preparing
for the examination, used to read his lessons aloud, which
were overheard by Ranganathan and thus memorized verba-
tim. This trick enabled him to pass the examination with
distinction. The headmaster, assuming that the boy had
cheated by copying, administered a sound thrashing to Ranganathan. Coming from a poor family, the uncharitable be-
haviour of his headmaster must have hurt him a great deal
and thus left its scar for the future.

        Those of us who knew Ranganathan found a charming
talker in him, with his bagful of anecdotes like interconnected stories narrated in the Puranas. The man who could
talk endlessly for hours together was a terrible stammerer
in his early years. He believed that he became one by unconscious imitation of one of his uncles. He developed shy-
ness into an art, the trait continuing even after he became
a teacher. The spell was broken when, as Secretary of
the Mathematics Association, Madras Christian College, he
was forced to propose a vote of thanks at a meeting. In
his own words, "Throughout the hour of the meeting, he felt
dazed and heard nothing; he was silently praying. Then
came the minute for proposing the Vote of Thanks. Ranganathan stood up, closed his eyes, imagined that there was
no audience before him and made a short speech. . . . He
was wet with perspiration. His stammering had left. " This
was a sheer act of willpower which he was to repeat time
and time again.

        In the later years of his life, it became a constant
struggle between the body and the mind. He had a great
willpower but it could not be sustained all the time by his
physique. In spite of the loving care of Mrs. Ranganathan
and a strict schedule prescribed by his doctors, he managed

to defy both. He was full of ideas which he was anxious to translate instantaneously. It was necessary to communicate with others for this purpose. All the same, he did not accept much discipline while talking to others. An interview granted for 15 minutes could easily lengthen to two hours. This tendency to over-talk may have to do with the earlier handicap of stammering. The same may be said about his writing. He wrote at great length, which seemed, besides conversation, his main preoccupation. A great deal of what he wrote was repetitive. Some of the repetition is pardonable because it helps to clarify abstruse statements. This can be overdone too. I wish that Ranganathan had had a good editor at his disposal.

Who knows whether discipline could have prolonged his life. There should be no regrets on this score because Ranganathan lived his life to the full. He was in a hurry in later years because he knew that his days were numbered. While we met for the last time in February 1972, he was full of enthusiasm for the 40-volume series that he had planned for the next few years. This was to consist of reprints of his earlier works, new publications by him and his colleagues at the Documentation Research and Training Centre, Bangalore. While I was carried away by the sheer magnitude of his proposal, I felt sceptical about executing the plan in time. I did not have the heart to tell him, and was content to remind myself of the stark reality that the man had already gone blind.

Indian Tradition

It was difficult for those who had visited him at his house to visualise the spartan life he lived. I had known him since he came to stay in Delhi in the late forties. His morning walks in Madras and Delhi are well known. I have heard from my friend Dr. M. S. Venkataramani of his morning walks on the famous Marine Beach of Madras. He accompanied him as a child because of the close association of his father, the late Prof. Sebesan, with Ranganathan. I have also known of early morning jaunts in Delhi accompanied by hangers-on, aspirants for jobs and the faithful. Every step taken by him was purposeful; major questions of classification and cataloguing, and pertaining to other departments of library science, were resolved during the walks. Then there was the famous Sunday discussion club held on afternoons at his residence in Maurice Nagar. The fore-

noons were usually spent in recitations from Valmiki's
Ramayana.   The recitations cut into the time of the discussion group.   The professional meetings went on till the late
hour of night, with no refreshment provided except for plain
water served in a tumbler.   I attributed this to niggardliness,
an opinion which I was glad to retract when I came to know
that his life savings had been donated in their entirety to the
cause of library science.   My wife and I were greatly
touched when we were served coffee and bananas on our
first visit to the Ranganathans at Bangalore in 1967.   This
was considered to be the highest mark of compliment to us
by our friends.   I was invariably served coffee on my subsequent visits to their residence.

    The health of Dr. Ranganathan was steadily deteri-
orating during the last five years, so much so that the last
year or two he was confined to his hard bed.   He was allowed to sit on a chair for restricted periods of time.   During my last visit in early 1972, I was horrified to realize
that he had virtually gone blind.   Yet he did not admit de-
feat and never breathed a word about his blindness.   I was
reminded of the writer Ved Mehta, who has shown his dis-
dain by never admitting the obvious.   My suspicion had been
aroused earlier because suddenly the signatures on his letters became illegible.   It was during the same visit that the
"brave new world" he was planning for the world of librarianship was taking shape in his mind.   Toynbee's challenge
and response were thus finding fulfillment in the work of
Ranganathan.   While Mrs. Ranganathan served him his spartan lunch, he reminisced with the visitor as well as giving
instructions to his charming lady secretary.   The conversations had usually the character of a monologue.   It revived
the tradition of old Rishis, who believed in guru-chela relationship at its best.   The student was part of the family
of the guru.   There were no regular hours for teaching.
The whole period of training was considered good enough
for education.   Ranganathan instilled the same spirit in his
students.   He was thus a peculiar amalgam of the modern
and the traditional.

Style of Writing

    Human beings can be divided into romantics and re-
alists.   There are the traditionalists, the modern, the con-
servatives and the radicals.   People can be divided into the
further categories of optimists and pessimists.   Modern

psychology has conclusively proved that the line of demarcation between two opposite categories can indeed be very thin in most cases. Human beings are said to have bisexual characteristics, with the normal person reflecting mainly the qualities of the sex to which he or she belongs. It is equally difficult to place Ranganathan into one category or the other. While Ranganathan started his career as a teacher of mathematics, it is not widely known that he also had a first-class degree in English literature. In one of his letters to me, he wrote that "the little strength I have at present is to be turned to my literary effort, to which I have already committed myself." In fact he was referring to his work in the field of library science in this letter, but in his subconscious he was expressing his subterranean wish to pursue his long-dormant literary pursuits. His best "literary" effort was his Five Laws of Library Science, which happens to be one of his earliest works. In fact, his advent into the profession was heralded by this remarkable piece of "literary" effort. The language is simple and extremely precise for expressing profound thoughts to librarians and non-librarians alike. This work is one of the best testaments to the library profession.

It is a pity indeed that in subsequent writings, Ranganathan began to cater to the specialist audience, thus narrowing his field of operation for communication purposes. Perhaps it is inherent in the very logic of any growing discipline. The field of knowledge advances by becoming abstruse, coining its own vocabulary of jargon, and through developing and refining concepts. The development of a discipline makes it logical and leaves it no choice but to shed its primeval virginity. The cramping of style of Ranganathan was inevitable with the development of his mental faculties. From literary excellence, he became a votary of logic. He was suited to this changeover because of his Brahmanic training. A great deal of Hindu literary and religious writing owes to the logical framework underlying it. Sutras are the best expression of it. The style of writing of Ranganathan has a great deal to do with this tradition. His numbering of chapters and paragraphs, irritating at times to the uninitiated, owes to the same tradition. His writings were thus an amalgam of literary style and logical abstruseness, with the latter predominating in his subsequent period.

Progressive Attitudes

Similarly, he was an admixture of the traditional and
modern. He was a typical repository of the Tamil Brahmin
tradition, with its predominantly Victorian ethos. Intellectual
arrogance in a proper sense of the term was his forte. This
attitude breeds an open contempt for the adversary and in-
tolerance of the opposing point of view. It also breeds a
certain amount of stubbornness, which inculcates the habit of
exclusiveness. The Brahmins of Tamil Nadu were on the
defensive during the prime of Ranganathan's professional career and he had to face considerable opposition on caste
grounds. The minority complex was thus highly ingrained in
him. The tendency to exclusiveness was accentuated by the
lack of social life and the strict observance of the rituals of
his community. His life had a set pattern, with no scope
for social communication. "Work, work and more work"
was his motto. This implied a total act of surrender on the
part of all those who worked with him. He sought to build
up the atmosphere of ashram around the Documentation Research and Training Centre (DRTC), Bangalore. No wonder
the students were refused a day off on the death of Jawaharlal Nehru. The local students of DRTC were required to
reside on the campus and were allowed to live with their
families on Sundays only. There was thus an element of
regimentation involved in all this. Individual personalities
had to be subordinated in an act of supreme personal sacrifice. It was thus hard on individuals with catholic tastes to
adjust to the implied regimentation. Many of us have other
interests than only the profession in which we are involved, and thus find it difficult to be wholetimers. It can
be argued that the cultivation of the mind in areas beyond
the professional expertise may be of benefit to professionals
in the long run.

All the same, he was not wrong in what he did in his
long but fruitful professional career. He could not have
achieved all he did in his lifetime but for his exclusive attention to the field of library science. It was his first and
last love. The same cannot be said about many of us. Even
the best of librarians would be willing to adopt library science only as their first mistress and no more. Ranganathan
was rooted deeply into the soil of the country and while his
methods were traditional, he was trying to achieve very progressive results. He wished to place India on the map of
the world. His intellectual contributions to library science
have implication much beyond the present, and the more so

because they are of international purport.   He was thus much
ahead of his times.   It is no exaggeration to say that he can
be listed as one of the very few Indian scholars who will
leave a lasting impression on the international scene.   It was
ironic to note that the Indian press consigned his obituary
note to an obscure corner of the newspapers.   God forgive
them, because they know not what they were missing!

Robust Optimism

        Ranganathan was an incorrigible optimist by inclina-
tion, with great hopes for the future of his country and the
library profession in India.   This optimism was tinged with
sadness at the present state of affairs in the country in general and the library profession in particular.   There were
moments when he turned to despair.   Luckily, such occasions
were only few and far between.   The robust optimism that
was the characteristic feature of the man hardly left him.
The hope for the future sustained him throughout his professional career.   He had, however, lost all hope in the older
generation.   He put all his trust in the younger generation--
the age-group of 20 to 35 years--terming them as the "sin-
cere sons of renascent India."   In his letter of September 5,
1969, he opened his heart to me in the following words:
"What I have written may produce the impression that I have
become a cynic and that I have lost all faith in our country.
No, not at all so.   I know that our country is gaining in its
viability through its younger generation.   To some extent it
is also true of our own profession.   The present harm done
by neo-imperialism and its Indian beneficiaries mark only a
passing phase according to me--probably between five and
ten years."   Let us hope that his prophecy comes true sooner than later.   His reference to neo-imperialism or neo-
colonialism is most appropriate.   It needs to be explained to
the uninitiated.   The pointed reference is to the high sales-
manship of American techniques in this country.   At one
time, there was a systematic attempt to superimpose foreign
library techniques, notwithstanding the fact that the indigenous
techniques were already available and being practised in Indian libraries and the schools of library science.

        This is one department in which we are self-sufficient
and need not import too much foreign know-how, thanks to
the pioneering work of Ranganathan.   In fact, we are in a
position to export indigenous knowhow to foreign lands.
Techniques of library classification, cataloguing and docu-

mentation by Ranganathan and his associates have received
much attention among documentalists and information scientists abroad.   The Classification Research Group in London
has been a pioneer in spreading the Ranganathan cult abroad.
The acceptance of Ranganathan abroad does not make the
task of local votaries easy.   Probably there is more resistance to his ideas, in this country than elsewhere.   In any
other country, Ranganathan's Colon Classification and the
Classified Catalogue Code would have received national acceptance by being adopted by the foremost libraries of the
country.   Neither any denigration of foreign techniques nor
chauvinism is being advocated through the forementioned
proposal.   The affirmation of faith in indigenous goods and
services is the first step towards national self-sufficiency.
Those who raise the banner of internationalism in this context are wide of the mark.   Ranganathan was a great cham-
pion of Swadeshi.   At the same time, he was an enthusiastic
advocate of international co-operation.   He never hesitated
to acknowledge his debt to his great predecessors like Melvil Dewey, Charles E. Cutter and W. C. Berwick Sayers,
all of whom happen to be foreigners.   The life of Ranganathan
was a living proof that there was no conflict between true
nationalism and internationalism.

Sense of Humour

Ranganathan had a great sense of humour.   His smile
was infectious.   He had the capacity to laugh at his own expense.   In his formal dress, comprised of long black coat,
white piece of long cloth around his neck, hanging down to
his knees, Madrasi turban, dhoti with black shoes, he looked
like a marionette.   He looked lovingly ridiculous in this
dress, being a hotch-potch of Hindu, Muslim and Western
styles.   One hardly notices his simple attire on other occasions.   The most impressive part of his physiognomy was
his face.   His eyes were gentle but they began to sparkle in
later years, turning stony hard after he went nearly blind.
Lying down on his bed, which in later years became his per-
petual abode, he reminded us of the Ancient Mariner or the
old grandmother who gathered young kids around her and re-
galed them with stories.   This is precisely what he did to
the younger generation of librarians visiting him at his residence.   He would tell us stories for hours and hours together, all of which were to do with his professional career.

The fun started on the first day of his office--to be

precise, on January 4, 1924--when his Assistant Librarian
told him that "an officer, sir, should not go into the reading room. " He followed the advice in the breach by spending a total of 91 hours on seven days of the week in the library, of which 50 hours were spent in helping the reference
staff or the readers directly. The library profession has
yet to establish its credibility in the public eye. This is as
much true today as it was at the time Ranganathan took over
as University Librarian 50 years ago. The following recom-
mendation that he received from a high-up is worth quoting
in full for its humour and the underlying hard realities: "The
bearer is a poor relative of mine. He belongs to a backward community. He appeared for the matriculation of the
earlier years several times and for the secondary school
leaving certificate. But he could not succeed. Where else
can I fix him up except in a library?"

     The great many humorous stories that he regaled us
with in private are not recorded. He told us of several fellow librarians who prostrated themselves before him, and
thus having cleared their conscience, worked against him in
actual practice. He had coined appellations for such characters. The one who obsessed him the most was designated
as the Syndicate Chief. Another character who proved to be
the most irritating to him was named as the Balding Joker.
The librarian who received a five per cent cut from booksellers under the counter was known to him as Five Per Cent
R.... He was fond of quoting the description of him by his
own teacher as a person who was "opinionative in matters
in which he had no experience. " The best story that he used
to tell was of his experiences on visiting the Islington Central Library during his first English visit, with the lady assistant librarian frightened to death because somehow she had
the feeling that the "Indians were a barbarous set of people--
quarrelsome, fearful and so on. " What a disappointment for
the lady to find a great charmer in Ranganathan.

Intellectual Intuition

     Ranganathan was a religious person. He believed in
mysticism, or what he termed as spiritual experience. Intuition was said to be the basis of spiritual experience. Intellectual work at its best owed a great deal to intuition. Intellectual activity for Ranganathan was religious duty resulting in spiritual experience. Creativity was equated by him
to mysticism. Excepting the great spiritual leaders, cre-

ativity, according to him, was released in short spurts after
imbibing rigorous intellectual discipline.   Hard work was the
foundation of all creativity for most of the mortals.   He included himself in that category.   There is so far no rational
explanation for creativity because if it were merely the question of imbibing all existing knowledge, the number of genuises
would have equalled the number of plodders in the world.
That it is not so requires no statistical proof.   Another thing
to be noted is that it is not sustained in individuals over long
periods of time.   Albert Einstein reached the prime with his
discovery of the Theory of Relativity at a very early stage of
his professional career, and was the ghost of himself in his
subsequent years.   The great Russian film director Eisen-
stein reached the pinnacle of glory after producing Battleship
Potemkin and he could never achieve the same heights in his
subsequent work.   The intellectual inventiveness is gained in
later years in the social sciences because of greater dependence on direct cumulative experience.   The break in tradition
is not as sharp in the social sciences as in natural and physical sciences.   Library science is also to be placed in the
category of social sciences as far as Ranganathan is concerned.

He entered the most creative period of his career
after retirement.   He had the leisure, resources and cumu-
lated experience at his disposal to take qualitative jumps.
The profession was dialectical because what he accepted today, he rejected the very next day.   The change-over was
so fast that it was difficult for most people to keep in the
race.   A considerable amount of intellectual dissatisfaction
in the library profession arose as a result of the inability
of traditionalists to catch up with him.   He had the mental
equipment but, sad to say, not the resources to translate
his thoughts into action.   Some of the potential creativity
was wasted because of the milieu in which he was caught up.
Living in this country also meant that the opportunities for
intellectual communication were limited.   The inhibitions that
came his way, to view them in a positive light, could have
been the propelling agent in his march forward.   His physique, that gave away in the end, was unable to curb his
creativity to the end.

It is not necessary to share his religious beliefs or
partake of his mystic experiences.   Intuition need not be accepted as an integral part of belief in theism.   Yet creativity
that is closely associated with intuition cannot be explained
away.   Scientific knowledge has yet to reach the stage when

it can explain the rationale of creativity. The science of
psychology has barely got acquainted with the working of the
subconscious. The inner recesses of the mind yet remain
to be probed. Until then any definitive judgment needs to be
withheld. The creativity of Ranganathan was perhaps of the
middle ranges. Yet it was of sufficient significance to be
noticed for its lasting impact on the library movement in
India, the discipline of library science and the emerging discipline of information science that may yet grow into the discipline of the future. There is no better way to sum up the
contribution of the man than in his own words, which I quote
in extenso from his letter dated September 6, 1971, addressed
to Dr. M. S. Venkataramani:

> I have had split moments of experience of intuition.
> My Five Laws of Library Science were 'seen,' in
> this way. My own other postulates, forming the
> foundation of my theory of library classification
> were seen like that. I had to slave a great deal
> to understand the Why and Why for of certain facts
> of experience. But when the intellect had done its
> best, and it appears for a split second and gives
> the postulates, etc. Once they are handed over by
> intuition, my intellect had to work out their impli-
> cations for days and days, with hardly any sleep
> for example, continuously for a few days. My
> theory of library classification, published as Pro-
> legomena to Library Classification, has been worked
> in this way.

Conclusion

      Dr. S. R. Ranganathan has been truly called the father
of library science in India. His contributions had international purport, an honour only a few Indians can claim. He had
the best of both East and West in him. He was deeply rooted
in the culture of this country. At the same time, he was
universal because his work was not confined to any geographical boundary. He has left a whole generation of his ad-
mirers all over India, with the tribe multiplying with accre-
tions from abroad. It is given to very few people to achieve
fulfilment in their lifetime. His death at the ripe age of 80
on September 27, 1972, is not to be mourned, but considered
an occasion for reaffirmation of faith in intellectual integrity.

CLASS AND PROFESSIONALISM*

Mary McKenney

I come from a working class family that became sub-working class when my father got multiple sclerosis and the government "supported" our family of five on $66 a month. But because of this society's insistence that there are no class barriers for young Horatio Algers, because of my mother's own thwarted dreams, and because of my early success in academic terms, I always knew I would go to college. Until a few years ago, my values were so middle class-defined that I despised my own family and all working class people for lacking the intelligence, perseverance, or whatever I thought it was that got me "out." I know now that moving out of a poverty background has more to do with linking up with middle class privilege than with personal intelligence or ability.

This article comes out of my experience in both economic worlds. It is directed to middle class librarians, but I hope that my working class sisters will see themselves here also. For me, class has been more difficult to understand and articulate than feminism, probably because the women's movement had from the beginning many well-educated spokeswomen. Class is not something you learn about in the suburbs or in college. As I discovered my class consciousness I also discovered anger, hostility, defensiveness. My aim is not to alienate or accuse, although I may do that also, but to alert middle class librarians to their unconscious class prejudice, embodied specifically in elitist ideas like "Professionalism." Understanding this prejudice and these ideas will, I think, help dissolve the barriers that keep librarians and their nonprofessional sisters from joining forces in the work place.

*Reprinted by permission of the author and publisher from Booklegger, Spring 1976, pp. 3-9.

Professionalism

Professionalism is an inherently elitist concept because it divides economic and occupational groups into the
thinkers at the top and the unthinking masses at the bottom.
Americans believe (contrary to our democratic pretensions)
that people with money and power are smart and people without money and power are not smart. (This even when allowances are made for disadvantaged minorities.) Professionalism rationalizes and disguises this belief by making it
seem that middle and upper class people just happen to be
intelligent, dedicated, and individualistic--or that they got
where they are because of these qualities. Their jobs seem
to bear this out: Doesn't it take brains to be a lawyer?
Likewise, working people's jobs enforce our socialization
that if it doesn't take brains to collect garbage, garbage collectors must be unintelligent. People in San Francisco are
outraged that some streetsweepers make $17,000 a year.
Their fury derives not from simple taxpayers' thrift toward
a high wage but from the social position of the worker who
earns it.

The middle class "pride of professionalism" is an
idealistic commitment to others or to the world. This commitment does not arise so much from personal virtue as from
encouragement, opportunity, and the economic security to be
able to afford the long, costly training and the lack of earning power in the interim. It is not just that the cost of education is prohibitive for poor and working class people but
that everything in our lives prepares us for other kinds of
work--just as women as a group have been confined to the
home and to low-status jobs. Professionalism, supposedly
service-oriented, still provides the means to control others
and maintain privilege over them. This is true because
poor and working people have no control over the services
professionals offer or the cost of those services. And we
have little opportunity to change the pattern because the professions are closed to all of us who can not or will not
abide by middle class rules.

Professions differ from occupations in their degree of
mystification and, consequently, in their social rewards and
apparent value. The mystification centers around what professionals do and who can be part of the group: Knowledge
and skills are closely guarded and credentials jealously
meted out. Professionals all have "larger questions" that
they mull over in their professional journals and at annual

conventions.   This public discussion sets professionals off
as being concerned with the more important things in life
and necessarily excludes nonprofessionals from the moral
realm and the decision-making process.

Professionalism is a big issue in librarianship.   (It
was certainly the major thrust of my library education: I
didn't learn a skill, I learned an attitude.)   Librarians do
not yet reap the rewards and enjoy the prestige of doctors
and lawyers, but then we are mostly women.   Teaching,
another popular profession for women, is more respectable
and mystified the higher the grade level--and the higher the
concentration of men.   If librarianship were predominantly
male, it would surely be a highly respected profession of
scholars and information specialists.

And maybe that's where it's headed.   To rectify their
second-class status, librarians try any and every means to
"upgrade the profession. "   "We are not merely custodians of
knowledge, " they say, "we have X number of degrees, we
have faculty status, we are one-to-one professors.   We computerize, theorize, specialize.   We will let technicians handle
the mundane work of the libraries and we will take the big
issues, the unsettled questions, the moral dilemmas and long-
range plans for ourselves. "   And someday we'll all need
Ph. D. s in Systems Research to shelve books.   I suspect that
the impetus for this flurry of self-aggrandizing activity comes
from the men who have flocked into the field and run most
libraries, not from the women drudges who have always
"manned" them and thought in simple terms of serving the
patrons.   Women librarians who jump on the bandwagon of
Professionalism are being used by the boys at the top, just
as the middle class in general is used as a buffer between
rich and poor.

People who are trying to make change in libraries
usually disparage ALA-style professionalism without realizing
just how deep the belief in middle class superiority goes and
how they themselves support the ideas that make Professionalism possible.

Class

I know that middle class people understand the economic advantages they have and that one doesn't have to talk
all the time about people starving in the ghetto to make them

feel guilty. But they don't understand the many behavioral
and cultural legacies of their economic comfort--how they
treat people, how they relate to the world, what they expect
from life. Classism is every bit as oppressive as sexism,
and just as "trivial" to the privileged. Just as the women's
movement politicized the battle between the sexes, working
class feminists have begun to make personal and political
sense out of where we came from--and why we've tried to
hide it.

Who is the working class? This is not India, and
class lines are not absolute and clear cut. But generally
speaking, a family network that is mostly uneducated (except
perhaps for the youngest generation) and employed in manual
or service trades is working class. Class always means
money or lack of it, but it goes beyond simple annual income:
It's a matter of how you make your money as well as how
much you make. A middle class artist may live in bohemi-
an-style poverty and a working class plumber may live in
relative suburban comfort. But access to money is always
greater the higher the class. Middle class people have access to financial help through relatives, friends, and business contacts, and through credit, stocks, pensions, and
other resources.

Depending on the kind and location of your library,
professionals and nonprofessionals may not be divided strictly along class lines. But the ideology remains the same.
Although we pretend to be an affluent, middle class society,
class differences are being acted out all the time. We don't
call them class differences, of course, we call them matters
of individual taste, personality, intelligence. We find ex-
cuses for maintaining any hierarchical relationship in which
we are the one on top. The most devastating excuse is that:
We Are The Norm. Everything in society tells us that those
in the middle and upper classes are more intelligent, more
talented, more cultured, more creative, more useful to humanity, more ethical than ordinary people. A middle class
woman said to me once that those who rise from the working
class to go to college and get good jobs are "the intelligent
ones." Although this statement would bring cries of outrage
from any liberal if directed at blacks, it is the prevailing
view of the white working class in all middle class institutions: media, schools, libraries, churches, government.
All reflect the middle class norm as surely as they do the
ideal of whiteness and maleness (and as conveniently). The
cultural realm reinforces it in movies like "Joe" and TV

shows like "All in the Family," which have us rolling in the
aisles with laughter at the stupidity, bigotry, and sheer bad
taste of the white working class.

At bottom, the oppression of the working class is
economic; but the glue that holds them at their jobs and in
their churches, not tearing up the streets, is the internaliz-
ing of society's values.   Working class people do resent
those with more money and power, they do know that the
middle class is born with a better chance, they do feel pride
in doing "hard honest work" rather than pushing papers and
controlling people.   But at the same time they believe the
myth that economic insecurity is an individual problem, a
personal inadequacy in one who doesn't work hard enough;
that working with the mind is more important than working
with the hands.   There is apology, defensiveness, and other
contradictions in white working class people because nowhere
is their culture validated, their opinions solicited, their efforts rewarded.

Middle class people tend to believe either that working class people are no different, just underprivileged (just
as men believe that women are weaker, less fortunate ver-
sions of themselves), or that they are different but would
rather be middle class.   Although the employed working
class is certainly upwardly mobile to the extent that they
want to have decent things, an education for their children,
and a secure retirement, they do not necessarily hunger for
the middle class life.   They don't hang around opera houses
and curse the god that made them prefer Dean Martin. They
don't covet gray flannel suits and have a secret compulsion
to sell insurance.   Working class life is demeaning because
of the lack of money, lack of opportunity, lack of job responsibility, lack of respect, lack of power, i. e., the shitty
treatment by other people, not because its culture or values
are inferior.   (Cf. penis envy.)

Because the middle class is assumed to be the norm,
middle class people don't think about class very much and
appear perplexed when the issue is raised.   They see workers only peripherally, and with a sense that "someone has to
do those jobs" but that the important work of society is done
by them.

As a correlate of "We are the norm," there are
various assumptions of middle class superiority:

We Are More Dedicated. The line is that professionals are more dedicated, more idealistic than others--not just
working for a buck, but truly concerned. Naturally, those
who make plenty of money can blithely pursue those ideals
that are beyond mere money, while those unimaginative file
clerks and shelvers just do their work and take home their
paycheck. A clerk-typist making $500 a month may care
less about community outreach or intellectual freedom than
about her annual raise, but she's never consulted about these
issues. She is no less "dedicated" for being dedicated to
survival.

Most professional librarians are unique in having the
time, the money, and the support by virtue of the kind of
work they do to be dedicated to humanity, scholarship, politics, etc. If their actual job doesn't challenge them, their
class background and professional rank tell them they deserve
and can demand more meaningful work. Nonprofessionals
have no such choice unless they want to go to library school.
The nonprofessional who is not politically oriented or library
identified is not a lost cause: No one is content to do boring,
non-responsible work. But she has no reason to believe that
professional or political ideas are in her interest unless
someone makes the connection, and makes it ring true to her
life and needs.

We Are Less Bourgeois. One of the contradictions
in our society is that the working class gets dumped on for
being "bourgeois," materialistic, security conscious, conventional, all classic definitions of middle class behavior.
Liberals and hip types are opposed to everything that's
"straight" or "plastic." But without a class perspective,
this approach lumps the working class in with those who run
the system and benefit from it. And it divides people in and
out of the library into those who are hip (politically right-
on) and those who are straight (conformists, rednecks, etc.).

People who have created their own subculture tend to
make stereotypical judgments of others on the basis of the
latest fashion or acceptable behavior in their own group. In
the middle class counterculture (a hot retreat for concerned
librarians), the code of behavior is that it is not done to:
follow big league sports, eat junk food, play cards, go bowling, watch TV except for serious programs, go to the movies except for heavy films. I guess after the Revolution
everyone will turn into Che Guevara and won't want to go
bowling.

Other morally superior, hip-middle class musts include downward mobility (pretending to be poor) and anti-consumerism. Downward mobility can be a genuine attempt to deal with privilege and to start change by changing one's own life. But paradoxically it takes money to be "poor" in the trendy subculture world. Anti-consumerism can be a genuine attempt to change living and buying habits born of economic comfort. But people who own vans and stereos, eat expensively, and live in nice neighborhoods are being hypocritical when they accuse the lower classes of being materialistic.

We Will Define Class. If an educated working class woman tries to confront middle class people about class, they will tell her that she is not working class any more so what's the fuss. According to all the stereotypes, she can't be working class if she: went to college, seems intelligent, speaks English properly, dresses well, cares about larger issues, has good manners, or likes the arts. If she acts and talks middle class, she must have "become" middle class herself. Education and a good job don't turn a black person white, and they don't negate a white person's background of poverty, her class identity, and her continuing financial needs. When a working class person is tracing her roots, don't make it more painful for her by insisting she has none.

Break Away

No one can control the class position she was born to, but there are ways to deal with it, if you don't want to be oppressive. Here are some to consider:

Align downward. (Not the same as downward mobility.) Aligning with the people at the bottom is essential if any change is to be made--you can't stop partway down and say, no, I draw the line at elevator operators. The system comes down on nonprofessionals harder than it does on librarians; of course they want to change it. Radical librarians have less in common with the administrators/management even though they speak the same educated tongue.

Resist professional privileges, or use them to advantage.

Fight for issues that will help all library workers, not

just professionals. Faculty status improves one's paycheck
and certainly helps the ailing professional ego, but what real
change does it make?

Fight for nonprofessionals the way you would fight for
yourself or other librarians. They too suffer from sex discrimination, layoffs, and firings. There is nothing more
noteworthy about discrimination at the director level than at
the clerical level.

Be aware of the "classist" nature of some demands.
It's common for a librarian to complain that she is being
treated like a clerical worker. This reinforces the belief
and the practice that clerical workers should be treated like
clerical workers. All workers deserve the dignity of responsible work and commensurate pay. Attack on the basis
that the shit-work is given unaccountably or exclusively to
women, professional or not.

Do not patronize those with less education or trivialize
their concerns.

Do not expect nonprofessionals to relate to professional issues. That they may not identify as library workers the way librarians do comes back to the cohesiveness
of the professions, with their national conventions, group
unity, and post-survival consciousness. Encourage political
involvement on the part of nonprofessionals but don't dis-
parge those who raise what you think are unimportant issues.
No one will consent to be "organized" if she suspects the
organizers will use her to get their way.

Share your skills and demystify librarianship. Most
librarians have definable skills, but to the uninitiated, librarianship is a vague discipline that does no visible good.
Information seeking and information organizing can and should
be common knowledge, not a hoarded job skill.

Because I have probably raised more questions than
I have answered in this limited space, I would be glad to
answer letters from any woman who disagrees with me or
would like me to explain further any of my points. I hope
other working class women will join me in working out this
analysis, and that middle class liberals and radicals will
take it upon themselves to learn how their world view dif-
fers from that of the people they want to help. All forms
of oppression feed on ignorance.

Readings

Class and Feminism edited by Charlotte Bunch & Nancy
        Myron. Diana Press, 1974. (see Bklg 10:30)
"Ways of Avoiding Class Consciousness, " Women: A Journal
        of Liberation, 2:3.
"Nowhere to be Found, A Literature Review And Annotated
        Bibliography On White Working Class Women, " by
        Victoria Samuels. Working Paper Series #13, Insti-
        tute on Pluralism and Group Identity, 165 E. 56th St.,
        NYC 10022, June 1975.
Daughter of Earth by Agnes Smedley. Feminist Press, 1974.
        (see Bklg 10:30)
Yesterday's Lessons by Sharon Isabell. Women's Press
        Collective, 1974. (see Bklg 5:31)

OUR LIBRARIES: CAN WE MEASURE
THEIR HOLDINGS AND ACQUISITIONS*

Fritz Machlup

We are a "knowledge society," a society that devotes
a large and ever-increasing part of its gross national product to the production and distribution of knowledge. The
"knowledge industry" has been growing at a faster rate than
most other sectors of the economy, and the number of people working in "knowledge occupations" is between two fifths
and one half of our potential labor force. Statements of this
sort were advanced fifteen years ago, and statistical research on "knowledge production" has been going forth ever
since.[1] Yet, on some rather elementary questions regarding "knowledge embodied in print" we know so little that we
must admit deep embarrassment.

Knowledge contained in books and journals has in fact
been the earliest object of measurement in this area. The
size and growth of our library collections have been taken to
be the most reliable and most easily obtainable indicators of
our engagement in knowledge production. For decades apo-
dictic statements have been passed around to the effect that
"knowledge" stored on the shelves of our libraries has been
doubling every ten years, or every seven years, or some
such number. A few of us have been skeptical about the
meaning of such assertions; we have asked, for example,
whether one hundred books really represented twice as much
knowledge as fifty books, and whether fifteen journals really
conveyed thrice as much information as five journals. But
we have not questioned the physical meaning of the measurement. We have not questioned the reported "facts" about the
rate at which the numbers of books and journals on the

*Reprinted by permission from the AAUP Bulletin, Vol. 62,
No. 3, October 1976, pp. 303-307. © 1976, American Association of University Professors.

shelves in our libraries have been increasing. We believed
the stories about the doubling every few years, because we
had not known that the librarians themselves were so very
unsure about the collections under their control. Now I
know a little more about the extent of my ignorance and I
want to share it with others. By sharing the realization of
my ignorance I may relieve my conscience as an investigator
of the dissemination of information.

Simple Questions, But No Answers

        I set out to get answers to what appeared to me as
rather simple questions. Relying on the most widely used
classification systems employed in library collections--say,
the system of the Library of Congress--I wanted to find out
the size of the libraries' total holdings, and the annual acquisitions, of books and journals in the various fields. Concerned with the economics of library services, I also wanted
to find out how much the libraries have been spending each
year for acquiring various kinds of materials in the different
fields. Call it the scholar's optimism or call it the fool's
naïveté, but I thought that all I had to do to get answers to
my questions was to ask the librarians. Alas, the librarians
did not have the answers, and the most I have learned from
them is why the answers were not available and how enor-
mously difficult, if not impossible, it would be to obtain
them.

        At first I was perplexed. If a grocery store can know
how much were the year's purchases of sugar, flour, vege-
tables, beer, bread, and all the rest, why should a librarian
not know his expenditures for books and journals in physics,
biology, mathematics, English literature, art history, and
so forth? What differences are there in keeping such records in a commercial business and in a research library?

        At last it dawned upon me that differences in the
mental habits of men of learning and men of business may
be at the root of their different practices regarding accounts
and statistical records. In contrast with businessmen, the
custodians of our scholarly publications are not under any
legal obligation to file annual returns to income-tax authorities, who may be curious to know the details of the expenditures and losses of the enterprise. The keepers of our
books in the libraries are not bookkeepers, and the subscriptions they pay for learned journals are not entered into such

lined journals and ledgers as are the bookkeepers' daily concern.

There may be another difficulty behind the lack of statistical records in library administration: the absence of an operational unit of measurement, apart from dollar expenditure. While groceries are bought in pounds and tons, pecks and bushels, quarts and gallons, such units do not apply to books and journals. Bewildering problems have to be solved before one can say how many "volumes" or "journals" are in the stacks of a library and how many have been added in any particular year.

The Units of Measurement

The most usual description of the size of a library collection, as we find it in the leaflets, bulletins, and reports of the institutions, is in terms of the number of volumes. The curious, surely, will immediately ask whether a two-volume edition of Adam Smith's Wealth of Nations is counted as two volumes while the Modern Library edition is only one volume. And since the Encyclopaedia of the Social Sciences is available in eight fat volumes but also in fifteen slimmer volumes, should it be counted as eight or fifteen volumes, or as just one reference work? Many libraries used to bind several paper-covered pamphlets by different authors of the nineteenth century--if they were addressing related subject-matters--into one hard-cover volume; should the number of pamphlets be counted or the number of bound volumes? If the library had bought multiple copies of a book that was assigned in an undergraduate course with large enrollment, should all the duplicates be included in the total? If a succession of administrators over the last fifty or hundred years had been keeping "accurate records" of acquisitions but had answered these questions differently, some counting the number of different titles acquired, some the number of bound books, some the number of pamphlets joined between hard covers, and so forth, the "accuracy" of the records would be of no avail and, if a consistent count of the total collection were wanted, a new stock-taking would be necessary--at a cost hardly justified by the benefits expected from knowing the "accurate" measure.

The problem of operational definitions is perhaps even more serious in the case of the serials: the journals, magazines, newsletters, newspapers, and other periodical publications. The library may have subscribed to a magazine or paper and put the issues into hard bindings, some annually, others semi-annually. Should the number of issues be counted or the number of the bound volumes, or perhaps simply the number of subscriptions? But what if the library does not have the complete set from the first issue of Volume I to the present? How should it count its collection of a journal if it possesses only Volumes XII to XXXII and again Volumes XLIV to LXI?

All these questions can of course be answered by some generally agreed convention. But can a library which has not kept consistent records afford the cost of taking a complete inventory? With library budgets so stringent that not all the wanted journals can be subscribed to and only a part of the wanted books can be purchased, should the allocation of funds for acquisitions be further encroached upon by expenditures for a stock-taking operation? Even a very curious researcher in library science or in information science could not have his priorities so distorted that he would vote for <u>measuring</u> rather than for <u>increasing</u> the stock of books and serials available in the stacks. We do not want to impede growth by an attempt to find out how fast it has been and how far it has gotten us.

I have deliberately drawn an excessively dark picture of the task of measuring the physical contents of our libraries. Readers quite unfamiliar with the problems of library operations may thereby be helped in shedding some of their illusions. But they should be told that some less expensive techniques of estimating the size of library collections have been developed. They include counts of the titles, copies, and serials as they appear in cards in the catalogue of the library. Since these cards are by author, title, and subject matter (often more than one subject for a single book), an estimate of the most likely multiple counting has to be made if estimates of the numbers of cards in the trays are used as the bases of the inventorization. Unfortunately, these techniques, though helpful to estimate the total number of titles held by the library, rarely help ascertain what the library possesses in the various fields of knowledge. Only specialized libraries, for example, a chemistry library, will be able by a simple count of catalogue cards to estimate its collection in the field of specialization.

Fields of Knowledge

My aim of obtaining information on the total holdings
and annual acquisitions by our libraries of printed materials
in the different fields of knowledge is not motivated by idle
curiosity. Important questions of national policy may be
raised by such information. If annual library budgets,
though increasing in dollars appropriated, can buy only fewer journals and fewer books at the faster increasing subscription rates and list prices, are the unavoidable retrench-
ments in real acquisitions equally distributed among the
fields of learning? Or are the priorities such that some
fields are given preferred treatment and other fields shut
out in the process? Are, for example, current acquisitions
in the social sciences being throttled, and acquisitions in the
humanities stopped, in order to allow the physical sciences
to be kept up to date? Since we know that subscription
rates for most journals in the natural sciences have been
raised at a spectacular pace--some by as much as 400 percent over the last six years--and that, as a result, the
number of books purchased by libraries had to be reduced,
how has this curtailment affected the different fields of knowledge? Clearly, these are not idle questions; we should do
our best to get the answers.

In consultation with various authorities, public and
private, my research associates classified books and journals published in recent years into thirty-one fields and have
been trying to develop accordingly disaggregated data on new
publications. Theoretically, the use of call numbers in the
libraries, for example, under the Library of Congress classification, could yield an even finer breakdown by subject
areas, subareas, and subsubareas. In actual fact, however,
we would be lucky if we were able to get a breakdown of library acquisitions by no more than ten areas. Thus we have
approached the members of the Association of Research Libraries regarding the feasibility of the following broad
classes: Science (Library of Congress class Q), Engineering and Technology (T), Medicine (R and S), Other Sciences
(U and V), Social Sciences (C, D, E, F, H, and J), Humanities (B, G, M, N, and P), Law (K), Education (L),
Other (A and Z), and Rare Books. In our innocence, we
thought that this rather general classification would be practicable without undue cost or effort.

Our hope was to obtain, from as many research libraries as possible, information, broken down by the ten

areas, on the size of their collection, annual increases in
size since 1970, annual purchases from various channels of
distribution, serial subscriptions, materials received at no
charge--and a few other things, such as outwide circulation,
rates of loss, interlibrary borrowing and lending, and
sources of funding.

He Who Asketh Too Much Will Get Nothing

I lost my innocence in my first interviews with the most
knowledgeable librarians and learned of the limits of the information they could furnish.   I discarded the carefully designed pages of an excessively nosy questionnaire that I had
drafted.   I realized that the administrators of libraries, like
most other human beings, would not undertake to complete a
questionnaire that asked too many unanswerable questions.   I
took a vow of modesty and decided not to request any data
before I found out how easy or how difficult it would be for
my respondents to respond to a request for information.

In line with this game plan, my research associates,
aided by officers and staff of the Association of Research Libraries, developed a "Preliminary Questionnaire," with the
subtitle in capital letters: "THIS IS NOT A REQUEST FOR
DATA." The instructions read as follows:

> Through the attached questionnaire we hope to obtain
> your evaluation of the level of difficulty and costs
> involved in gathering annual statistical data about
> your library for the period 1970 through 1975.
> Please select the response which best describes
> the accessibility of the various types of information
> listed and enter the corresponding code in the ap-
> propriate box.   The responses are as follows:

Code	Response
1	Data are available at little or no cost (under 1 man-hour).
2	Data are obtainable at moderate cost (1 man-hour to 1 man-day).
3	Data are obtainable at substantial cost (1 man-day to 1 man-week).
4	Data are obtainable at excessive cost (more than 1 man-week).
5	Data are not obtainable.

The questionnaire was sent to ninety-nine librarians; returns were received from sixty-seven--which I regard as a good rate of response. I may take this opportunity to commend the respondents for their cooperation and to thank them for their understanding and helpfulness. The findings, however, give no cause for enthusiasm; the scores show that most of the data will be either unobtainable or obtainable only at excessive cost. I have never seen so many 5s on a computer printout: 72 per cent of all boxes exhibited this number, conveying the message "data are not obtainable." Only 7.6 per cent of the boxes showed the figures 1 or 2, indicating that the data would be available at little or moderate cost.

As a matter of fact, these percentages still exaggerate the availability of information, because they include the boxes for responses regarding "data not broken down" by various subcategories, such as channels of acquisition, sources of funds, and, especially, subject areas. If we focus only on responses regarding the availability of data "broken down by subject areas," we see the figures 4 and 5--standing for virtual or actual unobtainability--in no less than 82 per cent of the boxes. This seems to close the door to the researcher who wants to find out what has been happening to the libraries as buyers and lenders of books and journals in different fields of science and scholarship.

This may sound like excessive defeatism. Yet it undoubtedly bars an inquiry that many answer such relatively simple questions as these: How are the book collections of our research libraries divided among natural sciences, social sciences, and the humanities? How many journals in each of these areas are being subscribed to by the largest and by the medium-sized libraries? How many book titles in science, in medicine, in technology, in the social sciences, in the humanities were acquired in each of the last five years? What trend in book acquisitions can be observed and what would happen if the trend continued for another five years? How have the library budgets been reallocated in recent years? Have acquisitions of books or subscriptions to learned journals been maintained in certain fields at the expense of other fields, regarded as less important or of lower priority or urgency?

Of course, we shall not give up so easily. If only a dozen of the large research libraries will be able to produce the data required for our research, we shall have to do with that small sample. Perhaps some sampling techniques will permit us to do some legitimate "blowing up" of small samples and obtain reasonable information about the "total population" of libraries. And, surely, if we cannot learn all that we ought to know about our libraries, we shall be able to learn a good deal about the few libraries that have managed to keep good records.

The Next Steps in Our Research

Our first reaction was not to bother many librarians with questionnaires on which they would be unable to answer most of the questions. The response rate would be so small that the whole inquiry might become worthless. It had become clear to us that different questionnaires have to be designed for libraries equipped with different systems of record-keeping and data-processing. Unfortunately, the libraries cannot be easily sorted into a few classes defined by degrees of availability of data. Most of the respondents to our feasibility test have indicated that they might furnish information on certain types of questions, but not on others, but the replies showed not only great inequality in the distribution of knowledge but also a wide dispersion in the distribution of hopelessness among different institutions regarding different questions. To fit each questionnaire exactly to the individual librarian's knowledgeability or ingenuity would help to get the highest rate of response, but would be quite unhelpful in providing comparable data for any meaningful analysis.

We tentatively concluded to design three questionnaires, one for the most knowledgeable of our respondents (ten or twelve), one for the middle class of about another twenty library administrators, and a third for the remaining seventy institutions from which we can and hope to get more than a minimum of information useful in our inquiry. If the response rate were high in all three classes, we would at least know how significant the answers of our first-class respondents would be in the total population of research libraries. Thus, the value of the detailed information obtained from the most promising providers of data would depend partly on the degree of cooperation by the members of the groups who can complete only the less demanding of our questionnaires.

The final decision on our procedures will be made in consultation with hardnosed librarians, seasoned specialists and experienced researchers in the field.

Improvements in Library Record-Keeping

Techniques for better record-keeping have been developed and tried out by a number of libraries. Some large institutions which in our feasibility test had to report only 4s and 5s--indicating that they are not equipped to answer our questions for detailed data--have installed or ordered computerized information systems with the capability of yielding virtually all relevant data, broken down in any way desired. But will they take full advantage of the physical capability of their equipment?

In a survey of university libraries in the United States with responses from 116 institutions (59 per cent of those queried), a researcher back in 1969 found that 51 per cent of the respondents had installed automated systems of some sort. Most of these systems, however, were used only for some "listings" and other isolated pieces of information.[2] Only a few libraries have developed computerized systems for all major operations: acquisition procedures, cataloging, serial records and controls, and circulation records.[3] And even those that have do not in general seek answers to all the questions which curious outsiders believe they need for their research.

There are no very stringent physical limitations imposed by the computer systems; the actual limitations lie partly in the interests and imagination of the administrators and their programmers, but chiefly in the time, effort, and money that can be allocated to the development of a comprehensive information program. Practically every additional piece of information increases the cost of the system, for its hardware, software, and for current operation. More expensive equipment may be needed to meet the increased demands for information, and each transaction in the various departments--acquisitions, cataloging, etc.--may require extra time for feeding the data into the system. Are the benefits from additional or more detailed information worth its cost? An outside researcher may be convinced that the answer is in the affirmative, whereas the library administrator, struggling hard to keep within his budget and, especially, to keep administrative expenses from increasing much faster than the cost of acquisitions, may have serious doubts or may even have concluded that the potential benefits of the additional information are not worth the incremental cost.

In these circumstances it will be necessary to em-

bark on some realistic benefit-and-cost analysis for information systems of various dimensions. I suspect that the
crunch due to fast-rising costs of urgently needed materials
(journals and books) and more slowly rising appropriations
will call for decisions which cannot be made wisely in the
absence of better information than is now available. The
budget crunch may, conceivably, suggest to some the desirability of economizing in "unproductive" record-keeping
and data-processing but, more likely, will impress decision
makers that they need better information in order to make
wiser decisions. As long as ample funds are available for
buying all the books and serials that look desirable, librarians may find it useless to spend time and money on information systems just to satisfy the idle curiosity of statisticians,
economists, and operations researchers. But when funds
get so scarce that every journal subscription crowds out the
acquisition of several books, and every purchase of a book
on physical chemistry shuts out the purchase of a book on
literary criticism, then it may be deemed imperative to
know the comparative needs and desires of students, faculty
members, and other constituents of the college or university
community for materials wanted for teaching and research.
The librarian, in such circumstances, may wish to know how
much he has been spending for books and journals in different fields and what use has been made of the collections
on his shelves.

We can trust the economic forces in operation to make
library administrators realize that the old saying "ignorance
is bliss" does not apply any longer to their management
techniques.

Notes

1. Fritz Machlup, The Production and Distribution of
   Knowledge in the United States (Princeton: Princeton
   University Press, 1962). Since the publication of
   this book, several other researchers have attempted
   to update the statistical findings. I myself, under
   grants from the National Science Foundation and the
   National Endowment for the Humanities, have been
   engaged in an inquiry to bring the study up to date.
   The present phase of my study focuses on publishing
   and library services.
2. James H. Byrn, "Automation in University Libraries:
   The State of the Art," Library Resources and Tech-

nical Services, 13 (Fall, 1969), pp. 520-530. The
report suggests that the sample may have been un-
representative, as libraries with well-known computerized systems had not responded to the questionnaire.
3. Ralph H. Parker, "Library Automation," Annual Review
of Information Science and Technology, 8 (1970), pp.
193-222.

THE IMAGE PROBLEM OF THE LIBRARIAN: FEMININITY AND SOCIAL CONTROL*

Jody Newmyer

> The central paradox--that the rise of
> images ... blurs rather than sharpens
> the outlines of reality--permeates one
> after another area of our life.
> > --Daniel Boorstin

Librarians who write on the subject agree that there is an "image problem" in the library today--and that the image is a "negative one."[1] The typical librarian is seen as a "kindly maiden lady in Red Cross shoes" and librarianship itself as a "female" occupation, weak, dependent, conservative, nonintellectual.[2] The image is not mere folklore; it is thought to be based on scientific findings and is discussed seriously in scholarly library journals by eminent librarians, some of whom argue that the library "should guard well its feminine qualities,"[3] and some (a growing body of critics) who believe that the library needs a more "masculine" personality.[4] The assumption that librarians, male as well as female, are "feminine" has been accepted almost without question; basic policy decisions are postulated on its validity. But there has been no examination of the historical origins of this assumption, how it was maintained, or what correspondence it has to the changing realities of the profession. Such an examination, which this study attempts, casts much light on the library as an institution in American society, for it reveals not only a curious pattern of occupational demography within the profession but also a dual set of theories of librarianship, one humanitarian, the other essentially

*Reprinted by permission of the author and publisher from The Journal of Library History, Vol. 11, No. 1, January 1976, pp. 44-67.

commercial, which have combined in an uneasy alliance and now dominate the philosophy and practices of library adminis- trators. To explore these aspects of the feminine image can give a useful historical and philosophical dimension to the ongoing effort for professional reform.

That there is nothing inherently "female" about li- brarians is evident from the prevailing assumption prior to the 1870s that the librarian was grim, grouchy, eccentric, and male. [5] Such an image found embodiment in such famous non-American librarians as Bulkeley Bandinel, Librarian of the Bodleian from 1813-1860, who "could lash with his tongue and had learned vigour of expression on the quarter deck of the Victory," and Edward Williams Byron Nicholson, Librari- an of the Bodleian from 1882-1912, a "tornado" whose "ca- reer saw one continual conflict with the world in general," or Chairman Mao, who was once a librarian and hardly fits the present "shy, retiring, quiet, reserved, withdrawn" image. [6] Neither, of course, do Panizzi and Melvil Dewey, those perennial tilters against the windmills of authority--nor the great American librarians Jewett, Poole, and Billings.

Not until the period 1876-1905, as Dee Garrison has shown, does the "kindly maiden lady" make her appearance. [7] During this period unmarried women began to flood the pro- fession; by 1910 78.5 per cent of library workers in the United States were women. The rapid influx of women into the profession and the terms on which they accepted their duties laid the basis for the feminine image of the librarian "as an inhibited, single, middle-aged woman." Women came into this admittedly ill-paid, fledgling profession because, while they met "resistance in other more established profes- sions," they were welcomed in a "new and fast-growing field in need of low-paid but educated recruits," for the library, "supported by taxes and voluntary donations, was by neces- sity obliged to practice thrifty housekeeping." Garrison notes that they were approved of by the males already in the field also because, since librarianship "appeared similar to the work of the home, functioned as cultural activity, re- quired no great skill or physical strength and brought little contact with the rougher portions of society," it was deemed "suitable" for women. Librarianship was really a kind of extension of the "domesticity and the guardianship of culture" to which the nineteenth century "myth of women's sphere" consigned the gentle sex. To move from domestic cathedral to this new cathedral of learning was appropriately female.

Furthermore, women were thought inherently suited to
the methodical, painstaking aspects of librarianship because
they "delight[ed] in self-sacrifice," "had greater ability than
men to bear pain with fortitude," and were thus more patient
and "could perform the most monotonous tasks without boredom."[8] Garrison, Schiller, and other historians of this
early period are fond of quoting Justin Winsor, speaking at
the 1877 conference of British and American librarians in
London, as an example of an important library figure who
summed up the prevailing attitude toward women in the profession: "In American libraries we set a high value on
women's work. They soften our atmosphere, they lighten
our labor, they are equal to our work, and for the money
they cost--if we must gauge such labor by such rules--they
are infinitely better than equivalent salaries will produce of
the other sex."[9]

Because the nineteenth century view of women was so
narrowly circumscribed, the entrance of many women into
the library profession at the turn of the century (especially
single women--and they were then the only possible candidates
for employment among the female sex) certainly initiated the
derogatory spinster image which so plagues librarians today.
The cultural assumption that women could not "be permitted
to work outside the home" because "their position in life was
defined in terms of a purity opposed to everything characteristic of the outer world"[10] led to other restrictions--wom-
en could not "testify in court, hold title to property, establish businesses, or sign papers as witnesses."[11] Nineteenth
century feminists rightly saw that economic subservience was
the root of female oppression and one of their major aims
became that of establishing the right of women to work outside the home. Ironically, to make their point, feminists
like the Bloomer girls used the "two-edged" idea of "feminine purity" by which males justified "the confinement of
women to a domestic role," bending the notion to their own
ends by arguing that, "if women were inherently more virtu-
ous than men, should they not use their influence to purify
politics, business, the world of public affairs?"[12] Thus
nineteenth century feminists conspired with men in the myth
that females were purer, more sensitive, more moral than
males--and used the myth to argue that women's entry into
a profession would "uplift" it.[13] Since one purpose of the
library was to provide "uplift" to the masses, unmarried
women won the right to enter librarianship long before they
were permitted entry into other professions: but they entered the profession just at a time when their purity, mod-

esty, and reserve had been established by a century of belief
and used as a basis for attaining opposing ends. [14]

Among the men most instrumental in assimilating
women into the library profession was Melvil Dewey, who,
as early as 1886, deprecated "the waste of women's intellectual force" in domesticity and urged fathers, who would
"not expect" "a group of idle sons, thirty or forty years of
age, hanging around your home" to "be contented," to open
to their daughters as well "the real opportunities of life."[15]
Some have asserted that Melvil Dewey sought the employment
of women in libraries--because of his "progressive (as well
as erotic) affinity for women"--but that he nevertheless saw
to it that, "while females from the library schools became
clerks and assistants and heads of small libraries, the most
honored and well-paid librarians were men."[16]

But such grudging praise leaves out account of Dewey's
protégées: Katharine Lucinda Sharp (1865-1914) who "established and directed the first school for the formal education
of librarians in the Midwest at Armour Institute, Chicago,
in 1893," and, from 1897-1907 "administered the Library
School and Library at the University of Illinois"; Misses
Robbins, Foote, and Kroeger who managed library schools
in other parts of the country;[17] Margaret Mann, cataloger
and teacher at the Carnegie Library and Library School and
the Paris Library School and author of Introduction to Cataloging and the Classification of Books;[18] Jennie Maas Flexner, who, at the beginning of the twentieth century, urged
the education of black as well as white librarians, headed the
Readers' Adviser's Office of the New York Public Library,
and authored books on circulation and readers' advisory services;[19] and Mary Salome Cutler, instituted by Dewey as
chairman of the permanent committee for the International
Library Exhibit over strong objections.[20] In fact, though it
took women some time to establish themselves in positions
of power in librarianship, as early as 1875 eighteen women
were "managing collections of over ten thousand volumes,"
no small collection by contemporary standards. By 1950 "the
majority (80 per cent) of the state librarians and state library agency directors were women"; by 1950 women edited
"about one half of the national library periodicals" and headed
many academic libraries. It is only since 1950 that "the
trend for women to be replaced by men ... has reduced
women's representation in leadership positions to an appal-
lingly low level."[21]

Because of his successful efforts to open librarianship
to women, Melvil Dewey has been castigated as the major
culprit in the creation of the feminine image which plagues
the library profession today. Certainly the presence of many
females in the profession helped to spawn the image. But
the fact that women were for a long time very visible members of the profession, both numerically and because of the
prestigious positions they held, does not fully account for the
persistence of the "old maid" image in a time when unmarried women no longer make up a majority of the profession,
when women hold few positions of power within it, [22] and
when "unisex" has made great inroads into traditional male-
female roles. [23] Ironically, however, Melvil Dewey can be
blamed for the durability of the spinster image of the librarian, not because he encouraged women to enter the field, but
because of another of his obsessions (held in common with
many others of his age)--his obsession with "efficiency. "

Dewey's interest in efficiency was evinced at first in
spelling reform (he even began to spell his name "Melvil
Dui") and the development of an efficient classification system. By 1911 he had institutionalized his interest in efficiency by becoming President of the Efficiency Society [of
New York], a somewhat diffuse organization which sought to
find an orderly terrestrial utopia through efficiency, and was
fascinated by the rising schools of scientific--and later human relations--management, the time-and-motion studies of
the engineers, the insights into personnel problems of the
social scientists. [24] Scientific management in general, and
the technique of the personality inventory specifically, was
what raised the feminine image of librarianship from that of
a momentary fact of occupational demography to a universal
by placing it on a "scientific" footing; the large female population among the librarians who were to be scientifically
"managed" provided a ready seedbed for this management concept; but it was scientific management as much as occupational demography which created and perpetuated a submissive,
dependent, spinsterish librarian image of such strength and
durability that it is now automatically assumed to have a real,
not just a mythological basis.

To understand the obsession with efficiency and scientific management of prominent Americans like Dewey, one
must consider the peculiar social characteristics of pre-
World War I America from which these movements sprang.
America had become an industrialized nation; the increasing
size and power of the business corporation had begun to be

accompanied by urban unrest; urbanization, a concomitant of
industrialization, brought with it increases in poverty, crime,
and disease; immigration continued but the immigrants were
no longer primarily from Western Europe but less "desirable," less oriented toward the Protestant Ethic: Chinese,
Japanese, Slavs, and Levantines, truly "foreigners." Turn-
of-the-century Americans saw the old ways and the old order
threatened everywhere, and the reformer of what has come
to be called the Progressive Era was spawned from the social unrest of the time, from the enormous social problems
which cried for solution, as well as from the evangelical and
charitable traditions of an earlier age. 25 The Progressive
Era was a period in which reformers worked to break the
trusts, tame big business, establish better working conditions, collective bargaining, unionization, and "industrial
democracy" for the working-man. The reformers addressed
themselves not only to economic problems but to social ones:
they worked for the conservation of public lands and instituted public schools, public libraries, the beginnings of a welfare system, and the reform school and asylum to meet the
needs of the urbanized common man. Some historians of
this period argue that the net effect of such reform was
basically conservative: by alleviating the symptoms of an
unjust social system but not altering the causes of injustice,
these reformers helped to maintain an inequitable status quo.
They worked against the trusts because "they rejected the
disorder of the uncontrolled market," but their answer to the
economic jungle was "to preserve middle-class independence
through expanding the realm of 'professionalism.' "26 In
every case they solved a social problem by establishing a
new institution, one in which the professional expert handed
down decisions about how the client would be served and his
problems solved. They developed such institutions as the
asylum and reformatory, 27 the public school, 28 and the social welfare system29 as much to control the immigrants and
prevent social disorder as to improve the lot of the poor.
Even the conservation movement was primarily "rational
planning to promote efficient development and use of all natural resources."30

     The library was, of course, affected by the institu-
tionalization of reform. The public library, like the school,
was to provide "moral uplift" as it served its role as a
"people's university." But Michael Harris has persuasively
argued that the public library in America was also seen by
the established power structure as a "conservator of order"
from its inception. 31 Andrew Carnegie, a library trustee of

some power, believed that "the result of knowledge ... is to
make men not violent revolutionists, but cautious evolution-
ists; not destroyers, but careful improvers."[32] The chain
of Carnegie Libraries built during the Depression years,
when the possibility of a working class revolution was for
many in the establishment a bogey that seemed to be taking
on flesh, attests to the seriousness of his belief in the library as a means of social control. Such critics of Harris's version of the origins and nature of the public library
as Harwell and Michener do not really shake the thesis that
the library was a subtle means of social control, for they
confirm that men like Ticknor and Carnegie "were skeptical
of the 'mob' and the influx of immigrants into American cities" and, denying "both the privilege of inherited aristocracy
and the sentimental romanticism of the emerging populism, "
left a vacuum into which the middle class expert and the scientific manager could move.[33]

     The reform impulse and the impulse to control the
masses were not a surprising combination if "efficiency" and
expertise are given the topmost priority in the scale of values, ranking above such other considerations as the quality
of life and social justice. The Progressives believed that
society must be made efficient to be good, for "efficient and
good came closer to meaning the same thing in these years
than in any other period of American history. " Efficiency
meant "a turning toward hard work and away from feeling,
toward discipline and away from sympathy, toward masculinity and away from femininity."[34] President Theodore
Roosevelt himself desired to supplant social conflict by solving "social and economic problems ... by experts who would
undertake scientific investigations and devise workable solutions"; he had "an almost unlimited faith in applied science."[35]
The elevation of the professional expert and the belief in science as a solution to social problems of all types led to a
concept of "scientific management," first in industry, then in
other social institutions. When industrial managers recognized the elements of social control implicit in the methodol-
ogies of the behaviorism prevalent in the psychiatry and psychology of the period,[36] they began to see in "psychology and
its expert practitioners" a possible "small measure of defense" against organized labor.[37] By the 1920s, industrial
managers saw that they could use the techniques developed by
the social scientists to manipulate their employees more sub-
tly and with greater social approval than by trying to gain
their ends through raw displays of power.[38] As Loren
Baritz puts it:

> Through motivation studies, through counseling,
> through selection devices calculated to hire only
> certain types of people, through attitude surveys,
> communication, role-playing, and all the rest in
> their bag of schemes, social scientists slowly
> moved toward a science of behavior. Thus manage-
> ment was given a slick new approach to its prob-
> lems of control. Authority gave way to manipula-
> tion, and workers could no longer be sure they
> were being exploited. [39]

The library's acceptance of social science techniques
in personnel administration, as we shall see, began only
after their effectiveness in industry had been well demonstrated. But some librarians--notably Melvil Dewey--had
prepared the way for the acceptance of applied psychology by
their early espousal of the ideals of efficiency and scientific
management as modes of curing social ills and improving social institutions. What Dewey and other exponents of efficiency failed to see was that such humanitarian institutions
as the library, the public school, the asylum, the reformatory, and the social casework system were built on premises
different from those of the business corporation. Social institutions which arise from a desire to uplift the masses, to
allay problems of ignorance, poverty, and disease, to open
opportunities for upward mobility to the poor, have within
them a built-in contradiction. Channeling humanitarian im-
pulses into an institutional framework and staffing that institution with professional experts especially trained in solving
the particular problem which the institution was formed to al-
leviate inevitably adds an element of social control to the
charitable impulse: it becomes the professional expert, not
the client served, who knows what the social desideratum is.
Increased size adds to the problem: large institutions, with
large numbers of employees, must become bureaucracies with
a separate administrative apparatus. And managing an institution, unifying a disparate personnel into an effective whole,
maintaining efficiency, and competing successfully for limited
budgetary funds induces a desire among managers to emulate
the methods of the successful American business corporation
which has had long practice in solving the same problems.
Espousing the business ethic in some ways becomes a practical necessity. But superimposing an "efficient" business
ethic on a humanitarian institution is in some sense a contradiction in terms; institutions which originate because of
sympathy for the lot of the poor and the oppressed begin to
find themselves with their own vested interest in maintaining

the status quo of the society which supports them, find themselves becoming more dominantly instruments of social control than vehicles of reform. [40]

Both the assumption that the twin goals of humani-
tarianism and efficiency could be merged (shared by the library with other social welfare institutions of the time and
illustrated in microcosm in the career of Melvil Dewey) and
the large numbers of female "professional experts" employed
in the library, then, encouraged the scientific management
and human relations schools of library administration, (after
all, if one is to "manage" efficiently, the weaker sex, presumably more docile and easily led, lends itself to manipulation the more readily). One social science technique apparently best adapted to personnel management, the paper-
and-pencil personality inventory (particularly its Masculinity-
Femininity Scale), when added to an employee population
which remained mostly female, gave durability to the librarian-
as-spinster image, for personality testing seemed to place
that image on a scientific foundation.

Applied psychology made its debut in industry, first
through its use as an aid in advertising, then, after World
War I, as a method of employee selection and placement. [41]
The efficiency notions embodied in scientific management
logically culminated, in the 1950s, in its more complex version, the human relations school of management, based on a
hierarchical pattern of human needs postulated by Abraham
Maslow and Richard Centers. [42] Exponents of human relations management argue that, since dissatisfaction on the job
creates poor performance, and poor performance results in
lessened output, the organization must make the jobs of its
employees as interesting and satisfying as possible, perhaps
going so far as to implement participative management methods and profit sharing schemes, [43] to give employees a sense
that the success of the organization is central to the fulfillment of their many manifold needs. [44] But these theories
soon took a curious turn. If pleasing employees was vital to
the success of an organization, why not simply hire employees
that will be satisfied with existing jobs in an organization?
Why keep changing jobs to suit people? Why not more accurately select employees who will suit the apparatus and
philosophy of the organization in the first place? How these
ideally suitable employees were to be selected posed a problem to which the predictive aptitude and personality testing
of the applied psychologists seemed to find the solution.

The "objective paper-pencil questionnaire" method of personality assessment was first constructed by R. S. Woodworth; his "Personal Data Sheet" was used to evaluate large numbers of draftees during World War I. The federal government judged it so successful that "a flurry of new tests" developed after the war, culminating, in the early 1940s, with the "most successful personality inventory to date," the Minnesota Multiphasic Personality Inventory (MMPI).[45] The MMPI was a direct descendant of the Woodworth Scale, as are its successors, particularly the Guilford-Martin Inventory of Factors GAMIN and the California Personality Inventory (CPI); the apparent success of such personality inventories in personality screening is evidenced by the large numbers of industrial, educational, and governmental organizations which rely on the results of such tests in their hiring and promotion practices.[46]

Although tests to measure those personality traits which make people successful in their work have become common placement and promotion instruments in American industry and are used as predictors of success in some colleges and in the military, the administrators of library schools and libraries have not yet joined the trend. They have placed their confidence in the more traditional methods of selection: acceptable scores on such achievement and/or intelligence tests as the Graduate Record Examination or the Miller Analogies Test,[47] academic grades, references from teachers or employers, and interviews[48] have been the sources from which admission to school or employment in the library field has been determined. We must not, however, be deceived by the fact that library administrators have not very often actually administered personality inventories to their employees or candidates for admission to their professional schools. The recurrence in piece after piece of library literature of adjectives from the Masculinity-Femininity Scales of the CPI or the GAMIN describing the traits of the librarian's allegedly "female" personality (feminine, meek, weak, gentle, helpful, dependent) indicates that the uniformity of the results in the few published studies in which librarians were given personality tests has convinced the library profession that there is a model librarian personality and that it is so well documented, so scientifically incontrovertible, that re-testing is not even necessary. (As a matter of fact, re-testing would only reaffirm the earlier results, since the items in the inventories are no true index of masculinity, femininity or actual trait-state concepts of the modern personality). Without paying individual library employees the

compliment of assuming that they might be unique were they
individually tested, the library profession has simply bought
the applied psychologists' package wholesale.

Librarians began to be given personality tests in the
1950s, not by library administrators but by other librarians
undertaking library surveys or doctoral research. The personality of the rather old womanish librarian which emerged
from these test results seemed for the first time to give the
old stereotypical image a scientific basis. Alice L. Bryan's
study of librarians, supported by R. R. Douglass's of library students five years later, showed that all librarians--
male and female--exhibit traits of orderliness, conscientious-
ness, responsibility, conservatism, and conformism, that
they lack vigor, ambition, and imagination, are introspective
rather than outgoing, somewhat insecure, more strongly interested in cultural and intellectual than in political and economic ideas, and that they rate high in femininity. [49]   It is
these early studies which have been the springboard for the
prolific literature on the "image problem" in library literature since then, though the way the test results were used
varied from decade to decade.

Until very recently, the personality test results of
librarians have been used only to make recommendations
about how best to fulfill the needs of these already in the
field, under the assumption that they were a fairly homogeneous group, as the personality tests seemed to indicate,
though there is a hint that, because they test out "feminine,"
they require careful "handling." Alan Brophy and George
Gazda's study is a case in point. [50]   These authors use the
personality profiles of librarians garnered by the Bryan and
Douglass investigations not to make a value judgment about
this personality type, nor to argue that new recruitment procedures should be instituted to produce either this model or
some alternate one, but to suggest personnel practices to
accommodate the alleged personality characteristics now scientifically unearthed. They are, in fact, rather cautious
about the validity of personality testing, and, though they
base their recommendations for personnel practices on the
librarians' "feminine" personality, these recommendations
are such common-sensical ones as any good personnel manager might elect without the benefit of any scientific findings
whatsoever. [51]

The 1960s and 1970s have, however, seen the advocacy
in library literature of a new use for personality tests.   The

argument is that personality tests ought to be part of the admission criteria of library schools, under the assumptions that certain personality profiles make people better librarians than others and that these personalities can and should be selected out by means of personality testing with only persons having the proper characteristics allowed to enter the profession. [52] Two quite recent studies which incorporate most of the results of various personality tests administered to librarians in their findings--those by Stuart Baillie and Howard Clayton--will illustrate the approach. Though they use the California Psychological Inventory (CPI) rather than the GAMIN used by Douglass and Bryan, Baillie and Clayton confirm the personality profile of the model librarian found earlier by Douglass and Bryan: librarians are not adventurous, clearthinking, outgoing, or daring--they are feminine, not masculine. Baillie concludes his work by arguing that the personality of the librarian is a crucial factor in later job success and that "attempts to isolate those types of personality most likely to succeed in libraries would be helpful"; he urges the "development of a personality scale to be used exclusively on librarians." [53] Clayton, distressed by the "feminine" results of personality tests he administered to male library students, argues that libraries should select more "aggressive," less "nurturant" personalities as employees in order that the library may become as "enterprising and ambitious, " as "central" as other educational institutions. [54]

Although much of the literature in psychological learned journals is profoundly skeptical of the validity of using personality inventories as a means of vocational prediction, [55] these tests have provided the scientific basis for the feminine image of the librarian in the twentieth century. An examination of the Masculinity-Femininity Scale which appears in all the personality inventories used on librarians will reveal the grounds on which the librarian--male and female--has been adjudged "feminine, " with all the nineteenth-century connotations of that term.

The striking similarity of the M-F Scales in the three major personality inventories used on librarians (the GAMIN, the MMPI, and the CPI) is obvious even on cursory examination; though the tests use slightly different terminology, they basically measure such personality traits as aggressivity vs. nurturance and amibiton vs. abasement as indices of masculinity and femininity. Further, they use many common questions to test for the traits alleged to separate males from fe-

males in our society. Thus, the MMPI 55-question masculinity-femininity scale has such items as "I would like to be
a soldier" (males mark true; females false) and "If I were
a reporter I would very much like to report sporting news"
(true for males, false for females). The CPI masculinity-
femininity scale also has the item "I would like to be a
soldier" and only alters the reporter question to read, "If I
were a reporter I would very much like to report news of
the theater" (false for males; true for females). The assumptions about what comprises masculinity-femininity in
these items are obviously identical. Psychologist Lewis R.
Goldberg, in his excellent history of personality scales and
inventories, accounts for the extensive item overlap in these
scales thus:

> Items devised around the turn of the century may
> have worked their way via Woodworth's Personal
> Data Sheet, to Thurstone and Thurstone's Person-
> ality Schedule, hence to Bernreuter's Personality
> Inventory, and later to the Minnesota Multiphasic
> Personality Inventory, where they were borrowed
> for the California Personality Inventory--only to
> serve as a source of items for the new Academic
> Behavior Inventory. As a result of the widespread
> practice of item borrowing, there is substantial
> item overlap between a number of present inven-
> tories. [56]

And Thomas F. Siess and Douglas N. Jackson find that personality inventories not only "have similar and often identical
items" and "scales possessing item overlap, " but they also
"use the same response format. "[57]

Because of the similarity of the M-F scales, a detailed examination of one of them (the femininity scale of the
CPI) will suffice to divulge their nature. Note that the correct answer to each item in this scale is keyed for female
respondents; males should respond to the items in the opposite way:

<u>Characteristic Items in the Femininity Scale</u>
<u>of the CPI</u>

I want to be an important person in the com-
    munity. (False)
I'm not the type to be a political leader.   (True)
I like mechanics magazines.   (False)

I think I would like the work of a librarian.   (True)

I'm pretty sure I know how we can settle the international problems we face today.   (False)

I must admit I feel sort of scared when I move to
  a strange place.   (True)

I like to go to parties and other affairs where there
  is lots of loud fun.   (False)

If I were a reporter I would like very much to report news of the theater.   (True)

I would like to be a nurse.   (True)

It is hard for me to "bawl out" someone who is
  not doing his job properly.   (True)

I very much like hunting.   (False)

I would like to be a soldier.   (False)

I think I could do better than most of the present
  politicians if I were in office.   (False)

I like to be with a crowd who play jokes on one
  another.   (False)

In school I was sometimes sent to the principal for
  cutting up.   (False)

I think I would like the work of a building con-
  tractor.   (False)

When I work at something I like to read and study
  about it.   (False)

I am somewhat afraid of the dark.   (True)

I like to boast about my achievements every now
  and then.   (False)

I think I would like to drive a racing car.   (False)

I must admit that I enjoy playing practical jokes
  on people.   (False)

At times I feel like picking a fist fight with someone.   (False)

The thought of being in an automobile accident is
  very frightening to me.   (True)

I think I would like the work of a garage mechanic.
  (False)

A windstorm terrifies me.   (True)

I think I would like the work of a dress designer.
  (True)

I think I would like the work of a clerk in a large
  department store.   (True) [58]

Of special interest to librarians is the [fourth] item, which is
keyed true only for females: people who have an interest in
librarianship are, ipso facto, feminine.   This professional
choice has been labeled feminine because, at the point in
history when the test item was constructed, more females

than males chose it for a vocation, a fact which may have
a certain statistical validity but is surely not indicative of
a profound psychological truth.

Yet the author, Harrison Gough, in his Interpreter's
Syllabus for the CPI, clearly intends this item, along with
the others, to fulfill these differentiating functions: "a) to
differentiate males from females; b) to distinguish between
deviant and sexually normal persons, and c) to define a
personological continuum that could be conceptualized as
"feminine" at one pole and masculine at the other. "59
Gough summarizes the model personalities of the two sexes
who score high in femininity (that is, they answer the items
mostly the way females should) in these terms:

> Males: appreciative, complaining, feminine,
> formal, meek, nervous, self-denying, sensitive,
> weak, worrying
> Females: conscientious, discreet, generous, gen-
> tle, helpful, mature, self-controlled, sympa-
> thetic, tactful, warm

And for males and females who score low in femininity,
Gough uses these adjective descriptions:

> Males: adventurous, aggressive, clearthinking,
> daring, impulsive, masculine, outgoing,
> pleasure-seeking, show-off, strong
> Females: coarse, dissatisfied, lazy, masculine,
> pleasure-seeking, restless, robust, self-
> centered, touchy, tough. 60

The normative tone of these adjectives is marked. Females
who feel unafraid of the phenomena of the natural world
(wind storms, the dark), who are pretty sure they could do
better than the Nixon administration did on Viet Nam or the
Ford administration on the economy but who would loathe
the work of a clerk in a department store and would much
prefer being important persons in their community are, then,
"coarse, dissatisfied, self-centered, and tough. " Males who
concur in all these likes and dislikes and share these opinions would, however, be "adventurous, clearthinking, and
strong. " But males who like the theater, prefer the work of
a dress designer or librarian to that of a soldier or mechanic, and are socially inclined are "complaining, meek,
nervous, weak and worrying. " Males but not females should
be "given to braggadocio and hyperbole, " should be aggressive

(they should like to hunt and have fistfights), should enjoy
loud fun, practical jokes, politics, and have decided views
on public affairs.[61]

The spillover of the adjective descriptions for
masculinity-femininity into the adjective descriptions of the
other scales of the CPI is high. Thus, males who score
high on self-acceptance are described as "confident, enterprising, imaginative"; women who score high are "bossy,
sarcastic, argumentative, and demanding. " Males who score
high on dominance are "ambitious, resourceful, self-confi-
dent, forceful. " Females who score high are "aggressive,
bossy, conceited, demanding. " On the other hand, females
who score low are "gentle, shy, trusting, " but males are
"apathetic, irresponsible, and submissive. "[62] The masculinity-femininity scale, then, incorporates other personality
traits tested for in the other scales of the CPI, and assumptions which underlie the choice of items selected to reveal
personality traits are common to all the scales.

Recalling that the bulk of these items were formulated
at the turn of the century, how accurate is such a personality profile for the model male and female of the 1970s?
Not very, says Lee Chronbach, a prolific and respected
psychologist:

> In an era of LSD, riots in the streets, the ubiqui-
> tous credit card, and new sexual standards, items
> that once betokened deviancy may today be within
> the normal range. Even in the 1940's the average
> adolescent had an MMPI profile much like that of
> the adult psychopath. Normality, defined em-
> pirically as the response typical of a mixed bag of
> Minnesota adults 30 years ago, cannot represent
> normality for all time to come, at all levels of
> age and education. [63]

Some psychologists argue that dated cultural biases are built
into the tests so deeply as to make them invalid for middle-
class males and all career-oriented females. Clark E. Vincent, for example, says:

> The items in many M-F tests and scales were
> selected initially because they discriminated sig-
> nificantly between the responses of the sexes at
> the time the tests were constructed. To the de-
> gree that these items reflect the concept of a tra-

ditional, male-dominant family and society; to the
degree that male-female role expectations are becoming more equalitarian; and to the degree that
role expectations effect socialization; it would appear to follow that M-F items need to be revised
and M-F scores reinterpreted within the context of
current male-female role expectations. [64]

Vincent argues that many items in the CPI scale are thus
"time- and culture-bound. " The traditional nature of the
items assumes a domestic role for women, not one in which
they are "expected to assume leadership responsibilities in
community, civic, political, and religious organizations, and
expected to make noteworthy contributions in a variety of occupations and professional pursuits. " Modern women "cannot afford ... to be very fearful of the dark, windstorms,
moving to a strange place, or being in an automobile accident, " and they will "tend to become accustomed to crowds,
parties, loud fun, excitement, and practical jokes. " These
women will score lower on femininity than "normal. "

Middle-class males as well as women are penalized
by the items in these tests, for men will tend to score high
on femininity as long as "items are included which formerly
described the female in a tradition-oriented society, but which
now tend to describe the 'other-directed, ' 'organization man'
in-the-gray-flannel-suit whose success depends more on a
psychological than on a physical manipulation of environment
and people. " Middle-class males who have been taught to
"avoid fighting ... and spitting on the sidewalk" will see
"little upward mobility involved in the work of building con-
tractor, garage mechanic, or soldier. " The masculinity-
femininity scale of the CPI thus has both socioeconomic and
sexist biases. [65]

Vincent's last point helps to explain why all college
males tend to score high in femininity and low in dominance
and aggression, as other psychologists also attest. [66] Not
only do college males tend to score high in femininity, but
so do the brightest elementary school children, male as well
as female, [67] and creative, high-achieving adults. [68] People
in all these categories tend either to be middle-class in origin or aspire to become so, seeing in various cultural and
educational pursuits ways to climb the upward mobility lad-
der.   Male librarians and library students fit this larger
pattern.

As males and females depart from stereotypical sex
roles, the sexes are becoming more similar;[69] when males
and females in the 1970's are asked to respond to the items
in the masculinity-femininity scales "in terms of their 'ideal
women'" the results "showed rejection of more than one half
of the items originally keyed as feminine, and little difference in response by sex."[70] A person who scores high in
femininity on a personality inventory is merely admitting that
he likes "feminine games, hobbies, and vocations" and denying that he likes their masculine equivalents; but labeling
such choices as characteristically feminine or masculine is
inaccurate because, as Jerry Wiggins notes:

> Here there is almost complete contamination of
> content and form.... Individuals may score high
> on this scale by presenting themselves as liking
> many things.... They may also score high by
> endorsing interests that, although possibly feminine,
> are also socially desirable, such as an interest in
> poetry, dramatics, news of the theatre, and artistic
> pursuits.... Finally, of course, individuals with
> a genuine preference for activities that are con-
> ceived by our culture as 'feminine' will achieve
> high scores on this scale.[71]

In short, for modern college-educated people, the turn-of-
the-century items which once discriminated between males
and females no longer do so because the roles of the two
sexes have become far more identical than they once were,
and interests once labeled as belonging purely to the one or
the other are now universally shared; of course, this uni-
sexuality does irreparable damage to the whole idea of discriminating between the sexes in the traditional ways which
are reflected in the items of the M-F scales.

Male librarians, then, quite logically test out "feminine" in these personality inventories; but, given the absurdity of many of the items, why do female librarians continue
to attain even median femininity scores? Vytautas Bieliauskas and Simon Miranda postulate one possible explanation:

> The obviousness of two masculinity-femininity
> tests [the GAMIN and the CPI] ... was examined
> by assigning three groups of 30 college men and
> three groups of 30 college women to three different
> conditions: a) standard administration, b) respond
> as college men would, c) respond as college women

> would. As predicted, both sexes could produce
> scores typical for either sex on the Fe scale....
> The data raise questions about the interpretation
> of both M-F tests under standard conditions....
> Their items are so obvious that some writers have
> questioned whether they assess the person's own
> psychological M-F or his awareness of the correct
> stereotypic response. [72]

Both William Whyte and Martin Gross, in their popular attacks on personality testing, [73] have shown their readers how
easy it is to fake on these tests; it is possible that such
test-taking chicanery is more natural to women than to men:
women, culturally brought up to please males by exaggerating
their feminine squeals at the sight of spiders and getting
lower grades than boys so as to make males feel superior,
might find "faking feminine" almost second nature; males
might need more instruction in "faking masculine," such as
they received from Bieliauskas and Miranda. Chronbach
confirms the obviousness of the CPI items in his review of
this test, when he notes that "twelve of the principal scales
are much affected by a desire to fake good and bad."[74]
Gergen and Marlowe suggest that women tend to fake their
responses to personality inventory items more often than
men because women have a greater "need-approval" and because "many personality scales are standardized on a male
population," are written by male psychologists who conceive
the theories behind them "with men in mind."[75] Male preconceptions and biases are intrinsic in the test items; sensitive, educated women who have coped with such biases from
infancy can hardly fail to detect--and respond--to them.

However obvious, even to a layman, the shakiness of
the concept of masculinity-femininity enshrined in the M-F
scales of the popular personality inventories, large "scientific" conclusions have been drawn from their use on librarians. It is the nineteenth century view of femininity expressed
in these scales which has nourished the spinster image of the
librarian.

The personality inventory, especially its M-F scale,
is in many ways the logical culmination of the social control
aspects of the Progressive Era, its delight in the use of science to promote social order. The danger to the library
profession is that the library administrator is urged to emulate the business ethos not only in the professional literature
he reads, [76] but, like all Americans, in the broad propa-

ganda attack of the business community itself, which prose-
lytizes its way of life to legitimize its position, to equate
the business ethos with "the American way of life."[77] Such
pressures encourage the staffing of libraries with personnel
who "fit in," by personality inventory screening, for such
methods are natural enough concomitants to making libraries
more like business corporations. Thus when Baillie and
Clayton argue that librarians should be more "masculine,"
they mean more ruthless, displaying more business acumen,
more of the businessman's "get-up-and-go" ethic. Then libraries can better compete for government funds, be more
efficient, attain an improved social status. These authors
do not recommend a more masculine librarian in the hope
that he will radically alter the status quo, for the personality
inventory makes no pretense that it can become an instrument for the radical renovation of institutions; the nature of
the assumptions behind what constitute normal patterns of
behavior for the two sexes are so tradition-bound that they
can only foster the old vested interests: employees will be
placed in existing positions to work for existing goals--and
kept happy there by capitalizing on their alleged traits.

A second danger lies in the fact that the library administrator seems to be placed in the happy situation of
having ready to hand large numbers of "female" employees,
often female in fact but also female by testable trait. The
alleged personalities of such employees can give managers
the comforting illusion that they secretly want to be dominated, that they will respond well to being "handled" by
"managers" who, giving full consideration to their tempera-
mental, childlike, feminine personalities, can give them an
illusion of "participative management" but make certain that
they are in fact firmly led. Ironically, of course, those
who hold the purse strings for libraries--college and university administrators, municipal governing boards, boards
of trustees--include the library administrator himself in the
feminine, manipulable category. Arguing "scientifically"
that professional people are dependent, timid, self-sacri-
ficing--in short, feminine (in the nineteenth-century sense)
--can only inspire domineering patterns of behavior in their
managers.

Until the personality inventory is viewed as scientifically unsound and the manipulative, social control assumptions behind the scientific management and human relations schools of administration of which it is so logically an
instrument are recognized as unworthy of a profession dedi-

cated to individual freedom and free inquiry, no change in
sexual occupation patterns, no alteration of the status of
women within the profession will enable the librarian to ease
off those Red Cross shoes--however much they are beginning
to pinch.

Notes

1. Ronald Benge, Libraries and Cultural Change (London:
   Clive Bingley, 1970), p. 216.
2. Jesse H. Shera, "The Compleat Librarian" and Other
   Essays (Cleveland: Case Western Reserve Press,
   1971), pp. 69-70; Anita R. Schiller, "Origin of
   Sexism in Librarianship," American Libraries 3
   (April 1972): 427.
3. Arnold P. Sable, "The Sexuality of the Library Profession: Male and Female Librarian," Wilson Library Bulletin 43 (April 1969): 751. Justin Winsor
   and Melvil Dewey were early spokesmen for this
   view.
4. Howard Clayton, "Femininity and Job Satisfaction among
   Male Library Students," College & Research Libs.
   31 (November 1970): 398.
5. Dee Garrison, "The Tender Technicians: The Feminization of Public Librarianship, 1876-1905," Journal of
   Social History 6 (Winter 1972-73): 152-153.
6. Benge, Libraries and Cultural Change, pp. 217-218.
7. Garrison, "Tender Technicians," pp. 131-134, 152-153.
8. Ibid.
9. "The English Conference: Official Report of Proceedings," Library Journal 2 (January-February 1878):
   280.
10. John Demos, "The American Family in Past Time,"
    American Scholar 43 (Summer 1974): 430, 433-434.
    For a more fully documented account see Demos,
    A Little Commonwealth: Family Life in Plymouth
    Colony (N. Y.: Oxford University Press, 1970).
11. William H. Chase, The American Woman: Her Changing
    Social, Economic, and Political Role, 1920-1970
    (Oxford: Oxford University Press, 1972), p. 5.
12. Demos, "The American Family in Past Time," p. 435.
13. Christopher Lasch, The New Radicalism in America,
    1889-1963 (N. Y.: Knopf, 1965), pp. 56-68.
14. Chase, American Woman, pp. 13-15, 100.
15. Grosvenor Dawe, Melvil Dewey: Seer: Inspirer: Doer,
    1851-1931 (Essex Co., N. Y.: Lake Placid Club,
    1932), pp. 91-92.

16. Garrison, "Tender Technicians," p. 152.
17. Laurel A. Grotzinger, "Melvil Dewey: The 'Sower,'" Journal of Library History 3 (1968): 315-17.
18. Laurel A. Grotzinger, "The Proto-Feminist Librarian at the Turn of the Century: Two Studies," Journal of Library History 10 (July 1975): 195-213.
19. Sidney Ditzion, "Flexner, Jennie Maas," Dictionary of American Biography, supplement three (New York: Scribners, 1941-45), pp. 280-281.
20. Dawe, Dewey, p. 91.
21. Anita Schiller, "Report on Women in Librarianship," American Libraries 2 (December 1971): 1215. See also Margaret Ann Corwin, "An Investigation of Female Leadership in Regional, State, and Local Library Associations, 1876-1923," Library Quarterly 44 (April 1974): 133-144. The changes wrought by the influx of married women into librarianship with their ambiguities about combining careers with marriage and their job discontinuity should be explored.
22. Valerie Kincade Oppenheimer, "Demographic Influence on Female Employment," in Joan Huber, ed., Changing Women in a Changing Society (Chicago: University of Chicago Press, 1973), pp. 184-199, especially pp. 197-198; a comparison of the U.S. census reports on professional workers for 1960 and 1970 and the ALA Membership Directory all indicate that married women are now a majority of the library profession.
23. The effects of the entry of married women into a profession are suggested in such articles as that by Matina Horner, "The Motive to Avoid Success and Changing Aspirations of College Women," in Judith M. Bardwick, ed., Readings on the Psychology of Women (N.Y.: Harper & Row, 1972), pp. 62-67; also see Ralph H. Turner, "Some Aspects of Women's Ambition," American Journal of Sociology (November 1964): 272; Mirra Komarovsky, "Cultural Contradictions and Sex Roles: the Masculine Case," in Huber, Changing Women, pp. 119-121; Juanita Kreps, Sex in the Marketplace; American Women at Work (Baltimore: Johns Hopkins Press, 1971), pp. 17, 42, 87; and Eric Bow, "Interrupted Careers: the Married Woman as Librarian," Ontario Library Review 56 (June 1972): 76-78.
24. Samuel Haber, Efficiency and Uplift: Scientific Management in the Progressive Era, 1890-1920 (Chicago: University of Chicago Press, 1964), pp. 73-74; see

also Dawe, Dewey, pp. 3, 117 for brief references
to Dewey's presidency of this society.   Haber, in
Chapters II and III, gives a succinct account of "industrial engineering" in the program of the Taylor-
ites; and Vernon K. Dibble, "Occupations and Ideologies, " American Journal of Sociology 68 (September 1962): 236 discusses the dissemination of the
business ethic in American culture.
25.   See Richard Hofstadter, The Age of Reform (N. Y.:
Knopf, 1956), pp. 171-184.
26.   Haber, Efficiency and Uplift, p. xii.   For a more detailed revisionist view of the Progressives, see Ga-
briel Kolko, The Triumph of Conservatism: A Rein-
terpretation of American History, 1900-1916 (Glen-
coe, N. Y.:   Free Press, 1963).
27.   David J. Rothman, The Discovery of the Asylum: Social Order and Disorder in the New Republic (Boston: Little, Brown & Co. , 1971).
28.   Michael B. Katz, The Irony of Early School Reform:
Educational Innovation in Mid-Nineteenth Century
Massachusetts (Boston: Beacon, 1968).
29.   Raymond A. Mohl, Poverty in New York (N. Y.:   Oxford University Press, 1971).
30.   Samuel P. Hays, Conservation and the Gospel of Efficiency: The Progressive Conservation Movement,
1890-1920 (N. Y.:   Atheneum, 1969), p. 2.
31.   Michael Harris, "The Purpose of the American Public
Library, " Library Journal 98 (September 1973): 2509.
32.   Ibid. , p. 2511; see also George Bobinski, Carnegie Libraries (Chicago: ALA, 1969), pp. 11, 104-105 and
Peter Mickelson, "American Society and the Public
Library in the Thought of Andrew Carnegie, " Journal
of Library History 10 (April 1975): 117-138 for more
information on Carnegie's motives and his critics.
33.   Richard Harwell and Roger Michener, "As Public as
the Town Pump, " Library Journal 99 (April 1974):
959-963.
34.   Haber, Efficiency and Uplift, p. ix. [emphasis mine].
35.   Hays, Conservation and the Gospel of Efficiency, pp.
3, 267.
36.   John C. Burnham, "Psychiatry, Psychology and the
Progressive Movement, " American Quarterly 12
(Winter 1960): 465.   The argument that science is
never revolutionary but always part of the evolution
of accepted social concepts is made by scientists as
well: See Stephen Toulmin, Human Understanding
(Princeton: Princeton Univ. Press, 1972): 98-117,

which counters the opposing views of T. S. Kuhn.
For an analysis of the uses to which science has
been put in America see also Michael Kammen, The
Contrapuntal Civilization (N.Y.: Cornell University
Press, 1971), pp. 23, 277-8 and Richard Hofstadter,
Anti-Intellectualism in American Life (N.Y.: Knopf,
1964), p. 51.

37. Loren Baritz, The Servants of Power: A History of
the Use of Social Science in American Industry
(Middletown, Connecticut: Wesleyan Univ. Press,
1960), pp. 21-22.

38. Milton Derber, "The Idea of Industrial Democracy in
America, 1915-1935," Labor History 8 (Winter 1967):
8, 27.

39. Baritz, Servants of Power, p. 209; Amitai Etzioni, The
Active Society (N.Y.: Free Press, 1968), p. 643,
makes the same point.

40. John Higham, "Hanging Together: Divergent Unities in
American History," Journal of American History 61
(June 1974): 26.

41. See Baritz, Chapter 2, "The Birth of Industrial Psychology," Servants of Power, pp. 21-43, for an account of the beginnings of the use of psychology by
management.

42. A lucid account of Maslow's theory of needs can be
found in Douglas M. McGregor, "The Human Side
of Enterprise," in Paul Wasserman and Mary Lee
Bundy, eds., Reader in Library Administration
(Washington, D.C.: Microcard Eds., 1968), pp.
210-216, especially pp. 212-213.

43. Frederick G. Lesieur, ed., The Scanlon Plan: A
Frontier in Labor-Management Cooperation (Cambridge: Technology Press of M.I.T., 1958), esp.
pp. 11-16.

44. See for example, Chris Argyris, Personality and Organization (N.Y.: Harper, 1957); Douglas McGregor,
"Human Side," pp. 210-216; Frederick J. Roethlis-
berger, Man-in-Organization (Cambridge: Harvard
University Press, 1968); Maurice P. Marchant,
"Participative Management in Libraries," in Elizabeth W. Stone, ed., New Directions in Staff Development (Chicago: ALA, 1971), pp. 28-38; and
Chester I. Barnard, "The Theory of Authority," in
Wasserman and Bundy, eds., Reader in Library Administration, pp. 182-192.

45. James N. Butcher, ed., Objective Personality Assessment: Changing Perspectives (New York: Academic

Press, 1972), p. 12; A. T. Poffenberger, Principles
of Applied Psychology (New York: Appleton-Century,
1942), pp. 580-581. For a more detailed account
of the history of the development of the personality
inventory, see Philip H. DuBois, A History of Psychological Testing (Boston: Allyn & Bacon, 1970),
pp. 94ff.

46. Martin L. Gross, The Brain Watchers (N. Y.: Random
House, 1962), p. 6, and James N. Butcher, Objective Personality Assessment, p. 13.

47. Stuart Baillie, Library School and Job Success (Denver:
University of Denver Studies in Librarianship 1
(1963): 15). Baillie finds the MAT far superior to
the GRE for predicting academic success.

48. See, as examples of the widespread faith in grades,
references, and interviews, Joseph L. Wheeler and
Herbert Goldhor, Practical Administration of Public
Libraries (N. Y.: Harper & Row, 1962), pp. 218-
233; Leigh Estabrook, "Job Seekers in a Buyers'
Market: How Library Employers Judge Candidates, "
Library Journal 78 (February 1973): 285-7; Robert
B. Downs, "Library School Administration, " in
Harold Borko, ed., Targets for Research in Library
Education (Chicago: ALA, 1973), pp. 86-99; and
Lucille Whalen, "Library School Faculty and Stu-
dents, " Ibid., pp. 100-110.

49. Alice I. Bryan, The Public Librarian (N. Y.: Columbia
Univ. Press, 1952); R. R. Douglass, "The Person-
ality of the Librarian, " Ph. D. dissertation, Univ. of
Chicago, 1957.

50. Alfred L. Brophy and George M. Gazda, "Handling the
Problem Staff Member, " in Wasserman and Bundy,
eds., Reader in Library Administration, pp. 218,
220.

51. Ibid., p. 224.

52. This "predictive" school seems to be gaining ground
rapidly. A check of the cumulative index for Vols.
1-29 of Dissertation Abstracts indicates that, of the
thirty-four dissertations listed in the Library Science
subheadings pertaining to personnel, nine are in the
area of predictive testing. Among them see, for
example, F. L. Adair, "The Development of a Scale
to Measure the Service Orientation of Librarians"
(University of North Carolina at Chapel Hill, 1968),
who advocates using the CPI for library school admission; G. S. Baillie, "An Investigation of Objective
Admission Variables as They Relate to Academic and

Job Success in One Graduate Library Education Program" (Washington Univ. of St. Louis, 1967); Eugene Holt Wilson, "Pre-professional Background of Students in a Library School" (Univ. of Ill. at Urbana, 1937). Baillie lists unpublished M.A. theses on the same subject, as do J. Periam Danton and LeRoy C. Merritt, Characteristics of the Graduates of the University of California School of Librarianship, "Occasional Papers," No. 22 (Urbana: Library School, University of Illinois, 1951).

53. Baillie, Library School and Job Success, p. 87.

54. Howard Clayton, "Femininity and Job Satisfaction," p. 398.

55. As examples of the large body of psychological literature dubious of the validity of using personality inventories as a means of vocational prediction see Mary Louise Griffin and Sr. M. Rita Flaherty, "Correlation of CPI Traits with Academic Achievement," Educational & Psychological Measurements 24 (Summer 1964): 370; E. E. Ghiselli and R. P. Barthol, "The Validity of Personality Inventories in the Selection of Employees," Journal of Applied Psychology 37 (January 1953): 18-20; N. Q. Brill and G. W. Beebe, "Some Applications of a Follow-Up Study to Psychiatric Standards for Mobilization," American Journal of Psychology 109 (December 1952): 402; Eli Ginzberg, The Ineffective Soldier: The Lost Divisions (N. Y.: Columbia University Press, 1959), pp. 178, 184, 187; Donald E. Super, Appraising Vocational Fitness (N. Y.: Harper & Row, 1962), p. 520, among others.

56. Lewis R. Goldberg, "A Historical Survey of Personality Scales and Inventories," in Paul McReynolds, ed., Advances in Psychological Assessment 2 (Palo Alto, California: Science and Behavior Books, 1971): 335.

57. Thomas F. Siess and Douglas N. Jackson, "The Personality Research Form and Vocational Interest Research," ibid., p. 111.

58. Harrison Gough, "Identifying Psychological Femininity," Educational & Psychological Measurement 12 (August 1952): 429-430.

59. Harrison Gough, "An Interpreter's Syllabus for the California Psychological Inventory," in Paul McReynolds, Advances in Psychological Assessment, 1: 73.

60. Ibid.

61. Gough, "Identifying Psychological Femininity," p. 431.
62. Gough, "An Interpreter's Syllabus," pp. 55-79.
63. Lee J. Chronbach, Essentials of Psychological Testing
     (N. Y.: Harper & Row, 1970), p. 532.
64. Clark E. Vincent, "Implications of Changes in Male-
     Female Role Expectations for Interpreting M-F
     Scores," Journal of Marriage & The Family 28
     (May 1966): 198.
65. Ibid., pp. 196-197.
66. Super, Appraising Vocational Fitness, p. 524.
67. Eleanor E. Maccoby, "Sex Differences in Intellectual
     Functioning," in Bardwick, ed., Readings in Psy-
     chology of Women, pp. 37-38.
68. John L. Holland, "The Prediction of College Grades
     from the California Psychological Inventory and the
     Scholastic Aptitude Test," Journals of Educational
     Psychology 50 (August 1959): 135-142.
69. Judith M. Bardwick and Elizabeth Douvan, "Ambivalence:
     The Socialization of Women," in Bardwick, Readings
     on Psychology of Women, p. 57.
70. M. M. Bott, "The M-F Scale: Yesterday and Today,"
     Measurement & Evaluation in Guidance 3 (1970): 92.
71. Jerry S. Wiggins, "Content Dimensions in the MMPI,"
     in James Butcher, ed., MMPI: Research Develop-
     ments and Clinical Applications (N. Y.: McGraw-
     Hill, 1969), p. 145.
72. Vytautas Bieliauskas and Simon B. Miranda, "Obvious-
     ness of Two Masculinity-Femininity Tests," Journal
     of Counsulting & Clinical Psychology 32 (1968): 314.
73. William H. Whyte, Jr., The Organization Man (N. Y.:
     Simon & Schuster, 1956); Gross, Brain Watchers.
74. Lee J. Chronbach, Review of the CPI in Oscar Krisen
     Buros, Personality Tests and Reviews Including an
     Index to the Mental Measurements Yearbooks (High-
     land Park, N. J.: The Gryphon Press, 1970), 5:37.
75. Kenneth J. Gergen and David Marlowe, eds., Person-
     ality and Social Behavior (Reading, Massachusetts:
     Addison-Wesley Pub., 1970), p. 32.
76. See, for example, a typical textbook used in library
     science administration courses, Wasserman and Bun-
     dy, Reader in Library Administration, which, both
     in the essays collected in it and the bibliographies
     which follow them, devotes itself largely to urging
     the use of business administrative methods--and the
     human relations school of management--in library
     administration.
77. Vernon K. Dibble, "Occupations and Ideologies," p. 234.

PART II

TECHNICAL SERVICES/ READERS' SERVICES

THE SELLING OF THE PUBLIC LIBRARY*

Fay M. Blake and Jane Irby

The Public Library and the Information Industry

In a talk at the 7th annual meeting of the Information Industry Association Barbara Slanker, Director of ALA's Office of Research, pleaded for a partnership between public libraries and the information industry. It is a line that seems to be creeping into the library world--the latest draft program of the National Commission on Libraries and Information Science also urges a stronger role for the private sector--and it is one that needs to be dissected. Public libraries and the information industry have a lot in common, says Slanker. They both provide information to persons who want and need it. The one big difference between the two groups is money, she says. As partners working together we could meet the total information needs of clients quickly and accurately so let's not take the narrow view that libraries providing information without charge and information industry members providing information for a profitable fee are competitors. [1]

Maybe Slanker sees the public library and the information industry as the lamb and the lion resting side by side in the Peaceable Kingdom but Paul Zurkowski, guru of the Information Industry Association, certainly doesn't. At the same conference he blasted free information in an intemperate speech, comparing it to the Berlin Wall and the Iron Curtain and accusing advocates of free information of threatening the very basis of our free enterprise system. (Free is not free and 1984 is almost upon us.) He's not about to engage in the sweet and loving partnership Slanker envisions. [2]

*Reprinted by permission from Drexel Library Quarterly, Vol. 12, Nos. 1-2, Jan.-April 1976, pp. 149-158.

While it is not out of the question for public libraries
to use the products of the information industry in a variety
of ways, it would be dangerous for advocates of free information (and one would naively assume the American Library
Association to be such an advocate) to propose or engage in
a "partnership" without a careful appraisal of the consequences. Otherwise, we might find ourselves in the kind of
partnership sharks and minnows enjoy. By the time the
minnow is ready to assess the partnership he isn't around
anymore.

Slanker asks us to accept a whole series of unwar-
ranted assumptions which need clarification and debate.

1. The assumption that money (or the lack of it) is
the only serious difference between private business and the
public library. Even an affluent library is headed in quite
a different direction from the neediest business. The public
library, funded by all its constituents, is responsible to all
of them and will always need to consider how equitably to
divide the funds available. A business is responsible to its
stockholders and only to them. So what seriously divides
the public library from the information industry is precisely
the profit motive which Slanker dismisses so lightly, leading
her to another assumption.

2. The assumption that the goals of the public library are the same as those of the information industry.
Not so! We do not assume that the goal of the meat packing industry is feeding the hungry, nor that the goal of the
pharmaceutical industry is curing the sick, nor that the goal
of the tobacco industry is bringing surcease to troubled people. Feeding and curing and comforting people are only by-
products of the drive for maximum profits. Upton Sinclair's
Jungle and the horrors of thalidomide and the fierce efforts
of the tobacco industry to suppress the Surgeon-General's
report on the relationship between cancer and smoking are
extreme but not unbelievable examples of the frail chances
safety or health stand in the face of the profit-making syndrome. It is a mistake to believe that the information industry is concerned in the same way as the public library
for the full, accurate and rapid provision of everyone's information needs. Only that portion of the information needs
which will yield the greatest rate of profit will receive first
priority from the private sector of the information industry.

Slanker admits that "the products of the information industry are directed primarily (though not exclusively) to business and industry." This situation is not an accidental or temporary one. The business and industrial communities are the ones who can buy information and therefore the ones whom the information industry has served. Why should Lockheed or SDC or any other profit-oriented information industry invest in the preparation of information that will be useful to people in prisons or in ghettos or in senior citizens' rest homes or in juvenile halls? Why should they worry about information for those who cannot possibly pay the tab? And that leads to still another assumption.

3. The assumption that the public library's clientele is essentially the same as the information industry's and that the information collected and processed by the information industry will serve the public library's clientele. Slanker says in her talk: "Public libraries need no definition," thereby passing up a good chance to spread some much needed education among the information industry types at the meeting. Who says they don't need definition? Even public librarians are not completely in agreement about the boundaries of service the public library should impose or accept. To most people the public library is still a bunch of books presided over by a Gorgon with a date-stamp and a fiendish set of rules designed to lock the books away from people. Most people have never set foot inside a public library. Most people don't realize a public library provides a variety of information services. And most people don't need books or bibliographies although lots of them are literally dying or living very badly for want of information. But the information industry does not serve most people. Neither, for that matter, does the public library. If we lock the public library into the definition of information developed by the information industry, we are helping to make it impossible for most people ever to obtain the information they need.

Not only does the information industry limit its services to those who can pay for them but, as a corollary, it must limit the kind of information it collects and it must limit the sources for that information. Let's take some examples. In a recent field study with COYOTE, the prostitutes' union in San Francisco, a library school student analyzed the kinds of information needed by the members of COYOTE and discovered that they needed most often and most desperately information about their legal rights and protec-

tion--not the formula read off by an arresting officer, not a
bibliography of articles on how to reform the criminal justice
system, not a duplicated page from the penal code but an up-
to-the-minute list of names and phone numbers of a great
variety of legal and social services in the city: someone
who will trot out in the middle of the night to negotiate a
release under the Own Recognizance program, someone who
will deliver a kid to a baby-sitter or a nursery school,
someone who gets a delay in her hearing about an eviction
notice.   This is all information; this is all information for
which the public library can and should be round-the-clock
mediator--if we accept as a definition of the public library
"that agency which provides access to all the information
needs for all the people in its community."   None of this information has been--or ever will be--of much interest to the
information industry.

Or, another example: a woman of 45 who has recently lost her husband.   She has teen-age kids in school,
no recent work experience and only limited education.   She
is in desperate need of information, one place where she will
learn where to go for food stamps, social security information, job or apprenticeship possibilities, educational counseling, psychological help, and maybe just a quiet competent
hand to help her fill in the countless forms she's undoubtedly
buried under.   The public library owes her the information
(a few even are beginning to provide it), but the information
industry has neither the will nor the capability to collect,
process and provide the information she needs.

Well, we can hear some of you saying, why not a
combination of the information services public libraries can
provide and those the information industry can provide?   And
that brings us face-to-face with the most dangerous assumption of all.

4.   The assumption that information for which a fee
is charged can be offered side by side with free services
with neither affecting the other.   Again, not so!   The fees
we're talking about are not, to begin with, chicken-feed.
For EDITEC the cost for an individual search is $125 and
costs for an extended DIALOG search (which is described
below) may go as high as $250.   What happens to the user
who cannot afford such fees?   Obviously, he or she will be
less extensively served.   Librarians are already discussing
arbitrary limitation of all free searches to 10 minutes.   Will

the library itself absorb search fees to be paid out of the library budget? Then what happens to the budget in the lean
years ahead? What is likely to happen is the erosion of the
whole concept of free public library services. No hard-
pressed city auditor or mayor or council is going to approve
a budget for a library's free services once he smells user
fees in the offing. And once fees become the norm we can
be sure that unserved or poorly served categories will be
even more unserved than ever. The problem is not a hypothetical one. Slanker comments in her talk on an obstacle
that has already emerged in the brief history of INFORM,
one of the information industry's services used by cooperating
libraries in the Minneapolis area. "The first obstacle," she
says, "was the belief held by staff and public alike that the
public library should not charge for its services; the fee
reimbursement basis of INFORM was considered inappropriate."

Services Libraries Can Provide

If we stop pushing for an unequable "partnership,"
however, it is important to recognize that public libraries
can make vital use of the computer and the kinds of sophisticated services which the information industry makes available for business and industry. Freed from the limitations
of the profit incentive, the public library could become the
single most important community information resource, calling on existing data bases when appropriate, creating additional data bases of its own and appropriate to its own community, using technology for the maintenance and updating of
current community information, and providing such extensive
information without user charges as the right of all and not
the privilege of those who can pay for it.

The examples cited by Slanker are examples of some
of the extensive services public libraries can provide, although her examples are limited to the business community.
Another example currently being tested in California is a two-
year experimental project funded by the National Science
Foundation.

Cooperative Information Network

Beginning in November 1974, four computer terminals
in Redwood City Public Library, Santa Clara County Library,

San Jose Public Library and San Mateo County Free Library
have made available the extensive data bases included in the
DIALOG on-line retrieval system developed by Lockheed Research Systems to the libraries within the Cooperative Information Network. DIALOG includes some 23 bases, ERIC,
Chemical Abstracts, Engineering Index, Psychological Abstracts, National Technical Information Service, Social Sciences Citation Index (but not the New York Times Information
Bank) among them. For the first period through May 1975
searches were free; during the second year half the regular
user fee was charged and after that the full fee. For $5 the
user receives a standard search during the second period,
that is, one data bank will be queried with a limited number
of terms. Customized on-line searches cost the user anywhere from $20 to $100 depending on the bank queried.
When full user charges are installed, the minimum fee for
the standard search will double to $10, and custom-tailored
searches can rise to $250. [3]

Even during the first free honeymoon period a few
troublesome problems have arisen. More than half of all
the searches at San Jose Public Library have been generated
by students of nearby San Jose State University. Librarians
are not overjoyed at this development since the students are
already served by their own university library and the DIA-
LOG installation was meant to reach a clientele hitherto
neglected by libraries. So rumblings are heard here and
there about limiting service to students.

Another development is, in a sense, even more dis-
turbing. Since the public library's collection is not meant
for an academic clientele, there was an expectation of a
huge increase in interlibrary loan requests--for books and
articles dredged up by DIALOG but not owned by the public
library--an expectation never fulfilled. There is practically
no discernible increase in the library's interlibrary loan
business although DIALOG users are routinely informed that
interlibrary loan service is available to them. So, librarians are inferring that students clutch their DIALIG bibliographies and head for the university library for the materials,
or, as the more cynical believe, students merely append the
DIALOG bibliographies to their papers as proof of "research."

The participating libraries in the Cooperative Information Network are watching their experiment carefully and will
be evaluating it throughout the experimental period. An
oversight committee has been meeting regularly and an ex-

ternal evaluator has been retained to monitor the success of
the program.   Questions like the effect of a fee structure
on number of queries, number of users, spread of users
and on other non-fee services have already been raised although it is too soon for any answers. [4]

Library-produced Products

Libraries cannot wait for the information industry to
supply them with information structured in the new technology.   They must be able to control the technology without
passively depending on the commercial information products.
People need information which cannot be supplied by an industry, giving top priority to profit-making.   Many information needs will not generate maximum profit; therefore,
products designed to answer these needs have not been developed by the information industry.   As one example, public
libraries have recently begun to identify the need for community information in urban, suburban and rural areas and
its deplorable lack in most communities. [5]   By definition,
data bases of community information will be largely local,
with considerable variation from community to community.
One community's file can not be marketed to another.   Obviously there is little profit to be made from such a specialized file, particularly since it will be used largely by
people who are not able to pay for information.   If libraries
sit back and wait for their "partners," the information industry, to develop tools which can then be purchased, community information will be a grossly neglected information
service in libraries.   Libraries must take the methods of
information storage and retrieval which have been in part
developed by the information industry and apply them imag-
inatively to serving community information needs.

Community Information Project

The Peninsula Library System (PLS) of San Mateo
County, California, is doing just that.   Its Computerized
Community Information Project received a two-year LSCA
grant for $83,000 in 1974 to develop a community informa-
tion file to serve the half-a-million residents of the mostly
suburban county immediately south of San Francisco. [6]   For
this project, the term community information was defined
as a file of public and social services, concentrating, to
begin with, on services offered by the county government.

The teletype system by which the eight PLS libraries now communicate is being modified to allow the teletype machines to act as terminals to a computer at nearby Stanford University. The Community Information Project is building its own data base within the Stanford system SPIRES (Stanford Public Information Retrieval System), a generalized information storage and retrieval system. SPIRES was designed to be extraordinarily flexible so that users may develop different types of data bases geared to their specific, generally academic, need.

The Stanford Center for Information Processing regards the PLS project as an experiment in extended educational uses of their system. Project staff and employees of PLS libraries have been able to enroll in courses which train them to use the system. Only a handful of librarians who are particularly interested in the project have taken the courses. The techniques of manipulation of the file can be taught to small groups in less than an hour. PLS libraries will be strongly encouraged by the project staff to send all of their public service staff to training workshops. Operation of the SPIRES system is simple enough so that intensive, expensive training is not required, thus making it possible for virtually every employee to be able to learn the techniques and to provide the service to the public. This simplicity is in marked contrast to the DIALOG system which required so much training and practice in the use of the data bases that only a few librarians have learned to search it.

The PLS Community Information File is on-line and interactive; that is, the PLS terminals hook up directly to the computer which responds to commands issued by the user. There are a number of advantages to this method of organizing a community information file which will serve a large population from several locations. Overnight additions or updates to the file are possible. After a change in the file is typed into the system, all users at all terminals have the correct and current information. Maintenance of the entire file can be centralized while the contents are available at multiple outlets. Updating, always a major problem in community information, is further simplified by the capability of the computer to generate letters to agencies in the file asking if the information is still accurate. Another attractive characteristic of the PLS file is that the items which fit the description fed into the computer are printed out at the teletypes and may be kept by the patron. This is a considerable

advance over searching through the indexes of printed directories and copying entries.

The PLS Community Information File is able to use
more index terms than would be conceivable in a manual file
or printed directory. There are, in fact, four separate indexed elements in the file: agency name, city, languages
spoken, and keywords describing the services. It is not uncommon for an entry to be filed by fifteen to twenty different
keywords, making access to items in the file much broader
than a manual file or directory could ever by. The fact that
neither the information industry nor the professions concerned have developed a thesaurus of terms describing the
provision of social services makes the assignment of keywords for services disturbingly arbitrary and demanding for
the file builders, but that is a problem common to accessing
manual files and directories also. At the 1975 National
Conference on Social Welfare, members of the Alliance of
Information and Referral Services, [7] an organization of social
workers, librarians, health professionals, and others involved
in community information, discussed the growing need for a
thesaurus. One participant, Thomas Deahl, has estimated
that development of a thesaurus comparable to those developed for the fields of education and psychology would cost
approximately $10 million and take several years. When
such a thesaurus is constructed, it is unlikely that it will
be done at the initiative or expense of the information industry.

The PLS Community Information Project is facing
several problems common to outreach and demonstration
projects. Only one seems to be related to the use of a
computer in the public library, and it is technical rather
than technological; the process of ordering and installing
equipment which will modify the PLS teletype system to allow
the machines to act as terminals to the Stanford computer
seems to take about six months. More typical problems are
the question of how to make the public aware of the new service, especially how to lead people to think of the library
as the place to look for community information, and the
problem of obtaining funding for the project when the demonstration period is over.

Public libraries need to make use of the extensive
technological advances developed during the last two decades.
Public libraries need to seek out the invisible members of
their community whom they have served only minimally or

not at all. Public libraries need to expand the amount, the kind and the quality of their services. [8] But not as partners of the information industry and not as fee-collecting brokers for the information industry. Since the inception of the free public library, we have provided free books and journals to users without suggesting that we needed to become partners of the publishing industry. On the contrary, we can take credit for maintaining an independent right to choose among any and all publications and to provide them as a free public service. The same independence toward the information industry and the provision of expanded information services without fees will revive the public library's honorable tradition of service.

Notes

1. Barbara Slanker, "Public Libraries and the Information Industry," a speech presented to the User Workshop, 7th Annual Meeting of the Information Industry Association, New York City, April 3, 1975. This speech appears in the Drexel Library Quarterly, Jan.-April 1976.
2. LJ/SLJ Hotline 4 (nos. 14 and 16, April 7 and April 21, 1975).
3. Ronny Markoe, "The Cooperative Information Network--A Report," California Librarian 35 (no. 3, July 1974): 17-21.
4. Cooperative Information Network of San Mateo, Santa Clara, Santa Cruz and Monterey Counties, Network News 1 (nos. 1-3, November 1974 to April 1975).
5. "Investigation of the Public Library as a Linking Agent to Major Scientific, Educational, Social and Environmental Data Bases--Quarterly Progress Reports to National Science Foundation," Palo Alto, California, Lockheed Missiles and Space Co., 1974, 1975.
6. "PLS Community Information Project Progress Report to Library Staffs," edited by Jane Irby, San Mateo City Library, 55 W. Third Ave., San Mateo, California 94402.
7. Alliance of Information and Referral Services, 1515 East Osborn Road, Phoenix, Arizona 85014.
8. "The Public Library as an Information Dissemination Center: An Experiment in Information Retrieval Services for the General Public," presented at the 12th Annual Clinic on Library Applications of Data Processing, Champaign, Ill., April 27-30, 1975.

LIBRARY AUTOMATION: CHANGING PATTERNS AND NEW DIRECTIONS*

Richard De Gennaro

In 1967, the literature of library automation was still very limited in scope and fell into two categories. At one extreme were the detailed technical papers written by systems librarians describing a specific application which was being implemented in a particular library. At the other extreme were general or visionary papers written by information scientists or librarians speculating on how computer technology was going to change libraries in the future. There was little in between to which librarians and administrators could turn for practical guidance on whether and how to plan, implement, and administer automation programs in their own libraries. In an attempt to meet that need the author, who was then responsible for systems development in the Harvard University Library, wrote a paper entitled "The Development and Administration of Automated Systems in Academic Libraries" which was published in the first issue of the Journal of Library Automation in 1968. It was reprinted in the ASIS collection, Key Papers in Information Science.[1]

The paper was in two parts. The first part made it clear that there were no canned formulas for automating a research library that were waiting to be discovered and applied. Each library was going to have to decide for itself which approach or strategy seemed best suited to its needs and resources. Three major approaches were described: 1) the wait-for-developments approach, 2) the direct approach to a total system, and 3) an evolutionary approach to a total system. The use of outside consultants and contractors was also considered. The second part of the paper dealt with the important elements of any library automation

*Reprinted from Library Journal, Jan. 1, 1976. Published by R. R. Bowker Co. (a Xerox company). Copyright © 1976 by Xerox Corporation.

program regardless of the approach that was used. There
was a section on the building of the capability to do automation, including considerations of staffing, equipment, and organizational structure. This was followed by a discussion of
the relative merits of the various kinds of projects that could
be selected such as serials, circulation, acquisitions, and
cataloging, and it concluded with some views on costs and
benefits.

Now, eight years later, the author was asked to write
another paper on library automation from an administrator's
point of view.[2] During those years remarkable progress has
been made in automation as well as in the scope and quality
of its literature. Gone are most of the hastily written descriptions of applications as well as the worst excesses of
the visionaries. They have been superseded by works of
solid quality in both areas and the gap in between has been
filled by studies such as Herman H. Fussler's Research Libraries and Technology, among others.[3,4,5]

In casting about for an appropriate focus for this paper, it seemed essential to review the earlier one to see
how well it had stood the test of time and how it could possibly be brought up to date. It came as no surprise that
much of what was written there about this rapidly changing
and developing field was no longer pertinent or useful.
Many of the most important and controversial issues of the
sixties have long since been resolved or have simply become
irrelevant. However, the main theme of the paper--the
identification and discussion of the various approaches to
automation and the strategies for pursuing them--has retained
its importance as the major current issue in library automation. It seemed appropriate therefore to use the basic approaches to automation that were outlined in the 1968 paper,
along with the other issues covered, as a vehicle and framework for highlighting the changes that have occurred and the
new approaches and directions that are discernible in library
automation in the United States in the mid-seventies.

Library Automation in the Late Sixties

In the mid-1960s there were two highly publicized
pioneering projects that did not fit into any of the three
most common approaches that were discussed in the paper.
One was the Florida Atlantic University project and the other
was Project INTREX at MIT. Florida Atlantic, a newly

founded university committed to using computer technology to
innovate new paths in higher education, decided to build a
totally computerized library apparatus in lieu of conventional
library card catalogs and other manual systems. [6] While
providing some useful experience, the project proved to be
entirely premature and was subsequently abandoned. The
task was simply beyond the state of the library and computer
art and technology of the time. However, the national and
even international publicity generated by this project created
tremendous interest, incentive, and pressure for other libraries to enter the field. It is hard to assess the legacy
of Florida Atlantic, but without it we may have had fewer
failures and a more orderly development of the field.

The motivating idea of Project INTREX was that
rather than attempt to automate existing libraries it would
be far more fruitful to use the advanced technology to build
a totally new kind of library which would parallel the conventional one and eventually transform or even supersede it.
In the words of its founder, "The goal of Project INTREX
is an information-transfer system to be installed by 1975 not
only at MIT but at a number of comparable institutions
throughout the nation and perhaps the world. "[7] After seven
years of expertly managed and reported experimentation and
development and the expenditure of several million dollars in
grant funds, Project INTREX declared that it had achieved
its objectives and quietly went out of existence in 1974. [8] On
the theoretical side its impact on library and information
technology was considerably less than its promise. On the
practical side it left little to show for its efforts beyond a
handsomely refurbished Engineering Library and a prototype
on-line interactive data and textual access system based on
computers and microfilm that is apparently still too expensive
and experimental for use in an operational environment. In
its highly sophisticated way INTREX may have been just as
ill-conceived and premature as the more amateurish Florida
Atlantic initiative.

The "Wait-for-Developments" Approach

The wait-for-developments approach to library automation was based on the premise that computer-based library systems were still in an experimental stage with questionable economic justification, and that it was unnecessary
and uneconomical for every large library to undertake difficult and costly development work. Most libraries should

wait until the pioneers with special grant funds had developed
workable systems which could be installed and operated at
reasonable costs.   Princeton was cited as the chief proponent
of this approach.

The 1968 paper suggested that this was a reasonable
course of action for smaller libraries, but that for larger
ones it entailed the risk of being left behind as technology
developed, and that in any case it would be difficult to hold
to this policy in the face of the then current pressures to
automate that were coming from all sides in that decade
when technology was riding high.   In retrospect, it is now
clear that the advice to wait for the pioneers to develop
workable systems would have also been appropriate even for
large libraries.   With the coming of austerity, the pressures
to automate subsided.   The fear of being left behind proved
to be groundless because the technology changed so rapidly
that many of the libraries that entered the field early were
locked into obsolescent systems while those who waited had
little difficulty entering at the current state of the art when
they were ready.   Princeton joined a fully operational
PALINET, the Pennsylvania regional affiliate of OCLC, in
1974, thereby avoiding the pains as well as the pleasures of
being in the forefront of a new movement.

In 1975 this cautions approach still seems like the
most prudent course for most libraries to follow with regard
to original systems development.   However, many of the developments that we have been waiting for are here and ready
for implementation.   The wait-for-developments approach
should be in fact an approach to dealing with technology, not
just an escape from it.

The Direct Approach to a Total System

This approach was based on the premise that since a
library is a single complex operating system and all its
varied operations are interrelated and interconnected, logic
demands that it be treated as such and that a single integrated or total computerized system be designed for it.   The
tasks could be designed and implemented as a series of
modules, but all must be designed as part of a whole.   The
University of Chicago and the Stanford University Libraries
were cited as the prime examples of this approach and both
had received substantial research and development grants
from government agencies and foundations.

The 1968 paper suggested that the total systems approach was somewhat beyond the state of the art of both library automation and computer technology; that while trying
it was a gamble that could pay off, it seemed doubtful that
the first models would be economically and technically viable
and that the best that could be hoped for was that they would
work well enough to serve as prototypes for later models.
It was suggested that while this bold approach would unques-
tionably advance the cause of library automation it presented
serious risks for the library that adopted it.   In retrospect,
this appears to have been a reasonably accurate forecast of
what actually occurred.   Only two large academic research
libraries, Chicago and Stanford, embarked upon this approach
(in 1966 and 1967 respectively) and both are persevering to
successful but diverging conclusions.   However, each has
found the task several times more difficult, costly, and
time-consuming than it had originally anticipated.

Chicago's first generation bibliographic data processing system allowed data to be input to an in-process file at
the time of ordering or cataloging either from local terminals or from MARC tapes and produced cards and other
printed products for the library.   Upon completion of this
system arounf 1968, Chicago made a new beginning with an
entirely new design concept.   The second generation system
performs a full range of administrative and reader services
via the library's Varian mini-computer, which has direct
access to a master data file in the university's large IBM
370/168 computer.   Chicago's comprehensive data management system is expected to achieve full operational status
in 1976 and be made available to other libraries under the
terms of a Council on Library Resources grant that it recently received. [9,10]   It should be capable of being used
either as a stand-alone system for an individual library or
as the central system for a regional network.

Developed at considerably greater expense, the Stanford system, called BALLOTS, is an on-line interactive
system with multi-file and multi-index capabilities and using
video display units in such a way as to allow for its extension, in phases, from technical processing support to other
areas of library operations and eventually to serve as a
central system for a library network. [11]   Although it has
been supporting the day-to-day acquisitions and cataloging
operations of the Stanford libraries since November 1972,
operational costs in this mode are excessively high and efforts are currently underway, as a result of a recent CLR

grant, to make the expansions necessary to permit the system to support a large-scale network for California similar to OCLC.

The original conception of the designers of these systems and the granting agencies that funded them was that they could be transferred to other large libraries when they were completed. There appears to be surprisingly little interest in this possibility now. Experience seems to indicate that these systems are too costly to operate in a single library environment, and most libraries have moved beyond the idea of having their own dedicated system and seem to prefer to join consortia such as OCLC and its affiliates. Stanford is actively trying to promote BALLOTS as a node for a western library network and this is undoubtedly where its future lies. Chicago is still trying to develop a system which can be used either by a single library or by a group of libraries. But in spite of Chicago's efforts, it can be said with considerable justification that the ultimate goal of library automation in the 1960's, the development of a total integrated system for a single library, appears to have been abandoned or at least set aside in the 1970's. However, there are indications that the advent of powerful and inexpensive minicomputers and storage capabilities will lead to a revival of this concept in the next few years. We will return to this point later.

The Evolutionary Approach to a Total System

The ultimate objective of the evolutionary approach was the same as the total system approach but the method of reaching it was different. In the evolutionary approach, the library was supposed to move from traditional manual systems to increasingly complex machine systems in successive stages to achieve a total system over a period of time with a minimum of cost and risk. It was viewed essentially as a series of do-it-yourself projects with librarians and computer specialists working together as a team designing separate batch-processing or on-line systems for various housekeeping functions such as circulation, ordering and accounting, catalog input, etc. This was and still is the most common approach to automation and was adopted by Harvard, Yale, British Columbia, and many others.

In 1968 this seemed to many librarians to be the most reasonable approach to computerizing the operations of a large academic library. By 1972, the state of the art of

library automation and computer technology had advanced to
a point where the objective of a total system for a single library as well as this conservative strategy for achieving it
both seemed irrelevant. Our perception of the task to be
done had changed from developing a single comprehensive
system to automate or computerize a library to making the
most effective use of technology to support library functions.
As the technology became more functional it began to lose
its aura of glamor, and librarians began to see it more as
a tool to do library work rather than as an end in itself.
Two new approaches to the use of technology were emerging.
The OCLC system had proved itself and the validity of the
cooperative on-line network concept for handling bibliographic
data while the inexpensive minicomputer package system for
handling certain local functions, such as circulation and acquisitions, was showing considerable promise. These new
developments and trends will be treated in more detail later.

Building the Capability for Automation

        Following the descriptions of the various approaches
to automation, the 1968 paper discussed some of the major
requirements for a successful automation effort regardless
of the approach that was selected. These requirements included staff, equipment, and organizational considerations.
This part of the paper has suffered the most from the pas-
sage of time and the course of developments. Much of what
was said is no longer relevant because it was assumed that
each library had to build an in-house capability to automate
its own operations and this basic assumption is no longer
valid. This do-it-yourself or localized era of library automation that characterized the 1960s is giving way to new approaches in which libraries join computer networks such as
OCLC or its affiliates for some functions and perhaps install
package minicomputer systems for others. In either case,
a highly qualified in-house technical staff is becoming less
essential as regular library staff members develop the competence and confidence to implement and operate these advanced on-line package systems.

Staff--"No One Is Threatened..."

        The question of who was to do library automation--
librarians or computer people--was one of those burning issues of the 1960s which simply faded away. The paper sug-

gested that a mixture of both types would be needed, but that
as systems and equipment became more sophisticated the
need for computer expertise would take precedence.   This
view was sustained by subsequent developments.   At present,
it is difficult to distinguish the computer people from the librarians as each has taken on the characteristics of the other
and no one feels threatened any more.   As a matter of fact,
many librarians who chose to specialize in computer work
during the heyday of the movement in the 1960s are reorient-
ing their careers back to regular library work which they
correctly perceive to be the main stream of the profession
in the long run.

The concern expressed over the shortage of experienced library systems people in the face of the "ever-growing
need and demand" seems particularly outdated in the face of
the current shrinking demand for computer specialists in libraries.   A small elite of highly skilled and dedicated systems people continues to be needed in the main centers of
activity such as the Library of Congress, OCLC, Chicago,
Stanford, Minnesota, the New York Public Library, and a
number of others.

Equipment--Turning to Networks

Another very live issue of the 1960s was how a library could gain assured access to the computer time that
it needed to test programs and run its routine jobs.   Computers were changing "generations" every few years and university computing centers were unreliable and unstable.   The
unresolved question was whether libraries would continue to
rely on computing center machines or whether their usage
would grow to a point where an in-house library computer
could be justified.   Since computers were growing in power,
size, and cost, and since it was clear that libraries would
require the use of powerful on-line systems, it seemed unlikely that a trend toward in-house library machines would
develop.   This proved to be the case, but instead of using
the general purpose machine at the computing center, an increasing number of libraries are turning to the computer-
based library network to satisfy their computing requirements.   Although few libraries want or need their own full-
scale computers, many are casually installing powerful in-
house minicomputers for circulation and other applications,
and this trend will surely continue.

Organization

It was assumed that large libraries which elected to
automate would require a permanent and growing systems
group, and it contained a number of ideas on how the group
might be organized, administered, and made to fit within the
regular library structures. It foresaw a future where the
library's automated systems were always being changed, enlarged, and improved, and program and system maintenance
were a permanent activity. This is very much the way it
was and still is for those libraries that have elected the
evolutionary approach described earlier. However, the continued viability of this approach is open to serious question,
as has been suggested, and some large libraries have already abandoned it.

Project Selection--End of an Era

This subject was of vital concern to the library automation fraternity in the decade of the 1960s, and the merits
of the various projects were widely debated. Some advocated
beginning automation with the serials check-in records because the most activity and the largest payoff was there.
Others thought that it should begin with the order records
because that is where the records first entered the system.
Circulation had its advocates because it was relatively risk
free. After some discussion of these questions, which are
no longer live issues, the 1968 paper suggested that the development and acceptance of the MARC II format in 1967
marked the end of one era in library automation and the beginning of another. In the pre-MARC period, because of the
lack of a standard format, every system was unique; in the
post-MARC period it was foreseen that automation would be
facilitated and expanded in the coming years. An input subsystem for cataloging in the MARC format, which individual
libraries could use, was promised as an imminent development which would enable libraries to make full use of the
MARC tapes to which they would soon be subscribing.

The MARC format and distribution service did in fact
signal the beginning of a new era of accelerating development in library automation, but the success of OCLC and
other on-line systems dramatically changed the direction of
that development. Instead of each major library subscribing
to and maintaining a file of MARC tapes and developing a
local system for utilizing them as was initially predicted, it

turned out that the emerging pattern is for libraries to utilize on-line terminal access systems and MARC data bases that are centrally maintained by networks or even commercial vendors.

Like many other issues which were critical in 1968, the issue of project selection has lost its meaning as library automation has evolved from an experimental localized activity in individual libraries to a service supplied to groups of libraries by a centralized consortium or network.

Costs--Still High

Many of the views about the costs and benefits of library automation in the 1968 paper still retain their validity. Attention was called to the high cost of developing original systems and software, and today one would confirm this and add a warning about the high cost of operating and maintaining such systems. Another major concern at that time was whether or to what extent automation could be justified on the basis of cost effectiveness. The paper suggested that computer-based systems as they then existed would not actually save a library money if all development and implementation costs were included. Their advantage lay in providing better systems with the greater capacity that was thought to be essential to enable libraries to cope with the steadily increasing growth rates and workloads which were overtaxing the traditional manual systems.

Unlike many of the other issues which have faded away with the advances in technology, the issue of costs and benefits has increased in importance. Although the argument that computer systems are needed to take care of increasing growth and workloads has lost some of its strength as library budgets and other growth indicators have begun to level off and decline, rapidly increasing personnel costs caused by rising salaries and benefits have given it a new force and urgency. Nevertheless, it is still possible to say that the actual cost savings of the localized systems that characterized the last decade were either minimal or nonexistent. The first really significant savings that have come to libraries from computerization have come from the OCLC system and its affiliates in the area of personnel costs in cataloging and technical services.

Less easily demonstrated, but still real and increas-

ing, are savings and benefits that will come to libraries indirectly as a result of the successful computerization of services, functions, and tools by organizations that serve libraries. For example, the computerization of the Library
of Congress bibliographical apparatus and subject heading list
facilitates the production of printed catalogs and lists and
other tools upon which libraries depend. The growing capability of the OCLC data base to serve as a location device
for interlibrary loan searches is another important example.
The computerization of the data bases of various indexing
and abstracting services has made it possible for commercial vendors and others to provide libraries with effective
on-line search services to expand their reference capabilities.

New Directions

          We come full circle and can now summarize and pro-
ject the four main lines of development that are discernible
in the mid-1970s:

          1) State and regional computer-based networks or
consortia are developing into a national system, not only for
sharing on-line processing systems, but also for locating and
sharing library resources.

          2) Parallel vendor-supplied on-line services and sys-
tems both for bibliographic searching and document access
as well as for supporting local library processing functions,
are developing.

          3) Transferable minicomputer systems designed to
support a wide range of library functions with a possible future tie-in to the network data bases and systems, have developed and made commercially available packaged minicomputer systems for specific functions such as circulation and
acquisitions.

          4) There is a trend toward in-house development and
transfer or adaptation of local systems.

The remainder of the paper will be devoted to a discussion
of these four main trends.

Networks--A New Maturity

Since it went on-line in 1971, the OCLC system has profoundly changed the nature and direction and quickened the pace of library automation in the U.S. OCLC has been the most significant development since the establishment of the MARC format and distribution service and has achieved a commanding and well-deserved lead in the area of cooperative computer-based library networks. The parent OCLC network serves Ohio while 11 other affiliated networks serve New England, New York, Pennsylvania and the Middle Atlantic, the Southeastern U.S., and Texas. Several other regional consortia are negotiating terms for participation. The ease with which libraries can participate effectively in the OCLC system has been chiefly responsible for the change in direction of library automation from the development of local systems for individual libraries that characterized the sixties, to the participation in cooperative networks that is dominating the seventies. It is clearly easier and less expensive for libraries to get the benefits of automation by joining networks than by attempting to develop their own stand-alone systems. Even the networks that are affiliated with OCLC, after an initial interest in replicating the OCLC computer system for use in their region, have largely abandoned this idea in favor of continuing to use the central OCLC system which is rapidly expanding its computing capacity to meet the growing demand. This willingness of libraries and even consortia to use an existing system signals a new maturity in library automation where the focus is on the product rather than on the process or the glamor of developing new systems. OCLC's demonstrated capability of serving as an effective library resource-sharing mechanism has also been an important factor in the rapid acceptance and growth of the network concept in the austere seventies.

Although OCLC clearly dominated the eastern half of the U.S., Stanford's BALLOTS system is making a serious bid to become the center of library networking in the West. Several consortia, including the University of California system, are seriously considering affiliating with BALLOTS, which is said to be technically equal or even superior to the OCLC system. Indications are that the University of Chicago system may also be available to support a major network.

As we try to assess OCLC's future, it appears that the two main capabilities upon which its current success is

based--shared cataloging and catalog card production and
distribution--may be largely superseded by advances in library automation and in the OCLC system itself. As the
Library of Congress and other major producers of MARC
cataloging abroad step up the currency and broaden the scope
of their output until near complete coverage is achieved, the
importance of OCLC's shared cataloging capability may diminish because libraries will draw virtually all of their cataloging from the data base and will only contribute original
cataloging for limited quantities of retrospective, locally
produced, and other special materials. Moreover, as the
Library of Congress and other major libraries begin to move
in the next several years toward closing their card catalogs
and implementing some combination of on-line and computer
output microfilm catalogs their need for catalog cards will
diminish. Smaller libraries will continue to need cards, but
they may be able to obtain them much less expensively from
other sources including commercial vendors. Thus, the
continued use of the OCLC system as a massive card production and distribution service in the next decade may be
seriously open to question.

On the other hand, the use of the OCLC data base
and system as a source for machine readable catalog entries
for use in local systems will probably assume the same importance that catalog card production and distribution now
have. In addition, the use of the system for union catalog
and interlibrary loan location and communication purposes as
well as for subject searching and other bibliographic reference functions is bound to increase and may well become its
dominant functions.

OCLC's ability to deliver and successfully operate the
long-promised serials control, acquisitions, and circulation
subsystems is not yet certain. Although work on circulation
has not yet begun, the serials control and acquisitions subsystems are under development and will soon be available.
What is much less certain is OCLC's ability to expand the
capacity of the computer system sufficiently to handle the
vastly increased storage and processing burden that will be
placed on it when several hundred member libraries try to
use these additional capabilities. It may well be that such
locally oriented functions as serials control, acquisitions,
circulation, and catalog maintenance and access will have to
be done on minicomputers which may be interconnected to a
large regional or national data base such as that maintained
by OCLC. This concept will be further developed later.

Vendor-Supplied Services and Systems

While this trend toward vendor-supplied services and systems is not yet as widespread and significant as library networking, it has much in common with networking and is growing rapidly. Just as it is more efficient and cost-effective for libraries to obtain certain services from a network than to try to develop the capability themselves, it may be equally advantageous for them to turn to vendors for other systems and services. Vendors in this context are not limited to commercial firms, they can also be large libraries, professional societies, government agencies, etc. This approach has not been important in the past because few vendors had any fully-tested operational systems or products to offer, but this is changing now. A number of vendors have developed effective systems and many libraries have begun to use them.

The System Development Corporation and the Lockheed Information Retrieval Service, among others, are providing libraries with access to a growing number of on-line bibliographic data bases, including the MARC file, on a fee-for-service basis. The commercial availability of these services appears to be resolving in a highly satisfactory manner what was once considered to be one of the most difficult problems in library automation, namely, how libraries could develop and offer computer-based information retrieval capabilities to their users.[12] Until recently, the end product of these on-line bibliographic searches was a list of citations which created as much frustration as they did satisfaction because they called attention to documents that libraries did not have or could not easily procure. Now it is possible to actually order copies through the on-line terminal of certain of the items that have been retrieved in a search. These are limited for now to National Technical Information Service (NTIS) reports and articles that are available through the Original Article Tearsheet Service (OATS) of the Institute for Scientific Information, Inc. However, this capability may expand as the indexing and abstracting services embrace the responsibility for providing copies as well as the opportunity for additional revenues that the service appears to afford.[13] The extension of these search services to include convenient access to documents in addition to citations could be one of the more significant developments that has occurred in library and information technology in the last several years. The availability of complete bibliographic access systems through on-line terminals would have a profound impact on traditional library acquisitions policies as well as on the future of scholarly journals.   However, the document ordering capability of these systems is still rudimentary and it is too early to assess the long-term significance of these developments.   It is quite possible that demand will be limited and that users will balk at paying the high fees that the suppliers will require to make the service profitable and viable.

The large book jobbers use computer systems for their own internal processing and are therefore in a favorable position to offer computer-produced cards, lists, and other services to their customers.   Customer libraries will soon be able to tie directly into the jobber's data base and system through on-line terminals and communication lines. By 1980, nearly all catalog data in Roman alphabets will be available through the MARC service, and international standard book and serial numbers will be widely used.   This will undoubtedly open new possibilities for system linkages between jobbers and libraries.

Other firms maintain the MARC data base on their computers and offer a variety of products and services including cards, book catalogs, and subject searches, thus making it unnecessary for small libraries to cope directly with any level of automation or technology to benefit from computerization.   As technology becomes more complex and cost-effective, and as book and journal prices along with salaries and personnel benefits continue to rise in the face of static budgets, some libraries may find it advantageous to buy products and services rather than to attempt to produce them in-house.

There are, of course, serious risks that come with purchasing vital library services from commercial vendors, and special caution is indicated to guard against the misleading claims and promises of the unscrupulous or incompetent entrepreneurs that exist in this field as in others.   Moreover, even reputable vendors with useful products and services can also fail or be forced to abruptly discontinue an unprofitable line, thereby exposing their customers to serious inconvenience and unrecoverable losses.

Minicomputer Systems

A third significant trend is the development of minicomputer systems capable of handling in an on-line mode a variety of library processes such as circulation, acquisition ordering and accounting, serial control, and catalog access. Two projects typify this trend; one is the Minnesota Bio-Medical Minicomputer Project and its application to the main library at the University of Minnesota, and the other is the efforts of C LSI, Inc. of Newtonville, Massachusetts.

The statement was made earlier that the ultimate goal of library automation in the 1960s, the development of a total integrated system for a single library, was largely superseded by the drive toward networking which was sparked by the success of the OCLC system and reinforced by the Chicago and Stanford experiences which showed that the cost of operating such systems was probably too high for one library to bear. Bucking this strong trend, the University of Minnesota Bio-Medical Library is attempting to achieve the total system goal of the 1960s by using the technology of the 1970s--the minicomputer and inexpensive mass storage. With a grant of $360,000 from the National Library of Medicine in 1972, the Minnesota Bio-Medical Library embarked on a three-year project to develop a low-cost, stand-alone, integrated library system which would be suitable for use in other libraries of a similar size. "The premise of the development is that an integrated acquisitions, accounting, in-process control system for all library materials coupled with an on-line catalog/circulation control system can be operationally affordable by a library or system of libraries in the 200,000 volume class using its own computer system."[14] Apart from the usual delays, the project appears to be progressing so satisfactorily that a proposal has been made and approved to apply the same concept to the main university library at Minnesota.[15] The design of these minicomputer systems calls for their being capable of interfacing with and being linked into the regional networks and their data bases. If this concept proves itself, it could become the dominant trend in library automation and networking in the next decade.

The other major line of development in minicomputer systems comes from the commercial sector. C LSI, Inc., of Newton, Mass., appears to be the leader in this field and is already offering standardized circulation and book ordering and accounting modules using its own software package and an off-the-shelf minicomputer and other components. It has installed several circulation systems but the acquisition system is not yet available. The entire system, software and hardware, is sold or leased to the library at prices which may be advantageous when compared with the cost of develop-

ing, operating and maintaining a local in-house system. The
installation and maintenance of these packaged or "turnkey"
systems are the responsibility of the vendor; the library
needs no machine-oriented systems staff, it is free from
the vicissitudes of dealing with a university computing center, and it retains a measure of independence and flexibility
as technology develops. CLSI will soon be joined by Check-
point-Plessey, Check-A-Book, and other vendors using a
similar approach as the market develops. The market for
circulation systems appears to be strongest since the networks are not yet offering this capability.

Development and Transfer of Local Systems

Closely related to commercially available packages
are complete systems for particular applications that have
been developed by certain libraries or centers for their own
use and are being offered for sale or transfer at cost to
other libraries. A few major examples can be cited. Ohio
State University's on-line circulation system is being transferred to the State University of New York System and Purdue
University, among others. The Hennepin County (Minn.) Library used the California Bibliographic Conversion System to
convert its catalog entries, and then processed them with
New York Public Library's book catalog system to produce a
book catalog. The New York Public Library is planning to
adapt and install the acquisition system originally developed
and used by the Columbia University Library. These and
other successful ventures suggest that systems transfer, after
many years of unfulfilled promise, may finally be possible
now that there are some systems worthy of transfer and technical people with the willingness and competence to make the
transfer. Libraries are beginning to overcome the "Not Invented Here" syndrome, and systems transfer may occur
more frequently than it has in the past.

Many major research libraries, including for example
the New York Public Library and those of the universities of
British Columbia, California (Berkeley), Minnesota, North-
western, Ohio State, Oregon, Washington State, and Toronto,
are continuing to retain systems staffs and to design, implement, and operate in-house systems for various library functions. Others are maintaining and improving existing systems
with in-house staff, but are not initiating new systems. Still
others, such as the University of Pennsylvania, have completely phased out their systems staffs and are relying com-

pletely on networks and outside sources for new systems and for the maintenance of existing ones. This latter course is a trend which may be expected to grow as networks, utilities, and minicomputer systems continue to develop and dominate the field.[16] Naturally, the Library of Congress, because of its enormous size and unique function, will continue as one of the major centers for research and development in library automation.

The Next Phase--Synergy

During the years under review we have seen the main thrust of library automation evolve from building total or integrated systems for individual libraries using local systems, staffs and equipment, to building regional library networks using the systems, facilities, and staffs of a few major centers such as the Library of Congress, New York Public Library, OCLC, Chicago, and Stanford. We have also seen the parallel emergence of a new concept at Minnesota, namely, the development of a powerful, flexible, and inexpensive minicomputer system for use in a single library. If this concept proves itself, it could combine some of the best features of the total systems goal of the 1960s with the major success of the 1970s--the cooperative network. This marriage could produce what may become the dominant thrust of the 1980s--the development of cost-effective in-house library minicomputer processing and catalog access systems capable of interfacing synergistically with an effective national library network for sharing bibliographical data and library resources.

References

1. Richard De Gennaro. "The Development and Administration of Automated Systems in Academic Libraries," Journal of Library Automation, March 1968, p. 75-91. Reprinted in: Key Papers in Information Science, ASIS, Washington, D.C., 1971.

2. An early version of the second part of this paper with the title "New Directions in Library Automation" was presented to the National and University Libraries Section at the IFLA Conference in Oslo, Norway, on August 15, 1975.

3. For example, one excellent and timely source are the proceedings of the annual clinics on Library Applications of Data Processing which are sponsored by the

University of Illinois, Graduate School of Library
Science, Urbana, Illinois, and edited by F. Wilfred
Lancaster. The 9th Clinic in 1972 was on "Applications of On-line Computers to Library Problems, "
the 10th in 1973 was on "Networking and Other Forms
of Cooperation, " the 11th in 1974 was on "Applications of Minicomputers to Library and Related Problems. "

4. Herman H. Fussler. Research Libraries and Technology; A Report to the Sloan Foundation, Chicago,
U. of Chicago Press, 1973, 91p. Although this
book is not easy reading, it is probably the most
thoughtful, authoritative, and comprehensive treatment of the subject currently available.

5. Allen B. Veaner. "Major Decision Points in Library
Automation, " College and Research Libraries, September 1970, p. 299-312.

6. Edward Heiliger, "Florida Atlantic University: New
Libraries on New Campuses, " College and Research
Libraries, May 1964, p. 181-184.

7. INTREX, Report of a Planning Conference on Informa-
tion Transfer Experiments. Edited by Carl F. J.
Overhage and R. Joyce Harman. Cambridge, M. I. T.
Press, 1965, p. 56.

8. Project Intrex. Semiannual Activity Report, M. I. T.,
Cambridge, 15 September 1972 (Intrex PR-14), p.
1-2.

9. Charles T. Payne. "The University of Chicago Library
Data Management System. " Presented at Clinic on
Library Applications of Data Processing, University
of Illinois, April 30, 1974.

10. CLR Recent Developments, May 1975, p. 1.

11. Project BALLOTS and the Stanford University Libraries,
"Stanford University's BALLOTS System, " Journal
of Library Automation, March 1975, p. 31-50.

12. Richard De Gennaro. "Providing Bibliographic Services
from Machine-readable Data Bases--the Library's
Role, " Journal of Library Automation, December
1973, p. 215-22.

13. James L. Wood. "NFAIS Document Access Activities, "
Presented at the 17th Annual NFAIS Conference,
Arlington, Virginia, March 5, 1975. Mimeo. 9p.

14. "Minnesota Bio-Medical Minicomputer Project, " Journal
of Library Automation, March 1973, p. 66. (Technical Communications.)

15. Glenn Brudvig. "University of Minnesota Libraries Automation Program, " June 30, 1975. Typescript of an
unpublished summary.

16. This point is enlarged upon in my editorial entitled
     "Library Automation: the Second Decade," Journal
     of Library Automation, March 1975, p. 3-4.

THE CARD CATALOGUE MADE SPECIFIC*

Doris Garton

I was happy to see my own feelings about the card
catalogue expressed in Liz Dickinson's article in Wilson Library Bulletin, February, 1976 ["Of catalogs, computers,
and communication," v. 50, no. 6, p. 463-70].

Having two small school libraries (one junior high and
one high), a small budget, and limited time, I--like thousands of my contemporaries in public schools--do all the
chores. I plan; purchase; weed; cultivate use; try to wed
faculty, students and library; and, yes, catalogue. The
large majority of my cards are homemade and scanty. Several people have served as part-time librarians before me.
After years of working with youth in junior and senior high
schools, I have discovered that most students in small libraries find the book they want by going to the shelves directly. Only a few tortured researchers use the card catalogue. The reason lies in the card catalogue.

To use the catalogue, one must know what a call number is and where and why. One needs to know names of authors and that they are listed alphabetically by last names.
And that there are pseudonyms. And that "du Jardin" is
listed by the "du." One needs to know that A, An, and The
are not alphabetized. If one knows the subject he or she
likes to read about, maybe the catalogue will be helpful,
maybe not. Mystery, adventure and detective stories are
easy to find, but the person simply wanting a "good book"
to read may be stuck. Asking the librarian may not be
helpful, either because the librarian is busy, or thinks differently about what constitutes a "good book." Any good

*Reprinted by permission of the author and publisher from
Hennepin County Library Cataloging Bulletin, No. 21, pp.
33-35.

books that find their way into the library are soon captured because children "know" about them in some mysterious way. Every librarian learns that the terrific books do not stay on the shelves long. The Hardy Boys and Nancy Drew series are perfect examples of that. They pass from hand to hand all year long, often overdue, always read, sometimes stolen. But the card catalogue is of no use in finding a good book.

But I am not one to give up. I purchased a lovely, pale-wood card catalogue with a nice new wood smell. I labeled the drawers neatly. I added new cards furiously, especially subject cards (for fiction in particular). I gave lectures on how to use the card catalogue. (Indeed, that's a regular part of my program.) We had book hunts. We memorized the Dewey Decimal system. There were posters around to demonstrate all the above. The students continued to go to the shelves to browse for a book to read. Nor am I against that. I purchased those plastic card holders which hold a card up above the others so that the title, author, or subject is evident. And I changed them to encourage interest. When the English class was trying to find autobiographies, I used these plastic holders to point out what we had in this area. When students were given the assignment to read an American historical novel, I used these "risers" to point out names of cities, states, areas, wars, movements, and times that have found their way into fiction. It helped, and some students did learn what the card catalogue is. Too many did not. They continued to go to the stacks, ride the stool, pull books, and browse. Since our library is small, why shouldn't they do it that way? Why have a card catalogue at all? I am a librarian and I do not give up easily.

One day, a few weeks ago, I was browsing and dreaming over the new National Geographic catalogue, a beautiful thing full of color photographs demonstrating all the films, filmstrips, and books they sell. A brilliant idea struck me and I want to share it with other librarians because it has been a spectacular success. I got students to cut and paste the small colorful pictures onto the right side of catalogue cards, leaving room on the left side for names, call numbers, etc. They cut and pasted. And I labeled.

I found a particularly fetching picture of an arachnid (spider to you). It had four, various-sized black eyes that gazed invitingly over its little tan furry "paws" directly into the face of the viewer. I labeled it "arachnid" and filed it in the A's. Anyone who opens the "A" drawer meets Mr.

Arachnid face-to-face.   There are nearly 300 students in
our junior high and at least half of them have not only asked
about the arachnid, but have gone to the shelf and found the
material we have on spiders.   It is "in" to know what an
arachnid is in our library.

As we glued and labeled, they got carried away and
began to label some of the pictures with their friends' names.
Then they found the picture of a cobra in striking position
and labeled it "Mrs. K- strikes again." Mrs. K- is the
math teacher, and she thought it was funny, too.   I put the
number for mathematics on the card and the students have
since found several entertaining books on crystals, the number one million, the psychology of numbers, etc.   A crab
became the principal, who was a good sport about it when he
learned that they now know what a crustacean is.   A group
of long-legged birds became the basketball team.   A small
bunch of mice became the cheerleaders, and the book we
have about that emerged.   A group of hyenas eating a zebra
became the lunchroom.   I hope the personnel of the cafeteria
won't mind because that card led the students to books about
cooking.

Talk about specificity!   What is more specific than a
picture?   And worth 10, 000 labels?   I have plans to use the
catalogues and other pictures I can find to demonstrate book-
subjects, especially for fiction that isn't getting noticed.   I
can think of at least a dozen pictures that will demonstrate
Sugarman's Seventeen Guide to Knowing Yourself better than
the subject heading ADOLESCENT BEHAVIOR.   I intend to
use cartoons, jokes, comics, and even photographs of the
students from old annuals to illustrate the card catalogue.
I intend to use different colored cards to attract students to
best sellers, classics, reviews.   I am now raising subject
headings above the cards to attract attention, changing them
often.   I have started making cards to use in the plastic
risers with headings like some of the following:

KNOW YOURSELF.... SEE 155. 5, Section 5, 3rd
shelf.

Got a date with Mr. Wonderful?   Read the book
with call # 395L

SO YOU ARE GOING FOR A JOB INTERVIEW!
Read 331. 1K

DO YOU KNOW WHAT GOES ON IN CHINESE
PRISONS TODAY?   Read 365. 6Y

FOR A CLEANER AMERICA READ 338. 4

Art can be especially appealing in the catalogue.
The problem is finding the time, the pictures and someone who likes to cut and paste.   (The latter is easiest to
find.)   Wouldn't it be great if LC would make a line of art-
ful, funny, psychedelic, captivating subject cards to go with
every card-set?   Line drawings are common in the books
and on the covers, but no one has ever added them to the
cards, have they?   I would like to find out if anyone has.
In the meantime, I never throw away any catalogues from
the dealers.

And it works!   My students give the catalogue such a
grand rush that I have to direct traffic.   They are saying,
"Gee, I didn't know we had so many keen books. "

LET THEM EAT CAKE
WHILE READING CATALOG CARDS
An Essay on the Availability Problem*

Daniel Gore

    I have long cherished the neat reason Will Cuppy gave
for not reading Thomas Carlyle's <u>Sartor Resartus</u>.

    "<u>Sartor Resartus</u> is simply unreadable," says Cuppy,
"and for me that always sort of spoils a book."

    Anyone who has worked in cataloging or acquisitions
will instantly perceive what Cuppy is getting at.

    Some books are simply unreadable, and it is a waste
of critical effort to explain why. I used to see so many
thousands of them in my years as a cataloger, I thought it
might be helpful if I compiled a bibliography of unreadable
books, with current supplements, of course, as a caution to
the innocent bibliographical voyager--a kind of buoy to steer
you away from shoal waters.

    The task was immense, but I was prepared to under-
take it, for strictly humanitarian reasons, until I realized
someone had beat me to it. I refer of course to <u>The National Union Catalog,</u> which, with a few scattered exceptions
here and there, accomplishes very nicely what I had in mind.

    Don't get me wrong. I have nothing personally
against unreadable books, so long as I don't have to read
them myself. I haven't had to read <u>Sartor Resartus</u> since I
escaped from graduate school 15 years ago, and even the re-
sentment I feel towards it is fading away. In fact, when I
look at all the unreadable new books on my FASTCAT shelves

*Reprinted from <u>Library Journal</u>, Jan. 15, 1975. Published
by R. R. Bowker Co. (a Xerox company). Copyright ©
1975 by Xerox Corporation.

I get a certain sense of subversive pleasure in knowing that I will never have to read any of them, while my friends on the faculty will.

Not only do I harbor no personal antagonism towards unreadable books, I don't even object to them from the professional standpoint, so long as the acquisition and maintenance of them does not seriously interfere with the provision of sufficient numbers of readable books for people who want to read them.

A readable book I define simply as one that people read--not implying in that definition any absolute exclusion of college faculties. And as a corollary to that definition, I might characterize a readable book as one that you have a very poor chance of finding on a library's shelves, even if you found it entered in the catalog, as you nearly always will. Most of us do a really splendid job of providing catalog entries for readable books.

Consider, for example, the amazing findings of the catalog-use study done at Yale several years ago, and reported on by Ben-Ami Lipetz.[1] Of the 50 million titles published since Gutenberg's time, the Yale catalog records some two and a"half million, or roughly five per cent. Yet the catalog-use study shows that nearly 90 per cent of the books that people want to read are entered in the catalog. That result is exactly 18 times better than you would expect from a completely random book selection program, and it demolishes the pessimistic claim that nobody really knows anything about book selection. If that argument were true, then the Yale Library would have to buy 42 million more books to achieve in a random unknowing way, the 90 per cent catalog-entry finding rate that a rational selection policy made possible.

Not that book selection is all that difficult a business. It is one of those blessed enterprises that nearly always turns out well when conducted by responsible people in a reasonably systematic fashion. I have good reason to believe that a catalog-use study at Macalester College, which owns about one-half per cent of all published books, would yield the same 90 per cent finding rate reported at Yale, and I suspect that most other academic libraries above the 200,000 volume mark would do about as well for their clientele, or better.[2]

What the Yale study does not tell us, to my considerable regret, is what happens after people leave the catalog, call-numbers in hand, and go to the shelves to fetch the books. Will they find all of them? 90 per cent? 80 per cent? Less?

If they go in quest of Sartor Resartus, I'll bet they find it--and leave it there too, for the next man's benefit.

But if it's Watership Down they're after, I'll give high odds they'll not find it this year, nor next either, unless they resort to heroic measures.

Before I started looking into the literature on the subject, I would have guessed the average rate of availability, among books actually owned by a college library, to be at least at the 75 per cent level, and perhaps better. That is to say, I would guess that three times out of four you would find on the shelves a book you found entered in the catalog. That guess would rest on two considerations:

1) In an academic library of any size, only five per cent or so of the total collection is likely to be on loan at any one time, leaving 95 per cent on the shelves waiting to be borrowed; and

2) I wouldn't think students would tolerate a failure rate in excess of 25 per cent. Why should we expect them to when you and I would not endure the same frustration rate in a drug store or supermarket?

To my considerable astonishment I found studies done in four different university libraries, all purporting to show the average failure rate to lie in the range of 40-50 per cent.[3] "If this is indeed generally true," I thought, "then the rebelliousness of college students has been much exaggerated." Either that, or they don't greatly care whether they find a book on the shelves, as long as they have a chance to read its catalog card.

Now though the latter proposition is plainly absurd, neither has the volatility of Macalester students been doubted in recent years--so I concluded that the failure rate in the Macalester Library must be a good deal lower than reported elsewhere. Either the 40+ per cent failure rate is not the rule, or if it is, we are, for reasons not easily guessed at, an exception to it. For there have been no riots in the Macalester Library.

In a survey we conducted, it was discovered, through reports on the outcome of a thousand efforts by students to find books that we owned, that the average failure rate in the Macalester Library is about 42 per cent--this is a library of a quarter million volumes, serving only 1800 readers! And with never more than three per cent of the collection on loan at any time. Given data like those, I believe something is seriously amiss with our management policies, specifically as they relate to acquisitions and loan periods, and that dramatic improvement in performance is both necessary and possible within existing budget limits. I marvel that we have got by so long with so scandalous a rate of failure as 42 per cent.

What has spared us, I suspect, is widespread student belief that the library is being systematically robbed. Assuming they were the victims of their own malfeasance, the students have indulged our shortcomings in a wonderfully high-minded way.

But a year ago we took a complete census of holdings, and found 10 per cent more volumes on the shelves than the inventory records showed we owned. While that put to rest all fears of theft, it did nothing to explain why students perceived us to be a thieves' paradise.

That's when I started looking seriously into the literature on availability rates.

Perhaps, as members of a profession that nowadays promotes the service aspects of its mission, with diminished emphasis on its more traditional curatorial functions, you will share my surprise in discovering that Library Literature has no subject heading whatever for availability rates, performance rates, success rates, satisfaction rates, or whatever language you care to cast the concept in.

The subject heading is lacking, of course, because the literature itself is almost nonexistent. Over a 50-year period I find only a dozen or so pieces directly concerned with this subject (entered under the heading "Duplicates"), most of them published in the last few years, and coming mainly from England and Canada, where the problem appears to be well understood and vigorously dealt with--at least among the new universities.

Arthur Hamlin raised a bright battle standard on this

field in 1966, for American librarians, but no one rallied
around;[4] and there is a remarkable series of statistical inquiries into the general question of library inventory control,
published in recent years by the industrial engineer R. W.
Trueswell.[5]   But, like Hamlin's paper, these too have been
ignored.

Eric Moon, in an LJ editorial of May 15, 1968,[6]
lambasted public librarians for their inattention to the availability problem; and the redoubtable Marvin Scilken addressed
a pungent note to the same audience in the Wilson Library
Bulletin of September 1971,[7] wryly observing that "Purchasing multiple copies violates Scilken's First Empirical Law of
Librarians' Science, 'that librarians much prefer buying
books that no one wants to buying books that they know everyone wants,' or, 'It's better to serve a possible reader later
than to serve an actual reader now.'"   Scilken protests that
"librarians use much verbiage, effort, and even some money,
on so-called public relations trying to convince patrons that
they should think well of an institution that rarely seems to
have what they want until the desire for it has disappeared.
As things are now ... it is good business and not very expensive to have the best kind of public relations--the books!"
Except for these few sallies, the rest is silence on an issue
which appears, at least from the patron's standpoint, to
dwarf all others in the field of library service.

Let me underscore the paradoxical indifference to the
availability problem in two related propositions regarding library services:

1) Through vigorous attention to the availability-rate
phenomenon, one can theoretically double the per capita loan
rate of an academic library.

2) By exploiting interlibrary loan services to the full-
est degree, in a geographical setting ideally suited to maximizing interloan services, one can theoretically increase the
per capita loan rate of books by about five per cent.

The first proposition, while stated theoretically, is
based on actual results obtained at the University of Lancaster Library, as reported on by Michael A. Buckland,[8]
who has written extensively on the subject.   When measures
were taken at Lancaster to raise the availability rate from
60 per cent to 86 per cent, per capita circulation rate more
than doubled.   While one swallow may not make a summer,

it does attest to summer's possibility and to a possible end of "this winter of our discontent." And what has actually happened in one library is at least theoretically possible at another.

The second proposition, relating to interloan services, derives from actual experience at Macalester College over the last four years, where with swift, reliable access to some two million titles in Twin Cities libraries, we have been able to add through interloan something like five per cent to the per capita borrowing rate. Without detailing my reasons here, I believe that is the saturation rate for us, and suspect it would be for most other libraries too, since our geographical and certain other circumstances are ideal for maximizing interloan service. Incidentally, our failure rate on interloan is only 17 per cent, or less than half the failure rate in finding on our shelves, on demand, books we actually own.

To recapitulate: By improving availability rates in your own holdings, you may improve use rates one hundred per cent. By maximizing interloan services, under ideal conditions, you may improve use rates five per cent.

How then do you account for the fact that over the past 50 years hundreds of articles have been written on the interloan question, while only a dozen have dealt with the availability problem?

Is it because we assume that availability is so routine a problem it should and must take care of itself, whereas interloan situations are sporadic, individualistic, and often rather interesting? Public health work goes on unnoticed and keeps the nation healthy, whereas heart transplants are glamorous and heavily publicized, and contribute absolutely nothing to the health of the masses. Interloan service is highly visible, and plainly grafitying to the rare patron who requests it. But making books available from your own collection is a task that goes on behind the scenes, and the patron never knows just whom to praise or blame on any occasion of success, or failure. The process is invisible, and our concern with it slight--beyond the one visible step of ensuring that we have cards in the catalog for all the right books. After that, who cares? Let them eat cake while reading catalog cards.

In giving such elaborate attention to the process of

borrowing books that we don't own, while largely ignoring
the enormous problem of delivering the books that we do
own, have we not been straining out gnats and swallowing
camels?

What we have <u>learned</u> recently from interloan networks may be more <u>valuable</u> than the loan service itself.
Data from the ACM Periodical Bank, the British National
Lending Library, and the National Library of Medicine illu-
minate an extraordinary imbalance in patron demand for
journal literature: most journals are read by practically no
one, while a very few journals seem to be read by everyone. [9] Of all the journals available through the ACM Bank,
those that receive the heaviest use turn out to be the very
ones that are <u>owned</u> by the libraries making a request for
them.   Those <u>that</u> receive the least use are those that are
owned by none of the ten libraries belonging to the Bank.
So far as journal literature is concerned, what the overwhelming majority of readers appear to want is not access
to an infinite variety of journal titles, but prompt availability of articles in an exceedingly small percentage (say
five per cent or less) of the journals that are available from
a lending center.

One may suppose a similar pattern of reader interest
obtains with respect to monographs as well.   Certainly the
Yale catalog study reveals an extremely narrow concentration of reader interest in books, when five per cent of the
world's publications satisfy 90 per cent of the catalog
searches.   The range of titles readers want to see may be
far smaller than we imagine.   Though I have no extensive
interloan data to bear this out, I have some general facts
that do.   Seven college libraries in the Twin Cities, owning
an aggregate 250, 000 unique titles, form an interloan network which calls upon the University of Minnesota Library
as a source of last resort.   Although the University of Minnesota holds nearly ten times as many titles as the college
network, it supplies only 25 per cent of the filled requests,
while 75 per cent of them are filled within the network.
Given the extraordinary fact that the collection that is ten
times larger fills only a quarter of the interloan requests,
it is hard to escape the inference that the interloan program
really satisfies a need not for esoteric or even uncommon
publications, but for rather obvious, commonplace titles that
<u>should</u> be available in the requesting library, but for some
<u>reason</u> are not.   At Macalester, for example, some 25 per
cent of book requests through interloan are for books that

we own ourselves, but for whatever reason cannot supply when the patron wants them. I estimate that another 25 per cent of the requests are for books that we should own but don't, leaving some 50 per cent as normal candidates for interloan activity. I suspect that we have been using interloan as a very poor substitute for effective inventory control, just as a profligate spender will go in debt to finance his food and shelter, having exhausted his own resources on baubles and trinkets.

The reason I consider even a highly effective interloan service to be a poor substitute for effective inventory management is this: The finding-rate survey I mentioned earlier indicates that students fail to find books we own when they want them on the order of 35,000 times per year. Yet the interloan data indicate that students will ask for only 500 of these books via interloan in the course of a year. That is to say, interloan makes up for only 1.5 per cent of the failures, and therefore seems hardly worth the candle.

One may well retort that if a student's interest in an unavailable book is so slight that he will request interloan backup only 1.5 per cent of the time, why strain yourself to accommodate so fleeting and flimsy an interest? I would answer such a question in two ways.

First, what we are seeing may not be a feeble interest on the student's part at all, but rather an overwhelming capacity on our part to convince him of the hopelessness of his quest. The 1.5 per cent we don't convince are just incorrigibly stubborn.

And second, I would cite again the results observed at the University of Lancaster Library when steps were taken to improve inhouse availability of high-demand books: the per capita circulation rate more than doubled.

While none of this absolutely proves anything, I find it powerfully suggestive, and that is about as close to certainty as we ever come with any of the fundamental issues in library management. Indeed I am so convinced by the little that has been said by others on the matter of availability, and by the appalling magnitude of the problem we have discovered in the Macalester Library, I regard the solving of this problem as our top action priority over the next few years.

There are several ways to tackle the problem, each involving so many imponderables that it is impossible to say exactly what the costs, or effectiveness, of any one of them will be.

Very briefly, the approaches are these: 1) shorten the general loan period; 2) shorten the loan period for high-demand titles only; 3) buy multiple copies of high-demand titles; and 4) some combination of the above.

The University of Lancaster reduced to one week the loan period of high-demand titles, with the result, as mentioned, of doubling the per capita circulation rate. This decision was based upon computer simulation of the problem, but the definition of what is a "high-demand title" appears to have been rather intuitively determined as covering the 10 per cent of the collection that exhibited the greatest recorded use. To identify that 10 per cent required the manual inspection of all 70,000 volumes then in the library, which has since grown to several times that size. I do not know whether Lancaster still takes that approach. I doubt it. With computerized circulation, which I assume Lancaster did not then have, identification of popular titles would be no problem. Re-processing them for shortened loan periods probably would be in any case.

At the University of Windsor (in Canada) a computer was used to identify popular titles and to predict the number of multiple copies required of each to achieve a 95 per cent satisfaction rate. [10] Out of a circulating collection of 200,000 volumes, only 40,000 different titles circulated at least once in the course of the academic year. And of those 40,000 the computer analysis indicated that 3,257 titles needed more than one copy to assure a 95 per cent availability rate. Of those 3,257 titles, only 570 needed more copies than the library already held, so there was no dramatic "before and after" result to report as there was at Lancaster. Presumably Windsor was already close to the 95 per cent satisfaction level before the study began (the general loan period for all books, incidentally, is one week), and that is indeed a very fine performance rate. The Windsor study, while extremely valuable for the rest of us, amounted to an enquiry into a problem that didn't exist at Windsor.

The least elegant approach to the problem is simply to shorten the loan period for all books, and do nothing else but that. The ultimate in that direction is to reduce the loan period to zero and then you have what used to be called a reference library. Maximizing availability in that way will also reduce your circulation rate to zero, which is not the goal at Macalester.

The other routes appear to require either computerized circulation, or tedious inspection of every volume in your library, to identify those that will either get an extra copy, or a shorter loan period, or perhaps both.

Macalester has neither computerized circulation, nor any disposition to make a wholesale inspection of the loan records in each of its quarter of a million volumes. That seemed to leave us with the sole inelegant option of simply reducing the loan period for all books to one week, or less.

Then we began to think about Richard Trueswell's remarkable discovery that 70 per cent or more of the books you lend on a given day will have circulated at least once in the previous year. Since the average circulation rate at Macalester Library is once every four years, it appears that 70 per cent of the books that are actually borrowed will exhibit a demand rate at least four times greater than the average. The majority of books returning from loan are ipso facto relatively high-demand titles, and potential candidates for duplication. By examining only those books that are being discharged from circulation, a student assistant can conveniently identify for you all books that meet any level-of-use criterion you may specify for high-demand titles. The criterion we are presently using, arrived at through highly sophisticated intuitive methods, is this:

Any book that has circulated at least four times within the last 12 months will be set aside and considered as a candidate for duplication, simply because it exhibits a demand rate at least 16 times greater than the average.

About six per cent of the books returning from loan meet this criterion, or roughly 70 books per week. These books are then submitted to a review process that is far more sensitive, responsive, and complex than anything a computer could do. The Library's associate director, Jean Archibald, looks at these books, and relying upon her vast knowledge of student reading habits, and of all the anomalies and idiosyncrasies of class assignments and individual tastes, and of the levels of transitoriness and durability of the various types and fields of literature, she makes an expert judgment

as to which of those 70 books per week shall be duplicated.
During the first six months of this undertaking, it turns out
that roughly half the books considered for duplication are in
fact being duplicated, or about three per cent of total general
circulation. At this rate the acquisitions costs for the first
full project year will run about $10,000, a figure that will
presumably decline in succeeding years as the saturation
point is approached.

Data from the interloan operation are also being continuously reviewed to identify titles in need of either duplication or first purchase. The circulation survey obviously
gives no clue about popular titles you never bought, or those
you bought only to have them immediately and permanently
sequestered on some professor's office shelves. Information
from interloan therefore makes a convenient hook for catch-
ing the relatively few titles you will never dip out of the circulation pool.

Selective reduction of loan periods for popular titles
appears too cumbersome to be practical in our situation, although Lancaster obtained excellent results through that approach, in a collection of 70,000 volumes.

We are considering, however, a modest blanket reduction in the general loan period, from five weeks to three,
as a means of multiplying the effects of systematic duplication. Before any such reduction is made we will of course
let the students know what we propose to do, and why. And
if the reduction is strongly resisted, and the present level
of duplication is not bringing the availability rate up to the
desired 80 or 90 per cent range, then we will seek additional funding for duplicate purchases, either through new moneys
for the book budget, or reallocation of ordinary funds.

Funding for our current duplication project came
mainly from reallocation, and with the blessings of the library committee, bestowed before either they or I knew
exactly how bad the failure rate is in the Macalester Library.
Now that we all know the shocking magnitude of that rate,
the prospects for continued and perhaps increased reallocation
in subsequent years are good.

Here is where the issue of spending money on unreadable books becomes a lively professional concern to me,
since budgets are always finite, and what is spent in one
place cannot be spent in another. Too many unreadable

books may mean too few copies of those that are read. In
libraries as in life, the essential thing is balance, and com-
promises must be made to achieve it. Much has been said
in the past about "balanced" collections, but that meant only
balancing titles in one area against those in another, not
weighing the demonstrable need for multiple copies of certain titles against the imagined need to maximize the number
of different titles by eliminating duplication altogether.

What sort of balance exists in the Macalester Library
when six per cent of our loans exhibit demand rates 16 times
greater than the average, yet supply of copies is not balanced
against measurable demand upon that fraction of the collection? That degree of imbalance in an auto parts inventory
would put you out of business in a week. But we get away
with it in libraries because there is rarely a competitor to
whom our frustrated clientele can turn.

Still we pay a price of sorts for our indifference to
the inventory problems caused by sharp differences in demand rates from one title to the next. When I think of those
35,000 searches in the Macalester Library that end in failure
every year, even though we own the books that are being
sought, I begin to understand for the first time how there
can be so many people who love books, and so few who love
librarians. With all that frustration, I think we're lucky just
to be tolerated.

Now that the shock of discovery is wearing off, and
I'm beginning to see how a well-stocked, well-supported, and
allegedly well-balanced library can routinely thwart its patrons on nearly half their quests, it occurs to me that we librarians have not an image problem, but a performance problem.

For rarely does an academic library show the slightest
concern for the availability problem, beyond the token ack-
nowledgment of its existence which the traditional reserve
operation provides. But the human condition that creates the
problem must be widespread, since most people want to read
readable books, and most aren't. So a lot of people are always pursuing a very few books, and numerous disappoint-
ments are bound to ensue. And since so very few librarians
have undertaken to solve the problem, the problem itself must
be as widespread as the human condition that begets it. No
wonder our public clings so tenaciously to the image of the
librarian as a forbidding, frustrating, and virginal figure.

Why should they think of us in images of helpfulness, and
generosity, and availability, when half the time we send them
away empty-handed? The extraordinary persistence of the
sour spinster image, decades after it lost all external rele-
vance, must carry some rather special message. I think it
does. I think it says that the pleasures we presume to offer
aren't nearly so available as our callers would like them to
be.

References

1. Ben-Ami Lipetz, "Catalog Use in a Large Research Li-
       brary," in Operations Research: Implications for Li-
       braries, ed. by Don R. Swanson & Abraham Book-
       stein ("University of Chicago Studies in Library Sci-
       ence"; Univ. of Chicago Pr. , 1972), p. 129-39.
2. A survey done recently in several English university li-
       braries indicates substantially poorer results (Carol
       A. Seymour & J. L. Schofield, "Measuring Reader
       Failure at the Catalogue," LRTS, Winter 1973, p. 6-
       24). The methodology employed, however, raises
       serious questions about the accuracy of the findings.
3. Three of these studies are cited in Richard W. Trues-
       well's Analysis of Library User Circulation Require-
       ments: Final Report (N. S. F. Grant GNO435, January
       1968), p. 1. The fourth is Michael Buckland's paper,
       cited below. A fifth study, done at Cambridge Univer-
       sity, yielded results quite different from the other
       four: the failure rate was in the 10-15 per cent
       range, rather than 40-50 per cent. Cf. J. A. Urqu-
       hart and J. L. Schofield, "Measuring Reader Failure
       at the Shelves," Journal of Documentation, December
       1971, p. 281.
4. Arthur T. Hamlin, "The Impact of College Enrollments
       on Library Acquisitions Policy," Liberal Education,
       May 1966, p. 204-10.
5. Richard W. Trueswell, "Two Characteristics of Circula-
       tion and Their Effect on the Implementation of Mecha-
       nized Circulation Control Systems," College & Re-
       search Libraries, July 1964, p. 285-91; "Determining
       the Optimal Number of Volumes for a Library's Core
       Collection," Libri, Vol. 16, 1966, p. 49-60; "Some
       Circulation Data from a Research Library," College
       & Research Libraries, November 1968, p. 493-95;
       "User Circulation Satisfaction vs. Size of Holdings at
       Three Academic Libraries," College & Research Li-

braries, May 1969, p. 204-13; "Article Use and Its Relationship to Individual User Satisfaction," College & Research Libraries, July 1970, p. 239-45.

6. Eric Moon, "Satisfaction Point," LJ, May 15, 1968, p. 1947.

7. Marvin H. Scilken, "The Read and Return Collection," Wilson Library Bulletin, Sept. 1971, p. 104-105.

8. Michael K. Buckland, "An Operations Research Study of a Variable Loan and Duplication Policy at the University of Lancaster," in Operations Research (Univ. of Chicago Pr., 1972), p. 97-106.

9. Daniel Gore, "Sawing Off the Horns of a Dilemma, or, How to Cut Subscription Lists and Expand Access to Journal Literature," in Management Problems in Serials Work, ed. by Spyers-Duran and Gore, Greenwood Pr., p. 104-14.

10. Robert S. Grant, "Predicting the Need for Multiple Copies of Books," Journal of Library Automation, June 1971, p. 64-71.

LIBRARIES AND ACCESS
TO THE LAW*

Linda Jewett

In Canadian society today most activities are governed at least to some extent by law. The citizen
is expected to know the law as it affects his or her
activities, and is liable to penalty if the law is not
followed. As a result, each day Canadians ask
thousands of questions involving law.

These questions are directed to government offices,
the police, lawyers, libraries, information centres,
social agencies and others. A great many of them
are not requests for legal assistance, but rather
attempts to find specific information about the law.

Aware of the public's need for information about
law, in 1974 the Law Reform Commission of Canada
asked the University of Toronto to examine the problem of access to the law. A study was undertaken
at the Faculty of Law by M. L. Friedland, Dean of
the Faculty, Peter Jewett, a lawyer with the law
firm of Tory, Tory, DesLauriers & Binnington,
and Linda Jewett, a librarian at the Metropolitan
Toronto Business Library.

With the assistance of an advisory committee, a research design was finalized. By late 1974, the research had been carried out, the results analysed
and certain conclusions reached about the nature of
access to the law in Canada and what could be done
to improve the situation. A report was submitted

*Reprinted by permission of the author and publisher from
Ontario Library Review, Vol. 59, No. 4, Dec. 1975, pp.
220-225.

to the Law Reform Commission early in 1975, and
is now available in book form from Methuen/Cars-
well.

The Access to the Law Study

What follows is not a detailed description of the research undertaken in the Access to the Law Study, nor of
the results obtained. The published report contains the
methodology and the complete results of the research. It
also outlines the suggestions of the investigators for dealing
with the problems of legal access identified in the study.
This description is presented in order to highlight certain
aspects of the study which are particularly significant for
libraries in Canada.

What do people do to get information about law? Do
they attempt to get information on their own, or do they
ask someone else? Whatever they do, is the question answered, and answered correctly? What problems are experienced by individuals and those assisting them in finding
legal information? And what can be done to improve the
whole process? These are the basic questions the study investigated.

The research was directed to two groups: the general public and those whose jobs entail provision of legal
information and/or basic legal assistance to others. Surveys and studies were undertaken to discover what people
do when faced with simple legal problems, and whether
members of the public can use statutes and regulations to
find basic information. In the second group, lawyers, libraries, police, government offices, information centres and
the like were contacted across Canada to obtain a picture of
their typical response to a question involving law, and to
hear their views about the problems in this area. In Toronto, representative organizations and individuals who had been
suggested by members of the public as sources to contact
were approached anonymously with test questions involving
law. Their success in handling the sample legal questions
was documented.

Finally, existing legal materials were examined and
their usefulness to both laymen and lawyers evaluated.
Readability and indexing were considered in particular detail.

The results of the research were illuminating. When faced with a simple legal problem, a majority of the members of the public surveyed would seek information or help from an organization or individual, rather than acting on their own. Roughly half of those seeking information or assistance would contact a government source; the remainder suggested a wide range of organizations and individuals to approach. Lawyers and legal aid were suggested, but much less often than government sources.

When researchers telephoned the sources suggested by the public and asked the test questions, it was found that the information and advice received often were inaccurate. In fact, an average of more than 25% of the sources called gave an incorrect answer or made a referral which led to an incorrect answer. In addition to incorrect answers, many sources gave incomplete answers. Further research indicated that on the average lawyers performed no better than other information sources when asked the test questions.

Tests of how successfully members of the public use statutes and regulations produced even more dismal results. Even using a relatively highly educated and motivated sample, only one person found the correct answer to a test question by using a procedure which could be expected consistently to produce the relevant sections. (It should be noted that all participants were given an introduction to the use of statutes and regulations similar to that used by reference librarians familiar with the material.) Four others who found the correct answer did so by luck. None of the remaining 30 participants succeeded in locating the answer to their test question.

Although unaware of the results of our other interviewing and testing, a number of the individuals we contacted whose jobs entailed providing legal information and advice reported uncertainty about their success with legal questions and problems. Those who were not lawyers described such problems as a personal lack of legal knowledge and inability to find answers on their own or referral sources. They also noted a lack of comprehensible legal materials.

Some lawyers complained about legal materials, while others indicated a tendency to "ad lib" answers to simple legal questions. This tendency appeared to be largely responsible for some of the incorrect or incomplete answers given by the lawyers tested.

It is possible to pinpoint some of the reasons for the wrong or partially complete answers these organizations give by looking at the internal processes they use to respond to an inquiry or problem. Perhaps the greatest difficulty lies in the almost-universal tendency to answer questions from personal knowledge. Even lawyers make mistakes because they do not check their answers to apparently simple legal questions. If people who receive inquiries about law from the public were trained always to check their answers, it seems likely that less incorrect and incomplete information would result.

Where can these individuals or members of the public check information about law to establish its correctness? This ultimately is the basic problem revealed by the Access to the Law Study.

Existing legal materials, particularly statutes and regulations, are neither widely available in Canada nor comprehensible. There are a number of areas of law not covered by statute, and for some of these there exists no text or treatise even for lawyers. Handbooks and other popular treatments of law are available only for the larger provinces. Where they exist at all, popular legal materials cover only a very few legal topics, and their contents may not be up to date.

Providing Better Access to the Law

It became clear that a new comprehensive source of law is needed. It should be written for laymen in enough detail that it would be useful to those who are approached by the public with questions and problems involving law. In fact, it seems likely that even lawyers would find such a source useful.

The study recommends a combination of four approaches to improving public access to the law: improvement of existing legal materials, basic education of the public about law, improvement of the quality of legal information dispensed by those whom the public approaches, and development of a new print source of law for non-lawyers. Each is necessary to make the other recommendations most effective.

Libraries' Role

What is the role of libraries and librarians in the
provision of public access to the law? Compared to the
number of legal questions handled by government offices and
the police, libraries get relatively few legal inquiries.
With the obvious exception of law libraries, most report that
fewer than 10% of their total reference inquiries concern
law.

Academic libraries get relatively few reference inquiries from outside the academic community, and as a result the number of legal questions they handle is directly influenced by faculty research and the courses taught. Political science, economics, business administration, social work
and criminology are among the subjects that produce requests
for legal information and materials.

Public libraries naturally enough are used more
heavily than other types of libraries by the public as a
source of information about law. In the public libraries of
Metropolitan Toronto this activity appears to represent between 30,000 and 40,000 legal inquiries annually. Thus, although not in the same league as government and the police,
urban public libraries at least handle a significant number of
legal questions.

Rural libraries in Alberta and New Brunswick were
studied intensively as part of the project. They typically
reported very few reference inquiries on any subject, but
when the population they serve is considered rural, libraries
appear to answer more legal questions per capita than do urban libraries. Many librarians rightfully are skeptical about
library statistics but it seems likely that rural libraries are
at least as important a source of legal information in the
community as urban libraries are.

Libraries are the only place where members of the
public can consult a range of legal materials rather than
getting verbal answers to questions. Students need published
material as a source of legal information, and some individuals prefer to look up law on their own rather than to discuss
a problem or question.

The fact that libraries contain legal materials means
that library staff members have access to the existing
sources of law in answering inquiries from the public. This

is particularly significant when the problem of checking answers to legal questions is considered.

A third important characteristic of libraries is their public service staff. Librarians are trained to avoid giving answers from personal knowledge. They generally are able to use published materials to find information, and are sensitive to the implications of place and date of publication. In theory, librarians should be able consistently to give correct and complete answers to some legal questions and to recognize situations where their collections do not provide the needed information.

Despite Library collections and staff, an individual who approaches the public library with a legal question may not receive useful information in response. Public libraries have more legal materials of all kinds than other non-library organizations in the community, but their collections tend to be spotty, out of date and lacking in basic legal tools.

Staff members are trained to check answers, but very few can use even the statutes and regulations successfully. This is partly the result of a lack of specific instruction in the use of legal materials, but it is also an indication of the glaring defects in the existing statute indexes. A combination of caution, unfamiliarity with the subject and inability to find useful information leads many librarians to refer inquirers to sources of legal information outside the library.

A good referral can be the best response to a legal question. However, libraries appear not to take sufficient care in referring inquirers to ensure that the question is likely to be answered correctly. Librarians tend not to check whether an outside organization is able and willing to assist a member of the public, or to know which organizations are appropriate. Library staff usually do not invite feedback by requesting that the inquirer call back if the question is not answered elsewhere. As a result, the librarian has little opportunity to assess the quality of information and assistance dispensed by an organization to which inquirers are referred.

No public library can afford to ignore its legal inquiries. For one thing, they represent approximately 3 to 5% of total questions asked. People who demonstrate faith in the ability of the public library to help them get information on any subject should be encouraged, if only to ensure continuing

financial support for what is rapidly becoming a multi-
million dollar institution.   The library is the interface between an individual and the information he or she needs, as
well as a storehouse for published material.   In order to
fulfill this responsibility in the area of legal information, it
appears that public libraries in particular should consider
carefully the recommendations of the Access to the Law
Study.

As we mentioned before, four suggestions were made
to improve access to the law in Canada: improvement of
existing legal materials, provision of basic public education
about law, improvement of the quality of legal information
dispensed, and development of a new legal information source
for non-lawyers.   Libraries can assist in the realization of
these goals.

Librarians use legal materials more than most non-
lawyers, and are thus in a better position than most members of the community to criticize shortcomings in present
materials, to point out gaps and to comment on proposed
new materials in an informed fashion.   For example, librarians use indexes in many subjects with reasonable success.   Why are legal indexes so difficult to use, and why
do we put up with it?   If we are aware of a lack of material suitable for use by non-lawyers, we should be pressing
the government and commercial publishers for more.

Many libraries already are active in continuing education programs in the community.   In Metropolitan Toronto
at least two public libraries have hosted public sessions on
law run by the Toronto Community Law School.   Local members of the bar could be encouraged to provide similar sessions in libraries outside the Toronto area.

The improvement of the legal information they now
provide is perhaps of greatest immediate interest to libraries.   Three basic steps in achieving this goal are collection building, staff training and coordination of effort
among cooperating libraries.

Collection building is discussed in Gail Dykstra's
article (same issue of Ontario Library Review).   At this
point it is only necessary to stress that at present a collection of statutes, regulations and other basic legal materials
is the only means by which legal information can be verified.
To ensure that they are dispensing accurate and complete in-

formation librarians must check it themselves. The research
described earlier indicates that most other sources of information are both less able and less inclined to do this at
the present time than are libraries.

Given the present state of Canadian legal publishing,
even a complete collection of materials is of no use to the
lay person without trained assistance in locating relevant information. All library staff responsible for dealing with
public inquiries need basic training in the use of the legal
materials in the library. This should include some knowledge
of other essential materials, such as case reports, which
may not be found in most public libraries. Library staff
members do not need to panic at the prospect of questions
involving law. They must be aware of the potential complexity of such questions, but should recognize their legitimate role in the location of useful information for inquirers.
This requires an appreciation of the absolute necessity of up
to date information where law is concerned.

Finally, accurate knowledge of other organizations and
individuals who can provide information about particular areas of law is as important for a public librarian as knowledge
of the library collection. There is very little practical difference between reading the wrong section of a statute to an
inquirer and referring the inquirer to someone else who will
read the wrong section of the statute. Obviously, no librarian can guarantee the accuracy of the information given by
someone else, but it is part of professional responsibility to
be informed generally about the quality of service given in
an organization to which library users are being referred.
This is an area where many community information centres
appear to be skilled, and librarians may want to rely on
these centres for assistance in making referrals.

Legal materials are expensive, and it may be difficult to arrange training sessions in the use of legal materials for the staff of a single library. Cooperation may be
the most practical means of upgrading the quality of legal
information and the service provided by libraries. All libraries offering reference service need certain basic legal
materials, but planning of in-depth collections to reduce
duplication is important where book budgets are not unlimited.
Library collections of legal materials within one geographical
area can be assessed and upgraded to allow overall access
to a better collection than any single library could afford.
Joint training sessions would assist in this area as well as

reducing the cost for each library. Regional courses and
workshops in legal materials and services for non-law libraries are an encouraging example of cooperative training.

    The Access to the Law Study examined a problem that
involves much more than libraries. However, the results
of that study are significant for any organization or individual involved in legal information. Because of their unique
characteristics libraries are likely to become more involved
in this area in the future. Now is the time to ensure that
the quality of information and service given by libraries
matches the potential.

THE LIBRARY CATALOG IN
A COMPUTERIZED ENVIRONMENT*

S. Michael Malinconico

The formative period of automated cataloging systems was characterized by an initiation ritual in which librarians were asked to explain and justify principles in terms of a linear, sequential, and statistical logic with which they were not entirely conversant. Principles developed over a century and a quarter of thought and experience (extending from Panizzi's defense in London [1849] to the 1961 Paris conference) were poorly defended by professional catalogers, and even less so by administrators harried by increasing personnel budgets. Administrators all too easily fall prey to the siren song of cost reduction, especially if words like innovation figure prominently in the lyrics.

The net result has been, to the largest extent, the automation of certain clerical activities ancillary to cataloging, without actual inclusion of the entire cataloging process, or the catalog itself, as part of the total system. The activities selected for automation, in general, were those for which costs could be easily ascertained and shown to be decreased by the new system. If the resultant machine-readable file bore no relation to a coherent catalog, that was of no serious concern, as the record-of-record was still the 3" x 5" card created more economically, but nonetheless filed in an off-line, manual catalog.

However, it doesn't take very long for the supporting machine file to attain greater importance than the manual catalog. This is especially so if the machine file is the product of cooperative input, because it soon becomes an

*Reprinted by permission of the author and publisher from Wilson Library Bulletin, Vol. 51, No. 1, Sept. 1976. Copyright © 1976 by The H. W. Wilson Co.

easily accessed union catalog of a consortium's holdings.   It
is at this point that the serious problems begin to occur,
when the apotheosis is effected from "file" to "catalog. "

A file, it should be recalled, in normal data processing terms is nothing more than a collection of related
physical records.   A catalog, on the other hand, should
manifest the attributes of a data base--that is, a file upon
which a coherent, logically consistent structure has been imposed.   Such a structure must be imposed from the outset,
and control over it exercised during any activity against the
data base.   Ad hoc attempts to impose a rigorous structure
will prove either impossible or so expensive as to render the
exercise impossible.

The questions raised by these developments and possible alternatives will form the subject of this discussion.
Specifically: 1) the need to impose a rigidly controlled
structure on a machine-readable catalog, 2) the capabilities
and limitations of machine processing in achieving this end,
3) some of the possibilities the machine might offer for control of the catalog, and 4) the extension of those possibilities
to permit a degree of control not possible in a manual system.

We have, perhaps, already been impelled toward a
definition of the future catalog by forces not especially con-
ducive to making it a more effective instrument.   Indeed,
the direction we seem to be taking may result in the negation
of a century of well established principles in favor of a
machine-negotiated, stochastic access to individual items in
the collection--a probabilistic access in which discrete,
known items will with good likelihood be found.

What Should a Library Catalog Be ?

One hundred years ago Charles Cutter began his ex-
position of a set of cataloging rules with the following:

OBJECTS

1. To enable a person to find a book of which
either (A) the author, (B) the title [or] (C) the
subject is known.

2. To show what the library has (D) by a given

author, (E) on a given subject [or] (F) in a given
kind of literature. [1]

These aims were reiterated in working paper No. 2 presented to the International Conference on Cataloguing Principles:

> The catalogue of a library must be designed not
> only 1) to show whether or not the library has a
> particular item or publication, issued under a cer-
> tain name of the author or under a certain title,
> but also 2) to identify the author and the work
> represented by the item or publication and to re-
> late the various works of the author and the vari-
> ous editions and translations of the work. [2]

These are, of course, Seymour Lubetzky's words. His
definition apparently found consensus among the participants
at the conference, since the following statement was adopted:

> The catalogue should be an efficient instrument for
> ascertaining:
>
> 2.1 Whether the library contains a particular book
> specified by
> (a) its author and title, etc....;
>
> 2.2 (a) which works by a particular author and
> (b) which editions of a particular work are in the
> library. [3]

What Should the Catalog Do?

Clearly, the basic functions of the catalog have not
altered, and indeed have been re-endorsed after a century of
experience. In the simplest terms the catalog should: 1)
provide access to a predefined item in the collection; 2) organize the collection; 3) attribute authorship responsibility,
when possible, to a work; and 4) assist the user with information regarding its own organization.

The first function is obvious. When a reader is seeking a precisely defined item which can be unambiguously
named, the catalog provides a location identifier. The second function is perhaps the most important, most difficult to
attain, and least addressed by automated systems. A library, of course, is not simply an aggregation of discrete

recorded materials; rather, it represents a <u>collection</u>, or more precisely <u>collections</u>, of works. A research library's value is in direct proportion to the comprehensiveness of its collections and the degree to which a rational collection policy has been developed and carried out. The catalog, if it is to serve an institution so defined, must be capable of reflecting, and assisting in the maintenance of, these collections.

The catalog entry, as we all know, is a surrogate for the item described. As a logical corollary, therefore, the catalog is itself a surrogate for the collection; more important, as a result of the added-entry structure, <u>several simultaneous surrogates</u>. The alternate access points created by an added-entry structure do provide assistance in locating a specific item; this structure, however, represents much more than simply an alternate route to a specific item. It permits the collocation, in one sequence, of all items that partake of a particular organizational attribute--all editions of an author's works, all works for which an author has primary responsibility, those for which he or she has secondary or tertiary responsibility, those works derived from his or her works, etc. It also permits the same item to take its proper place in several such sequences. From the point of view of the catalog's utility, the ability to present a comprehensive sequence under a given heading, or headings, is at least as important as its ability to provide the location of a precisely specified item.

Note carefully that this idea of drawing entries together is quite independent of the medium supporting the catalog. Whether the sequences are created by filing multiple copies of a unit card in a card catalog, or created dynamically by having a computer draw together various unit records in response to a query is irrelevant. The only difference is that in the case of the card catalog, complete sequences exist whether or not someone is actually viewing them, while on a CRT screen they exist only so long as the phosphors continue to glow.

More Than an Index

The point is that the catalog is not simply an index to the collection; in a sense, by its ability to create the collocation of entries, it assists in defining the collection. By an examination of its various sequences the catalog permits us to determine what has been written about a particular subject, how a particular idea evolved, how a particular author's thinking evolved, how a particular author's works affected others, what manifestations of an author's works the library owns, and so on. The importance of this idea of collocation appears even when we try to define what an author's work is.

Lubetzky has noted "that the materials of a library ... are representations of the works of authors, not the works themselves; ... a given work may be represented in a library in different forms or editions, under different names ... or under different titles."[4] I am inclined to go one step further and trest the entire corpus of an author's writings as his or her work. T. S. Eliot offers an interesting observation in his attempt to explore the difference between a major and a minor poet: "Whatever a minor poet may be, a major poet is one the whole of whose work we ought to read, in order to fully appreciate any part of it."[5] One can only wonder what Eliot's reaction would have been to the suggestion that some of Dante's works could be found by looking under Dante, while others might be found under Alighieri. And that works by F. H. Bradley, the subject of Eliot's doctoral dissertation, could be found by looking under F. H., Francis H., and Francis Herbert Bradley; or that he should examine all of the Bradleys in the Harvard University library catalog in order to determine what other works by that philosopher the library holds. I would venture to guess that he would have characterized these suggestions as the "eructation of unhealthy souls."

If the catalog is to fulfill any of the requirements just enumerated, it must be capable of responding to a user's query in a manner which is complete in terms of the collection and yet does not result in extraneous citations. In addition it must be capable of displaying the relationship among items in the collection. Creating and maintaining these relationships is, after all, what the acquisitions librarian attempts to do when defining and carrying out a collection development policy. It is also the function of the cataloger, who attempts to integrate each new item into the catalog in the context of what already exists.

Throwing the Computer Some Curves

How does this relate to an automated system? The

answer lies in an examination of the capabilities of the machine, made without losing sight of its limitations. The machine is indeed quite adept at creating alternate access
points and customized sequences. But it performs these
feats within the rigid discipline of Boolean logic, and then
only on data in the form in which it receives it. That is,
the machine can provide very rapid and novel accesses to
information, but it cannot impose an order that is not already
there. It has no capacity, for example, to make the intellectual decisions that attribute publications by <u>Puschkin</u>, <u>Pus-
kin</u>, and <u>Puszkin</u> to the noted poor marksman <u>Aleksandr Ser-
geevich Pushkin.</u>

There is one fundamental attribute of the machine that
should be borne in mind: <u>machine</u> <u>logic</u> <u>is</u> <u>of</u> <u>the</u> <u>most</u> <u>liter-
al</u> <u>variety.</u> By way of illustration: It is the machine's habit,
in its rush to complete bit by bit comparisons, to perform
remarkable feats, such as augmenting Western musical heritage with the discovery that the eighteenth century gave birth
to two contemporary composers named Mozart, one <u>W. A.</u>
and the other <u>Wolfgang Amadeus.</u> If we instruct the machine
to ponder this question in a more leisurely way, it will quickly try the user's patience with digressions concerning the
less illustrious senior Mozart--Leopold. A rather simple
solution could be found to this particular problem. The
search key could be formed from the last name plus the ini-
tials of the first two names. Mozart did have a habit, however, of sometimes identifying himself as <u>Johann Chrysostom
Wolfgang Amadeus Mozart</u>, yielding a key of Mozart, J. C.

It might be argued that we are here dealing with a
rare example, a classical, voluminous author. This may be
so, but we might consider as another case an author whose
first published volume appeared only 24 years ago: Evgeniĭ
Evtushenko. A perusal of the 1967-72 quinquennial of the
NUC would reveal the following variants of this name as
used by publishers of his works: Evtouchenko, Eugène;
Evtushenko, Evgeniĭ Aleksandrovich; Jewtuschenko, Jewgeni;
and Yevtushenko, Yevgeny.

This illustrates dramatically how failure to adopt a
single well defined form of name can spread entries throughout the alphabet. In this simple case of four entries, we
could have two sequences under E, one under J, and another
under Y.

The same arguments apply to subject access. We

might all easily agree that LITERATURE, IMMORAL is not
particularly descriptive of, and an anachronistic euphemism
for, PORNOGRAPHY. Nonetheless, the indiscriminate use
of both terms in a data base creates a situation in which the
serious scholar is either deprived of access to half of that
material in the collection, or must consult two sequences.
Lest this be considered a facetious example, consider the
effect of the indiscriminate use of LATIN AMERICA and
SPANISH AMERICA. [6] This not only creates split sequences
for anything listed under the heading or any of its subdivisions, but it can appear itself as a subdivision of other
headings, thereby proliferating such split sequences throughout the alphabet, e.g., PRESS--SPANISH AMERICA and
PRESS--LATIN AMERICA.

What the Computer Can't Do

It should by now be obvious that the machine cannot
by any of its logical processes draw together such variants
into single coherent sequences. The order must be imposed
by the cataloger. It is only by human intervention at the
time of data creation that sufficient normalization can be effected to make innovative machine access meaningful.

Note the distinction between organization of the data
and methods of access. The machine is indeed capable of
providing very rapid access based on combinations of data
elements--combinations that a human could scarcely keep in
mind while reviewing entries in a static, manual file. Interactive on-line systems do permit the user to renegotiate
the search as it proceeds; CRT displays, which produce their
replies out of pure light, do provide rapid response. These
factors, when combined with the computer's ability to select
all (and only) those items meeting a bewilderingly complex
set of conditions, do provide an access capability unimagined
with Cutter's catalogs. But keep clearly in mind that we are
describing only access. The more important question is, access to what? We have already noted that the machine cannot create an order not already intrinsic in the data, no matter how sophisticated its methods of access become. This
is an immutable axiom that can be assumed to hold true for
the foreseeable generations of computing systems--and systems analysts. Access techniques and data base organization
are logically separable facets of a system. They mutually
contribute to the quality of a system's response.

Sufficiently sophisticated techniques already exist that
will determine if a single well defined record exists in a data
base.   Computers are quite adroit at such simple yes/no responses, and without much prodding.   In fact, such levels of
sophistication were attained at least ten years ago.   But this
is not the sole function of a library catalog.   By conscious
or unconscious fixation on this single, already passé facet of
data processing technology we risk ignoring the other functions of a catalog: To show, in some efficient manner,
"which works by a particular author, and which editions of
a given work are in the library," or "what the library has
on a given subject. "

To Err Is Human, to Retrieve, Divine

There is a rather simple and obvious fact concerning
computing systems whose significance, nonetheless, is all
too often ignored: When data are encoded into machine-
readable form, they can only be retrieved again by machine
logic.   This results in an imbalance of error tolerance.
Any transcription process, as we all know, is susceptible to
error.   An examination of the MARC file, for example, will
show that the fields which can form headings--main entry,
uniform and series titles, added entries, and subjects--com-
prise on the average 116 characters of data/record. [7]   Given
a 99. 9 per cent accuracy rate (the norm for good master
typists), approximately 11 per cent of all records would
have at least one faulty access point.

Even so, a manual system often corrects itself.   Assume that a cataloger has transcribed Yeats, William Butler
as Yeats, William Bulter.   It is highly likely that this error
might escape the notice of the reviser, the typist, and the
proofreader.   It is even more likely that a filing clerk, influenced by all of the other cards that read Butler, would
file the card correctly.   If so, the user doubtless would find
the card, probably never noting the error.   The moral of
this little story is that at each of the critical steps in the
cycle--the creation of the data, its placement into the data
base, and its retrieval--the error tolerances were compati-
ble.   The system therefore functioned despite the error.

This is not so with an automated system, since a
similar error would result in the parthenogenesis of a totally
new author in the file.   Since Bulter sequences ahead of
Butler--and given the limited scan range of a CRT display

(approximately 25 lines of 80 characters each)--this record
could easily become lost. It is not difficult to imagine a
slightly more serious error that would place the record
completely out of reach.

It should be realized that the nature of machine retrieval and the limitations of display devices make any computer-based catalog equivalent to a large catalog. This is
true even when a Ruecking algorithm (3, 3 key)[8] has reduced
the search to a seemingly manageable set of ambiguous
choices, because it is still the same inexorably literal logic
which must ultimately glance into the chaos, and small differences create infinite displacements between records.

The Authority File to the Rescue

Clearly the only solution to the problems posed is to
use the machine itself to control the data. The techniques
for accomplishing this are not new to computing systems or
to libraries. Under manual systems libraries have traditionally maintained authority files, either as separate files
or embedded in an official catalog. Authority files are just
that: the authority for all personal, corporate, conference,
and place names; uniform and series titles; and subject headings. By the use of these files one could be reasonably assured that all headings used in the catalog were in conform-
ity with an existing structure. Any new heading must be
established in this file in a logically consistent manner,
thereby guaranteeing the continuing integrity of the catalog.

The computer allows us to extend this concept in several important directions. For instance, were we to render
this file machine manipulable:

The machine could verify all headings used in the bibliographic record. We would then have a system in which
human data entry is verified with the same logic that
will subsequently be used to retrieve it and have established thereby the sought-for balance of error tolerance.

The heading data would be created and stored only once.
Only a single copy of the name, subject heading, etc.,
would be maintained in the system and referenced by
every bibliographic record using that heading. Having
entered the authority data correctly once, we could thus
be sure that no matter how many bibliographic records

used it they would all do so with mechanical consistency.

The machine could be programmed to control the internal structure of this file, guaranteeing a degree of internal consistency within the authority file itself not feasible in a manual system.

The Two Aspects of the Catalog

The incorporation of such features into a system would permit us to create a machine-based catalog rather than a reference file of bibliographic records. This should be our first concern, not the gadgetry that allows us to peer into it. Only such a controlled data base, when combined with sophisticated access techniques, permits us simultaneously to address both major functions of the catalog--access and collocation. Virtually any system can satisfy the former requirement, but only by addressing the question of integrity of the data base can we even hope to satisfy the latter.

Mechanically this can be accomplished in a rather straightforward manner. First, whenever a new bibliographic record is entered into the system, all elements susceptible to authority control are identified. In simplest terms these can be defined as all elements which are potentially common access points for a group of records (e.g., author main, and added entries; series titles; subject headings; linking entries for serials; etc.). The bibliographic title for a monograph (unless analyzed) pertains only to that single item, hence it would not be controlled by an authority file. These elements could then be alphabetically compared with valid headings already in the authority file. If no valid match is found, the system would signal the cataloger of this fact. This would imply that either an invalid form is being used or a keying error has occurred, or that the heading still needs to be established. The cataloger may then take appropriate action. If a valid match is found, the system automatically replaces the text for that field with an identification number for the appropriate heading.

The Catalog Lives

Unlike most machine-based files, however, a catalog must relate data entered over a long period of time, if it is to continue to function as an effective tool. Catalogs, further, usually represent very large data bases, hence, any procedure that requires the alteration of records already in them can prove quite difficult, time-consuming, and thus expensive.

At present, when we are faced with situations that require that a significant number of entries, already in the catalog, be examined and altered, we either defer doing so or find some less than satisfactory solution. (The Library of Congress itself has been forced to contrive many of these less than ideal solutions. See, for example, Cataloging Service Bulletin No. 106, relating to pseudonymous authors, and the classics, Nos. 79 and 80, announcing superimposition.)

The Only Permanent Thing Is Change

Let us consider some typical examples of change and how catalog departments might handle them.

1. Subject heading changes. As usage of the language causes terms to become anachronistic, or as increases in our level of consciousness reveal undesirable connotations, we seek to change subject heading terms. So WOMEN AS POLICE becomes POLICEWOMEN[9] or SPANISH AMERICA is changed to LATIN AMERICA. In many catalogs these would be handled by a see also reference, in lieu of actually changing every card. The net result is a heavily overburdened cross-reference structure.[10] The see also reference was intended to inform the user that there are related headings in the catalog that might be considered, not that the search should be continued in some other part of the alphabet.

2. Name changes. We often find it necessary to change the form of a name used in the catalog. This is because an author has become better known by some pseudonym, or variation of name; names of women authors frequently undergo transformations as a result of marriage or divorce; political jurisdictions also are annexed or gain independence; etc. For example, Gordon Davis, Robert Dietrich, and David St. John are all discovered to be Howard Hunt, or the New York Times informs us one morning that in all subsequent issues the Congo will be known as Zaire.

3. New information causes a heading to change. These changes actually fall into the previous categories. The following common example of this type of change, however, indicates the scope of the category; it presents no

problem under a manual system, but would wreak havoc in
an automated one.   A bibliographic record created after
1973 for W. H. Auden would include his death date, thus:
1907-1973.   Records created earlier, of course, would show,
1907- .   In a manual system the new entries would be filed
correctly.   In an automated system, though, we would have
a difficult time, at best, convincing the machine that Auden's
death was not the cause for a sudden appearance on the literary scene of a new poet.

    4.   Changes to avoid conflict.   These usually require
that fuller forms be substituted for names already in the
catalog so that a new name can be distinguished from other
similar names.   The appearance of John M. Powell, for instance, requires that the middle initial or middle name of
an already established John Powell be supplied.   In a modest
file of only one quarter million records (1975), the NYPL
research libraries had already recorded seven John Powells.
In manual systems there is no way to avoid the tedious effort required to change the headings.   But once the main
entry cards are changed there is a great temptation to cut
corners by not changing all the added entry cards.

    5.   Changes in cataloging rules.   Anyone using LC
copy and the AACR is well aware of the stimulating challenges provided by superimposed headings.   The catalog
user is perhaps not quite so amused by his inability to divine
why it's Galerie Mikro Berlin on some cards and Berlin.
Museum für Völkerkunde (West Berlin) on others.   Recently
AACR 98 was changed and 99 was dropped, creating more of
these fine conundrums.

    Each of these changes, if we were to deal with them
in an adequate manner, creates severe workload problems
for the cataloging department.   If ignored, the problems are
only passed on to all users of the catalog.   On the other
hand, if we had a system in which each heading was represented by a link to a single authority record, then by a single maintenance transaction we could change the form of that
heading throughout the catalog.   Furthermore, because of the
nature of that link, we could be certain that the change had
been effected uniformly throughout the catalog.

Ringing the Changes

    It is clearly quite useful to be able to change all occurrences of a heading with only a single transaction. This by itself would prove a great labor-saver. But we would still not wish to hunt through the file in order to change all subdivisions of that heading.

If we set up our system in such a way that any subdivision of a heading is always mechanically referred to the next higher level heading, then any change made to a primary heading could be made to have a global effect on the entire authority file and hence the catalog. With such a system we could change AEROPLANES to AIRPLANES and at the same time change every subdivision of AEROPLANES.

Likewise, if all place names, either subdivided for direct regionalization or used as subdivisions of other headings in indirect regionalization, were maintained as links to a single record defining the authorized version of that name, we could affect all subject headings that used it with a single action. In this way all occurrences of CEYLON, for example, could be changed to SRI LANKA, both in headings of a direct form as in CEYLON--POETRY, and those indirect ones such as ART--CEYLON.

Similar considerations could be extended to the cross-reference structure. If this structure were treated as a network of mechanical links between proper headings and their associated cross-references, then we could always ensure that there would be no blind references, and that any change of a heading would be automatically reflected in all reciprocal records.

Freeing the Cataloger

The ability to perform these operations with such relative ease affords the cataloger the freedom to make decisions to restructure the catalog whenever it becomes necessary. The number of bibliographic records, entries, or other headings are of no concern, since the effort required is generally no more than a single manual action. The cataloger, by being relieved of the onerous clerical burden formerly required to reorganize the catalog, is free to do it. Attention can thus be devoted to making the catalog a more responsive and useful tool. Equally important, the cataloger can rest assured that changes will be made with mechanical consistency, without any possibility of clerical error.

The maintenance of complex networks of incorruptible
links among disparate records is one of the fundamental attributes of any computing system. Here we are simply using
it to make explicit those relations already intellectually implicit in the catalog.

There is yet the other capability inherent in data processing systems--the literal verification of data--that we can
employ to guarantee the integrity of an authority file. Within an authority file we wish to maintain rigorous consistency
of headings. For the most part this is still a human responsibility. Only a human can decide if two names actually
represent different individuals, or if different subject terms
represent distinct concepts or are synonymous. Once these
human decisions have been entered into the system, however,
we should be able to use its magnetic memory to assist us
in guaranteeing that we do not, in the future, create logical
inconsistencies.

Once informed that Gordon Ashe is in fact John
Creasey, for instance, the system should, on its own limited
initiative, be capable of correcting the error if an unauthorized form of name is used as a form of entry. Likewise, it should be capable of either correcting or refusing
to accept headings constructed illogically within the context
of the rest of the file. If we inform the system that MUSIC
DRAMA is in fact OPERA, it should treat MUSIC DRAMA--
COSTUMES as at least suspect. And if the system contains
a reference ST. PETERSBURG, see LENINGRAD, it should
automatically reject the illicit proposal to establish the heading OPERA--ST. PETERSBURG.

Consistency Is All

Rigorous mechanical control of the machine-based
catalog of a single institution is indisputably desirable. But
such control is indispensable in any attempt to collect a coherent national bibliographic data base in machine-readable
form. This is especially so if input is to come from disparate sources.

The problem of consistency of data has always
plagued attempts to create a national union catalog. Such
problems exist in manual systems and are only exacerbated
by automated systems. John Cronin, former director of the
LC processing department, in discussing plans for publica-

tion of the pre-1952 NUC noted the enormous benefits to be derived from such a catalog. But he went on to state that "the editing of the catalog is essential and presents the chief problem. "[11] Cronin was only addressing the problems of editing and creating a static national data base: the printed catalog could only represent a frozen moment in time. A machine-readable national data base, or for that matter any catalog, should be capable of existing in time. It must be capable of responding to a dynamic reality in which terms "strain, crack and sometimes break under the burden, under the tension, slip, slide, perish, decay with imprecision, will not stay in place, will not stay still. "

The techniques presented in this discussion are neither new nor purely theoretical. Henderson and Rosenthal, in a 1968 study[12] undertaken to determine the future of the NYPL card catalogs, proposed a very similar system. Most of the features described have been included in the Automated Bibliographic Control system[13, 14] developed as a result. Those not implemented were excluded only because of the hardware limitations of the NYPL computer configuration in 1969. They have, however, been made a part of the design for conversion of the system to an on-line mode of operation. The National Library of Canada, early last year, implemented a similar system of linked authority and bibliographic files. [15] The Library of Congress, too, has included similar considerations in its new automated system. [16]

Living with the Code

The application of a new technology to an existing procedure, if it is to be done effectively, requires that we thoroughly understand the unique properties of the medium and relate them to the basic tasks to be performed. In the case of the computer, data are reduced to machine-readable form for two major reasons: 1) to provide efficient, instantaneous, decentralized access, and 2) to make it possible to manipulate its elements. The latter reason may be further subdivided into a) those operations that synthesize new data from existing data, and b) those in which we wish to alter and restructure existing data.

It is the great expense and difficulty involved in changing a record, once filed into a manual catalog, that has proved an anathema to the framers of cataloging codes and created a schism between technical and public service

librarians. Catalogers are sympathetic to the needs of catalog users, but are subject to pressure to refrain from altering existing records. Reference librarians, on the other
hand, want a tool that is reflective of a current user's needs,
not the needs of a user who might have flourished at the
time the record was made.

Cataloging codes, and the principles espoused for
their development, have attempted to recognize the users'
needs. These laudable sentiments are all too often couched
as exceptions with phrases like, "use unless better known
as." The intent is to create a mechanism that recognizes
the needs of the user, rather than simplifies clerical procedures in the cataloging department. The problem arises
when the record is being created. The cataloger, being unaware of the sign-on procedure that would put him or her
on-line to Delphi, cannot realistically make such predictive
decisions. Thereupon, due to the difficulty of altering a
manual file and the pressure to catalog more new books
faster, catalogers are administratively enjoined from attend-
ing to such details when the situation does resolve itself later. By then the record has already been created and filed.

Theory Good, Practice Poor

The ALA code of 1941, despite its deficiencies, did
attempt such a practical approach to the users' needs. For
example, ALA 5A counsels that collections should be "enter[ed] under the compiler or editor, individual or corporate."
But it provides the following exceptions: 1b) "enter under
title ... when they are generally referred to by title"; or
1a) "enter ... collections under title ... if there are frequent changes of editor." The Paris conference put forth
similar exceptions in its statement of principles, and the
1967 AACR in rule 40 requires that a person be entered
"under the name by which he is commonly [emphasis supplied]
identified."

The principles are excellent. Unfortunately, under a
manual system they are difficult to apply. Just as the pilot
of an aeroplane is usually the first to arrive at the scene of
a crash, the cataloger is often the first to see a new title.
Nonetheless, the cataloger is asked to make decisions that
require that the title's future behavior be predicted. In general the cataloger is asked to create a structure that is
simultaneously consistent, permanent, and responsive to the

users' needs. The inertia of an existing structure tends to make these requirements incompatible. Changes in the external world, furthermore, render judgments that were valid when made into errors.

It is here that the computer can provide the greatest potential for a truly innovative advance in the maintenance of catalogs. Rather than concerning themselves with the requirements of the computer, the framers of cataloging codes could instead utilize machine capabilities to create a code responsive to users' needs. The potential is enormous, but so are the problems.

What about the Little Libraries?

It is easy to predict that a majority of large or affluent libraries in this country will employ some form of catalog under machine control in the foreseeable future and thereby be able to respond to a dynamic environment. But how are the libraries of more modest resources to be accommodated in this scheme? What, for example, will be the impact on the library community as a whole if LC closes its existing catalogs and replaces them with an automated system employing linked authority control? How will the rest of the community keep up with the relatively complex changes LC will be able to make in its own catalogs? After having become the de facto national library--as a result of the technological innovation of the printed catalog card--will LC be forced to abdicate its role? Or will it--in order to continue that role--be forced to forego the opportunities this new technology presents?

Technology certainly exists that will permit us to create machine-based catalogs without giving up any of the quality and integrity traditionally striven for in manual catalogs. Indeed, the technology is actually capable of creating an even more precise level of bibliographic control than was feasible in manual systems. At the same time it allows the incompatible requirements imposed on the catalog to be amelioriated. Permanence and change can be achieved by utilizing the computer's sophisticated access techniques with a rigorously controlled and easily reorganized data base.

Catalogs in Computerland

The intrinsic nature of the computer does not negate any cataloging principles. Not only are these principles still valid, but the computer can actually provide us with the means to apply them in a far more consistent manner. Desiderata contained or implied in cataloging codes, abandoned because of the expense or difficulty of application, can be implemented with relative ease by properly employing the computer's capabilities. Further, rules can be framed with greater regard for the convenience of the user without imposing undue burdens on the cataloging department.

We can permit ourselves to be hypnotized by the gadgetry for access, and by illusory cost reductions, or we can use the computer effectively to transform the catalog into a truly responsive instrument. Finally, we can use the century and a quarter of experience in conjunction with the fundamental properties of the machine to implement and extend the principles developed, or we can turn our backs on them with fatuous arguments, which posit their anachronism and the nonexistent intelligence of computing machinery.

Library automation has become a multimillion-dollar industry. We can no longer treat automation projects as interesting experiments that are disposable if they fail. We have too much invested, and the new systems are too intimately integrated into the everyday operation of the library for us to assume any longer that we can, by sheer force of will, temper their influence on emerging standards. We can program the computer to implement a system of well considered and established purposes and principles, intended to enhance the usefulness of the library, or use the computer simplistically to manipulate a hodge-podge of names and titles, words and phrases, and call it progress. The choice and responsibility for it is ours. The only realistic approach is to establish the standards for quality as part of the system's design. We can program the computer to insure adherence to intelligently established principles, or permit it to establish them in its own image.

References

1. Charles A. Cutter. Rules for a Dictionary Catalog, 4th ed. Washington, D. C. , Government Printing Office, 1907. First edition appeared as: U. S. Bureau

of Education. Public Libraries in the United States of America: Their History, Condition and Management, Part II. Washington, D.C., Government Printing Office, 1876.

2. Seymour Lubetzky. "The Function of the Main Entry in the Alphabetical Catalog--One Approach," International Conference on Cataloguing Principles, Paris, 9-18 October 1961. Report. London, 1963, p. 139-43.

3. International Federation of Library Associations. Statement of Principles Adopted at the International Conference on Cataloguing Principles, Paris, October, 1961. London, IFLA Committee on Cataloguing, 1971, p. xiii.

4. Lubetzky, op. cit.

5. T. S. Eliot. "What is Minor Poetry," in his On Poetry and Poets. New York, Noonday Press, 1961, p. 44.

6. U.S. Library of Congress. Cataloging Service Bulletin No. 65. August 1965.

7. Statistics derived from the LC/MARC file in July 1973 by the NYPL Systems Office (unpublished). The file contained, at that time, 329,354 records. There was an average of 3.39 authority fields/bibliographic record. The mean length of these fields was determined to be 34 characters. Thus with a keyboarding accuracy rate of 99.9 per cent, one could expect 36,229 records to have at least one faulty authority access point.

8. Frederick Ruecking, Jr. Bibliographic Retrieval. MARC Pilot Project Progress Report No. 3. Rice University, Fondren Library, Advanced Library Systems Project, Aug. 10, 1967.

9. U.S. Library of Congress, Subject Cataloging Division. Supplement to LC Subject Headings: Quarterly Cumulative Supplement to the 8th Edition. March 1975, p. 368.

10. Maurice F. Tauber. Technical Services in Libraries. New York, Columbia University Press, 1953, p. 172.

11. John Cronin. "The National Union and Library of Congress Catalogs: Problems and Prospects." Library Quarterly, 34 (January 1964), p. 77-96.

12. James W. Henderson and Joseph A. Rosenthal, eds. Library Catalogs: Their Preservation and Maintenance by Photographic and Automated Techniques (MIT Report No. 14). Cambridge, Mass., MIT Press, 1968.

13. S. Michael Malinconico. "Role of a Machine-Based

Authority File in an Automated Bibliographic System," Automation in Libraries: Papers Presented at the CACUL Workshop on Library Automation, Winnipeg, June 22-23, 1974, Ottawa, Canadian Library Association, 1975.

14. S. Michael Malinconico and James A. Rizzolo. "The New York Public Library Automated Book Catalog Subsystem," Journal of Library Automation, 6 (March 1973), p. 3-36.

15. National Library of Canada. Accessible, 3 (November 1975).

16. Henriette D. Avram et al. "Automation Activities in the Processing Department of The Library of Congress," Library Resources and Technical Services, 16 (Spring 1972), p. 195-239.

INFORMATION POWER FOR
INNER-CITY COMMUNITIES*

Major R. Owens

.The concept of information power is readily understood in government and business circles. Governments all
over the world and industries in every area of production
continue to invest heavily in information systems. Multi-
national corporations, utilizing satellites for telecommunications, are able to act with a speed and thoroughness greater
than that of most governments. Major decision-makers no
longer have to be "sold" on the need for such systems.
Present concerns focus more on the improvement, expansion and safeguarding of information systems.

Consider the fact that at least ten nations of the
world which do not now possess nuclear weapons definitely
have the physical capability needed to produce such weapons
and would do so if only they had the necessary information.
Ponder the paradox of the Russian consumer buying cheaper
and better bread than ever before as a result of his government's purchase of American wheat, while the American consumer pays far more for bread and meat produced from
grain-fed livestock. The notorious Russian grain deal was
manipulated by the Russians for their benefit by withholding
certain crucial information such as the extent of the Russian
crop failure and the overall amount of grain they wanted to
buy. Reflect also on the recent energy crisis which on the
East coast had reached the stage where motorists literally
fought each other at the gas pumps. A national debate continues to rage on this issue and no one, including the office
of the President of the United States, has yet been able to
offer the public a reasonable set of facts and statistics on

*Reprinted by permission of the author and publisher from
The Southeastern Librarian, Vol. 25, No. 3, Fall 1975, pp.
9-16.

the extent of the shortage.   We know for a fact that oil
company profits have increased by as much as seventy per
cent, but we do not yet know whether there is really an oil
shortage in this country.   One industry-financed institute
hoards and controls information on oil production and distribution.

Not only are research and data necessary to win wars,
but men with the right information at the right time may utilize it to become millionaires.   Grain dealers and oil execu-
tives have obviously reaped large profits; however, imagine
for a moment that you are one of the declining number of
middle-class Americans who, after meeting ongoing living
expenses, has funds left over to dabble in the stock market.
Imagine yourself having advance information concerning the
impending energy shortage.   Think of what a killing you
might have made by purchasing Exxon or Standard Oil stock.
In national defense, in basic dollars and cents economics
and in matters of federal, state and local politics, information is power.

Projecting Priority Needs

Just as generals and businessmen need data before
they decide, inner-city residents, both leaders and average
citizens, need information for decision-making.   The level
of information may range from straight facts and simple statistics through complex expositions and interpretive explanations to basic background and theoretical works.   Materials
utilized may vary from a resource file card which provides
the address of an agency, to a pamphlet or booklet which
describes activities and programs in great detail, to a book
or major reference work concerned with the problem or issue
in question.   While the average citizen's quest for information may be satisfied by simple facts and statistics, the needs
of opinion makers and community leaders will require more
complex materials.   Those misled proponents who argue that
libraries are obsolete and that information centers can only
be developed as entities separate and distinct from libraries
must be reminded that at one end of this continuum one must
have books and basic reference works.

To better serve the needs of the inner-city residents
it is useful to set up special categories or classification
schemes which focus on the priority areas of need.   Any
such outline of needs should be viewed only as a general set

of directional guidelines and all tendencies to freeze lines
and force all information into such a funnel must be resisted.
Interesting outlines have been developed by the IRMA system
in New York City and by the Appalachian Adult Education
Center. The students and staff of the Columbia University
Community Media Librarian Program developed the following
set of information priorities for inner-city residents:

1. General Know-How and Community Action
2. Community News, Studies, History
3. Job Training, Employment and Career Development
4. Education: Formal and Non-Formal
5. Social Services and Income Maintenance
6. Health and Environment Protection
7. Civil and Criminal Legal System
8. Housing and Community Development
9. Economic Development
10. Consumer Education and Protection

Although the emphasis may vary from city to city and
neighborhood to neighborhood, we find that most information
needs can be fitted into these categories. Inner-city communities are alike enough to enable us to generalize and
state that even within this set of ten categories, certain
needs can be further pinpointed as being particularly critical
within all inner-city communities.

Because of the high degree of dependency upon the involvement and interaction with federal, state and city agencies, the category of General Know-How and Community Action assumes a special importance. Needless to say all citizens in all neighborhoods--low, middle or high income; suburban or urban--should know how to obtain the delivery of
services and benefits from government agencies to which
they are entitled. Inner-city communities, however, usually
lack the normal and regular liaisons and channels of communication with public agencies. Because of their lack of
economic power and voting strength such communities usually
do not have elected officials who are responsive to their
needs and who will serve as their advocates in their quest
for services. Inner-city communities have traditionally suffered from a drain on their leadership which leaves them
weak and unorganized, openly exposed to every form of economic and political chicanery. Exploited, oppressed and deprived of the means available to other American communities, the inner-city must rely on alternative methods. Community action thus becomes a vitally necessary activity, one

of the few last legal ways to obtain justice by working within
the system. Information which facilitates such action must
be assigned top priority.

Certain other categories appear to be self evident,
but history and experience show that libraries have not responded to these obvious needs. The category of Community
News, Studies, History assumes a special significance as
mass media increase their domination of communications. As
the media broadcast and edit for more and more people, inner-city communities receive less and less attention. The
community of Bedford-Stuyvesant in Brooklyn contains nearly
300,000 residents of all races and income levels. It also
has a rich social and institutional life filled with vitality.
Each day this densely populated area generates more news
than the average American city; however, it has no daily
newspapers, no radio and no television stations. The significant events which occurred in this community a month ago
have already vanished from history except for what remains
in the memories of a few individuals.

Job Training, Employment and Career Development
is a category which has always received considerable attention in collections for young adults; however, a dynamic and
rapidly changing world of work necessitates the availability
to adults of a variety of up-to-date information on job opportunities. The need for information on Social Services and
Income Maintenance is a critical one for a large percentage
of inner-city residents. Eligibility requirements, application
procedures, waiting periods, locations of offices are examples of the kinds of information residents should expect to
be able to find in their neighborhood library.

The Civil and Criminal Legal System is a maze which
even college-trained citizens find difficult to get through.
While one expects to utilize the legal profession for trials
and complex suits, there is evidence that a more widespread
dissemination of basic information concerning court procedures
would end the near total dependence on lawyers. One statistical forecast predicts that as many as eighty per cent of the
young Black males in the country will acquire an arrest record. Unfortunately, there is no parallel forecast that adequate free legal aid will be made available. Civil and criminal justice is too often a dollars and cents proposition for
the inner-city resident; when they are unable to pay for it,
they do not get justice.

Consumer Education and Protection is another priority
information category which involves law enforcement and the
courts. If residents could imitate the corporate structure
and retain lawyers to constantly protect their rights, the
systematic and institutionalized swindling and exploitation
which is commonplace in most inner-city communities would
be eradicated. Already there are substantial laws available
to protect consumers. More information about these laws
and how they work is the vital need of those who definitely
lack the funds to retain a constantly vigilant corporate at-
torney. For poor people such information has an immediate
dollars and cents value.

Information for Decision-Making

To save money and to lubricate the often arduous task
of everyday living, information can play a major role in the
life of individuals. Residents continually pay for what they
could obtain freely if they were better informed. They pay
employment agencies which are often less competent than the
free U. S. Employment Service. They pay unauthorized income tax preparers for simple advice which is often available at no expense from the Internal Revenue Service. Too
often they pay for medical care, correspondence training
courses, apartment rental fees and legal advice when such
services are unpublicized but available in government-funded
agencies and institutions. Inner-city residents also pay a
price in their physical, psychic and emotional health as a
result of the consumption of great amounts of spoiled food-
stuffs; as a consequence of inadequate housing and environmental conditions and as a result of the benign terror fos-
tered by exploiting salesmen or professional hustlers. For
individuals, information cannot provide total salvation, but
more information increases the chances that an individual
will be able to help himself and find his way through the urban jungle. Despite poverty, individual families survive with
greater dignity and less anxiety and pain when they better
understand the workings of our modern complex society.

More important than assistance to individuals is the
utilization of information to encourage and support group and
institutional efforts to improve living conditions in the inner-
city. Such efforts usually involve no more than a raising of
the level of awareness of existing rights and an increased
understanding of how to utilize existing laws, administrative
structures and procedures. It is sometimes necessary, how-

ever, for such efforts to press for basic changes in the
laws and administrative structures. Regardless of the type
and level of change attempted, information becomes a vital
tool and weapon.

Like individuals, groups must decide. Such decision-
making involves the use of existing information to develop a
set of options and the selection of one or a combination of
these options as a strategy for solving the problem or reaching an objective. Without adequate information the group
problem solving is faulty from the beginning. Consider the
following cases:

About nine years ago, a certain organization of parents
and citizens in the Brooklyn community of Brownsville had
envisioned an elementary school on a site near a complex of
housing projects. When the news reached the group that construction for the school was about to begin on another site,
they immediately formed a delegation and visited the head-
quarters of the Superintendent of Schools. The Superintendent
was not available; however, the group did gain an audience
with an administrative assistant. They were told that although plans had already been developed, their protest would
be considered and they would be contacted for a subsequent
meeting. Only partially satisfied with this response, the
group decided to expand their protest activities. They initiated a letter writing and petition signing campaign.

At the unfavorable site, however, construction activity
increased. Further inquiries at the school board headquar-
ters went unanswered. The group decided to escalate their
activities by picketing the Superintendent and by appealing to
community residents to stage an all-night vigil at the construction site. Large numbers of community residents and
outside sympathizers supported the vigil which took place on
one of the coldest nights of that year. Shortly after the well-
publicized vigil, the Superintendent's office issued a detailed
statement explaining why it was impossible to reconsider the
decision and change the site for the school. The provisions
of the state and city laws were such that the decision had
been irreversible for nearly two years. In other words, the
survey, planning and bidding process had been set in motion
two years before, following a decision by the city's Board of
Estimate. Abandonment of the project at the point when the
protests were initiated would have meant not only the loss
of several million dollars, but it would have also required
legislative action.

The organization of parents and citizens was almost wrecked by the disappointment, anger and bitterness which followed this revelation. To influence the selection of a site, the information was needed two years prior to the first delegation visit to the Superintendent's office. Information about the process, timetable and legally prescribed sequence would have prevented the waste of tremendous amounts of community time, energy and spirit. Several years were needed to rebuild community confidence and counter the apathy and defeatism which followed this failure.

The Welfare Rights movement of New York City represents an even more tragic case where an organization was wrecked partially because it relied heavily upon a strategy based on faulty information. The local movement deliberately determined to maximize the number of people on welfare and the benefits they were receiving. In addition to the appropriate moral position, which stated that all persons eligible for benefits and in need should receive benefits, the group took the political position that an inadequate system should be destroyed by packing the rolls. The city administration which administered the program became the primary target of the group's very effective pressure campaign. Within a few years, the number of people on welfare and the overall costs of public assistance had doubled. A sympathetic city administration obeyed the law and granted assistance to all who were eligible. Final decisions concerning welfare programs, however, are not made at the level of the city government. Although the city is responsible for administration, final decisions on regulations and budgets are made at the state level with federal approval. The local Welfare Rights movement had failed to consider the impact of their actions on the ultimate decision-makers. The leadership displayed no understanding of the decision-making process until after the governor and the state legislature had set in motion one of the most regressive state welfare programs in the country. Under the label of "reforms" the state political machinery wiped out all of the gains realized at the city level.

A final case focuses on the much heralded changes in the South's political structure and climate. While the South has definitely shed many of its obvious oppressions, a recent compilation of information has brought a quite significant issue of exploitation to the surface. Despite the very real gains made by Blacks as evidenced by the large number of Black elected officials who are now decision-makers at vari-

ous levels in local and state government, an old problem of
regressive and oppressive taxation of the poor still persists.
The New York Times recently summarized a report by the
Southern Regional Council which showed that the poor pay a
greater percentage of their incomes for taxes and while this
is a national problem, this form of government exploitation
is worst in the deep South. Mississippi, where the percentage of poor and the percentage of Blacks is greatest,
has the most regressive tax system.

Why has a problem which touches so many remained
a non-issue? Why is tax reform not presently on the agenda
of the Black elected officials of the South? These are obvious questions which may be partially answered with the plea
of lack of information. A research and study organization
has not only reminded the public that there is a significant
problem being neglected, it has also stated the intensity and
the exploitive implications of the problem. The existence
and the publication of the information have projected the problem into the mainstream of discussion. Whether or not this
matter becomes a hot political issue worthy of election campaign debate will depend upon the extent to which the information is publicized. Will the people who are the victims really know the facts? This is the key question and the information problem.

Public Library as Optimum
Information Agency

Inner-city residents need information to make significant individual and group decisions, but information may be
received from a variety of sources through a number of
channels other than the public library. There are alternative
organizers and disseminators of information; however, such
alternatives are seldom accessible to inner-city residents.
The growing number of agencies organized to sell information
may provide an adequate solution to the ongoing information
problems of those able to pay; however, the increase in
commercial providers of information poses a threat to the
development of a free public information system. In the inner-city information services must be free or they are not
accessible to inner-city residents. Arrangements which meet
the needs of the affluent while ignoring the needs of the rest
of the populace erode the intensity of the public demand for
a modern and free information network.

A few publicly financed alternatives have been launched. Information and referral centers financed by the Department of Health, Education and Welfare are perhaps the most soundly based of these alternatives. Such centers are usually integral parts of a social services system and are operated by social workers. Information and referral services have been federally reimbursable activities for many years; however, widespread efforts to use this authorization have only recently been launched. It is important to note that except in Brooklyn, where the Community Urban Information Centers (CUIC) are being planned, public library systems are not involved in these new efforts to set up social services-oriented information systems. It should also be noted, that at the moment when the greatest enthusiasm has been kindled for information and referral programs, the federal government proposes to discontinue the funding of this activity. Regulations issued by the Secretary of HEW, in 1973, proposed to eliminate the function; however, these regulations have undergone several revisions and been subjected to intense congressional scrutiny thus delaying a final decision. It is expected that there will be some form of compromise permitting the individual states to decide whether or not they wish to continue funding information services from their social services allocation.

Independently financed information centers have also been launched with varying degrees of success. As it is with most youthful private institutions, the survival, growth and productivity of such centers is heavily dependent upon the dedication and intensity of individual workers. Special problems such as drugs, alcoholism, draft counseling and women's liberation have often stimulated the development of independent information centers. Deprived groups such as migrant workers and prison inmates have often been the beneficiaries of such independent centers.

For the millions who live in the inner-city, only a publicly financed information system is worthy of discussion. Such a system does not have to be the public library. Municipalities could choose to contract with community agencies for the operation of information systems. Local public libraries might be forced to compete with commercial information agencies through the utilization of a voucher system similar to the one tested by the Office of Economic Opportunity for public schools. The present period of fiscal and administrative conservatism is such that most localities will probably choose to utilize their public library system to pro-

vide information services.   Unless it insists on playing the
role of the defiant dodo, the library profession will continue
to be the primary body of people determining the scope,
shape and thoroughness of information services throughout
the country.

   At this point in history the library is the optimum
choice for the provision of information services to inner-city
communities.   Very practical facts of funding, public administration and politics support this conclusion.   Some of
the factors which must be considered are:

  1. Public library systems already exist in most cities.
      They have linkages with a local tax and budgeting
      system, and they have an accepted administrative
      structure.
  2. Because of their established place in the system,
      both private and government funding sources are
      more likely to view their financing more favorably.
  3. No special start-up and no capital construction costs
      are needed to initiate or to expand information ser-
      vices.   All new funds made available may be utilized
      for materials and personal services.
  4. Branch libraries which already exist within the inner-
      city provide a convenient dissemination and distribu-
      tion network.
  5. The basic administrative and technical services sys-
      tems developed by the library profession have func-
      tioned successfully and would have to be replicated
      at considerable cost by any alternative system.
  6. Alternative systems will find it difficult to survive
      and sustain themselves in a situation characterized
      by uncertain, spotty and haphazard financing.

   For the public library, nearly everything is in place
except the most vital ingredient.   To expand and fully embrace the provision of information services as a priority responsibility and duty, the public library needs a new understanding of its mission.   As long ago as 1924, William S.
Learned, in The American Public Library and the Diffusion
of Knowledge, clearly and forcefully stated that part of the
mission, part of the justification for the existence of the
public library was the provision of practical information to
the public.   Clearly, there is nothing new and revolutionary
in the call for libraries to provide information power to the
people.

Public Library as Information
Management Component

A new understanding of its mission, a new professional attitude is needed before the library can begin to effectively serve the inner-city. All of the myriad of detailed problems may be solved after the basic issues of sense of purpose and "reason for being" are reexamined. Among publicly financed institutions, libraries are not alone in their need
to reexamine fundamental goals and basic operations policies
and procedures. The myriad of programs and services which
presently are located within most inner-cities must also examine their isolated positions and consider ways to function
in unison and with productive coordination.

Service programs evolved in a helter-skelter hap-
hazard manner, and it is therefore easy to understand why
they are operated as separate and distinct agencies and not
as components of an overall system. For the good of all
concerned, however, it would be useful to view all such programs and agencies as part of an overall delivery system.
The basic components of such a delivery system would be the
health, housing, planning, economic development, job training
agencies: protective agencies such as police and fire; regulatory agencies such as the licensing bureaus and the courts;
social service agencies such as Day Care and Senior Citizens
Centers; educational agencies such as public schools and colleges. Within this overall service delivery system the public
library should serve as the information management component.

The effective provision of information to inner-city
communities requires that there be a steady and timely flow
of information from those programs and agencies which play
a major role in and have a continuing impact upon the lives
of the residents of the inner-city. The information should
flow through and be processed by the library. Selection of
what is most pertinent and significant and selection of the
format which most effectively communicates it would be the
awesome responsibility of the public library.

How should the library manage such information and
what formats should it employ to effectively communicate it
to inner-city residents? One basic comparison, although it
may take us to the brink of over-simplification, will help to
clarify the approach to meeting the need and providing information power. Consider the world of business and industry

and the ways in which it meets its information needs. For
the sake of this example we will skip over the hourly and
daily computer and telecommunications. It would be useful
to focus on a more static part of this information system:
the weekly newspaper summary or the weekly business magazine. An examination of a variety of such publications reveals the following categories as standard features: personal
finance; business briefs; quotations on stocks and bonds; industrial averages; commodities index; summaries on law,
legislation, advertising, taxes.

     Paralleling this approach, an inner-city library sys-
tem might publish a weekly information newsletter or bulletin
or produce a weekly radio or television show which contained
the following features: personal finance; consumer's cost of
living index; employment summary; local news briefs; courtroom briefs; long term job forecast; medical guide; family
health news; community safety and crime prevention tips;
apartment vacancy listings; public school news briefs; welfare
department changes in rules and regulations; calendar of important public hearings; calendar of local community meetings;
understanding your city budget; review of free and inexpensive
information material; community people in the news.

     If this approach with popular headings is considered
confusing or vulgar, then a straight and simple approach
which lists each function and major agency of government and
provides a weekly (or monthly or quarterly) news summary
might be attempted as a more suitable one: News from the
Welfare Department; Information from the State Employment
Agency; News from ...; Information from ...; Facts from
...; Statistics from ...; Laws, Rules and Regulations of....

     For individual and group decision-making, from the
huge volume of information being generated daily, weekly,
monthly, what should be assigned priority and communicated
in the simplest and/or the most dramatic format? For certain types and amounts of information, a weekly radio or
television show may be absolutely essential. In other cases
the provision of audio slide presentations, may be needed.
A video-tape camera may capture and preserve a local community event ignored by all of the press and electronic media.

     For modern inner-city communities the effective
management of information may prove to be as important as
the effective management of light, gas and water systems.
The mission of public libraries is as serious as the mission
of the public utilities.

Need for an Information Movement

In order to keep abreast in the complex post-industrial society, maintain a reasonable individual and family equilibrium, and maximize the effectiveness of the group process in solving community problems, inner-city residents must have the services of a well functioning information system. It is not exaggerating to state that in the post-industrial society, in addition to food, clothing and shelter, information has become the fourth necessity.

Although it is presently recognized by only a few, the right to information is as necessary as the freedom of speech, assembly and the press. Citizens are not stimulated to speak, to write, to assemble for action when they lack information. Whether it is by accident or by deliberate design, the preservation of the ignorance of the people sabotages the democratic process. Without information we are mere mice in a laboratory maze. The food price crisis and the energy crisis will be followed by many other crises as parts of the labyrinth. International forces are at work determining the state of our economy; what we eat; what we wear; where we sleep and many other detailed aspects of our daily lives. Citizens attempting to find their way out of the maze without the necessary information to guide them may find the frustration unbearable. Periodic seizures of collective madness will replace rational decision-making. In the inner-city, gang violence and spontaneous community rebellion are expressions of such collective madness.

The kind of access to information services needed within inner-city communities is a micro model of what is needed in the nation as a whole for all communities. To create a climate for change, to move the entire country off dead center away from the existing monumental inadequacy and toward modern and relevant information services, nothing less than a "movement" is necessary. To generate broad, sweeping and deep changes, bold positions must be taken; geometric increases in library and information resources must be demanded; strategies to shape public opinion and command the attention of public officials must be developed. The library profession should declare itself an oppressed profession and demand a massive government investment to revamp and expand. A Marshall Plan for the development of public information systems should be immediately set forth in bold and imaginative design.

Since the primary need is for a change in outlook and
attitude among the members of the library profession, some
movement in the direction of improved information services
is immediately possible without waiting for such national
master plans. Any inner-city library in a small way may
participate in the start-up of a new "movement" by reviewing
its present service capacity--staff, budget, physical facilities,
etc., to determine how they may be reorganized or refocused
to meet information needs. It is important to go to work
analyzing needs and setting new priorities. The resources
will remain the same until changes begin to occur in the
budget allocation patterns; therefore, the first concern must
be a new and better utilization of existing resources. The
first aim and objective must be to make a breakthrough to
the public. Inner-city residents must be made interested
and excited about information services. Their present
apathy and alienation is neither natural nor inevitable.

We must find a way to break out of the vicious cycle
of irrelevant services leading to lack of use, and lack of
circulation causing cutbacks in budget and staff allocations
which result in a further reduction in services. Special
efforts are needed to break the cycle but such attempts
should not continue the erroneous approach which greatly reduced the impact of many of the projects financed by the
Library Services and Construction Act. In many instances
such projects have been conducted as isolated super shows
apart from the regular library system. Basic and lasting
change requires that there be support from the entire library
system. In addition to change in the attitudes of individual
librarians, there must be a change in overall library policy.
The decision-makers within each library system must decide
that the effort to develop adequate information services will
receive top priority. We understand, of course, that overnight such a decision will not produce sweeping changes. It
is absolutely essential, however, that we accelerate the pace
of our steps in the right direction.

By simply doing our job in a better and more imaginative way, we may spark a new awareness within inner-city
communities. Since true power is not vague and illusive,
the residents, individually and collectively, will begin to
feel the power that information brings. A critical point of
revelation will be reached and the pressure for more and
better information services will become the force which
keeps the "movement" in motion. Information is automatically advocacy. Without projecting a point of view or partici-

pating in local organization activities, librarians automatically assist the process of change by offering choices, options which initiate the process of decision-making. Such legitimate assistance, however, makes the library a partner with the community in the quest for improvement. When the citizens acquire this changed perception of what adequate information services can do for them, they will have arrived at a point of full understanding of information power.

COPING WITH BUDGET ADVERSITY:
THE IMPACT OF THE FINANCIAL
SQUEEZE ON ACQUISITIONS*

Marion T. Reid

The problem of reduced or virtually frozen library budgets is a national one. Indeed, William S. Dix warns, "This is the day of adversity, and most university libraries are going to have to make do for a while with relatively less money than we have become accustomed to."[1] H. William Axford concurs, urging more efficiency: "Real progress in making the library a vital and dynamic center for inspiration and information ... cannot be gained during a severe budget crisis unless our labor-intensive organizations can achieve a higher level of manpower utilization than is now generally the case." He further observes, "It is clearly in the interest of the profession and its users that the motivation for change be internal."[2]

If libraries have less money to spend, they are presumably buying fewer titles. Without as many books to process, what are they doing with the acquisitions personnel left? For the most part, there is no leftover personnel. In some cases, technical services staffs were not increased when book budgets were in the 1960s. Acquisitions personnel had more to spend; they began buying books in exotic languages that were more difficult to obtain; their card catalogs and order files became more complex as more entries were added, so more time was required for searching. In other cases, acquisitions staffs have been cut as much as 20 per cent--primarily by attrition. In still other cases, libraries have reorganized, shifting positions from acquisi-

*Reprinted by permission of the author and the American Library Association from College & Research Libraries, Vol. 37, No. 3, May 1976, pp. 266-272. Copyright © 1976, the American Library Association.

tions functions to other areas. Such manpower loss seems to exceed the amount of work lost through budget cuts. So how are acquisitions personnel coping with this situation?

To "take a hard look at the whole sequence of functions and procedures in this area"[3] of acquisitions, the author visited libraries at the following ten universities: Columbia University, Cornell University, the University of North Carolina, the University of Oklahoma, Pennsylvania State University, Purdue University, Southern Illinois University, the University of Tennessee, the University of California at Los Angeles (UCLA), and the University of Utah. According to Association of Research Libraries (ARL) statistics from 1969-70 through 1972-73, the total expenditures for books and binding for nine of these schools were reduced at some point or remained virtually static, thus causing a loss of buying power. Although the library at the tenth school--the University of Tennessee--had not suffered financial acquisitions setbacks within the past five years, it was included in the study because it is practicing economies that should be considered by research libraries that are affected by budget adversity. In addition to the information gained from interviews with over 100 people at these ten universities, the author has drawn on information in the literature, thirty current annual reports received from ARL libraries not visited, and personal experience at the Louisiana State University (Baton Rouge) Library.

ORGANIZATION AND PROCEDURES

Several libraries have made organizational changes in an attempt to smooth the flow of work in technical services. Two of them have established groups to act as buffers between acquisitions and cataloging. In one library this group is a section of the acquisitions department; in the other it constitutes an entire department. The primary functions of these groups are to locate Library of Congress card information for titles lacking it and to funnel the books to the proper person or group in the catalog department. One library has a bibliographic search unit which does all searching and verification for acquisitions and for cataloging. To "improve the flow of materials through units, working on backlogs, preparing for automation of processing procedures, processing bulk collections, and serving as a productivity 'yardstick' or procedure evaluation agency and change catalyst to improve methods of handling materials," the UCLA Library estab-

lished a task force during the 1968-69 year. In 1972 its
duties expanded to include collection development and public
service assignments. The task force, which was at first
under the supervision of the assistant university librarian for
systems and technical services, is now a unit of the regular
library administrative network with full departmental status. 4

Staffing

In many acquisitions departments the searching staff
is inundated with work during the first fiscal quarter and at
loose ends by the end of the year. Two acquisitions librarians stated that, if the searching work load were spread out
more evenly during the year, fewer searchers would be needed. Two suggestions for achieving a more even acquisitions
work load are: (1) Work out a schedule so (a) the bulk of
the more difficult-to-obtain items (geographically hard-to-get
or bibliographically hard-to-verify) are handled first; and
(b) the remainder of the orders to be processed are distributed more evenly over the first half of the fiscal year.
(2) Give the acquisitions unit more manpower during its
heaviest ordering season by hiring part-time personnel on a
temporary basis and/or shifting other library staff to ordering duties on a short-term basis.

To combat the paucity of salary money while being
faced with a great amount of work, two libraries have con-
verted each of several vacated professional positions into
two support staff positions. Such action requires an evaluation of the remaining professional positions within the department as well as the positions being downgraded so that a
general retrenchment of duties occurs, with the most routine tasks delegated to the new support staff.

Two acquisitions departments stress in-depth training
of their staffs. Each job can be handled by two or three
people. Two people can train others for any support job.
Such versatility allows each staff member to understand his
department better, and it permits work to continue in spite
of professional meetings, illnesses, vacations, and resigna-
tions.

Searching Considerations

Stevens suggests verifying entries only for items

above average cost, for corporate entries, and for items with difficult personal names. [5] Axford agrees that the main entry should not be established prior to ordering: "A considerable amount of wasted time can be avoided if the acquisitions department confines itself to determining if the library has an item, if it is on order, or if it exists, and leaving the descriptive cataloging to be performed by the catalog department after the item arrives."[6] If the search unit is responsible for providing the catalog department with card information (and the majority visited were), then acquisitions personnel should at most look for card information in the two LC/NUC sets in which a card would most likely appear. For example, a 1906 imprint would be searched only in A Catalog of Books Represented by Library of Congress Printed Cards Issued to July 31, 1942 and in The National Union Catalog, Pre-1956 Imprints, while a 1957 imprint would be searched only in Library of Congress and National Union Catalog Author Lists, 1942-1962 and The National Union Catalog for 1963-67. A card search for an out-of-print item should be made only after the item's availability is verified or after the book has been received.

Nine of the ten libraries visited estimate the cost of a title whose search reveals no price rather than making an exhaustive search in available tools and/or requesting a price quotation from the publisher. Estimates can be based on average trade prices presented in the most recent edition of the Bowker Annual. Instructions accompanying purchase orders to dealers can request notification before shipment if a title is more than the estimate shown, thus safeguarding a library against getting a $300 book for which it expected to pay $15.

Items designated "rush" require special handling and stop the normal flow of work, thereby reducing productivity. Available percentages of rush orders in the libraries visited covered the wide range of 2 per cent to 21.6 per cent. Perhaps more libraries should consider handling fewer titles on a rush basis.

Approval Plans

In four of the eight libraries that had some sort of approval plan, acquisitions librarians emphatically stated that without an approval plan they would not be able to spend their book budgets. This may seen contradictory--if there is less

money to spend, why rely on an approval plan? The chief
advantage of an approval plan to an acquisitions area is the
savings in paperwork: no purchase orders need be generated, for the necessary slips are supplied in the books.
There appears, however, to be little savings in the time
taken for review of books supplied on approval. Most of the
libraries visited have established a routine for the review of
approval books by subject librarians. Such a review seems
to remain most valid over a long period of time if subject
librarians are required to initial the slips of those books
they wish to accept. Thus, all books not reviewed are automatically returned rather than automatically retained.

When determining whether or not to maintain an approval plan, the prime concern should be: Is a library's
static book budget large enough to include that approval plan?
Shepard points out that "the key question is whether the
amount you have allocated, or might normally spend on a
certain subject area, approaches the estimated cost of books
published during the year in that subject."[7]

Forms and File Arrangement

Ford points out that the use of forms in acquisitions
work "is an important feature in saving time in repetitive,
routine operations and in assuring that work is done accurately and as completely as necessary."[8] Two libraries use in-
house forms for problem receipts so that receiving clerks
can quickly describe for problem-letter writers what is
wrong with a book by checking off appropriate items. This
practice allows both the receiving clerk and the problem-
letter writer to work independently without having to make
time for verbal discussion of each problem. One library
has adopted the multilingual several-purpose form letter proposed by Shinn to achieve uniformity in exchange communication.[9]

Two libraries have changed their order file from
main entry arrangement to title arrangement for greater
speed in checking new orders against the order file. It took
twenty people five working days to realphabetize 85,000 slips
in one of these libraries. Its file is now displayed in open
drawers on waist-high tables so that no user wastes time
pulling drawers out in order to look at their contents.

Metcalf points out that "a record should not be kept

unless in the long run it saves more time or money than it takes to make and use."[10] One library is removing branch library serials information from its serials Kardex record, for branch holdings are already listed on a computer printout. Two of the eight libraries do without any publishers' and/or dealers' catalogs file, relying on existing searching tools and advertisements or catalogs submitted with orders.

BUDGETARY CONSIDERATIONS

Obtaining Additional Funds from the University

Aside from doing what one university library did--ordering as usual and then cancelling all outstanding orders midyear when funds are exhausted (a most extreme procedure which is effective as a bargaining tool once at most), it seems that the best possible approach for getting more funds is to assure the university that any additional funds given the library will be spent--and then spend any that appear, no matter how late in the fiscal year they are received. One library has a list of priority items already selected so it can spend up to $200,000 extra within a week's time toward the end of the fiscal year.

Dealer Discounts

One library has a bond arrangement with its approval plan dealer whereby the entire approval fund is given the dealer at the beginning of the fiscal year and treated as a deposit account. In return, the dealer gives the library an additional 1 per cent discount on approval plan items. Another library bargains with out-of-print booksellers for a discount, assuring a certain amount of business in a given year in exchange for a given discount. One library is using the same dealer for approval plan and continuations as a bargaining point for higher discounts.

Encumbrances

Several public-service area librarians with small funds expressed deep concern that encumbrances from the past fiscal year are being reencumbered against their funds for the present fiscal year. This charges such funds twice

for each book not received during the year in which it was
ordered.   One effective solution offered is that all remaining
encumbrances for books ordered during the prior year be de-
ducted from the total book budget at the beginning of the new
year and that the remainder then be divided among existing
funds.

Serials Economies

The following trends have appeared in reaction to
ever-increasing serials commitments: (1) Four of the libraries visited conducted organized reviews of their current
serials, with an eye to removing duplicates and/or cutting
off any fat that had accumulated during the more lucrative
1960s.   (2) Four libraries dissolved their serials budgets by
attributing each serial title to a subject fund and giving that
fund an appropriate portion of the serials budget to cover the
cost of that title.   This action makes each subject fund co-
ordinater responsible for cutting old titles to obtain money
for ordering new ones.   (3) Two libraries notify the appropriate subject bibliographer if a serial title's cost increases
drastically.   The next renewal is not honored unless that
bibliographer has approved continuation.

Gifts and Exchanges Economies

Various libraries make money on unwanted duplicates
by selling them to dealers on a bid basis; giving runs of
serials to out-of-print dealers in exchange for credit; and
selling them to their own faculty and students or to other libraries at bargain rates.

Galejs points out that "libraries should not ignore the
possibility of exchanges as a means of serial acquisitions--
especially in periods of austerity and reduced funds."[11] One
of the libraries visited is converting as many serials as possible from purchase to exchange.

Librarians faced with meager rare book budgets might
follow the method used at the Washington University (St.
Louis) Library to build its special collection of modern literature.   Matheson points out that this library has developed
a most valuable collection with very little capital outlay by
purchasing books by and requesting literary papers of contemporary writers and poets designated by consultants as

people "whose abilities they particularly respected and who they felt stood a good chance of being important in fifty years. "12

Other Economies

Several libraries have realized savings in other budget areas in order to maintain or add to their book budgets. One library puts book replacement fees directly into the book replacement fund. If a processing charge is added to the cost of the lost book (one library adds a $5 processing fee; another adds $9), this provides a considerable amount of replacement money. Another now contracts its supplies and binding on an annual bid basis. Two libraries are revising their binding requirements to stretch the binding dollar, using cheaper, light adhesive bindings for some titles and having others bound as they are.

Postage Savings

Some postage-saving practices are: Using lightweight stationery for airmail letters; using aerograms for foreign correspondence not typed on form letters and without enclosures; batching correspondence and sending it on a weekly basis; sending all domestic rush orders airmail except those mailed on Thursdays and Fridays; sending no domestic correspondence by airmail; and using postcards for serials claims and catalog requests.

SELECTION

Bruer, in his 1973 review of acquisitions, suggests that a new emphasis on collection development "seems to symbolize the response by acquisitions librarians to the strained budget conditions of recent years. "13 Reduced budgets are forcing changes in selection perspective and level of expectation. Collection development is harder; for although the same quantity of literature must be considered, fewer items may be purchased. Blanket orders are being reviewed annually. Sale and remainder catalogs are used more heavily. Some libraries are ordering reference books on an every-other-edition basis as suggested by Strain.14 More microforms are being purchased in the interest of economy.

Library administrators expressed grave concern about
what the diminishing budget is doing to quality education. A
library cannot be a viable research institution if it provides
everyday instructional materials alone. Special collections--
the research library's most important area--cannot be meas-
ured in immediate productivity and may, therefore, be sacri-
ficed for immediate instructional needs, which must be met
first. Lyman urges coordination in any dismantling of collections, for "if the job is done on an individual basis, each
institution thinking only of its own programs and assuming
that no one else is contemplating cutting back in the same
area of study, the results will be very bad. "[15]

To keep special collections support reduction to a
minimum while meeting current patron needs, research libraries are turning to cooperative programs. Eight of the
ten libraries visited practice some means of cooperative acquisitions. These vary from a simple exchange of main entry cards between two libraries to the sophisticaled coor-
dinated acquisitions program being developed by the Research
Libraries Group. Members of the Center for Research Libraries are becoming more dependent upon that center for
little-used titles. Dix states that "it is becoming increasingly clear that one of the most promising means of slowing the
growth of library costs is the sharing of resources among institutions. "[16]

SUMMARY

Librarians are examining structural organization,
work procedures, budgetary operations, and selection practices, seeking the most economical measures in this financially bleak era. Such self-examination should be done on a
continuing basis to assure that library operations are as
streamlined as possible. However, a library can reach a
point of efficiency beyond which it can recognize no great
budgetary savings. If the internal efficiency is maximized,
the only economy measures that can be made are cooperative
ones. Perhaps the most valuable result of budget adversity
is that it is forcing the still quite imperfect national network
of research libraries to emerge as a "coherent, integrated
whole"[17] much more rapidly than it would have, had libraries continued to receive the kind of financial support
they did in the 1960s.

References

1. William S. Dix, "Reflections in Adversity; or, How Do You Cut a Library Budget?" [Louisiana State University] Library Lectures, nos. 17-20 (1972), p. 10.
2. H. William Axford, "Performance Measurement Revisited," College & Research Libraries 34:250 (Sept. 1973).
3. Ashby J. Fristoe and Rose E. Myers, "Acquisitions in 1971," Library Resources & Technical Services 16: 173 (Spring 1972).
4. Roberta Nixon, "UCLA Library Task Force," Library Resources & Technical Services 18:289-90 (Summer 1974).
5. Rolland E. Stevens, "The Relationships of the Acquisition Department to the Library's Total Program," in Herbert Goldhor, ed., Selection and Acquisition Procedures in Medium-Sized and Large Libraries (Champaign, Ill.: Univ. of Illinois Graduate School of Library Science, 1963), p. 133.
6. Axford, "Performance Measurement Revisited," p. 255.
7. Stanley A. Shepard, "Approval Books on a Small Budget?" in Edmond L. Applebaum, ed., Reader in Technical Services (Washington, D.C.: NCR Microcard Editions, 1973), p. 74.
8. Stephen Ford, The Acquisition of Library Materials (Chicago: American Library Assn., 1973), p. 172-73.
9. Isabella E. Shinn, "Toward Uniformity in Exchange Communications," Library Resources & Technical Services 16:502-10 (Fall 1972).
10. Keyes D. Metcalf, "The Essentials of an Acquisition Program," in Edmond L. Applebaum, ed., Reader in Technical Services (Washington, D.C.: NCR Microcard Editions, 1973), p. 57.
11. John E. Galejs, "Economics of Serials Exchanges," Library Resources & Technical Services 16:519 (Fall 1972).
12. William Matheson, "An Approach to Special Collections," American Libraries 2:1151 (Dec. 1971).
13. J. Michael Bruer, "Acquisitions in 1973," Library Resources & Technical Services 18:239 (Summer 1974).
14. Paula M. Strain, "What to Do if the Money Goes," Sci-Tech News 27:38 (Summer 1973).
15. R. W. Lyman, "New Trends in Higher Education: The

Impact on the University Library," College & Research Libraries 33:301 (July 1972).

16. William S. Dix, "The Financing of the Research Library," College & Research Libraries 35:256-57 (July 1974).

17. Ibid., p. 255.

THE LIZARD OF OZ:
The Adventure of a Self-published Fable*

Richard Seltzer

A year and a half ago, when the 13th rejection notice arrived, my wife, Barbara, said, "Why don't we do it ourselves?" That was all the encouragement I needed.

We had no experience in book publishing and no money. But in the back of my mind, I had always wanted to start a little book publishing company; so why not start with our own book?

College had instilled in me a respect for the editorial judgment of established publishers. I saw the role of the writer as an extension of the role of the student: you submit your work and patiently await approval or rejection.

But The Lizard of Oz was a unique story that had evolved in ways that gave me confidence that the public, young and old, would enjoy it. Over the three years of collecting rejection slips and kind but confused letters from editors, I had also been getting helpful feedback from a wide variety of people, and rewriting and rewriting again.

The story of the story began when I visited the elementary school class of a friend, Judy Morgan, to read the kids some stories I had written. I wound up visiting a number of classes in the same building. And there's no better audience in the world than fourth and fifth graders. When I finished reading, they'd swarm around with questions. One time they asked what I was going to write next, and I popped off with a couple titles: "The Quest for the Holy Mackeral,"

*Reprinted by permission from The Self-Publishing Writer: A Quarterly Journal for Writers, Vol. 4, No. 1, Spring 1976, pp. 48-57.

"The Lizard of Oz" ... they wanted to hear "The Lizard of
Oz"; so I started writing a story with that title with the kids
themselves as characters.   I went back a couple of times to
read them new chapters, then school ended, but the story
kept growing, going its own way, until it became a "fable
for all ages," a story intended for adults that kids like too.

That summer I went around with some musician-
friends to coffee-houses in the Boston area, reading the
story aloud to audiences of strangers, getting immediate reaction to new chapters and revisions.   By the end of the
summer I was two-thirds through, quit a librarian's job I
had at the time, and went to my parents' place in Pennsylvania, where I wrote the last third in about two weeks.

As the manuscript followed its meandering path through
the mails, I returned to Boston, did some free-lance Russian
translating at a penny a word, and then went to grad school
in comparative literature at the U. of Mass. in Amherst.
Each publisher typically took 3-4 months to return the manuscript.   I'd address it to the trade book department, saying
that this was a story intended primarily for adults, although
children would like it too.   And I'd get back a rejection note
from the children's book department, saying that they were
sorry, but this didn't really seem like a children's book.
Frequently, I ended up trimming and revising before mailing
the story off again.   All in all it was a valuable experience
(frustrating as it seemed at the time) forcing me to rethink
what I intended to say and reconsider whether the words I
had chosen conveyed what I meant them to.

While at the U. of Mass., I chanced upon a note on
a bulletin board.   Christin Couture needed a book to illustrate for a course.   I got in touch with her, and once she
started drawing the characters it was hard for me to imagine
them any other way.   The Humbug, the Redcoats, the Witch,
Mr. Bacon, Sir Real, Prince Frog, the Weatherman, the
Mothers of Fact, Joan of Noah's Ark, and the Lizard himself all took on new life in her drawings.   So copies of the
illustrations accompanied the manuscript in its rounds from
publisher to publisher, until my wife and I decided to go
ahead and start our own company.

We weren't totally ignorant of printing and preparing
copy for printers.   I was working for Benwill Publishing
Co., writing and editing for Circuits Manufacturing, a monthly technical trade magazine.   And on my own, back when I

first started writing The Lizard, I had handlettered on a couple of my children's stories ("Now and Then" and "Julie's Book: the Little Princess") and had had them printed and stapled together like pamphlets.

I had seen The Publish-It-Yourself Handbook in bookstores. Now I bought a copy, read it quickly and brainstormed with my old roommate from Yale, David Gleason. Dave had recently gotten his MBS from Harvard Business School and was in the habit of taking a hard practical look at business projects. He also had experience in dealing with printers and had done some silk-screen printing himself.

Handlettering, I thought, would suit the child-like tone and anti-machine content of the story. It would also enable me to put the words where I wanted them on the pages, ending the page where a thought ended and shaping the words to fit the shape of the illustrations. But, as Dave pointed out, production costs depend largely on the number of pages, and normal handlettering would leave a lot of wasted space on the page. He suggested lettering it large and have the printer reduce it. So long as the reduction was the same on each page, the printer could do it with a single camera setting and there would be no extra charge. I settled on a reduction to two-thirds, which brought my lettering down to about the size of regular type (10 or 11 point).

I used a felt-tip pen and regular typing paper, stopping and cutting off strips when I made mistakes. Barbara lined-up and pasted the pieces together on large sheets of paper. Inside of two weeks, working nights and weekends (we both had full-time jobs at the time), we got the camera ready copy together and delivered it to the printer, a "book manufacturer" that would both print and perfect bind the books--Semline, in Braintree, Mass.

Dave designed the cover starting with Christin's line-drawing of the Lizard. And he handsilkscreened the covers for the first printing. (Silkscreening 1,200 covers with two colors of ink is not the simplest task in the world. I wouldn't advise anyone doing it to save money. We did it this way because The Lizard was our very first book, and we wanted the first copies to be unique, collector's items).

All in all, we kept the production cost of 1,000 copies (128 pages) to about $1,000, which we borrowed

from a bank as a personal loan. We had decided to start a
company on August 15. On October 4th we picked up the
finished books at Semline and dashed into the Globe Book
Festival, where we had rented an exhibit table for $50.

Two other decisions that we made at the very beginning have proven particularly helpful. First and most important was the price. On Dave's advice, we started with
the price, what we felt would be reasonable to charge for a
paperback intended to reach the general adult, college, and
high school market--$2.95. Our production decisions were
based on the knowledge that we had to keep costs low enough
so that even after bookstores took 40% or distributors took
50% (or even more depending on the quantity ordered), and
even after postage and printing up fliers and other promotional material and other operating expenses, we had to be
able to come out ahead with a $2.95 retail price. With too
high costs, we could end up losing money with every book
we sold. We were excited enough not to figure in the value
of our labor, but we simply couldn't afford to go ahead with
a project that had no chance of breaking even.

My initial calculations were based on average receipts
of about $1.50 per book and operating expenses running
about 50% of production/printing expenses. As it turned out,
for the first printing we had many more direct sales than
anticipated, giving us higher average receipts per book. But
our operating expenses also exceeded our expectations leaving
us about where we had hoped to be. Then with the second
printing, the production cost per book dropped from $1 to
about 50¢; but we began dealing more with book stores and
distributors than individuals, so our receipts per book
dropped, leaving us a little bit ahead.

In 1975, our first full calendar year of operation, we
ended up spending $70-200 per month in addition to the cost
of the second printing. Our receipts that year ranged $150-
450 per month. In other words, there was no simple way to
relate printing expense to operating expense. The bills flow
in at a relatively steady rate, and the rate of sales and receipts has to keep pace. Success depends not just on the
total number of books sold or the total amount of receipts,
but rather on how fast these sales are made. If we were
to sell 1,000 books in a month, we'd make money. And if
it were to take us two years to sell them, we'd lose money.
For 1975, our receipts totalled $3,380, and our expenses
(including the second printing costs, but not including a per-

centage of rent and utilities and phone as allowable under
IRS regulations) amounted to $3,195. ("Receipts" here
means cash received, and does not include accounts still
owing.)

The other important decision we made at the beginning was the company name: the B & R Samizdat Express.
B = Barbara, R = Richard. Samizdat means "self-published"
in Russian. The name sounded so much like a train that we
called it "Express" instead of "Press." This unusual name,
with its unusual explanation, as well as the unusual title of
the book, made potential buyers and reviewers give the book
a second glance. Opening the book, the handlettered format
caught their eye, and they took a few moments to sample the
text and get involved.

We could see this process in action at the Globe Book
Festival in Boston the very day we got the first copies from
the printer. Walking by our table, people would do a dou-
ble-take at the word Lizard, come back, stare at the striking
cover design, open the book and start reading. Or they's
ask questions: "B & R what?" "Why did you handletter it?"
"Is that really 'Lizard'?"

Managers of a couple of small bookstores met us
there and ordered. And a sales representative, Sumner
Dane, saw people gathering around our table and indicated
that he wanted to handle our book. He regularly goes the
rounds of stores in New England representing a wide variety
of books and book publishers, ranging from operations as
small as ours to Bellerophon Books. He takes orders, for-
wards them to us, and we pay him a percentage of what the
book store pays us. We give him a relatively hefty cut
(20% of net, or about 35¢ per book) to keep him interested
in our small operation. Inside of a couple of weeks, he
placed our book in a couple dozen stores, and got an order
for 100 from Paperback Booksmith, a bookstore chain that
also acts as a distributor to other stores. (For bulk orders
like that, we give the chain/distributor 50%; and, in our arrangement, the sales rep. gets 10% of net).

In succeeding weeks we picked up a few extra stores
by going personally and talking to store managers. But
more often than not the book buyer wouldn't be in, or would
look askance at an author peddling his own book, or at any
booksalesman with only one title to sell. We didn't have
much time to spare what with our regular jobs, so we con-
centrated our attention on direct mail sales.

We had had fliers printed up so we would have something to hand to people at the Globe Book Festival. And a trickling of mail orders came in from people who had picked up the flier. More importantly, we did a mailing to about 200 friends and relatives, offering a 50¢ discount if they ordered (prepaid) directly from us before December 1. We have never charged for shipping/handling/postage. We like to encourage people to order directly from us, since such orders save us the percentage that would go to bookstores and other middlemen, and also give me a chance to get direct feedback from readers. By the way, for single copy orders we give bookstores a 20% discount, to make it worth their while to act as middlemen on special requests from customers. They have to order five copies to get 40%. It being Christmas time, that mailing sold 60 books directly, then friends and relatives and friends of friends and friends of friends of friends who had read the book spread the word. We sold about 190 books directly by that snowball effect in the first couple months. In addition we had sold about 60 books at the Globe Book Festival, 55 at a Christmas craft fair, and 25 at another (poorly attended) craft fair.

We also tried a direct mail campaign to a few local colleges to see what kind of response we'd get. First, we contacted the administration for permission. Then we delivered fliers with the 50¢ discount-December 1 deadline cards stapled on and college personnel put them in the students' boxes, saving us the cost of postage. It seemed like a good idea, but 1,000 such fliers brought us only 6 direct orders. (It's hard to measure the secondary effect of students buying the book in stores after seeing the flier or after hearing about it from somebody who bought it on the basis of a flier.)

Meanwhile, we could see by November 4th, just one month after we had received the first copies, that we would run out of books in a month or two. So we ordered a second printing of 3,000, which was ready December 4th.

After Christmas came a lull. There we sat with 3,000 books in our living room.

Following the advice of The Publish-It-Yourself Handbook, we had set out "official publication date" a couple of months after the date we first received the books from the printer and had sent out review copies to major review sources and also to local papers around Boston and in other areas where I had lived. We hoped/expected that when December 1st arrived, a few of these publications would review our book, and orders would start coming in from strangers around the country. But by January 1st, as far as we knew, we had only been mentioned in a paper in Greenfield, Mass., where a friend had brought the book to the editor's attention. And that review only brought us an order for two books from a local bookstore.

We had used the Literary Marketplace (an R. R. Bowker publication) to get our reviewer mailing list, and had sent out about 100 review copies in the first mailing, together with 100 form letters to another set of reviewers asking them if they would like to see the book. (Since then we've sent out about 100 more review copies, following up miscellaneous leads.) Two local newspapers in Tennessee (the state where I was born) asked for review copies, and then didn't send clippings and didn't answer follow-up letters. A Chicago reviewer asked for a review copy and in reply to a follow-up letter indicated that he had just lost his job due to the "economic crunch." The Washington Post was kind enough to acknowledge receipt of the book and to say that they would consider it the next time they ran a children's book section; but to the best of our knowledge, they have not yet run a review.

With a disproportionate expenditure of time and money for phone calls and correspondence, my mother managed to place the book in half a dozen stores in her area of Pennsylvania. And I wrote a flurry of letters to distributors and bookstores, but got zero response.

The advice in the Handbook didn't extend beyond production and the first promotion push. It seemed like we had reached a deadend.

Then a form letter arrived in the mail from Library Journal. At first it seemed like an ad. Then I realized that a review clipping was attached: The Lizard was to be reviewed in the January 15 issue. A few days later a similar letter arrived from The Booklist, a publication of the American Library Association. Their review would appear February 1. Both reviews were very favorable, and both treated The Lizard as a book intended for adults.

I immediately wrote follow-up letters to all the reviewers who had received copies, asking if they had scheduled

or already published reviews.   A few answered.   Publishers
Weekly indicated that they "review only those books which
have a widespread national circulation. " (Catch-22:   you
need widespread circulation to get reviewed, and you need
to get reviewed to get widespread circulation.)   The Boston
Globe indicated that, as a rule, they don't review paperbacks.
(A strange criterion of literary merit.)   A few others said
simply that they didn't plan to review it or that they had no
way of knowing which of their reviewers might have picked
it up or whether anything could be written.   A Harrisburg,
Penn. paper sent a clipping of a brief mention that had already appeared.   The Philadelphia Daily News also ran a
brief mention.

    The book editor from the Philadelphia Bulletin replied
with a question: "Tell me something about your business--
who you are, what you are, and where you got that name. "
I replied with a lengthy letter, and on January 26th the lead
review in the Sunday Bulletin was a very favorable commentary on The Lizard and our company.   Wanamaker's department store in Philadelphia telephoned the next day to order
25.   A couple more stores and a few individuals ordered by
mail.   And letters to stores listed in the Philadelphia Yellow
Pages brought a few more orders from that area.   The Bulletin review also led, with the prompting of friends and relatives, to reviews in half a dozen local papers in Pennsylvania and New Jersey and a few more store orders.

    About this time, the Library Journal and Booklist re-
views began to take effect, and we started getting library
and book jobber orders from all over the U. S. and Canada.
(We charge libraries full price, and give jobbers a 20% discount to make it worth their while to act as middlemen.)   A
year after the appearance of those reviews, we still get a
trickle of orders directly attributable to them.   All in all,
those reviews have directly sold us about 300 books to libraries and jobbers (including over 100 to the various offices
of Baker & Taylor).

    Large East Coast distributors, such as A & A, re-
buffed us, saying it wasn't worth their while dealing with a
company that has only one title.   But a handful of stores reordered and reordered again.   (Booksmith has reordered
twice, 100 copies each time.)   And our sales rep. has kept
getting a few new stores a month.   Meanwhile reviews appeared in The Valley Advocate (western Mass.), The Lancaster (Penn.) Independent Press, and Aspect (a bimonthly
literary magazine published in the Boston area).

Then we began to make contacts with other small publishers, joining the Committee of Small Magazine Editors and Publishers (COSMEP) and following up the helpful leads in their monthly newsletter. But more importantly, we exhibited at Book Affair, the small press book fair that was held at Boston University last April (scheduled for May 7-9 at Harvard this year), and the New York Book Fair in NYC (scheduled for April 30-May 2 this year).

Follow-up from contacts made at those events brought half a dozen more store orders and orders from two small press distributors for 100 copies each: Atlantis in New Orleans and Bob Koen in New Jersey. (It's still too early to tell how well those arrangements will work out in the long run.) More important than these orders and direct sales to the public was the opportunity to meet and talk to other small publishers. And the growing realization that we weren't alone, that others were running up against the same obstacles with distributors, reviewers, bookstores, and were trying to work out solutions, and in any case were enjoying publishing what they wanted to publish the way they wanted to publish it. There was a sense of excitement, that all these little individual efforts were part of a "movement," that in the universe of publishing the center was shifting, and we were watching it and making it happen.

At the N.Y. Fair I tired of telling about my book and started asking the visitors about their lines of business. One visitor was a reporter from the New Republic who subsequently mentioned me in a brief account of the fair. Another was an agent who said he wanted to handle the foreign rights to The Lizard. (He's still working on that, but nothing concrete has developed yet.) Quite a few were editors at large publishing houses, and I had an opportunity to ask questions that had often puzzled me (like--Why has Doubleday been letting valuable and popular Anchor paperbacks drop out of print?)

In the fall, on the basis of the previous publicity I had received, my mother managed to get me scheduled for two local TV appearances in Lancaster, Penn., and Hank Grissom of the Illusion in Lancaster (a store that had repeatedly reordered) got me scheduled for a radio interview show and an autographing session at his store. I was scared stiff, never having appeared on television or radio; but it all worked out beautifully, in three jam-packed days, complete with a prominent story in the Lancaster New Era. We sold about 50 copies in four hours of autographing at the Illusion,

and the store took three dozen more for follow-up sales.
We also got orders and reorders from half a dozen other
stores in the area.

By now it has become difficult to trace the source of
sales. We have had orders from about 150 book stores,
distributors, and jobbers from all over the U.S. and Canada.
(Three bookstores, for instance, in Calgary, Canada.) For
the most part, they have contacted us. We've found that
mailing promotional material for a single book to a bookstore
simply does not pay, unless you have some special reason to
expect them to be interested. Some stores order just one
or two copies; other half a dozen or a dozen. A few reorder
at odd intervals. (Follow-up letters don't seem to bring reorders. They happen on their own or they don't happen at
all.)

Although we've gotten orders from a number of individuals on the West Coast, we still haven't made any inroads with the bookstores or distributors there. Small Press
Traffic in San Francisco has a few on consignment, but Book-
people, the distributor, has continually ignored our correspondence. RPM on the East Coast also doesn't answer.

Returning to the Globe Book Festival in 1975, I was
one of the scheduled speakers and had an opportunity to talk
to an audience of about 100 for an hour. WBUR--radio interviewed me there and one of the broadcasters took an interest in The Lizard. I've since written a radio script of
The Lizard for them (20 episodes, 3-7 minutes long). It
looks like the series will be ready for broadcast sometime
this summer.

This Globe Festival appearance also led to two brief
mentions in Publishers Weekly (in a story on small publishers in New England and in a writeup on the Festival). Shortly thereafter we got a request for a review copy from a syn-
dicated columnist in NYC, Joan Orth. Her story should be
appearing soon, and she also wants to interview me on her
radio show "Hear-Abouts."

Orders have started to come in as a result of a recent review in the newsletter of the International Oz Club
(The Baum Bugle). An elementary school in Sharon, Mass.,
will be performing The Lizard as a play next month. (The
drama teacher worked out a script with the kids.) A junior
high in Penn. and another in Conn. are using The Lizard as

an English text.   We've also gotten inquiries from high
school teachers and a college professor interested in using
it for freshman English.

The second printing is nearly exhausted now; so we're
ordering a third printing of 5,000.   We're also putting together a short collection of children's stories written by me,
including my favorites: "Now and Then," "Julie's Book: the
Little Princess," "The Little Oops Named Ker Plop," and
"Mary Jane's Book: the Book of Animals."   It looks like
this second book will be 64 pages, paperback, handlettered
(same-size rather than reduced, to make it easier to read
for kids).   Title: Now and Then & Other Tales from Ome.
Price: $1.95.

It's like we're starting all over again.

PART III

COMMUNICATION AND EDUCATION

PUBLIC LENDING RIGHT*

Eric Clough

Authors have been claiming a public lending right in
the United Kingdom for 25 years; unfortunately, that fact
does not give it the respectability that usually comes with
advancing years. The idea was misconceived in 1950 and
the years have demonstrated that it remains wrong-headed
and impracticable. The fact that public lending right has
gained a measure of political support over the last quarter
of a century merely serves to demonstrate that authors have
become increasingly effective at organizing an influential lobby. Because politicians have recognized the strength of the
writer's lobby, it does not follow that this strengthens and
supports the authors' arguments for PLR. But it does serve
to demonstrate that if you say something often enough and
loudly enough for a long enough time it will be accepted as
true.

John Brophy first made the claim of a "penny for the
author on each library loan." Since that time the main thesis advanced by authors has been that their interests were
damaged by making their books available through a public library. It followed, they maintained, that if their books
were not so available more copies would be sold through
booksellers. But the proposition has never been properly
researched.

Since we are in the area of subjective judgements, I
contend that public libraries serve as a show place for books.
Many members of the public see books they wish to buy in
a public library and then go to a bookshop and purchase

*Reprinted by permission of the author and publisher from
Canadian Library Journal, Vol. 32, No. 6, Dec. 1975, pp.
423-425. Copyright © 1975, The Canadian Library Association.

them. It has been the experience of many of my colleagues
that where you have a town with an effective public library
service you are likely to find a successful bookshop. I have
been fortunate in enjoying an excellent public library service
for the whole of my professional life--a public library service of a standard that everyone should enjoy--and yet I have
consistently bought new books and sometimes bought old ones.

Subjective, certainly, but it is a theory supported to
some extent by the steady increase in the number of books
published in the United Kingdom annually over the past 25
years. But, ask authors, what about the novel? The poor
old novel does not show any increase in the number of titles
published in recent years. Authors say this is due to the
activities of the public library in making novels freely available. I can only reply that each and every week for 20
years from 1954 to 1974 I looked at a large portion of books
published in my country and it occurred to me that possibly
the art of writing a novel was in decline. After looking
through the week's output, our experienced team of book se-
lectors would declare a bumper week if there were ten novels out of forty worthy of serious consideration. An average
week would produce five or six.

This is not meant to be an attack upon authors; it is
meant to be a statement of the case against a public lending
right. In a free-market economy authors are paid what they
command. Some are paid generously, some are paid poorly,
but that is the way the market operates. The only alternative is state control and few of us would welcome that. Possibly, the harshness of the system, by which I mean free-
market economy, could be alleviated by financial aid from
the state to artists producing outstanding work of obvious social value. To some extent financial assistance is given
through our Arts Council which supplies rather meagre
grants for this purpose. I wish it would make larger grants,
but I can see no justification for the state disguising such
grants as public lending right, with the size of the grant related to the popularity of the work. This is not élitism on
my part but rather an expression of concern. For example,
publication of each and every volume of that monumental
work by Sir Nikolaus Pevsner on The Building of England
was made possible by the support of some charitable trust.
Here we have an outstanding contribution to our knowledge
of the architecture of this country; I for one would be happy
to see such works given a measure of encouragement by the
state. But should the state subsidize the popular novelist

regardless? When I look at most of our fiction I think
not.

Some of the authors in my country point out that
they are deplorably paid. Not all of them, some of them.
Many years ago Richard Findlater claimed that on an average authors earned £600 a year. Even allowing for infla-
tionary increases since Findlater wrote that, it is still poor
pay. But what does it mean? As with many of the authors'
arguments, it is poorly based. What is an author? One
engaged wholly in writing as a means of earning his/her
livelihood, or, all those who write books: politicians, academics, even librarians? Are we to assume that all authors, full-time and part-time alike, are grossly underpaid?
If this is so, what are the publishers going to do about it?

Having served on the Technical Investigation Group
appointed by the Minister for the Arts to look into the feasibility of administering a public lending right, I find my doubts
about both the desirability and practicability of such a scheme
reinforced. First it was decided that the scheme could only
be implemented if it were limited to the sole author of a literary work. There would be no right for joint authors,
compilers, editors, illustrators or whatever. To counter
the criticism that a public lending right would result in the
rich authors getting richer and the average authors getting
very little, the Minister and the authors agreed the scheme
should be modified. Payments could be tapered in such a
way that the successful author would not get quite so much
and the less successful author would get a little more. But,
the least successful authors who came below the cut-off
point would get no payments. An odd right, some might
call it a rather arbitrary payment by the state to authors of
average mediocrity.

Could it be made to work? It might if you allowed
three years for it to be implemented. It might if you were
prepared to accept a sample of loans from 32 service points
out of a total of 6,500. It might if it were found to be possible to print bar codes giving International Standard Book
Numbers in all new books published and if it were then possible to install suitable machines in appropriate libraries.
It might if the state were prepared to pay something of the
order of £400,000 a year to administer such a scheme. It
might if you were prepared to accept an arbitrary loan factor
for books in reference libraries. This is the point that a
high-level committee of senior civil servants, statisticians,

data research specialists, publishers, authors and librarians
have reached after 18-months' deliberation. It would seem
that the proposed scheme is inequitable, administratively
clumsy and probably unworkable, apart from the basic objection that it is misconceived.

It is too easy to go on picking holes in this patched-
up cobweb of a public lending right, but there remain two
or three issues which librarians of all countries may care
to consider.

Why are only public libraries to be used as a basis
for assessing the proposed public lending right? If it is a
right should it not apply to national and academic libraries?
Should it not apply to school, hospital, and prison libraries?
Might it not apply to any form of book anywhere? Certainly
it would be the authors' hope to extend the right to all libraries as soon as this became practicable. But knowing
something of the difficulties that have been experienced in
trying out a limited scheme, I am doubtful about the feasibility of the present proposals. Whatever the authors'
wishes, it seems highly unlikely that it will be extended to
cover a wider range of libraries or authors.

Public librarians are understandably concerned that
if such a right were established the payments for it would,
sooner rather than later, prejudice the financial support
given to public libraries. An assurance has been given that
the state will pay the cost of administering the scheme entirely out of the Exchequer; this would cover the cost to the
local authorities of administering the scheme, fund the sta-
tutory authority and, of course, pay the authors. It seems
likely that these monies would come out of those made available for the support of the Arts. It also seems reasonable
to suppose that it would not be long before such payments
were reflected in a reduction of the financial support made
to public libraries.

Let us look briefly at the supposed legal basis for
the right. Authors emote the plea that the right is merely
"common justice for which they have been appealing for 25
years." Originally authors claimed that loans through the
public library were an infringement of copyright, or that the
matter could be dealt with by an extension of the law of
copyright. A working party appointed by Lord Eccles looked
into the possibility of amending the Copyright Act in this way
in 1956; as a result the Government of the day abandoned

any such proposals. But the working party went further;
they decided that any scheme for a public lending right was
impracticable.

Another question is whether the authors have any
property rights over their books that are loaned by public
libraries. A fundamental part of the concept of public lending right claims that authors do have property rights. But
authors do not own their books in the public libraries: they
cannot lend them: they do not have a lending right. It
could even be argued that books are merely the physical
form by which a reader may discover what the author wishes
to communicate. Even the copyright protection given to an
author's literary works, in the sense that there exists a
monopoly to make copies of the work for distribution, has
usually been assigned to a publisher in return for an agreed
payment. The logic of a public lending right would entail
authors' publishing their own works and retaining possession
of all copies. They would then have an incontestable right
to charge a fee for each book borrowed. But as long as authors continue to let the publisher take the commercial risk,
they cannot in fairness expect to be compensated by the state
when profits accruing from the writing of a book are disap-
pointing. This concept that the corporate ownership of books
should carry with it some compensation for the writer is a
principle that could quite logically be extended to a wide
range of resources that are in corporate ownership for corporate use.

The authors make their case sound more persuasive
by comparing it with a performing right, but this too is a
confusion of thinking. Reading is not a copyright offence.
The confusion arises because both writing and the composition of music use printing or writing as their means of communication. With books, the multiple aspect of communication is met by the payment of royalties on the number of
copies of a book sold. With music, fees are paid in relation to the number of people who listen to a public performance.

Although public lending right is misconceived, un-
wieldy, unfair, and expensive it may possibly become law in
my country before the year is out. It has been on the statute book in Western Germany for three years but it has not
yet been found possible to implement. Perhaps Canada can
demonstrate that logic can best be combined with advancing
the interest of authors by resisting this proposal for a public
lending right.

THE HUMANIZATION OF INFORMATION SCIENCE*

Stanley A. Elman

> When we run over libraries ... what havoc
> must we make? If we take in our hand any vol-
> ume, of divinity or school metaphysics, for in-
> stance, let us ask, Does it contain any abstract
> reasoning concerning quantity or number? No.
> Does it contain any experimental reasoning con-
> cerning matter of fact and existence? No. Com-
> mit it then to the flames: for it can contain noth-
> ing but sophistry and illusion.
> --Final paragraph from An Enquiry Concern-
> ing Human Understanding, by David Hume,
> published in 1751, one year before he be-
> came Librarian of the Advocates' Library
> in England.

Science has made significant progress in the two hundred years since Hume and his followers suggested book-
burning as a solution to rid the world of equivocation and
hypocrisy. We have, at least, reached a point at which individuals in allied fields, although disagreeing on methods
and priorities, and even fundamental principles, cooperate
with each other to effect common goals.

The relatively specialized and somewhat detached
character of science is perhaps a function of its short history. Science is young when compared with human life on
earth. It has quite recently reached a relative state of maturity. Evidence for this maturity is demonstrated by the
increasing number of scientists who are asking what the actu-

*Reprinted by permission from Special Libraries, Vol. 69,
No. 9, Sept. 1976, pp. 421-427. Copyright © 1976 by
Special Libraries Association.

al and potential roles of science are in the modern world. They urge that scientists fully recognize and accept responsibilities for the consequences of their efforts.

Information science is one of science's youngest subdivisions. It is even younger than the older science of librarianship. Already, however, it has made a substantial impact on society.

An Interdisciplinary Science

Both Borko (1) and Cuadra (2) stress the interdisciplinary aspects of information science in defining it:

> What is information science? It is an interdisciplinary science that investigates the properties and behavior of information, the forces that govern the flow and use of information, and the techniques, both manual and mechanical, of processing information for optimal storage, retrieval, and dissemination (1).

The growing field of information science and technology "draws on fragments and fringes of a number of sciences, technologies, disciplines, arts, and practices. The element that provides whatever degree of cohesiveness now exists in the field is a shared deep concern with 'information'--its generation, transformation, communication, storage, retrieval, and use" (2).

Artandi (3) claims that "these and other definitions and observations are somewhat less than adequate because they are too broad, or too narrow, or because they fail to distinguish between information science and librarianship." She adds that, "in information science we are often concerned with problems that are qualitatively the same as library problems at the same level, except that we are considering these with more sophistication in order to cope with and utilize changes which have occurred in the environment in which we now need to operate."

Horn (4), in a more eclectic and conciliatory spirit, states that despite many efforts "to clarify and urge agreement upon definitions of such terms as librarianship or library science, special librarianship, documentation, information science, information engineering or technology, sci-

ence information, etc., there remains a tendency for individuals and organizations to use whatever terms appeal to
them in describing, identifying, or differentiating their own
efforts or programs."

Computer Technology

Information science and the new technology of the
electronic computer have made their impact in spite of the
reluctance and skepticism of many librarians. Scientists,
and especially information scientists, became convinced that
librarianship, particularly information retrieval, was too important to be left to the primarily humanistic librarians,
many of whom as Shera (5) put it "were fearful and distrust-
ful of science" and lacking in a professional philosophy.

Information science, while still struggling to define
itself and its membership (6-9), already has some internal
revisionists and iconoclasts. Borrowing the notion of the
scientific paradigm for Kuhn's essay on the nature of science
(10) and capitalizing on the vagueness of its definition, Rosenberg (11) urges the rejection of what is his notion of the
basic components of the paradigm underlying information sci-
ence--that is, the integration of the "gestalt of the computer"
with behaviorist psychology and the Newtonian world view.
Not only does Rosenberg urge their rejection but he attributes
to these notions basically deterministic, reductionist, and
mechanical values--scientific values which inhibit the consideration of concepts that are social, cultural, or spiritual.
He also claims that many of the premises which constitute
the currently held paradigm of information science are socially and politically pathogenic.

"All truth begins in a minority of one," claims Watson (12). "A paradigm is never developed by one man, but
rather by a community of scientists," counters Rosenberg
(11), suggesting merely a few avenues of research which
might be productive. First, he insists that information science must abandon its deterministic approach and recognize
the computer as an historical accident rather than as a scientific organizing principle. "We must get out from behind
the computer," he pleads. Rosenberg also urges that we pay
more attention to the social, cultural, and spiritual aspects
of human communication and that we must admit as scientific
evidence the intuitive, the subjective, and the experiential
(11). [Rosenberg was one of those featured in "Ten Informa-

tion Scientists as Human Beings," <u>Wilson Library Bulletin</u> 47 (no. 9): 753-762 (1973). He was described as a sensitive, low-profiled activist, concerned with human rights.]

Rosenberg's notion of pathogenic premises comes from Harmon's (13) definition that a pathogenic premise is one which is problem generating even though in other ways it may produce useful consequences. One such premise is that the summed knowledge of experts constitutes wisdom. Perhaps Alfred Lord Tennyson expressed it better in "Locksley Hall" when he wrote "knowledge comes but wisdom lingers." Some information scientists, although very knowledgeable in the manipulative aspects of information science, may at times lack this lingering wisdom. Roszak (14) is much less sympathetic, referring to them as imitators of natural scientists and as scientific-technical experts "purporting to know as the scientist knows."

There may already exist a lower echelon of technocrats and supersalesmen who may be advancing a new pseudo-paradigm not based on science but related solely to the profit motive. These unscrupulous individuals are making vast inroads into the areas of industrialization and dehumanization of information science and libraries. "They would turn libraries into factories in which units of production would determine the effectiveness of librarians," noted Mason (15). They, it seems, may be adopting the world view of the American industrialist--anything can be justified in order to sell more computers.

Humanization Needed

Let us plead for humanization at the level of the pragmatic working information scientists and librarians who must deal with the daily human aspects of information and its seekers. Many such individuals must often work without much benefit of theory, without understanding paradigms or even computerized Boolean logic; they are driven only by a desire to help and a dedicated commitment to serve. Rosenberg's (11) plea to admit as scientific evidence the intuitive, the subjective, and the experiential is long overdue. Often intuitions, subjectivism, and experience are all the working information scientists and librarians have left after forced staff-reductions and budget cuts. The ghetto story-telling children's librarian, the perspicacious literature searcher and analyst, the harassed school librarian--all rely on the social, cultural,

and spiritual aspects of primarily human communication. The
"gestalt" of the deterministic machine--the computer--is still
unknown to many of them and those they serve.

It is not the intent here to challenge the small group
of super-sophisticated computer-revering cognitive simulators,
artificial intelligence probers, game players, computerized
language translators, problem solvers, and pattern recog-
nizers--men like Simon, Minsky, Newell, Shaw, Feigenbaum,
McCarthy, Rosenblatt, etc. Rosenberg is undoubtedly correct that these men (the leaders, the innovators, the experi-
menters) are the most influential and, therefore, potentially
most dangerous of the dehumanizers. They must be challenged when their over-zealousness threatens us with premature and unproven mechanistic manipulations and glorified
predictions of matching intelligence and computer competence.
Those challenges are better left to men like Dreyfus, Bar-
Hillel, Oettinger, and Rosenberg. Most of us are barely
able to cope with the lower echelon of dehumanizing influences.
It is at this lower level that we find our immediate threat--
at the working level of the operations researcher, the systems analyst, the computer detailman, the library automator.

It is the level of one such glib manipulator/automator
who claimed that most library problems "can be reduced to
one of inventory control as in an independent shoe store" and
effectively solved by proper application of the current state-
of-the-art of the computer (16). He apparently failed to realize, for example, that unlike the shoe store owner, the librarian does not own the library which itself is a complex
system within a system, within a system, etc. Neither did
he realize that, seemingly unlike the shoe on the store shelf,
each element on the library shelves consists of priceless
sub-elements of information which interrelate with other such
sub-elements of information elsewhere. These sub-elements,
in turn, may or may not be within a larger entity called
knowledge or wisdom. It is from this system that the information scientist or librarian must retrieve the kernels
for a user whose needs are often unexpressed or unexpressa-
ble.

These automators suffer from a common semantic
confusion caused by inability to discern between effectiveness
and efficiency. As pointed out by Griffen and Hall (17), library effectiveness is not synonymous with efficient collection
management. While collection management is an important
element of effectiveness, it is only one dimension of the pro-

cess of giving and receiving service. Perhaps it gets so
much attention because it is more easily quantifiable than
other elements, such as the information scientist's ability
to assist the user in defining an information need, or the librarian's skill in assessing the information needs of the community in relation to the information services provided by
the library.

Information scientists and librarians must continue to
prepare themselves to better challenge those who omit the
essential human variables within the equations, graphs, programs, diagrams, statistics, probabilities, etc. , tossed at
them. It is worth noting here again some of the admonitions
of that professional perennial peripatetic iconoclast, Mason
(18): "... the more we multiply the number of people
through whom a process must work, the more dehumanized
the response becomes. " And, again from the same source:
"We tend to substitute organization for personal effort, to
keep our chain of command straight rather than our humanity
straight. We confuse Randtrievers and computers, and other
machines, with libraries, which they are not. We confuse
buildings with libraries. We confuse book collections with
libraries, and even book collections are not libraries. "

Information scientists and librarians must explore all
available avenues--self-study, seminars, publications, professional societies, etc.--to learn the battle tactics to apply
when confronting those who would dehumanize them.

The Systems Approach

The most important tactic to learn, of course, is to
distinguish friend from foe, and that is difficult for they all
tend to speak the same language, and their sample wares
and glittering promises are overwhelming. Their own inter-
pretations of past successes are impressive. Perhaps the
best way to evaluate them is to establish a credibility scale
on which expected performance would be in inverse ratio to
promise. The honest systems analysts, operations researchers, or computer sales representatives are usually cautious
in their predictions, forthright in discussion costs, and critical of their systems capabilities. Such competent specialists
are helpful. Without them we would be unable to learn of
the new potential applications of statistical, mathematical,
sociological, and computerized tools of research.

It would be ludicrous to reject out-of-hand the many
real and proven advantages which a computer can bring when
judiciously applied. Much of the criticism and distrust of
computer systems is aimed at those systems in which computers operate on their own. When man and machine work
together in cooperative systems--in a symbiosis, as described
by Kemeny (19)--attitudes often change completely.

Dreyfus (20) ignores the many meretricious prophets,
concentrating instead on dissecting artificial intelligence and
synthesizing, evaluating, and countering the often speculative
and exaggerated views of the top level of the most prestigious
information scientists. Dreyfus shows that, in general, in
the areas of cognitive simulation such as language translation, problem solving, game playing, and pattern recognition
there has been a characteristic repeated pattern of early
dramatic, but often relatively minor, successes based on the
easy performance of simple tasks or of low-quality work on
complex tasks, grandiose promise and predictions, then dis-
appointments, diminishing returns, disenchantment and finally
silence as the research bogs down and the promises remain
unfulfilled. Dreyfus organizes and synthesizes a large amount
of information and presents it in an efficient manner.

What Dreyfus does to the hierarchy of dehumanizers
at the top of the information science pyramid, Hoos (21)
does to the systems analysts on the lower level--the level
most closely associated with the working information scientist and librarian. In her denunciations of systems analysis
she leaves herself exposed to severe criticisms. In her
overzealousness she often overgeneralizes and oversimplifies
and denounces some sensitive and highly placed systems,
organizations, and individuals.

Churchman (22) examines the validity of the "systems approach" in the climate of a debate. Conceding that
the systems in which we live are too complicated for our intellectual power and technology to understand, he concludes
that "we have every right to question whether any approach--
systems approach, humanist approach, artist's approach, engineering approach, religious approach, psychoanalytic ap-
proach--is the correct approach to the understanding of our
society" (22). He introduces applications of program planning and budgeting (PPB), management information systems,
planning and anti-planning. Wildavsky (23), in a witty and
provocative article, points out the failures of planning.

Librarians, traditionally concerned with people, are often considered utopians. In the late forties and fifties their world was suddenly invaded by (24), "new utopians, concerned with non-people and people-substitutes.... Their planning done with computer hardware, systems procedures, functional analyses, and heuristics...."

Churchman (25) reaches the frank conclusion that "it may very well be that operations researchers are solving the wrong problems because the existing system--for example, the library--may itself be faulty in its design with respect to the real clients."

In the last two decades the profession has witnessed the exhilaration of unparalleled rapid growth of information science and librarianship. Suddenly the profession faces a crucial time. There is the paradoxical situation of, on the one hand, statistical evidence, presented by Bourne, et al. (26), to the National Commission on Libraries and Information Science which implies that over 90% of blue collar workers, 85% of the retired, almost 70% of the unemployed, and, what is most startling, well over half of all students (primary, secondary, college) are still unserved by libraries and, on the other hand, of zero-funding or budget-vetoing at the national level for libraries and information science by a completely insensitive federal bureaucracy.

What Can Be Done?

It is not the intent here to propose scholarly new paradigms or utopian solutions. However, nobody will dispute the assertion that whatever can or will be done to help the profession can be done more quickly, more efficiently, more economically if information scientists and librarians begin to understand, communicate with, and cooperate with each other to a greater degree than they do now.

The proposals that follow are based on the view that the principal "raison d'être" for both information scientists and librarians is to bring together the information seeker (the human element) and the information sought. This contrasts starkly with Rosenberg's (27) observation about the "predominant preoccupation of information scientists with mechanical and deterministic solutions to information problems."

Librarians and information scientists are among the
key members of the fastest growing group of the nation's
work force--the group Drucker (28) calls "knowledge workers. " In a bold hypothesis Parker (29) even suggests that
already more than 50% of the labor activity in our post-
industrial society may be information processing rather than
industrial production. In fact, he further suggests a direct
relation between the current national economic crisis and the
rapid growth in the production of new knowledge and information and the rapidly changing information needs of society.

Now during the times of rising expectations and consciousness, countercultural revolutions, sensitivity training
and encounter groups, transactional analysis, job enrichment,
affirmative action programs, various liberation movements,
participative management, and other innovations, we must be
released from the boundaries of our habits of thought and accept the gamut of patterns possible in human interactions.
What is urgently needed as a starting point for our profession is an honest open dialogue between information scientists
and librarians on a regularly scheduled basis to discuss one
common element--the human one.

It is therefore suggested that continuing seminars be
established within one or more graduate library and/or information science school, to take place regularly, to which
information scientists and librarians would be invited to discuss the human element in information science and librarianship.   Until the seminars become reasonably well established,
the presentations would be invited ones.   Later, refereed
volunteer papers would be presented.   Perhaps the theme of
the first seminar could be the humanization of the information science aspects of the proposed network-oriented national
program of library and information science outlined by the
National Commission on Libraries and Information Science
(NCLIS).   Perhaps NCLIS could be persuaded to schedule and
support such a dialogue which could then become the nucleus
for a continuing series of such "humanization of information
science" encounters.

The second proposal is not as simple as the first.
Programs could be established at various schools, again with
the same main objective, i.e., the humanization of information science (and to a lesser degree, librarianship), in which
there would be an exchange of positions between faculty and
working librarians or information scientists, for a quarter
or a semester on a rotating basis.   The first to participate,

it is hoped, would be those faculty members who had never had the opportunity to experience the human element in a library or information science situation through a professional working level or administrative position. Excluded from consideration as fulfilling the requirement would be special tasks performed at libraries or information centers as consultants or while on special projects or while doing research on a special assignment. Discounted also would be library or information science positions held on a part-time basis, or employment while undergraduate or graduate students.

An additional benefit from such programs would be the opportunity to publish articles on overall experiences with the program. The benefits for information scientists of real-time, real-life experience with libraries and the human beings that use them or work in them, and vice versa, would be extremely valuable to participating faculty and their students.

It is believed that these proposals would help "return information science to a more reasonable position vis-a-vis library science" (27) and that they would bring information science "closer to humanistic concerns" (27). They would help to show, as Klempner (30) put it, that "the field of information science is concerned with both man and machine" and that "the humanist as well as the technologist can make worthwhile and significant contributions to this field. "

Literature Cited

1. Borko, H. "Information Science: What Is It?" American Documentation 19 (no. 1):3-5 (1968).
2. Cuadra, C. A. "Introduction to the ADI Annual Review." In Annual Review of Information Science and Technology. C. A. Cuadra, ed. v. 1. New York, John Wiley & Sons, 1966. p. 1-14.
3. Artandi, S. An Introduction to Computers in Information Science, 2d ed. Metuchen, N. J., Scarecrow Press, Inc. 1972. p. 16-17.
4. Horn, H. A. "A Separate Degree Program in Information Science: The Degree 'Master of Science' in Information Science at UCLA." Libri 18 (nos. 3-4): 283-311 (1968).
5. Shera, J. H. "Librarians Against Machines." Science 156 (no. 3776):746-750 (1967).
6. Vagianos, L. "Information Science: A House Built on

Sand." Library Journal 97 (no. 2):153-157 (1972).

7. Artandi, S. "Information Concepts and Their Utility."
Journal of the American Society for Information Science 24 (no. 4):242-245 (1973).

8. Heilprin, L. B. "Outline of a Theory of Information Science." Address on the occasion of the 1st anniversary of the establishment of the Special Interest Group on Foundations of Information Science (SIG/FIS), American Society for Information Science, Annual Meeting, Los Angeles, California, Oct. 24, 1973.

9. Williams, J. G. and C. Kim. "On Theory Development in Information Science." Journal of the American Society for Information Science 26 (no. 1):3-9 (1975).

10. Kuhn, T. The Structure of Scientific Revolutions. 2d ed., enl. Chicago, The University of Chicago Press, 1970.

11. Rosenberg, V. "The Scientific Premises of Information Science." Journal of the American Society for Information Science 25 (no. 4):263-269 (1974).

12. Watson, D. L. Scientists Are Human. London, Watts and Company, 1933.

13. Harmon, W. Alternative Futures and Educational Policy, ERIC #6747-6, prepared for Bureau of Research, U.S. Office of Education by Stanford Research Institute (Feb. 1970).

14. Roszak, T. Where the Wasteland Ends: Politics and Transcendence in Post-Industrial Society. Garden City, N.Y., Doubleday & Company, Inc., 1972. p. 34.

15. Mason, E. "Brother, Can You Spare a Dime?" Unpublished paper presented at: Survival! An Institute on the Impact of Change on the Individual Librarian, Sixth Annual Institute of Library Institutes Planning Committee, Palo Alto, Calif., Nov. 2-3, 1973.

16. Kountz, J. Untitled presentation at: Survival! An Institute on the Impact of Change on the Individual Librarian, Sixth Annual Institute of Library Institutes Planning Committee, Palo Alto, Calif., Nov. 2-3, 1973.

17. Griffen, A. M. and J. P. Hall. "Social Indicators and Library Change." Library Journal 97 (no. 17):3120-3123 (1972).

18. Mason, E. "The Sobering Seventies: Prospects for Change." Library Journal 97 (no. 17):3115-3119 (1972).

19. Kemeny, J. G. Man and the Computer. New York, Charles Scribner's Sons, 1972. p. 10-13.
20. Dreyfus, H. L. What Computers Can't Do: A Critique of Artificial Reason. New York, Harper and Row, 1972. p. 3-11; 12-40; 197-210.
21. Hoos, I. R. Systems Analysis in Public Policy. Berkeley, Calif., University of California Press, 1972.
22. Churchman, C. W. The Systems Approach. New York, Dell Publishing Co., Inc., 1968. p. x-xi.
23. Wildavsky, A. "If Planning Is Everything, Maybe It's Nothing." Policy Sciences 4 (no. 2):127-153 (1973).
24. Boguslaw, R. The New Utopians--A Study of System Design and Social Change. Englewood Cliffs, N.J., Prentice-Hall, Inc., 1965.
25. Churchman, C. W. "Operations Research Prospects for Libraries: The Realities and Ideals." Library Quarterly 42 (no. 1):6-14 (1972).
26. Bourne, C. P., V. Rosenberg, M. J. Bates, and G. R. Perolman. Preliminary Investigation of Present and Potential Library and Information Science Needs. Berkeley, Calif., University of California, Institute of Library Research, Feb. 1973.
27. Rosenberg, V. "The Teaching of Information Science to Nonscientists." Journal of Education for Librarianship 13 (no. 2):94-103 (1972).
28. Drucker, P. F. "Managing the Knowledge Worker." Wall Street Journal 16 (Nov. 7, 1975).
29. Parker, E. B. and M. Porat. Social Implications of Computer/Telecommunications Systems. Stanford Univ. 1974 (ERIC ED 102978).
30. Klempner, I. M. "Information Science Unlimited? ... A Position Paper." American Documentation 20 (no. 4):339-343 (1969).

PUBLISHERS VERSUS LIBRARIES:
SOME HIDDEN DIMENSIONS
IN THE CURRENT DEBATE*

Walter J. Fraser

Two apologies are owed the audience at the beginning
of this speech.

First, it does not begin with a joke. It would have
been nice to have had one; but I could neither think of one
nor find one. This is a session about "libraries" in a conference on scientific journals and this is a double bind. Almost a decade ago, when invited to speak about the automation of serials, I searched my memory and the literature of
librarianship for something humorous with which I could begin my remarks. The only thing I found, at that date, that
even connected libraries, periodicals, and humor were some
remarks by Don Culbertson, now at Argonne National Labora-
tories. He had made a similar search, found nothing, and
concluded that, to a librarian, periodicals are just not funny.
Neither my professional experience nor my reading in the
succeeding decade has done anything to challenge that position. As a matter of fact, periodicals are, if anything,
much less funny to librarians in the 1970s than in the 1960s.

Part of the reason that journals are less funny today
than in years past is that librarians now find their efforts
to make such items available subject to attack from publishers, who wish to employ the sanctions of the copyright law
to make librarians' efforts ineffective. As the copyright law
has provision for fines, treble damages, and jail terms, it
is difficult for librarians to view this attack as even vaguely
humorous. [1]

*Reprinted by permission from IEEE Transactions on Profes-
sional Communication, Vol. PC-18, No. 3, Sept. 1975, pp.
200-206. Copyright © 1975 by the Institute of Electrical and
Electronics Engineers.

Having mentioned the current controversy between publishers and librarians, I am led to the second of my two promised apologies. I must ask your indulgence in relation to the subtitle for this paper, "Some Hidden Dimensions in the Current Debate." Earlier this year, just before being asked to plan my talk here, I had been reading quite a few articles on the copyright controversy which seemed to me to miss several rather important aspects of the whole debate. With that rashness which is proverbially ascribed to fools rather than angels I wrote down that my remarks would reveal some hitherto "hidden dimensions" in the debate. That phrase, hidden dimensions, has plagued me ever since. Each reference I checked, each article I stumbled across since writing those words, has contained one or several of my hidden dimensions. At this point it seems likely that even the few hidden dimensions which were not conspicuous in the articles I checked must be present in the literature somewhere. At least that is the way I felt when preparing this speech before the conference; but, having been here and listened to some of the earlier presentations and discussions, I am concerned anew that some of the things that seem clear to librarians are actually hidden to others. Since this conference is intended to provide a forum for people of diverse backgrounds, what I would like to offer is a summary of librarians' positions in the debate. I no more represent all librarians than the spokesmen of William and Wilkins represent all copyright holders; so what is being offered here is one librarian's view of the debate.

Having offered the caveat that my insights are neither universally hidden nor universally accepted, it is nonetheless disconcerting to this librarian that many of the articles on this controversy read as though there were only two participants. Two examples might help. Last November, Richard R. Lingerman in the New York Times Book Review column, "Last Word,"[2] attacked the Court of Claims decision in Williams and Wilkins Company vs. The United States.[3] The villains clearly were the librarians and the beleaguered heroes were the publishers and the authors, whose interests were viewed as coincidental with those of the publishers. In the same month, Publishers Weekly printed Barbara Ringer's Bowker Memorial Lecture for 1974, "The Demonology of Copyright."[4] Ms. Ringer is currently the U. S. Registrar of Copyrights and, in addition, an internationally recognized authority on copyright. Nonetheless, the piece reprinted in Publishers Weekly emphasized the author's interest in the copyright controversy and mentioned the publisher's position

very infrequently.   Perhaps a few quotes will help to convey
the thrust of her remarks:

> I believe that it is society's duty to go as
> far as it can in nurturing the atmosphere in which
> authors and other creative artists can flourish. [5]

While she does refer to the need for dissemination, she also
says that

> ... it seems to me that, in the long pull, it is
> more important for a generation to produce a hand-
> ful of great creative works than to shower its
> school-children with unauthorized photocopies. [6]

Later, in discussing "Copyright's Ultimate Goals,"
Ms. Ringer lists one:

> ... which may be the most important copyright
> goal of all.   It can be stated very simply: a sub-
> stantial increase in the rights of the author, con-
> sidered not as a copyright owner but as a separate
> creative individual.   It involves a recognition that
> committees don't create works and machines don't
> create works.   If for the sake of convenience, of
> companies or societies or governments, the copy-
> right law forces individual authors back into a col-
> lective straightjacket or makes them into human
> writing machines, it will indeed have become a
> tool of the devil. [7]

Quotations such as these were what originally prompted
me to assert that some aspects of the debate were hidden.

Admittedly, both Lingerman and Ringer were discussing all authors and all publications; but many librarians reading these and similar remarks feel that the problem is not
being discussed in real world terms.   Certainly not in real
world terms if the literature of science and technology is being discussed.   This feeling may have also communicated itself to the majority of the Court of Claims in Williams and
Wilkins vs. The United States.   The court noted in its decision that some of the authors of the representative articles
which were specifically the subject of litigation testified at
the trial that they were in favor of photocopying as an aid to
the advancement of science and knowledge. [8]   The court also
noted that medical society authors, with rare exception, are
not paid for contributions to such journals. [9]

This then is the dimension hidden from Lingerman and Ringer. In broad classes of literature, copyright is of little financial interest to the author. This dimension seems to many librarians to receive inadequate discussion, particularly in relation to the production of scientific materials. It might be helpful in this connection to review the usual status of the scientific-technical author. The author-researcher is usually forced to surrender all rights to the publisher as a condition of publication. This practice is so pervasive that the surrender is often never explicitly agreed to by the author but implied by his submission of material for publication. The enforced surrender of copyright by the author-researcher is certainly one of the most pervasive practices in all scholarly publishing. The researcher, having surrendered all rights, is then frequently requested to pay page charges to get his material published at all. Usually, the author is not only not paid, but also charged for reprints. Whatever case can be made for broadening the traditional meaning of copyright in this society, it seems difficult to support any contention that the abrogation of fair use would be of any immediate financial benefit to the author-researcher of scientific-technical materials. In Williams and Wilkins vs. The United States and in much of the debate, the party most loudly defending the author seems to be the publisher who has charged him to publish.

While Ms. Ringer does mention the schoolchildren on whom, according to her, it is unimportant to shower photocopies, Lingerman never seems to see any user of photocopies beyond the librarians. Indeed, in much of the discussion, it never does seem to come out that librarians are not in fact copying for other librarians. Even in the case of so-called systematic copying involved in interlibrary loan, even in the case of the respectable numbers of copies made at the National Library of Medicine, each of those photocopies has been and is made in response to a specific request from a specific member of the public. And that member of the public could, if he or she chose, write to the publisher for that photocopy. Most individuals would probably not write; but if a small percent did, most publishers would find it financially unrewarding to deal with the volume of paper work. The Court of Claims noted that Williams and Wilkins, up to the time of the suit, published a notice to the effect that it did not attempt to keep back issues and that requests for reprints should be directed to the authors of the articles.[10] Parenthetically, it should be noted that after the suit, Williams and Wilkins made an agreement with, I be-

lieve, the Institute for Scientific Information (ISI) of Philadelphia to supply offprints, photocopies, etc., of articles.
If that information is not correct, there are enough representatives of ISI here today to insure prompt correction.
Before proceeding further it seems well to emphasize the
main point. Libraries photocopy articles not for themselves,
but for users. Users who in the case of scientific and technological literature may be and often are researcher-authors
themselves.

In addition to authors and users, the two more frequently discussed participants in the debate are the libraries
and the publishers. The libraries speak with many voices,
but, in many cases, have indicated some willingness to ac-
cede to the publishers' recent demands for royalties for copies, if some reasonable collection system could be designed.
However, Nicholas Henry has estimated that at least one
such system might carry a price tag of $300 million for the
clerical work alone. 11 The principal common position of librarians, in my candid opinion, is one of fear. Librarians
fear that they would have to pass such costs along to their
users, resulting in a reduction of patronage, or absorb them
resulting in--well, in nothing that we librarians can really
see at all in an era when our traditional budgets buy so
much less and require so much more effort to wrest from
those who fund our operations. Librarians fear that such
costs would constitute a burden which would destroy the effectiveness of any conceivable system of dissemination of
scientific-technical information. A collection system that is
very expensive to administer would be almost as effective a
constraint on traditional copying as a legal prohibition.

The publishers assert that they do not wish to prohibit photocopying but merely to profit from it. But at the
time Williams and Wilkins went to court, the law was clear.
The copyright holder who could exact a charge could prohibit
any copying at all. Indeed, copying without his express prior
permission was actionable. No publishers' clearinghouse
existed; there was no provision for compulsory licensing; and
each librarian across the country would have had to personally contact each publisher or every journal and get prior
permission for each copying action. The result would have
been a prohibition on traditional copying in libraries. Even
if the librarians could find the amateurs who publish many
high quality scientific journals but are difficult to track down
for missing issues, the expense involved in obtaining the permission, and paying the royalty, and clerically monitoring

each page copied, would have been monumental regardless of
whether the requisite permission was forthcoming at all and
irrespective of the actual amount of the royalty payment demanded. The result of a Williams and Wilkins victory, up
to now, would have been the strangulation of the historic scientific-technical information dissemination system.

Publishers say that the libraries should pay a larger
share of the cost of disseminating scientific and technical information. Librarians believe that the inflated institutional
rates which they have been paying for scientific and technical
journals constitute a major, perhaps the major, subsidy of
the scientific and technical information dissemination system.
Librarians begin to despair that any amount of money will
be enough. Librarians begin to fear that the logic of the
publishers' arguments will only be satisfied when libraries
no longer exist.

That leaves us with the publishers. They seem to
be saying that if they don't get more money there won't be
any scientific journals. This particular librarian is bemused
by their expectation that the additional revenue should come
from libraries. This particular librarian is bemused by
the publishers' bland assumption that the other participants
in the system must continually make larger payments to
them, the publishers. The publishers of scientific and technical journals have charged the author to print, they charge
the reader, they charge the libraries (much higher rates as
a rule), then they have charged the authors for reprints.
It would seem that the publishers' only recourse may be to
devise ways of charging the paper manufacturers, the printers, and the U.S. Mails: then everybody would pay the publisher.

In Look Homeward, Angel, Thomas Wolfe, instead of
just giving the customary disclaimer that no references were
intended to persons living or dead, wrote a beautiful piece
on the nature of the novel. He admitted weaving his past
with his fiction but asserted that he mediated no man's portrait and went on to assure those who had known him that
he wrote from middle distance without rancor or bitter in-
tention. Unfortunately, I cannot offer all those assurances
today. I do not speak from middle distance but from a position of fear. My fear is that the publishers' assault on fair
use is just the beginning of a more fundamental assault on
the very concept of libraries. That basic concept is that
readers may band together to make multiple use of a single
purchase.

Perhaps this last fear can be defended in advance
from accusations of paranoia by reference to some quoted
remarks. Some of these remarks cause me pain as well as
fear because they have been attributed to Dr. Eugene Garfield. As an information scientist, I am quite sensible of
the debt which the entire field owes Gene Garfield. My students all seem to believe, in error, that he invented citation
indexing. In this case, however, their error is profound,
because Gene Garfield did in effect "invent" citation indexing
as far as modern, nonlegal bibliographic practices goes.
In addition, he is responsible for several other innovations
which are so well known as to not require listing here.
Nonetheless, in spite of his reputation, or perhaps because
of it, the summary of his remarks as board chairman of the
Information Industry Association (IIA) before the National
Commission on Libraries and Information Science (NCLIS)
that was published in American Libraries[12] did engender
fear. According to the summary, Dr. Garfield stated cate-
gorically that "user-based charges must inevitably prevail."
He was quoted as deprecating

> ... the depression type psychology that dominated
> library training [and that] cultivated the concept
> that library service should be a labor of love and
> that service to the user should be free. [13]

Fear has also been created among librarians by an
earlier American Libraries[14] summary of an IIA draft statement which was not delivered at NCLIS but circulated, according to IIA's then executive director, Paul G. Zurkowski,
as "... an admittedly provocative piece written to stimulate
member company thinking."[15] The internal, unused draft,
as reported on by American Libraries, introduced the concept of the "for-profit library" called the "information supermarket" complete with "parking meters" to assess fees for
time spent in the reading room. It did suggest some free
service. Students were to be issued "information vouchers"
for a limited period of time only for the purpose of training
and introduction to the "real world" kind of information for
which charges would be exacted from all. [16]

It should be remembered here that what is being discussed is fear. Fear on the part of librarians. To understand that fear it is not necessary that the reports mentioned
earlier be true. It is merely necessary to understand that
librarians believe that such assertions constitute the real aim
of the publishing world. Quite clearly, Fay Blake, Lecturer,

School of Librarianship, University of California, Berkeley, and Edith Perlmutter, Assistant Professor of Economics, Loyola University, Los Angeles, did believe that such statements typified the intent of the publishing community. In a January 1974 article in Library Journal titled "Libraries in the Marketplace," they cited and rejected the suggestions attributed to Garfield and Zurkowski.[17] In February 1975 Richard De Gennaro, Director of Libraries, University of Pennsylvania, also writing in Library Journal, described the earlier Blake-Perlmutter article as emotionally charged. De Gennaro, writing with the title, "Pay Libraries and User Charges," seemed a good deal less fearful and suggested that libraries of the future might have some sort of mix of services made up of those for which charges are assessed as well as those which are free.[18] He had some other things to say which I would like to reserve for the moment, since the main thrust of these remarks parallels that of his paper.

A great deal has been said up to now about fear. I should not like to leave you with the picture of the librarians of the world cringing behind their bookcases. They see themselves as providing a useful social service; and attacks, such as the ones retailed above, seem to them to be unfair and destructive of an institution which they perceive as having social worth. They further see themselves, in relation to our reasons for being together today, as providing a vital link in the chain of scientific and technical information dissemination. They fear that if their institution is altered in the direction suggested, the entire system would be deleteriously affected.

The Court of Claims decision in Williams and Wilkins vs. The United States has been criticized as bad law, but librarians would agree with one of its findings of fact. The court concluded as a finding of fact that a library is essential to the conduct of medical research.[19] Most librarians would go further and assert that a library is essential to all scientific and technical research.

Librarians believe that their institution is based on the fact that scientific and technical materials are expensive in relation to the income of researchers and that libraries have been established to facilitate multiple use of the items purchased. Furthermore, librarians believe that such multiple use of purchases is legal, moral, and clearly within the public interest.

Librarians believe that charging for user services would inevitably stratify the use of information and intensify class differentials within the society.

Publishers, defending the very high institutional rates they charge libraries, frequently produce graphs such as the one offered by Art Herschman, then Director of Information at the American Institute of Physics, at the last meeting of this group.[20] That graph shows clearly that individuals drop out of the market for individual purchase of information products very rapidly as the price increases. Librarians wonder about the strength of individual, personal, economic demand for information services. The question here is not need, but the amount of money individuals have and are willing to spend for information services. If individuals were really willing to pay high prices for information services, the publishers might now be able to derive a larger portion of their income from individual subscriptions. Their financially sobering experience has been that individual, economic demand does drop very rapidly with each price increase. In view of the publishers' experience, their proposals that libraries subsist on direct user charges hardly seems comforting to librarians.

In this light, it may be understood that librarians are skeptical about the joys of the information supermarket with parking meters in the reading rooms. They are skeptical because such systems have repeatedly been tried and have failed. Subscription and/or circulating libraries were tried both in Europe and on the North American continent before the American Revolution. In the early days of the new republic they may have been the dominant form of library service. They have long since ceased to dominate the American library scene. They ceased to dominate because of the fitful and undependable income they were able to generate. And contrary to the myths of the IIA, subscription libraries ceased to dominate before the coming of the public library and not because of it. The very existence of the free public library is a function of the fact that information supermarkets could not do the job even without any competition from free libraries.

Librarians are bemused by the repeated assertion that they believe that information is free. On the contrary, it would seem that the free public library is a reflection of widespread acceptance of the idea that information is costly, too costly for individuals to be able to obtain as much as they need. The free public library's existence indicates clearly that citizens have been convinced that information costs are beyond the means of individuals and that the provision of information is a corporate, public responsibility. Even suburban New Jersey communities (such as the one I live in), which do not governmentally support a fire department, support free public libraries. The concept of the corporate purchase of a few copies of costly material for economic use by a number of individuals is the philosophy behind all libraries, public, academic, and special.

Before leaving the wonderful world of the information supermarket, it should be made clear that librarians believe that this idea would be a disservice to the scientific and technical community. We are generally, and I am in particular, unable to convince ourselves that the information supermarkets of this world would find it economically advantageous to cater to the poor individual or to service scientific and technical specialties which do not boast large numbers of workers willing and able to pay personally for each piece of information which they need to read. In short, some people and some ideas would be priced out of the market.

Public and academic librarians, with a great deal of reluctance, have been forced to charge directly for some services, for instance, photocopying. But, where resources are adequate and the funders are interested in promoting the use of information, as in most special library situations, the institution bears such costs, and each service is free of personal charge to the user.

Librarians are also bemused by assertions that giving free services is unfair competition with the information industry. De Gennaro, in his February 1975 Library Journal article, reviews some of the remarks attributed to Gene Garfield and observes that

> Garfield asks how anyone can make money selling information if libraries are permitted to continue to give it away free. Well, libraries were here first giving away information before there was any question that it might be profitable to sell it. No one disputes Garfield's right to sell information, but it is hard for librarians to understand why they should not be permitted to 'compete' with him, and why tax support for libraries should be withdrawn in favor, perhaps, of subsidies for the private sector. [21]

Librarians, working in institutions which were legal
before the Constitution and copyright laws were written and
which have been legal for 200 years since the Constitution
was written, wonder if new times really demand that these
documents should now be read as forbidding the multiple use
of a purchaser's copy and, by extension, forbidding the existence of all libraries.

What I have been saying here may have sounded as
though I have been taking an adversary position. I have,
but I haven't taken the publishers to court; I haven't threatened them with treble damages and a jail term. If things
continue as they have in the recent past, what seems likely
is that the adversary relationship between librarians and publishers will continue and deepen. Again, while much has
been made of the fears of librarians in these remarks, publishers should be warned that not all librarians are palsied
with terror. Institutions which, mutatis mutandis, have
existed since Babylonia are unlikely to depart from the
scene without a struggle.

Librarians have yet to take a publisher to court; but,
somewhere, there may be a librarian unabashed enough to
go to court with a scholarly journal over the issue of differential pricing. If the adversary nature of the relationship continues, some other librarian may meditate on the
Constitutional purpose of the copyright power, i. e. , "to
promote the progress of science and the useful arts...."
And, after meditating, that librarian may be brash enough
to suggest to the courts that the public interest is not served
by allowing publishers to retain control over out-of-print
materials and that such materials should be in the public
domain. The suggestions above may not sound persuasive
this afternoon; but, if copying which has been legal for 200
years is suddenly now illegal, maybe the librarians' lawyers
can devise some new illegalities.

De Gennaro has some wise and conciliatory comments:

> Perhaps, we take ourselves and each other
> too seriously. We need some perspective. All
> signs indicate that our 'industry' is being put
> through the economic wringer by forces that we
> did not create and that we cannot control. Li-
> brary photocopying of copyrighted materials is
> not the cause of the publishers' economic woes;

libraries' giving away free services in competition
with certain commercial vendors is not the true
cause of their profit problems; and the diversion
of some public money to subsidize certain for-
profit information activities is not the cause of
acute budget crises that libraries are experiencing.
The information industry, of which libraries are
also a part, does not exist in a vacuum; it is part
of the national and international economies which
are experiencing very serious dislocations. This
is the true source of our problems. It does us no
good to blame each other or to try to profit at each
other's expense. We are allies, not adversaries;
our interests are complementary, not competing. [22]

Earlier, I apologized for not speaking from middle
distance and without rancor. I would now assert that I do
indeed speak without bitter intent. Even though I have taken
an adversary stance today, I agree with De Gennaro. I believe that the adversary stance, if long continued, will hurt
us all. If the publishers continue to attack libraries in
court, they can expect attacks back eventually. The hard
things that I have said today should be taken as an attempt
to lay out quite clearly the level of anxiety that librarians
are now feeling. We have to reduce that level of anxiety.
If we can stop going to court over these problems and start
talking together about them and make a united request for
the funding which the dissemination system requires, we may
all find our problems eased. Librarians need to remember
that publishers may indeed be telling the truth when they assert that they are being put out of business. If our interests
are those of the scientific community, then we need to remember that society at large has an interest in the dissemination of scientific and technical information. United, publishers, author-researchers, librarians, technologically based
industries, and other users might be able to convince the
legislatures of the land that information does indeed cost
something and that all of us need support if the scientific,
technological, and human environment in which we are all
trapped is to be serviced, improved, or even maintained.
But, if the publishers continue to take us on, they may find
that more and more librarians and their supporters in every
city and town across the land will also assume an adversary
position. And that could be nothing but bad for the publishers, the libraries, and the future of scientific and technical
information dissemination in this country.

Notes

1. In the discussion which follows presentation of this paper,
    several comments were made about the fact that pro-
    ceedings under the copyright statute are civil rather
    than criminal proceedings. The author's slight ex-
    posure to legal matters leaves him convinced that
    reading laws demands professional competence. Both
    before and after speaking, the author has relied on
    the copy of the copyright law as amended which was
    reprinted as Appendix 1 in Copyright--the Librarian
    and the Law (Proceedings of the 8th Annual Symposi-
    um, sponsored by the Alumni and the Faculty of the
    Rutgers University Graduate School of Library Ser-
    vice), George J. Lukac, ed. (New Brunswick, N. J. :
    1972). Any naive reading of the law would support
    the publishers' current contention that all copying of
    any sort without prior permission is prohibited. But
    the 1909 law was written with the assistance of the
    Librarian of Congress, Herbert Putnam, who was al-
    so one of its principal public sponsors, and Putnam's
    library permitted copying throughout his tenure which
    only ended in 1939. Obviously the text cannot be our
    only guide. Again on naive reading, the sections out-
    lining the harsh penalties mentioned in the text are
    prescribed for particular types of abuse. But the
    law, and this is one of the points being emphasized
    in the text, does have sharp teeth. Furthermore, in
    any resort to the courts the plaintiff is clearly seek-
    ing to have his position backed by the full majesty
    and coercive power of the state. The salient point
    then, is that by going to court over this matter Wil-
    liams and Wilkins voluntarily left the arena of polite
    discussion in an appeal to force. Had they won, it
    is impossible for this nonlawyer to know which of the
    available penalties they and other copyright holders
    would have requested and been granted in future ac-
    tions against libraries and librarians.
2. New York Times Book Review, p. 63, Nov. 17, 1974;
    and New York Times Book Review, p. 47, Nov. 24,
    1974.
3. Williams and Wilkins Company v. The United States,
    U. S. Court of Claims, no. 73-68 (decided Nov. 27,
    1973).
4. Publishers Weekly; vol. 206, pp. 26-30, Nov. 18, 1974.
5. Ibid., p. 26.
6. Ibid., pp. 26-27.

7. Ibid., p. 30.
8. Williams and Wilkins v. The United States, op. cit., p. 23.
9. Ibid.
10. Ibid., p. 19, footnote 17.
11. N. L. Henry, "Copyright, public policy, and information technology," Science; vol. 183, p. 390, Feb. 1, 1974.
12. "IIA Urges User Fees for Libraries in NCLIS Testimony." American Libraries; vol. 4, p. 335, June 1973.
13. Ibid.
14. "Information industry promotes libraries 'for-profit,'" American Libraries; vol. 4, pp. 79-80, Feb. 1973.
15. P. B. Zurkowski, "Protestations," American Libraries (letter to the editor), vol. 4, p. 258, May 1973.
16. "Information industry promotes libraries 'for-profit,'" op. cit., pp. 79-80.
17. Library J., vol. 99; pp. 108-111, Jan. 15, 1974.
18. Library J., vol. 100; pp. 363-367, Feb. 15, 1975.
19. Williams and Wilkins v. the United States, op. cit., p. 79, finding no. 13.
20. "Session V: Roundup and critique," IEEE Trans. Pro. Commun., vol. PC-16; p. 159, Sept. 1973.
21. Library J., vol. 100, p. 365, Feb. 15, 1975.
22. Ibid., p. 367.

THE MEDIA JARGON JOYRIDE:
PROGRESS BACKWARDS*

Leonard H. Freiser

Today, while the rest of the country is trying to find
out why so many of our young people cannot read nor write,
the school media specialists have exorcised books and libraries. In the January issue of the Wilson Library Bulletin, a "media-minded educator" writes that: "... Those
persons presently known as librarians must also accept new
roles. They must become learning facilitators and minimize the observable role of 'keepers of books' (p. 394). "
Further, she teaches that, "Media ... is an amalgamation
of objects, models, life realities, live representatives, real
or magical experiences, print materials, simulations, charts,
sound effects, and all visual, aural, and tactile resources of
multiple descriptions and uses (p. 392). "

All of this is easy to lampoon, but who among us can
afford the luxury? The schools have our children, and it is
disquieting to have to remind library and media specialists
that reading is important--frightening to realize that many
disagree. (A media director at this preconference claimed
that reading is "elitist. ")

The problem is not that schools use films and electronic equipment, but that they blur intellectual and aesthetic
distinctions when they adopt communications analogies from
industry. The notion that watching television and reading a
book are merely parts of a process is a denial of the unique-
ness and values of both forms. This doctrine, as it operates in the schools, is also patronizing and mischievous:
invoking McLuhan and future-schlock writers to deny that

*Reprinted from School Library Journal, Vol. 23, No. 2,
Oct. 1976, pp. 80-81. Published by R. R. Bowker Co. (a
Xerox company). Copyright © 1976 by Xerox Corporation.

reading and writing are essential to thought, essential to inquiry, and essential to education. The effects of television on children have been studied and reported on, but I wonder if we have begun to understand its effects on educators, particularly on school librarians. I believe we have been had. McLuhan, the professor of English, the Joycean scholar, announced that the new technology would help us understand the old--he was wrong. We still do not understand the book.

Why do school librarians apologize for books? "The library is more than just books," has become their rallying cry. The answer could be that they see the book as a teaching device, in the same way that they see slide projectors and plastic overlays. The library becomes "more than just books" when it is no longer a library, but a place where the teaching tools are: a media center, a toolroom. If these workrooms help students, let us have them--but we cannot afford to have them displace the library. What we lose is irreplaceable: an opportunity for children to have access to book collections and to be in a place that is not determined by educational technology but by the pleasure of reading.

In criticizing the language of the media movement, I am well aware that its roots are in the jargon of education and in industrial and military management. Here are some examples of this typical jargon: input, parameters of instructional design, maximize, minimize, transmittal process, teaching strategies, learning facilitators, and interface. As librarians and readers, as filmmakers and film buffs, as photographers, and as television producers, we have abandoned ourselves to a bloodless pedantry.

To those who may say that this is quibbling, that it is merely a question of semantics, I ask that you consider that our language represents our ideas and the quality and flavor of our thought. Media jargon levels all forms and works of expression to the mechanics of teaching machines. The language and practices of the school media movement have had a negative influence on the use of literature and books in the schools and, ironically, have done little to help the students' understanding of films, photography, and television.

As teachers, as school librarians, we are concerned about the effects of TV on children, or how to use TV in the school curriculum and in library programs. A number of us are also concerned about being caught napping in the midst of change, or being left outside the "communications revolution." What is this interest in media all about, and what is media?

In 1975, the American Association of School Librarians (ASSL) and the Association for Educational Communications and Technology (AECT) issued Media Programs: District and School, a 128-page set of standards, with only one reference to books in its index. It defines media as: "... all of the forms and channels used in the transmittal process. The point at which an information transfer or exchange occurs is an interface. The media program, therefore, can be described as patterns of interfacings among program components, e.g., people, materials, machines, facilities, and environments managed by media professionals who establish and maintain relationships between or among the components (p. 110-11)." Although this allows the media professional a wide latitude in establishing relationships, Media Programs... does not evoke Alice's looking-glass or Huck's raft.

Looking back, we can see that there were a number of reasons for the AASL and the AECT to join forces. The library and the audiovisual practitioners in schools were both involved in direct support of classroom instruction. Librarians taught library skills and helped students with their assignments. Audiovisual people ran the projectors and made transparencies (these teachers occasionally introduced students to the art of the film, but their professional interests were with equipment and instructional materials). And although a number of librarians worked with the child as reader, too many acted as if their sole responsibility was to supply lesson materials--a unit on climate or transportation took precedence over the discovery of books.

The postwar boom in film and electronics gave audiovisual teachers (then predominantly male) more equipment and larger budgets to play with. This also gave them greater standing in the school hierarchy and served to put them a notch above the school librarians (traditionally female). The librarians felt threatened: they feared that administrators would lump both groups together and put the audiovisual men in charge. With this writing on the wall, libraries soon had collections of software and closets of hardware. Audiovisual teachers, in the meantime, found respectability in the "parameters of instructional design" and in similar concerns of the education profession.

The '60s brought Federal largess to the schools and a
bonanza for the education industries. Every conceivable
combination of films, slides, plastic novelties, tapes, models
--a peddler's pack--was sold to the schools, sometimes at
the last hour of the government deadline for spending. If the
product was advertised "to meet a curriculum need," it was
purchased. Schools had lots of money to spend and limited
time in which to spend it; evaluating the material before it
was put into the school was not always possible. The purchases wound up in the library, in the instructional materials center, and also in the classroom. School administrators,
however, preferred to have this inventory under a single control. Therefore, in order to survive and to justify their
growing share of the school's budget, the librarians and the
audiovisual teachers developed their own rationales for a uni-
fied program. Out of this came the "media center," an
amalgam of products and activities dedicated to communication and to the proposition that all forms of communication
are of equal weight.

Part of the impetus for the programs of the '60s
came from educators who wished to modify the highly structured classroom and curriculum in order to instruct children
on an individual basis. At that time, the library was ideally
suited for this purpose. Where classroom structure directs
students, the library calls for self-direction; where the classroom is part and parcel of the school, the library transcends
its locale. Ironically, as libraries were caught up by waves
of innovation, they gave way to the directed and instructional
milieu of the media center--they progressed backwards.

Educators do not understand books when they use them
as teaching tools. That's not what books are. The love and
the mastery of language, of ideas, of books, stands with the
foundations and goals of education, not with its hardware.
A library does not support a curriculum, the curriculum supports the library. The curriculum succeeds when students
realize that the library is the cathedral of their mind, the
definition of their civilization, the spinal column of their
freedom--that without the language of literature they are not
human--and the library is a celebration of their humanness.
Is it possible that as educated people we know this, but as
librarians we do not?

How can we, as librarians, say that we are not librarians, that libraries no longer exist? How did we adopt
standards that read like a bastard child of an education text
and a SONY catalog?

In this year of celebration, I call upon the AASL to adopt new standards, written in English and on one page. Something like this:

> By design and function, school libraries celebrate language, ideas, and books. The selection of school principals is based upon their understanding of libraries. School librarians are selected from book people who can get children and books together. Librarians are different from one another and each library is different from the next. A child does not need a basic collection, but the basic discovery of the triumphs and disappointments of human intelligence. The library shall be carpeted.

This is a reasonable statement of standards. It provides the child with a distinctive place to discover and enjoy books. The guidance of knowledgeable and sympathetic adults is available. The statement is only 76 words long; it even has a hint of philosophy and a touch of interior decorating. It talks of books, but what of films, photography, television?

Certainly all three should be available to children. They can appreciate and work in photography, film, and television, as they now do in art, dance, drama, and music. I would hope that we could provide them with the proper space for these arts--studios and darkrooms.

But we can violate space as well as endow it. A library alive with books and a studio bustling with activity are endowed spaces. But space is violated when studios, classrooms, viewing rooms, workshops, reading rooms are all merged. The excitement generated by the different activities in their own space is lost in this melting pot--in a space with a severe identity crisis.

What about instructional materials? Instruction belongs in the classroom, not in the library. I am talking about instruction, not learning. Wherever instruction takes place in the schools, you have a classroom. When you give over the library to instruction and instructors, you lose the only library you have and what you gain is only another classroom. And when librarians do this, they are not telling the world that the library is more than books, but that it is less than a classroom.

THE "BACK TO BASICS" CONTROVERSY*

Robert F. Hogan and Stephen Judy

We don't know what news dominated the front page of
The Washington Post on Thursday, May 20, 1976. Nor do
we recall the articles on page one of The Post's separate
Virginia section. But we do know what was on page eight of
the Virginia section. We saved that. Latticed across the
page is a series of tables listing the school by school
achievement scores for Fairfax County. In almost every
category, the students are above the 50th percentile. Consequently, the report is on page eight of the Virginia section, scrunched into microscopic type. The moral is clear:
good scores don't make good news stories. If Fairfax County wants to make page one, it will have to do much worse.

But all right, the test results from other districts
are not such happy ones. Let's grant that point for a moment, and ask why. The popular logic says it's because
the kids can't read, can't write, and can't 'rithmetic, and
the solution is the "back to basics" movement. Now that's
the kind of reasoning people can understand. Direct, simple,
no complexities, no ambiguities, no cautions. It's the logic
of hype: Fred the football flash won't give you a tumble?
Don't waste your bucks on those trendy threads. Swish
your teeth in whitewash. Then watch Fred stop in his
tracks.

It's not that simple, of course, not even for Fred
and Heart-throb. It's much less simple for raising student
achievement. We don't want to douse everybody's fireworks,
but there are some questions that need to be asked of the
"back to basics" group. Can it be proved that low test
scores mean low achievement levels? And if in some in-

---

*Reprinted by permission from Media & Methods, Vol. 13,
No. 1, Sept. 1976, pp. 17-18, 54-56.

stances this can be demonstrated convincingly, might the
drop in skills perhaps be attributed to roots other than recent changes in educational content and process? Are we
jumping from symptom to cure without asking what the cause
might be? It's worth wondering about.

Let's follow, for the moment, the validity of some
scores. Strong forces affect these scores that the public
has not heard much about. For example, the average daily
attendance rate is now higher than ever before. If we check
the 1973 statistics in last year's World Almanac, we find
that during that year nearly ten per cent more school age
children attended class on any given day than did, say, in
1960. The increase is not in the lower grades, where enrollment is dropping off, but in the higher grades. One
probable reason is that as the high school diploma becomes
a more universal minimum job prerequisite, more and more
kids who might have dropped out at age 16 are now staying
to finish high school. While we're glad to see them stay,
we must recognize that they are often from the lower achievement levels and will therefore pull down any broadly based
test scores.

Another probably little known variable that affects
test scores is fluctuation in family size. The research into
the effect of birth order on I.Q. and achievement is massive. An interesting roundup report appeared in "The End
of the IQ Slump" by Carol Tavris (Psychology Today, April
1976). She showed that as the number of children in a
family increases, intelligence and achievement diminish for
the younger members. The birth rate, which showed a resurgence in 1960, has been steadily declining. A turn-
around in test scores has already been reported on the Iowa
Test of Basic Skills for children born after 1962. By 1980--
when the kids born in '62 reach their senior year--the SAT
scores will have begun to rise, and we'll all look better.

Also affecting the schools--though they lie beyond the
educator's control--are social and political pressures. During the recent busing uprising in Boston, for instance, a lot
of kids didn't make it to class everyday. Those who did
come to school had to endure an emotional climate that can
surely--and generously--be described as hostile to learning.
At the risk of appearing so safe as to be silly, one might
conjecture that the students in South Boston and Roxbury
won't do as well as they might have a couple of years ago.
The problem is not what or how they are taught, but the

climate in which this teaching was forced to take place.
Was there ever a setting in which the sins of the parents
were more surely and severely visited upon their children?

Much of the national lamentation over loss of basic
skills is coming from the colleges and universities. But
look at what's been happening there: open admissions, lowered admission standards by institutions struggling to survive, and the rapid expansion of open-door public community
colleges enrolling people who would never have gone to college otherwise. We do not advocate a return to the elitist
past where only the wise or the wealthy went to college, but
we do point out that these changes will result in lowered test
scores despite what is being taught in the classroom.

A look inside that classroom--not just on college
campuses but in high schools and elementary schools as well
--reveals another hidden cause of drooping test scores: the
teacher-pupil ratio. Irrespective of what is being taught,
it stands to reason that kids will learn less when there are
40 of them in a class than when there are 25, and that
teachers will teach less when they have a 25-hour class
schedule than when they have a 15-hour one. (The "back to
basics" folks don't like that argument because smaller class
size means hiring additional teachers. And some of the
more cynical among us have the nagging feeling that "back to
basics" is just a watchword for budget cuts.)

All right, so maybe there are some hidden causes for
the lower test scores, but there's still a clear drop in basic
skills, right? Maybe. On the Berkeley campus of the University of California, about 50 per cent of the incoming
freshmen--according to recent press stories--fail the famous
Subject A Examination. What was it like in the good old
days? Let's go back to 1950. What was the failure rate
then? About 50 per cent.

Down the peninsula at Stanford, the admissions formula is, as in most such institutions, quite complex. Considerable credence is given to college boards and the like.
Yet, for all the screening devices--including scores of at
least 700 on the C.E.E.B. tests--Stanford has discovered
that it still cannot be certain that students write sufficiently
well. So, like the University of California, it administers
its own writing placement test. Interesting. Maybe Stanford and UC know something that the general public and
some test makers do not.

Few, if any, published tests call for samples of student writing. They include questions on usage, spelling,
editing, etc., and extrapolate from these some putative assessment of the students' actual writing ability. And there
are examples too numerous to mention of students who score
poorly on tests of reading skills, but in situations outside a
formal school setting demonstrate a reading level far above
what their scores indicate.

Our point here is not to claim that there are no problems. Throughout the country, language arts teachers are
dismayed at the lack of communications skills shown by some
students who falter in their attempts--or have already stopped
attempting--to express themselves and to comprehend the expressions of others. The crisis goes beyond grammar and
spelling, phonics and comprehension quizzes. The problem
involves literacy, and latter on in this article we will propose some concrete strategies for rectifying it.

In the meantime, there are the "back to basics" people to contend with. So far, we have argued that they are
working from a faulty base: test scores do not infallibly reflect skill levels, and the level of learning is influenced by
many variables beyond what and how the teacher does in the
classroom. A further complication arises from the fact that
while "back to basics" has become a national chant, there
is no widespread agreement about what the "basics" are and
how they should be taught. Even in Kanawha County, West
Virginia--the place where, for many, the "back to basics"
cry was first hears--there is no solid agreement. Some
advocates there called for an emphasis on fundamentalist
Protestant values and morality, while others in the same
area wanted training in critical thinking and cross-cultural
comparison. For some in the Northeast, "back to basics"
means stressing a cluster of abilities and information that
will make a student admissible to a private, selective university. Others take it to mean a school experience that
will guarantee acceptance in the job market after high school.

As we said earlier, money plays a central role in the
call for a return to the basics. Taxpayers are using the
slogan as a device for cutting school budgets by concentrating
on the most rudimentary learning tools and techniques.
Teachers are demanding an increased share of available
funds for salary increments, even though this means larger
class size and reduced funds for purchasing teaching and
learning materials.

And finally, we must raise a question about the inflated reliance placed on the tests themselves. The current "crisis" was spawned by the release of data showing a decline not in actual skills but in test scores presumably related to those skills. There's a big difference. Comprehension and vocabulary are not the sole components of reading; usage and spelling are but two elements of writing--and have scant influence on the more central matters of interest, impact, and creativity. If the schools are to gear their curriculum toward improving test scores, they will not be educating students, they will be cloning them.

The only group we know of that has successfully integrated public opinion and educational policy is the Amish community. It has defined for itself what is basic, designed its schools to teach what is basic, and insulated itself from the larger world which has different beliefs and concerns. However, the pluralism of the United States makes it unlikely that the rest of us will ever develop the stamina, the courage, the intellectual consensus, and the social unity of the Amish.

What, then, are we to do? Or, more specifically, what is the individual classroom teacher to do? Parents are demanding improvement in the teaching of English. Administrators have developed a distinct distrust of those of us who teach English and communications; they want change. Even students are lamenting their training in English for the benefit of reporters and cocktail party gossips. How can teachers cope with the "back to basics" movement?

Unlike the basic skills advocates, we do not have a simple, one-shot solution to offer. But we do want to suggest some priorities which, we feel, can help teachers deal positively with the situation, while keeping their values and heads together. Here are a few of our "topic sentences." They are based on our conviction that the real answer lies not with a return to technical skills (the "basics"), but with a resurgence of the more fundamental and all-encompassing educational goal of literacy.

We need literacy programs that are based on doing, not on studying peripheral skills. Practicing grammar exercises is not writing. Memorizing spelling rules is not writing. Studying logic is not writing. Correcting other people's sentence errors is not writing. Learning phonics is not reading; nor is filling out worksheets or studying work-attack skills or answering comprehension questions or learning how

to use a dictionary or card catalog. While such activities
may (or may not) have some direct or indirect connection
with learning to read and write, and although the study of
them may (or may not) be a major focus of the literacy
program at some time, they are clearly no substitute for
actual language experiences--putting pen to paper to write,
putting nose in book to read. We're convinced that English
teachers as a profession have already spent too much time
on the peripheral "basics, " too little on the fundamentals of
having students read (and read and read) and write (and
write and write).

We need programs that extend, rather than restrict,
the dimensions of literacy. Although the colleges regularly
complain that the schools don't do enough to prepare students
for freshman work, the typical K-12 school curriculum gives
strong evidence that teachers are concerned with preparation
for college, perhaps too concerned. We find it interesting
that in the elementary grades, children are pretty much free
to read and write in a wide range of forms and genres; they
do poems and stories, playlets and letters, fiction and non-
fiction--and nobody worries about it. However, at the junior
high level, teachers suddenly become concerned about "getting ready" ... for high school, for college. The broad
writing program of the elementary years frequently becomes
reduced to the study of a single form, "the essay" (with its
topic sentences and supporting evidence, with its methods of
paragraph development, with its reliance on the formal outline)--a program which finds its culmination in the preparation of a research paper. In reading, the program too often
becomes restricted to the purely "literary, " the "good stuff, "
and as a consequence, the reading young people do in school
becomes increasingly isolated from what they might read outside.

We don't want to diminish the importance of the essay,
for many young people do need to learn how to write one;
nor are we promoting pulp literature at the expense of "the
classics. " However, we do argue that diverse experiences
in reading and writing give students a flexibility in the use
of language not found in narrower programs. Thus we'd
like to see secondary teachers consciously broadening their
notion of literacy, offering students as many different kinds
of languaging experiences as possible: composing letters,
diaries, journals, scripts, songs, stories, and essays;
reading newspapers, magazines, monographs, leaflets, ads,
and good books, contemporary and classic.

Media exert an important role here. The introduction
of "media composition" and "media literacy" in the English
classroom has gone a long way toward breaking down traditional conceptions of literacy. During the basics "crisis,"
the use of media has come under attack as representing a
cop-out from the more "difficult" task of teaching reading
and writing. While media and nonverbal projects have been
misused in some classes (certainly the construction of col-
lages has become an overdone exercise), the well-integrated
use of film, video, radio, and photography adds to an English program simply by increasing the number of ways young
people can send and receive messages.

We need school-wide programs in literacy. Our
skepticism of the notion that "every teacher should be a
teacher of English" is based on practical, not philosophical
grounds. Most science and history teachers received virtually no training in teaching writing, and their inclination
is to teach via the red pencil, precisely the kind of teaching
many English teachers are trying to escape. We're also opposed on practical and philosophical grounds to the notion of
having subject teachers grade for content, then forwarding
papers to the English teacher for correction of mechanics
and usage.

What we do suggest is that English teachers take the
lead in sponsoring school-wide discussions of literacy. How
much writing is actually being done in history and science
and math? What kinds of writing? To what extent can English classes help prepare students for those assignments?
Is the school administration willing to support a broad program in literacy? If English teachers begin asking such
questions, criticism and sniping can be replaced by productive
cooperation.

We need a professional commitment to teach the skills
of literacy at whatever level they are needed. Blaming
teachers at lower levels of the system has gone far enough.
A more productive attitude is for teachers to borrow Harry
Truman's phrase, "The buck stops here." Literacy can be
and must be taught at all levels. There are important skills
required for success in assignments that cannot be mastered
until students are actually in college, and it is long overdue
for the universities to identify and teach those skills. Similarly, at the secondary level, teachers need to look closely
at the skills demanded for high school reading and writing
assignments and teach them. Writing in English Journal

(October 1975), Suzanne Jacobs of the University of Hawaii
summed it up nicely for writing: "Most of us need to take
a course just at the time when we discover how difficult it
is to say those things we really have some reason or desire
to say.... The writing course should be offered to students
of all levels, and it should be essentially the same course.
A student should be encouraged to take the course as often
as he feels that his growth in reading and experience has
outpaced his growth in writing." The same attitude can be
applied to reading; whenever students move into a new reading area, they need help on the spot. Blaming the alleged
failures of earlier teachers simply delays solving the problems.

Further, we might well reverse the traditional pattern of articulation between levels of schooling, where the
upper levels set expectations for the lower ones. For example, we recently heard a sixth grade teacher say to her
junior high colleagues: "Tell me what skills you want and
I'll teach up to them." While that attitude is a positive one,
we think it has the query going in the wrong direction. Better if the junior high teachers took the initiative and said
"Tell us what you have been able to do with your sixth
graders; we'll take it from there."

We need to encourage journalists to write about the
schools as they are, not as they are imagined to be. Many
of the journalistic outpourings about the literacy crisis have
obviously been written by people who haven't been inside a
school in years, who fancy that the "progressives" have
taken over, who believe that they, the journalists, are the
last people in the universe to care about language standards,
who tend to forget about their own "on-the-job" learning to
join in a cry for more "grammar." In its infamous feature,
"Why Johnny Can't Write," Newsweek magazine reported:
"Willy-nilly, the U.S. educational system is spawning a generation of semi-illiterates." No person thoroughly familiar
with American schools would make such an unsupportable
statement. If journalists come into the schools, they may
not like everything they see, but they will at least avoid
making preposterous statements that are harmful to teachers
and to the cause of improving instruction in literacy.

We need responsible standardized testing and testmakers. Educational Testing Service has issued numerous
cautionary statements about the interpretation of the SAT
score decline and has admitted that it doesn't know precisely

why the decline has taken place. (See Ruth Stokes, "Assessing the Assessors," English Journal, March, 1975.) Yet
one has to ask why testmakers are issuing public reports on
test data for which they are not willing to be held "account-
able." The public expects that an organization the size of
ETS (or the National Assessment of Educational Progress, or
the American College Testing program) is releasing reliable
data, and the response of the public to the announcements of
test score declines was predictable.

It is not enough that testmakers are trying to do a
good job, that they are concerned with collecting information
on the reliability of their tests, that they are forming blue
ribbon panels to look into the exams. Until such time as
the testmakers can offer adequate explanations of their data
in language that will not arouse irrational fears in the mind
of the public, we suggest that they go, not to the reporters,
but back to the drawing boards.

The literacy crisis has placed enormous burdens on
already-overburdened English teachers. Faced with impos-
sibly large teaching loads, insufficient supplies and materials, and a public that is, at best, ambivalent in its attitudes
toward literacy and literate people, teachers find themselves
confronted on all sides. One possible (and easy) solution is
for teachers to retreat back into the grammar books, to give
the public what it says it wants--a route which will, of
course, do nothing to solve the crisis and may even heighten
it.

The alternative is for educators to assess the outcry,
to sort through the sense and nonsense, and to move on to
develop imaginative, sound, broadly-based programs in reading and writing. We submit that both the public and the profession will be better served if teachers move not back to
the "basics," but forward to the fundamentals.

"THIS INCREDIBLE STREAM OF GARBAGE":
THE LIBRARY JOURNALS, 1876-1975*

Graham Jones

There have since the foundation of Leypoldt's Library
Journal in 1876 been dozens of English-language serials published by and for the library/archive/information fraternity.
In these, not hundreds but thousands of articles have appeared. It thus seems likely enough that out of this several
thousand a handful at least will have been devoted to the library periodical press itself--its characteristics, course,
and crises. If, however, so as to avoid saying again what
has been well said before, any commentator in 1976 sits
down with Cannons or later indexes to find out what his predecessors thought, immediately he finds himself subject to
the stinging rebuke of the expatriate Englishman, one-time
Liaison editor, and latterly publishing executive, Eric Moon:
that he is guilty of "scissors and paste research," a "grub-
by composite," the best example of which, the Library Quarterly, "still thought of by some as a 'scholarly' periodical
... looks to me more like a collection of ... antiquated
gentlemen examing their navels."[1]

To linger around in the midst of this cannonade, de-
bating whether one finds juxtaposition with the University of
Chicago's LQ a flattering accolade, would be less than stupid.
For Moon's curt, crude words reveal, with the brilliance of
a lightning flash illuminating ruined stairs and a gaping abyss
at our feet, the depth of the division across which different
professional elements confront each other. Without help
from Robert Shallow's friends the sociologists, we might
guess that Moon is talking about a gap not so much between
generations or countries as between strata which can be described only in terms of educational, perhaps even social,

*Reprinted by permission from The Indexer, Vol. 10, No. 1,
April 1976, pp. 9-14.

class. Such divisive issues have never been candidly discussed either side of the Atlantic. Yet they can hardly be
ignored: and it is as well at the outset of some innocuous-
seeming comments on type, margins, paper and other trivia
to set down some obvious points, derived from map reading
over British professional terrain.

A profession gets, obviously, only the press it can
produce and, directly and indirectly, support. Thus in 1877
a profession of first-generation librarians was ready for only
the briefest records of fact or experience, while in 1947 a
profession trained--and well enough trained, largely on the
job--could look to its journals for (a) basic educational material and (b) continuous reporting of innovation. By 1967,
with that complete absence of abstract discussion which char-
acterizes change in Britain, almost every would-be entrant
to the profession was confronted with full-time college or
university courses of two or three years' duration, such as
Moon had escaped. The education of librarians was now
coming, as never before, under the influence of political scientists, management teachers, "communications" lecturers
and others of university background. Nor should it be forgotten that for the first time librarianship students, however
detached--or indifferent--by inclination were encountering
amongst their fellows political activism that would have ap-
palled Roy Stokes no less perhaps than E. A. Baker. Thus
within the generation born between 1945 and 1955 there are
probably more differences of background and training--more
variant ideas as to what librarianship is about--than in any
previous age bracket. Even if librarians, British and American, had not since at least the 1930s cultivated the habit of
denigrating their professional press, one cannot easily imagine a journal or an editor capable of satisfying any bare majority of practitioners as LJ attains its centenary.

Let us at this point, then, pluck up courage to nail
some highly personal colours to a hypothetical mast. We
may say at the outset that a profession which wants to talk
nothing but shop is pathetic, but one which wants never to
talk shop is sinister. The overall "feel" of a periodical is
thus important. It conveys immediately a sense of rightness
or of wrongness: we react favourably or unfavourably towards it as to the dress or speech of individuals. Periodicals important to our world of practitioners and practitioner-
academics must make some positive claim to our attention.
There is a moment for the current issue of a periodical, as
for spring or a young girl in bloom: once past, attention

moves elsewhere. We may say further, with considerable
sympathy for editors in their travail, that the options open
to those who control library periodicals are severely limited.
There are few such arresting journals, but many good practices in use which are no longer striking when employed in
any newcomer. To this we must add that to manage any
journal adequately over a long period calls for every dimension of an editor's social and intellectual being, every scrap
of his ability. Lastly we should not imagine that the success
or failure of any periodical is the same thing as its balance
sheet. What organ did one choose if in the early '70s one
wanted to provoke a major professional debate in Britain?

The road to Hell is paved with them, of course: with
the good intentions which, though there is no unanimity in
their direction, serve to unite Booklegger (San Francisco),
Librarians for Social Change (Brighton), and Assistant Librarian (Stevenage, until further notice). Visually, much
the most convincing is Booklegger, with its vari-coloured
covers and the three brassy beauties who edit (? used to
edit) this feminist magazine which occasionally tolerates selected male contributors. There is about it something of the
smell of wholemeal bread: about LfSC, by contrast, a whiff
of instant coffee. Duplicated, with rather less than the
splendour of an office equipment demonstration, the latter
suggests all too faithfully something of the quality of British
life as seen by transatlantic eyes since '45, and much about
the British economy since '71. The Assistant too is visually
symbolic, for with its symmetrical two-column page, justified margins, and dependable advertisers it never quite manages to walk naked in the dew, however much it may try to
throw off the trammels of the psyche. Its covers, on the
other hand, although rarely dramatic, illustrate another aspect of the Assistant: particularly that celebrated cover
which showed a lady technical librarian acting as checker in
a motor-cycle rally. Rarely has the soul of a profession
been bared so effectively, though unconsciously. There have
been covers exemplifying certain humanitarian sympathies,
or campaigns, which in a newspaper might be considered
promotional (Nieswand, Palatnik), and covers designed to
stop the serials librarian in his tracks: that, for instance,
showing a supposedly drug-stricken couple strewn across the
floor, the girl displaying generous areas of kneecap (it would
be pleasant to speculate that the inevitable letter from a lady
reader wishing to receive the Assistant no longer was the
work of the editor). There is an overall impression of
trying hard, if sporadically; and indeed it is remarkable

how well the file of the Assistant emerges from a not particularly sympathetic scrutiny.   So for that matter, after
making the necessary allowances, does the Camden Libraries
staff Newsletter: duplicated, yet done with verve: clearly
enjoying, as LfSC cannot, a massive tacit subsidy, yet equally clearly practising remarkable freedom of speech on sensitive internal issues, some with political colouring.   Yet the
Camden staff, who tell the editor when he solicits copy from
them "we are a dull lot here: nothing ever happens at this
branch," are evidently saying something with which editors
are very familiar.   There are always critics of the librarianship press to indict its dullness: but if it is the profession
which is dull, if there are no newcomers with divine discontent or unexpected fact, what is the critic criticising but himself, his own stature, personality, and interests?

     The professional press thus has a difficult job, al-
though one often performed with flair and panache: a job
spelled out in some detail by Henry Guppy in the newly
founded Library Association Record in January 1899.   For
perhaps one-third of its subsequent history the LAR has been
edited by altogether able men; for another sixth, by men
whose contacts and interests were inadequate; and for the
rest by unremembered figures of average competence.   Guppy's Record was full, well informed, and superbly indexed:
Esdaile's was stately: Hilton Smith's and Walford's were
comprehensive, but the Record in 1968, with its new format,
entered an era about which it is still difficult to be objective.
There were of course good reasons to be advanced in committee for each of the major decisions taken.   One reader,
condemned apparently for years to some private typographic
torture chamber, is said to have hailed the new look as
"sheer visual delight."   Let one other reader at this point
remark that he never took kindly to the three-column page,
presenting as it did a forbidding mass of type at most open-
ings--save where articles ended abruptly in white spaces
complete with see-through--while paradoxically making most
contributions look skimpy.   The use of blank space he found
mechanical; the correspondence section over long, lacking a
firm editorial pruning-knife; and the limited use of type to
distinguish between different features ineffectual and unimaginative.   Nor for that matter did he warm to the simulated
mateyness of the "People" feature, which replaced bare appointments lists.   Let us remember that the overall design
concept was that of a professional (lady) consultant.   It is a
far cry from the days when the revamped Assistant, with a
cover drawn by John O'Leary, so impressed J. W. Robert-

son Scott, then starting The Countryman, that he wrote off
post-haste to ask for its source of visual inspiration.

At this point let us introduce a personal heresy.   Advertisements are essential for the continuance of the average
periodical.   They are also an essential ingredient in its appeal.   They have, however, to be worked for, and also integrated in the design of the journal.   Curious, incidentally,
that no librarianship periodical appears to have experimented
with the gratis non-commercial advertising which has com-
mended itself to, amongst others, The Shropshire Journal,
Car Mechanics, and the AUT Bulletin.   Yet advertising is
but one possible periodical feature: and it is a general rule
that journals with most features--articles, reviews, appropriate correspondence, news, bibliographic sections, illustrations, supplements, special issues--will be cast least per-
functorily into the "out" tray.   Curious again, then, that
whereas Aslib has never worried about dividing book reviews
between its two periodicals, the Library Association has consistently impoverished The Journal of Librarianship by con-
fining its regular books section to the Record.   Most mainstream librarianship periodicals anywhere run to most main
features, although latterly one might have wondered what had
happened to illustrations in LAR.   Something very wrong--at
a cursory glance, at least--if, then, a journal with every
expected feature nevertheless generates consistent criticism.

If such be the case with the Library Association Record in recent years--and this is by no means proved--one
must add at once that it would seem to have been the sport
of external circumstance.   "Experience, " the editor declared,
preparing his readers for change, "in the first half of 1967
indicated clearly an acute pressure on ... limited space."[2]
Hence the decision to launch a quarterly comparable to the
Journal of Documentation, intended to be commercially self-
sufficient, whereas in '66 and '67 the Association's monthly
--distributed without charge to every member--had lost
something like £6,000 each year.[3]   For the Record itself a
brave future with articles of 3,000-7,000 words was envis-
aged; yet by the end of '72 the editor had to point out that
at the hands of the accountants his periodical had "gone
ghastly thin."   Since editors can publish only what they have
been sent, and have money to print, the freedom of action
of the LAR editor would seem to have been greatly circumscribed during these years.   Moreover, one must not
underestimate the courage required to do certain things that
were done during these years.   It would not need great au-

dacity to devote a whole issue of RQ to a review of an encyclopaedia, or to print four-letter words--again--in Booklegger: to do both in the Record was the act of no docile apparatchik. It may not have gone unnoticed in Britain that John Gordon Burke departed precipitately from the editorial chair of American Libraries in 1974 when the ALA found itself diplomatically embarrassed by certain enquiries undertaken by his staff into Federal subsidy policies.

So far we have spoken only of those periodicals which can at best hope to do no more than break even financially: a few, of course, ostensibly seek to be commercially lucrative. The oldest is certainly LJ. At the outset, in Leypoldt's hands, this in fact lost money for several years: by now it is visibly a remarkable commercial achievement, providing a rich, though not perhaps always nourishing, diet. Its latest English equivalent, New Library World, provides a good-humoured one-man attempt at a current awareness service extending towards information science territory ("God knows what all this means: Don Davinson provided the information"). About its current financial position NLW is commendably frank, having by its own account lost money about as often as it has paid its way. [4] With The Assistant Librarian it shares the problem of finding month by month suitable blocks for its cover: and since contemporary library buildings are anonymous in character, and few prominent professionals facially remarkable (BLLD has had its share of exceptions), one wonders whether the effort is justifiable. Certainly W. H. Smith's Library World, which pioneered photographic covers, achieved impact--in, for instance, February '66 and February and March '69--hardly practicable now.

Typically, a trade journal (a) administers ceaselessly a thousand pinpricks to the association or union to which most of its readers must belong, and (b) speaks up lustily at any hint of government encroachment in their domain. The present reincarnation of Duff Brown's Library World ("NLW says NO to PLR") wears this particular cap happily enough. Major trade journals can do a great deal more. The Farmers Weekly runs half a dozen demonstration farms, and stages competitions with tractors or Range Rovers as prizes. Even the recollection of the old LW publicity awards is, unhappily, fading into the past.

If we consider the whole range of library and librarianship periodicals to be found on the racks in a good collec-

tion, perhaps only two possess that touch of class which
could enable them to sit with self-assurance beside, say,
Country Life or Penthouse: the New York Public Library
Bulletin and LC's Quarterly Journal. That this is so derives, no doubt, from the variety of material each carries:
text, bibliographic matter, footnotes, genealogies, notes on
contributors, maps, facsimiles, portraits. They are not of
course "about" librarianship at all: but few librarianship
journals, surely, can afford to exclude such bibliographic
and archive studies as these contain. There are no others
so likely as these to turn on the sensuous librarian, if such
librarians there be: in fact, the evidence suggests instead
a remarkable degree of asceticism and a remarkable ignorance of such books as Ruari Maclean's Magazine Design.
For years without number American professionals have put
up with two of their best periodicals appearing in the soporific
uniformity of a two-column glossy page with justified margins; but it must be conceded that a new standard of visual
tediousness was established with the foundation of Library
Trends, which made things considerably worse by failing for
long to grapple with the problem of guiding readers adequately through its bound volumes. The several lessons of LT
were not lost on Drexel Library Quarterly when this, too,
adopted the policy of single-theme issues. Perhaps surprisingly the Journal of Documentation, so familiar and so
respected as to be taken almost for granted, turns out to be
little better than its most sober American contemporaries.
With these no-one could confuse Library Quarterly, which
with its warm yellow cover and invariable reproduction of
some old printer's device has always, for one reader, ward-
ed off visual monotony, contriving to appear precisely what
since 1931 it has aimed at being, the premier research periodical in librarianship. It goes without saying that a benign
influence from the Chicago University Press is strong: was
the less welcome introduction of broad measure not long ago
a wind blowing from the same quarter?

There is much to be said for a cover contents list
like that of The Library; a pity that this restricts severely
the choice of colour. The Journal of Librarianship uses in
its cover three bold colour elements, and promptly vitiates
this arrangement by placing its title in the centre panel, so
that it is lost to sight in many a magazine rack. Library
Review has an adequate symbolic cover design, but dissipates
its effect by changing colour quarter by quarter. Between
1968 and 1975 two issues of LAR had specially designed
covers. Every cover of LJ, Wilson Library Bulletin, and

American Libraries--and, for that matter, of the Journal of
American Society for Information Science--is individually designed. There is no need to stress the effort involved in
this--or its value.

Within the exiguous budget in which most unsubsidized
librarianship periodicals operate it is not surprising that
there has been almost no experiment with massed effects of
black or of empty internal space, but it seems odd that in
Britain virtually no one has toyed with unjustified margins,
with differential type size, with italics, with the selection of
key paragraphs for top-of-the-page emphasis, or the other
devices to be found in Maclean's book. Unexpectedly, IFLA's
Journal has taken one cautious step in this direction: Catalogue & Index uninhibitedly goes further. Ontario Library
Review instead prefers cream paper, sepia type, and a generous lefthand margin sometimes used for subheadings. It
goes without saying that in magazine design open space is a
precious commodity; not, however, when it occurs with predictable regularity, or when it has the air of deriving from
a contributor's drying up. Some editors, unable to bear such
space, or unable to employ it artistically, fill it up with
brief reviews or with notes and miscellaneous news: not of
necessity a bad thing, since collected news and notes sections
can flow on with mesmeric regularity. This is of course
much less true when such material is handled by contributors
supplying an individual column. One holds no brief now for
those venerable wraiths with classical names who in another
era used to pontificate in The Library World: nor is it altogether clear that the pseudonymous voices extolling mediocrity
are altogether stilled even now. It seems curious in a free-
spoken age that anyone should be ready liberally to criticise
individuals and institutions without being prepared to do so
under his own name. Those who have supplied specialist
columns over the past four decades have of course included
exceptional men such as Herbert Woodbine, J. F. W. Bryon,
and Frank Smith; and this is to omit many of almost equal
competence.

To a small degree, such columns reach out in the direction of a reviewing section, but neither can suffice as a
substitute for the other. Like advertisement, reviews must
be worked for: and few periodicals indeed can afford to
leave their reviewing section to the whims of commercial
book publishers. With purchasing by their own libraries to
complement the distribution of review copies by issuing
houses, both Aslib and the Library Association are in a for-

tunate position. It is thus of interest that over the years
1972-1974 the number of signed librarianship and information
science reviews in LAR was 195, in Library Review 160, and
in the Journal of Documentation 143. It does not take long
to sense that Aslib does better for foreign publications, the
LA for less obvious public library material. Some books of
importance are reviewed, as if grudgingly, only in off-centre
contents: Richard Fothergill's A Challenge for Librarians?
and Ronald Benge's Communication and Identity are striking
examples.

        In general it is a fair proposition that, unless a peri-
odical has something in its cover, contents or general appearance to induce us to stuff it into our homeward-bound
briefcase at night, it has lost the first round of the battle
to contribute to professional thinking: for few, surely, are
prepared to leaf through each fresh issue of the Abstract
Journal: Informatics or LISA. Yet the backward glance for
ill-remembered items is essential, even in lush jungle growth
such as that of LJ before Library Literature has hewn this
into shape. One cannot report that many journals help greatly in any extensive retrospective search. Scottish Library
Association News (SLAN) has a cumulative index covering
issues 1-82; the Camden Newsletter has at the moment of
writing one covering forty-two issues; Education Libraries
Bulletin lists authors and titles of articles, and authors of
books reviewed, over volumes 13-16; and LfSC has what is
called an "exhausting index" of its first six issues by a mysterious, and possibly sinister, Lauren Ban Foon. NLW in
October 1972 announced its decision to index no more: an
understandable decision, but one which implies the necessity
for a more informative contents page than is currently the
case. And what are we to say of those journals which over
a period of ten years exhaust almost every possible option
as to what to include, what use to make of form headings
such as "obituary," and what abbreviations to introduce into
the index? Perhaps only this: that a prefatory note explaining indexing practice would not only help the user but
would tend to stabilise practice over a period. The Library,
which has before now provided such notes, also helps one
through its normally generous entries by picking out subject-
headings in bold type. But he who has to search through a
long periodical run in which indexes are sometimes bound
at the front of the volume, sometimes at the back, and sometimes omitted altogether, might well wish for instructions directed as much at library staff as at binders, which are obvious, unequivocal and foolproof. No-one will of course be

helped much if like the British Library Lending Division
Review--in the hands of HMSO, one of the dreariest English
serials--a periodical prints an undernourished index as an
integral part of the first issue of the following year.

Regretfully, as one comes to concede that there are
social classes, so one learns ultimately that distinctions
exist between levels of indexing accepted in different contexts;
and that the level which will suffice for Eric Moon's bête
noire, the "scholarly" journal, will not do for the omnibus
news medium circulating through a scattered profession,
such as LJ once was for Anglo-American librarianship as a
whole and Inform, that lusty, tabloid-echoing news sheet, is
for the Institute of Information Scientists--if indeed these are
indexed at all. "Scholarly" journals, even LQ, can get by
with authors, titles, and review entries: the bulletins and
magazines of membership organizations must treat every personal name with democratic impartiality, every committee
with decorous solemnity. The strain on American Libraries,
the closest equivalent to LAR, is evident. In November
1972 it provided separate indexes of ALA committees and of
the individuals serving on them. In the December issue
were "Authors and subjects" and "People" indexes for the
year. Exhausted apparently by the effort, it has since then
--unless our Serials Department is greatly mistaken--indexed
nothing. And to such policies one resigns oneself, as the
issues of the LA Information: Weekly Newsheet and its like
pile up or fail to come back from circulation.

To return almost to our starting-point. "We are all
conscious of the complaint," wrote Carnovsky two decades
ago, "that library literature is so dull!"[5] Perhaps it is no
more than a populist slogan which, for a deceiving moment,
allows the many fragmented specialist interest amongst li-
brary/archive/information workers to imagine themselves on
one thing at least united.[6] But is what is dull to the ARLIS
Newsletter reader dull to that of Audio-Visual Librarian?
Substitute for one of these titles Library History, LEG News,
Focus on International and Comparative Librarianship or any
one of that strong-limbed brood whose departure from the
parental roof has of late left the Record so forlorn, and the
equation looks equally tricky. Even so, dross by any analysis remains dross.

A prominent librarian has stated that many people
complain that library literature is dull. An answer to this is the production of stimulating and

challenging manuscripts which contain new ideas
and information.

This, from the ALA Bulletin in the '60s, manages to be
simultaneously dull, trite, and pretentious. Another answer?
Read New Society--or, better still, just look at the art-work.

Source Notes

1.   The "stream of garbage"--Moon's description of the
     quality of material submitted during his nine years'
     editorship of Library Journal--is drawn from the
     same article (Moon, E. The library press, LJ 94
     (20) 15 Nov. 1969. pp. 4104-9). Characteristically,
     the emphasis of Carnovsky, eighteen years managing
     editor of Library Quarterly, is altogether different:
     "Get a footnote right. " (Carnovsky, L. Publishing
     the results of research in librarianship. Library
     Trends 13 (1) July 1964.
2.   LAR 70 (3) Mar. 1968. p. 57.
3.   LAR 70 (5) May 1968. p. 135.
4.   NLW 75 (887) May 1974. p. 101.
5.   Carnovsky, L. Standards for library periodicals. LJ
     80 (3) 1 Feb. 1955. pp. 264-9.
6.   The future of the Library Association Record was de-
     cided in 1974 after 1199 usable replies had been re-
     ceived to a questionnaire circulated to an 11% sample
     of home personal members of the LA, asking them
     to grade in broad categories 35 possible varieties of
     subject-matter. The kind judged "essential" by the
     highest number (715) was "Standards for library ser-
     vice. " Essential, yes: but interesting? (Informa-
     tion supplied by courtesy of Michael Yelland, LA Re-
     search Officer.)

CHILDREN'S BOOKS IN A PLURALISTIC SOCIETY*

Donnarae MacCann

The long-standing debate between the American Library Association and some of its members over racist and sexist children's books has placed children's librarians in a painful position. Everyone in the dispute seems dedicated to the same ideals of individual growth through freedom in reading, but we need to ask what kind of freedom each side considers valid, and whether one segment of society should define freedom for all others. [1]

The ALA policy about providing "diverse views, ... including those which are strange, unorthodox, or unpopular" sounds like an indisputable statement of the liberal tradition. But if a racist children's book is merely defined as strange or unpopular, the policy creates enormous problems. In 1972 a junior high school teacher in Waterloo, Iowa, was using Little Brown Koko and the Preacher's Watermelon as an exercise in her speech class. The black community did not consider the references in the book to "nice, good, ole, big, fat black Mammy," "black woolly head," and "little, fat, brown face" as simply unorthodox.

Similarly, one cannot toss off the implications in children's books that Africans and monkeys are indistinguishable: "That girl looks just as much like a monkey as I look like a girl," according to Chee Chee, the monkey in The Voyages of Dr. Dolittle by Hugh Lofting. A similar comparison with a black child is made in P. L. Travers's 1971 publication, Friend Monkey.

Children do not have the secure sense of themselves

*Reprinted by permission of the author and publisher from Wilson Library Bulletin, Vol. 51, No. 2, Oct. 1976, pp. 154-162. Copyright © 1976 by The H. W. Wilson Company.

that can withstand this kind of "unorthodox" viewpoint. Derogation of this sort is an attack, rather than an opinion, when
it is directed at children and their physical traits.

Until recently racism and sexism were not challenged
by America's dominant group--the white middle class.
Therefore, in tracing the history of children's book contro-
versies, one finds little relevant to a debate on those subjects. Critics were first concerned about religion, morality,
and gentility, but they were chiefly selecting books for Sunday School libraries and not trying to determine the criteria
for general collections. [2]

In this century special interest groups have been concerned about violent comic books, "subversive" history books,
and increasingly explicit books about sex and/or sex education. [3] These topics do not have the same bearing upon the
child's emerging self-concept as do racism and sexism. The
latter deal with qualities in a child that are invariable, and
this fact places a different kind of responsibility upon those
working with children.

Questions of morality and patriotism call for discussion and the presentation of diverse viewpoints. There are
many opinions to weigh and perspectives to balance. Children as well as adults have the right to encounter the various
presentations. But a child's self-image in terms of race or
sex is not a matter of degree. It is a necessary part of a
child's being, and future development largely hinges upon it.
In the long run society's future hinges upon it also, and the
community therefore has the right to concern itself with children's self-concepts. [4]

The line between selection and censorship must be
drawn differently in juvenile and adult book collections, because in the latter the issue of identity-formation isn't one
of the librarian's concerns. For an adult library the dif-
ferentiation has been put in these terms: "The positive se-
lector asks what the reaction of a rational, intelligent adult
would be to the content of the work; the censor fears for the
results on the weak.... "[5]

Children are by definition inexperienced; although they
can respond to a work with as much intelligence and ration-
ality as an adult, they cannot be expected to know the historical forces that lie behind a racist or sexist presentation
in a book. There is little in their background to mitigate the

suffering of self-rejection when the characters they identify
with are degraded. Nor can other children escape an un-
founded sense of superiority. Therefore, it seems that input
from members of Third World and feminist groups is clearly
necessary in the selection of children's books.

It is the child's involuntary group membership--by
race or sex--that underlies our seemingly contradictory response to complaints from a group such as the National Association for the Advancement of Colored Peoples on the one
hand and a segment of the Kanawha County (W. Va.) Citizens
Review Committee on the other. The circumstances that require action in these instances are in no way related. In the
NAACP cases argument has rested upon involuntary group
membership and the self-image of children in that group.
The right-wing section of the Kanawha committee was demanding a limitation of experience for children based chiefly
upon social and political theory, about which there are many
conflicting views. The National Education Association's investigation concluded that had there been no multicultural and
multiethnic content in the books questioned in Kanawha County, these books would not have generated such a protest.

Foolish Inconsistency

Richard L. Darling, dean of Columbia University
School of Library Science, worries about the inconsistency in
removing Little Black Sambo from children's libraries, but
refusing to remove Sylvester and the Magic Pebble by William Steig. 6 In the Steig book all the characters are animals;
but a group of police officers made a complaint about pig
characters in police uniform. Children are the audience for
both books, but in the latter book there is no offense directed
at a child. Even if one accepts the contention that pigs-as-
police-officers is automatically offensive (given recent sarcastic uses of the word "pig"), the recipients of the slur are
nonetheless adults. For them a developed sense of identity
can be presumed, and there is the additional fact that being
a member of a police force is a voluntary association and
therefore basically different from racial group membership.

Darling warns that we face a 1984-type society if we
censor books like Little Black Sambo. His argument fails
to take notice of the principal threat treated in George Orwell's novel--namely, the conditioning of an individual through
propagandistic manipulation. 7 Racism in a child is not an in-

herent characteristic. <u>Little Black Sambo</u> and many other books have imposed racist condemnation--condemnation that says to the child, "You should be ashamed that you were born."

If <u>Little Brown Koko</u> and <u>Little Black Sambo</u> represented only political opinions, we would still dislike the books. We know, though, that political opinions change under many different influences, and their impermanence reduces their threat in the long run. But the shock of self-rejection in a child doesn't change easily. There is ample empirical evidence from those who have felt the brunt of racism. Marjorie Hammock tells about her experience of hearing <u>Little Black Sambo</u> read in school:

> I remember how some of my classmates would re-
> fer to me as Black Sambo after hearing the story
> (they were too sophisticated to say nigger) and
> how for the first time I didn't want to go to school
> ever! To this day I hate the teacher and the prin-
> cipal who told my mother it was harmless. The
> only good thing it did was put me on guard for my
> remaining years in public school. No, the book
> can only be used as an example of how to destroy
> a child. [8]

And Ernest W. Chambers cited his memories:

> I wasn't born from the womb with the attitudes I
> have now.... I sat through <u>Little Black Sambo</u>.
> And since I was the only black face in the room,
> I became Little Black Sambo. [9]

Socialization and Authenticity

Educators are properly concerned with socialization--the process that fits people for getting along with others. In school and out, children are under the tutelage of others and are adopting new attitudes. Experiences in living and in reading are producing either positive or negative change. If this were not so, teachers could be selected indiscriminately and libraries acquire children's books through some random method of acquisition. But here is the irony: Children's librarians search for books of value, yet sometimes acclaim those that run counter to socialization. This problem stems from the fact that socialization through literature is unlikely

without authenticity, without a depth of understanding in the
writer and in the book.

Even stories that try to deal positively with interra-
cial understanding have sometimes had negative effects.   The
lack of authenticity has not been recognized by the writer or
by librarians.   The veracity of the characters has not been
defined in conjunction with people from the specific culture.

In The Empty Schoolhouse by Natalie Carlson, a black
adolescent compares her physical traits with her younger
sister's: Her "skin is like coffee and cream mixed together,
and she has wavy hair to her shoulders.   Me, I'm dark as
Daddy Jobe, and my hair never grew out much longer than
he wears his."   She is told that she should wear berets so
that she will look less like a boy.   Instead of bringing out
the idea that black and white Americans are equal, the treatment of the characters suggests that integration with the
white community is a good idea because that way one can get
away from the black community, which is inferior.   The latter is shown as a place where people are superstitious, foolish; where an elderly black man looks "like a popped cotton
boll"; and where the 14-year-old narrator's sole aspiration
is to continue being a scrub girl at the Magnolia Motel.   At
the end of the story, the wavy-haired sister is happy because
she has established friendships with white people.

Some writers claim that although their perception of
the Third World is from outside, it is as valid as any other
because all perception is personal and in some degree confined.   Sandra Weiner, the author of It's Wings That Make
Birds Fly, writes: "I see no reason to apologize for a sympathetic interest in an ethnic group, no matter how incomplete the portrait that emerges might be."[10]   But even when
the portrayal is sympathetically motivated and even when the
white author claims a genuine imaginative experience, the
ultimate question remains: Does the book reduce the child
in his or her own eyes, and does it set one reader against
another?   An incomplete portrait can have this effect if the
missing qualities are the ones needed to convey self-respect
or mutual respect.   In such cases the book does not serve
the aims of education or socialization.   But since the writer
by necessity writes only what he or she perceives, it falls
to librarians to judge the work and to recognize either subtle
or blatant forms of racism or sexism.

Librarians are all too aware of the fine line between

censorship and book selection. Some are self-critical enough
to put in this way: Selection is the process carried on by librarians when they make value judgments about the books
other people will read; censorship is the same process when
it is carried on by nonlibrarians.

A new dimension in this self-awareness developed in
the 1960s, and skepticism about book selection increased.
During those years of the black revolution, people began to
understand how difficult it is for non-Third World members
to evaluate representations of the experiences of Third World
communities and populations. Librarians, like many other
white-collar professionals, tend to belong to one class of
people in both an economic and racial sense. They bring
that perspective to bear on judgments of Third World books.

The late Arna Bontemps, author and lecturer at Yale,
used the tale of Ole Sis Goose to illustrate the miscarriage
of justice that is associated with libraries as well as other
institutions in a predominantly white culture. After the fox
captures Ole Sis Goose when she's sailing on the lake and
threatens to pick her bones, she says: "You got your nerve,
telling me I can't sail on the lake. This is a free country.
We are going to tell this to the judge." But then Ole Sis
Goose looked around inside the courthouse and saw the sheriff, and he was a fox. "She noticed that the judge, he was
a fox, and the attorneys, they were foxes, and all the jury-
men, they were foxes too. So they tried Ole Sis Goose, and
they convicted her, and they executed her, and they picked
her bones." Regarding books, Bontemps noted:

> The editor is apt to be a fox. The publisher, like
> as not, could turn out to be a fox. The critics
> who review the book, the editors and publishers
> of the publications that carry the reviews, they're
> foxes. The salesmen who put the book on the
> market, the booksellers, the selection committees
> --even most of the readers are all foxes, too. [11]

The average citizen has entrusted book selection to
librarians because of their special training; but Lester Asheim, former dean of the University of Chicago Graduate
Library School and currently at the University of North Caro-
lins/Chapel Hill SLS, pointed out that "we demand that those
to whom we delegate such authority shall demonstrate the vir-
tues which are the basis of that trust." A profession, he
said, exists when a group "has the earned confidence of

those it serves."[12] When monocultural assumptions were
applied, over the years, to a multicultural society, the resulting damage eroded that trust.

There is no way around this dilemma when adding
books to an adult library collection. Even when a white librarian seeks out expert advice from Third World advisors,
someone has to make the final decision, and the responsibility lies with the librarian. But the hazards of this arbitrary selection process are minimized when the librarian
does attempt to have all viewpoints represented.

The hazards of selection in a children's library must
be handled differently because a book can focus a child's attention on his or her identity. In the case of "I'm Glad I'm
a Boy! I'm Glad I'm a Girl!" by Whitney Darrow, Jr., a
contemptuous bias about sex roles is imposed on children;
and through the library it reaches them with all the power
of authority that children usually attribute to books in general and library books in particular.

The Darrow book provides historians with a succinct
catalog of antifeminist attitudes. But it was removed from
several school libraries in southeast Iowa because review
committees decided unanimously that the content could reinforce feelings of inferiority.[13] Typical statements in the
books include "Boys are doctors. Girls are nurses.... Boys
are policemen. Girls are meter maids.... Boys fix things.
Girls need things fixed."

Nancy Schimmel, children's librarian at Half Moon
Bay Library in San Mateo, Calif., has suggested that more
guidance be given to children about the racist and sexist
books within their libraries. She writes: "Wanting to make
clear that our own values are not the same as those in a
book we hand to a child, some of us feel we must say
something before the book goes out."[14] Such guidance might
reduce some of the authoritative aura that a library book has
for children, but it would be difficult to practice unless the
library had a very large, well informed staff.

A more practical correlative of this idea is to keep
the extreme examples of racist and sexist books in an adult
research collection. Then when guidance is available, or a
discussion group is planned on racism or sexism, the books
can be freely used. In some school libraries books with
racist and sexist content are being transferred to the special

collection connected with the unit of study on those subjects.
This practice may contradict the ALA policy on "labeling,"
but the policy, as presently interpreted, disregards the rights
of children in a pluralistic world.

The Intellectual Freedom Committee's position that
parents make the decisions about what the child reads is not
borne out. Many parents don't read or know the content of
children's books. The library would need to inform each
parent about the books in order to provide some background
on racist and sexist content. The IFC position is also unrealistic in that it implies that no child visits a library except in the company of a parent.

The need is for clarification of children's librarianship as a specialized field, with a detailed description of
what that specialty entails. Children's librarians need to
explain clearly to other librarians the differences between
adult and child readers. Of course it is more convenient
to have a uniform policy, but surely it is better to have a
separate policy suited to children. Freedom is not absolute.
To shout "fire" in a crowded theater is illegal; to downgrade
a child's sense of identity or encourage a false sense of superiority among other children is also a seriously irresponsible act.

Furthermore, the different kinds of children's books
should be understood. Otherwise political censorship might
be mistakenly accepted in the guise of a legitimate complaint
about racist or sexist content. Children's librarians have
the professional training to make these distinctions and better qualified than other ALA groups to administer a selection
policy for a children's library. It would be incredible if
people unfamiliar with the books were setting the policy.

In arguing at the ALA midwinter meeting for rescind-
ing the Statement on Reevaluation of Library Materials for
Children's Collections, Dianne Farrell stated: "Admittedly,
books in our children's collections reflect racist, sexist, and
puritanical attitudes. But removing these books from our
shelves will not eradicate racism, sexism, or puritanism."[15]
Nothing could lead to greater confusion than the lumping together of racism and sexism with puritanism. Attacks based
on race or sex and those based on ideology affect us in fun-
damentally different ways. Puritanism is a philosophy and
is as mutable as any system of thought; racism and sexism
are connected with irrevocable physical conditions. In chil-

dren the impact of racial or sexual derogation is intensified manyfold because children are much less secure about their place in society.

Pro Status Quo

Farrell argues on behalf of the status quo because, in her view, books can't eradicate problems. The National Council of Teachers of English takes the opposite position:

> To be sure, the school experience is not the sole force that shapes self-images and attitudes toward others. But in the measure that school does exert this influence, it is essential that the materials it provides foster in the student not only a self-image deeply rooted in a sense of personal dignity, but also the development of attitudes grounded in respect for and understanding of the diversity of American society.
> The accomplishment of these ends is a responsibility and obligation of those involved in English and Language Arts programs. [16]

The NCTE statement acknowledges that institutionalized racism and sexism must be overcome in the schools. The library profession should be able to make the same admission. An additional article to the Library Bill of Rights and revision of other articles would set a new course. A statement along these lines is needed:

> The child's right of access to books is similar to that of adults in areas of political, social, and religious opinion. Identity-formation involves inferences about race and sex. Slurs and demeaning images related to these subjects deny the child's freedom to exist as an individual of equal worth with others. Books containing such content should be relegated to research collections maintained for historians and other scholars.

Because such a basic human right is at issue in this proposal, the ideas should be explored by ALA in conjunction with lawyers and child psychologists who represent feminists and Third World peoples.

More than One Amendment Involved

Naturally, upholding the free speech provision in the
First Amendment takes constant alertness.   But equal care
is needed to uphold the Fourteenth Amendment's "equal protection under the law. " Violation of equal protection is perhaps even easier to perpetrate than violation of free speech,
because it is instinctive for many of us who are white to
sustain our own values and monopoly of power.

Some of the legal precedents that have a bearing on
the censorship debate include three cases in which youthful
audiences were judged by the court to be obviously separate
from adult audiences and the standards different with respect
to what is said and read to the two groups.   These cases
(Jacobellis v. Ohio, U. S. Supreme Court; State v. Settle,
Rhode Island Supreme Court; and Keefe v. Geanakos, 418
Fed. 359 First Cir.) involved disputes over obscenity in
films and books and are not parallel with disputes over racism and sexism.   However, Supreme Court Justice Brennan
stated his opinion in very general terms: "We recognize the
legitimate and indeed exigent interest of States ... in prevent-
ing the dissemination of material deemed harmful to children. "

According to the National Organization of Women's
Project on Equal Education Rights, Secretary of Health,
Education, and Welfare Caspar W. Weinberger was advised
by HEW lawyers that limited antibias procedures for elementary and secondary schools in the area of textbooks would
not violate free speech guarantees under the First Amendment.
The antisex-bias rules for education under Title IX of the
Education Amendments were finally drafted without the inclusion of textbooks, but Weinberger's decision ran counter to
a number of legal opinions. [17]

As much as we value the concept of children's rights,
it would be unrealistic to claim that the actual experiences
of children are not circumscribed by adult decisions (including
those of publishers).   Librarians have the capacity to change
some of these decisions--to eliminate selection practices that
have caused agonizing experiences for many children.

In urging that the Statement on Reevaluation of Materials be rescinded, Dianne Farrell noted with dismay that
one librarian had used the statement to justify the removal
of Laura Ingalls Wilder's books. [18]   Many librarians auto-

matically responded with horror at this revelation; but the
librarian at the University School of the University of Wyo-
ming described Wilder's <u>Little House on the Prairie</u> in these
terms from a different vantage point:

> ... Indians and wolves are classed together, and
> red men are described as naked, wild men with
> eyes like snake's eyes and with speech, when they
> weren't silent, as short harsh sounds in the throat.
> But perhaps most objectionable is the fact that the
> stalwart, upright family of the story moves into
> Indian country with wanton disregard for Indian
> rights because, of course, the government is going
> to make the Indians move further west. 'Treaties
> or no treaties, the land belongs to folks that'll
> farm it.'[19]

Farrell asks if we are ready to give up the Wilder books.
If we think the white majority has the same superior claims
with respect to children's libraries that it demanded in the
history of the frontier, the answer will always be "no."
Either we are a pluralistic society, fully including Native
Americans and their actual history and human characteristics,
or we are not. Either we acknowledge that others have the
right to exist with the human dignity that we ourselves take
for granted, or we maintain a white cultural monopoly by
saying that popular books that force on readers a racial or
sexist bias are sacrosanct.

A book that demeans and sets one child against an-
other--does this make no difference to a profession that
proclaims a "Bill of Rights"?

References

1.   The organizations best representing the two points of
     view are the Intellectual Freedom Committee of the
     American Library Association and the Council on In-
     terracial Books for Children (1841 Broadway, NY
     10023).   The council opposed rescinding the 1973
     Statement on Reevaluation of Library Materials for
     Children's Collections at the 1976 ALA midwinter
     meeting.   That statement proclaimed the obligation
     of children's librarians "to introduce to the child
     those titles which will enable him to develop with a
     free spirit...."

2. Richard L. Darling. "Censorship--An Old Story,"
    Elementary English, 51 (May 1974), p. 692, 694.
3. Ibid., p. 694.
4. Studies in education and psychology with findings on
    negative self-concepts include "Emotional Factors in
    Racial Identification and Preference in Negro Chil-
    dren" by Kenneth B. and Mamie P. Clark (Journal
    of Negro Education, 19 [1950], p. 341-50); "The
    Social World of the Slum Child: Some Early Find-
    ings" by Suzanne Keller (American Journal of Ortho-
    psychiatry, 33 [1963], p. 823-31); Race Awareness
    in Young Children by Mary Ellen Goodman (Addison
    Wesley, 1952); They Learn What They Live by Helen
    G. Trager (Harper, 1952); Black Self-Concept: Im-
    plications for Education and Social Science, edited by
    James A. Banks and Jean D. Grambe (McGraw-Hill,
    1972).
5. Lester Asheim. "Not Censorship, but Selection,"
    Wilson Library Bulletin, 28 (September 1953), p. 63.
6. Darling, op. cit., p. 695.
7. Ibid., p. 696.
8. See Little Black Sambo--A Closer Look by Phyllis J.
    Yuill. New York, Council on Interracial Books for
    Children, Inc., 1976, p. 22.
9. "We Have Marched, We Have Cried, We Have Prayed,"
    excerpt from a report of the Kerner Commission on
    Civil Disorders. Ebony (April 1968), p. 31.
10. Sandra Weiner. "Who Speaks for a Culture," in Read-
    ing, Children's Books, and Our Pluralistic Society,
    ed. by Harold Tanyzer and Jean Karl. Newark,
    Del., International Reading Association, 1971, 1972,
    p. 35.
11. Arna Bontemps. "Ole Sis Goose," in The American
    Negro Writer and His Roots. New York, American
    Society of African Culture, 1960, p. 51, 52.
12. Asheim, op. cit., p. 67.
13. The procedure by which this book was deleted from
    public school collections is worth studying. The de-
    cision was neither in the hands of the complainant
    nor the librarian who purchased the book. A stand-
    ing committee appointed by either a city council or
    school board reviewed the evidence and voted by
    secret ballot. On one committee five members had
    connections with educational institutions (including
    two high school students) and six were from the
    community. An allowance was made for two per-
    sons with special knowledge or competence to be

added on an ad hoc basis; and in accordance with
Iowa law, all meetings were open.
     This procedure provides a method of "due
process" that safeguards free discussion and offers
a recourse to anyone who feels that a poor judgment
about racist or sexist content has seriously reduced
a child's chance for free development. The school's
selection policy rejected racist or sexist books, and
the committee's function was a judicial one. Its decision could be appealed to the school board. In
this connection it should be noted that in Epperson v.
Arkansas, 393 U.S. 97 (1968), the court ruled that
"it would seem clear to us that books which become
obsolete or irrelevant or were improperly selected
initially, for whatever reason, can be removed by
the same authority which was empowered to make
the selection in the first place. "

14. Nancy Schimmel. "Reading Guidance and Intellectual
     Freedom, " Top of the News (April 1975), p. 319.
15. Dianne Farrell. "CSD Intellectual Freedom Committee:
     Statement to the CSD Board January 21, 1976, "
     Top of the News (April 1976), p. 231.
16. "Criteria for Teaching Materials in Reading and Litera-
     ture of the NCTE Task Force on Racism and Bias
     in the Teaching of English, " in Searching for Ameri-
     ca, ed. Ernece B. Kelly. Urbana, Ill., Conference
     on College Composition and Communication and the
     National Council of Teachers of English (1111 Kenyon
     Rd., 61801), 1972, p. xvi.
17. "Ford to Act on Sex Bias Rule, " Peer Perspective
     (April 1975), p. 1.
18. Farrell, op. cit., p. 232.
19. Laura Herbst. "That's One Good Indian: Unacceptable
     Images in Children's Novels, " Top of the News (Janu-
     ary 1976), p. 193.

COMICS, COKES, & CENSORSHIP*

Norma Fox Mazer

When I was growing up, my mother didn't allow comics in our house. My parents were readers, and nothing else printed was off limits. I read everything, without discretion, as long as it contained words: my parents' books, the Sue Barton nurse series from beginning to end, Gulliver's Travels, and dreadful Pollyanna whom I adored, all in the same big gulp. But no comics, I had to go across the street to Buddy Wells' house and read his Wonder Woman and Elastic Man on the sly. I guess my mother thought comics would corrupt my sisters and my brains the same way she firmly believed Cokes would poison our insides.

When my children began to read, I decided they could read anything, including comics. I hewed to the line that no printed word, sentence, or story ever killed or maimed anyone, that reading leads to more reading, and that, finally, given time, the kids would develop their own tastes which, hopefully, would include much more than comics.

All this was fine and liberated, but I didn't anticipate some of the reading material my four offspring would choose. Comics of all kinds, war comics, horror comics, even funny comics, were big in our house. My nine-year-old son had a collection that stood taller than he did, and which he read avidly, day after day after day. Despite my theories I had never shaken off a faint queasiness about comic books, a feeling that they were, yes, bad for you. (In the same way I've never been able to really relish a nice frosty Coke without a pang of guilt. It tastes good, but what is it doing to my insides?)

*Reprinted by permission of the author and the American Library Association from Top of the News, Vol. 32, No. 2, Jan. 1976, pp. 167-170. Copyright © 1976 by the American Library Association.

One day I went into my son's closet where he kept
his comic collection and leafed through a few. I had forgotten, or maybe, as a child, had never recognized, how
lurid, violent, racist, and sexist comics could be. (Besides,
their literary style was a bit purple. "Alone ... so terribly,
hideously alone! The surrounding silhouettes of mountains
ripple in the heat ... the moon is a fading ember ... the
wind whispers DEATH ... a shadow blackens the sky ... as
the dread BATMAN awaits a doomful destiny along the HIGH-
WAY TO NOWHERE!")

Reading my son's comics, so far removed from the
mixture of approved classics and bland kids' fare I'd been
nurtured on, I grew definitely uneasy. What sick festering
notions were already rotting in his young mind? He was a
delicious looking little boy, round cheeked, rosy faced, a bit
plump, the sort of kid you like to hug and squeeze. But you
couldn't tell anything by that, could you? The comics could
really be mucking up his mind. Good Lord, what would be
the use of all my efforts about nutrition and diets, enough
sleep, yearly checks with the pediatrician, and always the
right shots and shoes if it were all sabotaged by these mis-
erable comic books? With a wave of guilt, I took a huge
armful straight to the garbage can. I never opened it. I
stared at that big pile of pulpy words and lurid pictures and
chose again the principle of no censorship. My son could
have his comics.

I was put to another test when one of our daughters
brought home a book that was, by anyone's standards, porno-
graphic. This daughter was only fourteen at the time, and
I still felt terrifically protective toward her about all sorts
of things, most of which I already realized I could no longer
control.

There was the usual mental struggle--Should I make
her take the offensive book out of the house immediately?
Should I ignore it? Should I read it? Should I say something, but lay down no law? I was not happy that she was
getting any of her sexual education this way, but a little
thought convinced me that banning a book from our house
didn't mean banning it from her eyes and mind. In fact,
she and a whole group of girlfriends were passing this book
around, generally secretly as far as parents were concerned.

More recently, I discovered a young daughter reading
scenes from Sybil, scenes which had so distressed me that

I had felt an actual physical shock to my system.   By this
time, after passing through all this and more with three
other children, I ought not to have felt even a jolt.   But I
did.   My first impulse was to throw out the book, protect
her from the knowledge that such a terrible thing as a
mother's attacking her infant daughter could happen in this
world.

Once again, although I spoke to her about what she
was reading, I refrained from taking the book from her.

Enough time has passed for me to feel more strongly,
not less so, about my position on the matter of reading.
My son, the comic book freak, has grown up to be a young
man who doesn't seem to have a violent bone in his body and
whose mind is clear and capable.   Along with a variety of
material that ran the gamut from Tolkien to Tolstoy, interestingly enough he was still also reading comics right into
his late teens.   I've noticed the same thing not only in my
daughters but in a lot of young people.   Comics--<u>Mad Maga-
zine</u> and <u>National Lampoon,</u> for instance--are an accepted
part of their culture.

Today there's a rather strong current alive in our
country devoted to screening, censoring, banning, and in
some cases even burning books that our children read.   And
the cry for censorship rings out not just against sex, for instance, but against books which contain certain words people
find offensive, certain attitudes and points of view.

As a writer for the young, as a reader, a parent, I
despise all censorship, even including things that enrage and
pain me.   I want to bite nails when I read yet another portrait of a silly, simpering, weepy, noncapable girl.   I find,
even in a book for the young that I otherwise admire, a gra-
tuitious, racist remark about Jews.   And in a book which
has been widely acclaimed, a black woman character who
might have come off the pancake box: unmarried, working
faithfully for a white family, deeply understanding, and always there when needed by the white children.

I don't like these things, I hate the blindness that
persistently ties us to such stereotypes, but I wouldn't keep
these books out of the hands of children who want to read
them.   And this is because I believe that children are people
with as much sense and an equal ability to sort out things
for themselves as adults.

Children are not imperfect copies of ourselves who magically come into the possession of our superior adult reasoning powers at a certain fixed age. Children, in fact, have remarkable sense from quite a young age and lack, most of all, experience. It's experience, I believe, which separates "us" from "them."

Of course there are other differences. The young are more intense, emotional, impatient, lusty, and zestful. Their time sense is quite different. And they can throw themselves into life in a wonderful way which we adults gradually lose. When my youngest daughter reads, for instance, I have to shout in her ear three or four times to pull her out of that world she's so blissfully fallen into.

Today, writers for adolescents are giving them stories about things that used to be verboten. Growing up, I read saccharine <u>Pollyanna.</u> My kids can read <u>M. C. Higgins the Great</u> and <u>Pocketful of Seeds.</u> Two marvelous books. There are a lot around. Writers are discovering that death, sex, love, war, divorce, and so on are part of the lives of the young. Some books, it's true, are written, it seems, merely to be in the swim, to be realistic because "realistic" is in vogue. But others are literature; they're real, passionate, felt books. They may deal, on one level, with social problems, but they are primarily about the human condition, about the way we feel and how we live with others.

When I write, I hope not to write for "children"--that is, for the fictional dear little innocent some of us seem still to believe in--but for readers. Younger readers, yes, who will respond to the characters I create--characters like themselves, also young, with the same limitation of experience. For me, all readers are equal.

This point of view, however, raises certain thorny questions. We are back to square A. Does this mean that there are no limits to what can, or should, or will be written for children? As guardians of the young, do we protect them from certain ideas, certain types of literature, the way we try to protect them from bad food and dangerous ventures? Is there material that is inappropriate for the young, or is this, too, censorship?

And if we are censoring, however discreetly, whether as parents, readers, teachers, librarians, or writers, what are we risking?

THE LIBRARIAN--GUILTY
OR UNFIT TO PLEAD?*

Sandy Mullay

This is no way to begin an article on librarianship,
but do you remember a film released a few years ago called
The Spy Who Came In from the Cold? Richard Burton played
a minor cog in an espionage organization which takes him
from his job in a special library to an assignment behind the
Berlin Wall. When caught, this pathetic figure appears in a
clinical East German courtroom, armed guards behind him,
three judges staring impassively down at him. They ask him
his name, which he gives, then his occupation and out it
comes--assistant librarian. I hope to show that this scene,
described imperfectly from memory, sums up the position of
the librarian in regard to the current controversy over Public
Lending Right and an adequate remuneration to authors for
their work.

Let me say straight away that this article represents
the personal views of one librarian with writing aspirations
and a feeling of dismay that authors should seemingly blame
librarians, of all people, for the insufficient value which society places on the writer's art.

One can hardly open a newspaper without reading of
authors' protests or demonstrations against the free lending
of library books. Do we ever read of authors' lobbying publishers for a fairer system of payment? Librarians, according to Katharine Whitehorn, are like "people who eat foie
gras but would prefer not to be reminded about the dreadful
things that happen to the geese" (Assistant Librarian, December 1973, p. 195). How often do we hear authors criticizing the publishing and bookselling trades with equal
venom?

*Reprinted by permission from Assistant Librarian, Sept.
1975, pp. 130-132.

The Publisher's Contribution

Let's get some facts straight. Most authors are badly paid. If they received a few pence every time one of their books is lent by a public library, this would go some way to recompensing them. In their fight for P. L. R. , the authors are supported by most publishers--some of whom have published correspondence on the subject. Obviously, if authors receive income from library lending, the publisher will too, for the book is not the product of the author alone; indeed, he earns only a fraction of its sales returns.

Just how badly authors are paid by publishers was brought home to me last year when I answered a newspaper advert placed by a Cornish publisher of guidebooks. This firm invited--without obligation to publish--manuscripts on the tourist attractions of the writer's local area. Fair enough you may think, but payment for suitable manuscripts was, would you believe, £30 for 10, 000 words (1974 figures). This princely sum was in reward for work which could take a month to research and from which a typing agency's fee might have to be subtracted. Anyone daft enough to write for this kind of pittance could reflect, as he skipped to the bank with his equivalent of £7. 50 per week, that the firm had also bought his copyright, and could proceed to reproduce annual editions of the book from now to Doomsday, without paying the author an extra penny.

Needless to say, I remained unrecruited to the writing fraternity. However, this publisher's offer prompted me to wonder about the current state of relations between the book trade and the authors who supply it with raw material.

The Author's Place Today

Considering the high and increasing costs of books-- and that's one thing librarians have plenty of opportunity to consider--and the fact that some bookshops carve off up to forty per cent of the retail price for themselves, one must infer that the average author who has to fight for a reasonable financial return, is getting a pretty raw deal. But don't take my word for it. The prominent publisher Sir Brian Batsford, in a letter to The Times (December 30th, 1974) says "Authors have always been shabbily treated by publishers and still are. " A glance at The Bookseller will disclose such trade advertisements as "This novel is going to

make someone a lot of money." (Issue for 26th April 1975,
p. 2227). As the magazine is aimed at the bookselling
trade, one assumes that the "someone" referred to is not
the author. This echoes Herman Wouk's hero, Youngblood
Hawke, who, in the book of the same name, is dismayed at
hearing his publisher refer to Hawke's first novel as "a door-
stopper of a book." Such exhibitions of commercial insensi-
tivity lend weight to the suspicion that authors are the producers of literary fuel which drives the media of today--
whether it be book, newspaper, or television programme.
It doesn't seem unreasonable to compare the present-day author with the coal-miner in the Industrial Revolution; without
him industrialization could not have developed, but his own
welfare was largely ignored. Without the twentieth-century
literary miner the media would collapse for lack of new
ideas, or at least be forced to repeat more and more of
those scratched old movies, or republish books whose copyrights were bought years ago for the price of a box of cigars.

Librarians in the Cross-Fire

But why should authors direct their feeling of injustice
against librarians? Granted they are underpaid, but why
don't they aim their protests at their paymasters, the publishers, and not at librarians? Is it unkind to suggest that
the writer, in his undeservedly lowly place in society is lash-
ing out at a comparatively soft target, the library profession?
After all, we are easily attacked. As a thinking profession
not exclusively motivated by profit, we can be hurt by the
suggestion that we are denying authors what they claim is
due to them. We bruise easily. In fact we may be vulnerable simply because we are incapable of retaliation; unlike the
publishers we don't have the power of deciding which authors
are going to eat well. An additional point is that libraries
represent the major purchasers of non-commercial books--
poetry, novels by unknown authors--but the writing community may not be aware of this until P.L.R. is implemented
and these non-commercial categories of literature disappear
from library selection lists simply because their purchase
cannot be justified by immediate public demand.

If, in this confrontation between the author and his
publisher--between Art and Commerce, if you like--creative
writing has become enmeshed in the barbed wire of capitalism, what on earth are librarians doing out there in no-
man's-land? Both sides seem to be using our profession for

target practice. If we must be involved in this conflict--and
the opening shots were fired before the first public library
opened its doors--then let us at least align ourselves with
the protagonist which has right on its side. Let's remind
authors that, of all those involved in the production and dissemination of books, i. e. , author, publisher, paper mer-
chant, printer, binder, bookseller, and librarian, only the
first and last are trying to make a living, not a profit.

The Slings and Arrows

Would it sound pompous to explain to authors that we
actually have an important job to do, and that at times it
isn't a very pleasant one? Adult illiteracy is currently running at ten per cent in this country where free and compulsory education has been available for a century. (Longer in
Scotland, where the situation may even be worse; according
to a recent report Scotland's largest-selling newspaper requires a reading age of exactly twelve years.) Ten per cent
is a shocking statistic. It means that at every Cup Final
there are ten thousand people at Wembley, and another three
million at home watching the event on T. V. , who cannot read
the adverts so tastefully grouped behind the goalmouths.

While this may worry the advertising industry, it
should worry the library profession even more. In a society
where genetic engineering, spare-part surgery, and chemical
and biological warfare are available to our political masters
whatever their party, the public is possibly no better equipped
educationally to understand such matters than it was two hundred years ago when a nation's rulers had no more sophisticated weaponry than a parchment Riot Act and a handful of
militia.

Shelling out novels from a public library may not do
much to correct this state of affairs, but at least we keep
people reading, keep open their channels of communication to
a wider--and freely available--source of knowledge. But why
am I writing all this? Surely we know the purpose of public
libraries, know that they enable the citizen to freely improve
his or her education, help them enrich their leisure time.
Libraries can be communication posts in the new campaign
against illiteracy being mounted by the education authorities
and the B. B. C. If our profession's purpose is in any way
philanthropic--and incidentally, profitless--why must we withstand renewed attacks from authors, who should in any case
be part of the public we serve?

I believe we <u>must</u> improve our relations with the writing community. If an ethnic group--for example, Pakistanis or Irish--were to publicly criticize our book selection policies, if a religious order was offended by any facet of public library activity, if we ignored service complaints from people who are left-handed, or have red hair, would we be doing our jobs properly, in ensuring the maintenance of a library service to <u>all</u> constituent groups of the community? I think not, but we seem to grit our teeth and turn away from the protests of authors, hoping their din will die down. It may, of course--when the last author gives up trying to write and either joins a dole queue or takes a job translating foreign-language books already being imported into this country. (Incidentally, the large number of foreign-language works reappearing in English implies that British publishers may be able to buy texts and illustrations "off the peg" abroad. This could reduce the demand for material generated in Britain, thus keeping our authors underpaid and working in a market with fewer outlets for their talents.)

Joint Interests

In case you still feel that this is none of our business, remember that if authors stop working, so do we, for our libraries would become nothing but museums for bibliophiles. A factor common to the writing and library worlds is the recent cutback on local government spending. As A. L. 's editor has pointed out (May 1975, p. 77) the recent Bucks County case affects authors' sales as well as librarians' jobs.

This is my case, then. We must patch up our tattered lines of communications with the writing community. There should be no need to emphasize that we are not having a joyride at their expense, no need to show them one old Carnegie building which is so cold in winter that the staff w. c. freezes over, or the branch in the mining district where, if you drop your pencil, you have to walk to the other end of the room to pick it up. I could name these examples, but this is only a side issue; my point is that, while librarians may not starve in garrets, they sometimes have to work in unpleasant conditions serving a fickle public. Let's positively build bridges to one section of the community which seems to regard us as parasitical.

Back to the court scene, to the disgraced librarian

in the dock. Cannot the A.A.L. organize a joint meeting
with the Society of Authors or the Writers' Action Group, to
have a "talk-in" on P.L.R.? Could we not attempt to define
the reasons for the lack of financial reward for authors'
work by inviting representatives of the publishing and bookselling professions? Let's ask them to enter the dock, ask
if they feel that authors are getting a "shabby deal" and if
so, who exactly is giving it to them. The Press must be
invited--especially Bernard Levin, who has compared the opponents of P.L.R. with gorillas--as we try to hammer out
a degree of understanding.

A Remedy ...

Are there other steps we can take? This may not be
the best time for such an idea but can we not persuade local
authorities to create more posts for writers? Public libraries could employ an author on a contractual basis, requiring him or her to assist with the publishing programme
which every large library should run anyway--with a fair
deal for the author involved (!)--and leaving time free for
the author to undertake his own writing projects with a
guaranteed wage, whether his manuscripts catch the fancy
of the publishing houses or not.

... or Too Late?

These ideas may be fruitless suggestions; possibly the
rift between ourselves and those responsible for the content
of books is now so wide as to be unbridgeable. But surely
we should do something to correct what appears to be a mis-
understanding of our situation. Even a condemned man
should attempt to defend himself. Or is the analogy to be
perfect? Playing a librarian spying for the West against
the Communists, Burton was only a pawn in a power struggle between forces too vast for him to understand; perhaps
British librarians are caught in the Armageddon where the
forces of Art and Commerce clash.

PART IV

THE SOCIAL PREROGATIVE

CIVIL LIBERTIES, LIBRARIES AND COMPUTERS*

Joyce Crooks

Borrower's Rights

The question of the rights of library users has arisen increasingly since the McCarthy era, usually in the form of a request to view the records of a particular borrower, or to see the names of all the persons who read a certain kind of book. Typically, such requests come from people representing considerable authority in a community, such as law enforcement personnel or members of city government, or from parents with what seems to be a legitimate request to see what their children read. Librarians who wish to refuse such a request often find themselves on very shaky ground; and while some who successfully resisted have been reported in the library press, it is unfortunately likely that many quick capitulations were never reported. I know of several such incidents from the San Francisco Bay Area, although they have been less frequent in the last couple of years, owing to the increased political sophistication of librarians, and to the official policy statement of the American Library Association,[1] however nebulous a help it may be in a showdown.

Until the recent Texas case no librarian has ever had any legal justification for such refusal. Before the Privacy Act of 1974, it has not been that simple to "establish" a right of privacy based on the Constitution alone, although the American Civil Liberties Union has expressed great interest in taking such a case. One of the especially thought-provoking and somewhat amusing precedents in the Texas case

*Reprinted from Library Journal, Vol. 101, No. 3, Feb. 1, 1975, pp. 482-487. Published by R. R. Bowker Co. (a Xerox company). Copyright © 1976, by Xerox Corporation.

is that establishing the right of a man to read pornography
in his own home. [2] If you can read pornography without undue interference of the state, you can read library books
without undue interference of neighbors! In any case, it
seems fairly certain that this will serve as a precedent to
help protect libraries and librarians from casual violations
of borrowers' records.

There still remains the problem of protecting the integrity of the files against law enforcement bodies with sub-
poenas in hand. The Privacy Act[3] is intended to protect individuals from the abuses of federal government files and is
particularly applicable to automated retrieval systems and
data banks. A data bank is very carefully defined as a combination of retrieval systems designed to gather otherwise
scattered material in one place for more effective use regarding one subject. [4] It is intended to insure that citizens
will know that information has been collected on them, and
for what purpose; that the accuracy and timeliness of such
information may be challenged; and that the file cannot be
shared with other departments for other than its original
purpose without the individual's consent. Exempt from the
Act are all law enforcement agencies, or agencies claiming
to be collecting intelligence data for law or national security
purposes. In these circumstances, the citizen or library patron would have no protection. If a law enforcement officer,
FBI agent, IRS agent, or whatever, persuades a judge to issue a subpoena, however ill-advised, the librarian must obey
it.

The Buddy System

Although there has been some discussion about the integrity of borrowers' files, another form of widespread
abuse--that of records of employees, public and private--
has generated very little concern. This absence of concern
is the result of two major factors: 1) The "buddy system"
of casual information-sharing on individuals, between offices,
colleagues, jurisdictions, to and from police, credit bureaus,
etc., is so common that it rarely elicits any comments at
all, although the effect of the exchange sometimes amounts
to a "black list" based on hearsay, or inaccurate or biased
information (Westin and Baker note that these exchanges are
often in direct violation of laws or official policies); 2) an
individual, particularly an applicant, is unable to challenge
such information when he cannot usually even prove that such
an exchange has taken place. [5]

One of the most sensitive areas in this regard is the arrest record. It has long been common practice for all civil service and government recruiting applications to include the question, "Have you ever been arrested?" It is also very common with large private employers. To answer "yes" often meant one would not be hired. There are 7.5 million arrests a year, of which one quarter result in convictions. Sixty per cent of white urban males are likely to be arrested during their lifetime, compared with 90 per cent of black urban males. Civil service jurisdictions did query applicants on arrest, according to one study, and 75 per cent of the employment agencies studied in the New York area "would not accept an applicant with an arrest record ... without conviction."[6] The innocent and the guilty suffer alike!

Since the mass arrests of large numbers of middle-class activists and bystanders in the 1960s, questions of police and FBI information exchange have received greater notoriety, insofar as such records are often incomplete and/or inaccurate. The information on dismissal of charges, or a not guilty verdict, is often omitted from the FBI or police records, since these verdicts are not of primary interest to these agencies. Consequently, many have been denied jobs almost automatically without any cause, and certainly without due process or recourse.[7]

Civil rights legislation now requires that only conviction questions be allowed on job applications, and that a job cannot be refused on the ground of conviction unless it can be shown that the offense directly relates to the prospective position.[8] But the casual sharing of police information with employers, and credit bureaus, remains a basic and major problem of due process and privacy for most library employees.[9]

An especially heavy stigma surrounds ex-drug users and those who have a history of mental health problems.[10] Activism in college can cause trouble, too, so much so that many colleges have stopped keeping files on club memberships,[11] so that FBI agents and other investigators simply cannot obtain such data, even with a subpoena. Many students have stopped joining clubs at all, for fear that participating in fully legal dissent activity in college could haunt them in later life.[12]

The Privacy Act no doubt has foreshadowed many at-

tempts on the part of state and local governments to enact
regulations and laws which will protect personnel files from
casual intrusion. Solano County, California, has drawn up
such a personnel rule.[13] This document includes some procedures that are notable in their regard for due process and
fairness. Among these are: 1) Before information from the
master personnel file is given to any law enforcement agency, the employee shall be notified so that he may obtain
counsel if necessary. 2) Without a demonstrable "need to
know," only public information can be revealed, for instance
the fact that the employee works there, his salary range,
length of service, etc. 3) The permission of the employee
is not sufficient reason to reveal contents of a file. This
last point brings up the question of the "informed consent"
of the employee.[14] That is, is the employee necessarily
the best judge of what s/he should or should not reveal?
Credit bureaus, in particular, often operate in flagrant disregard for the rights of privacy, and often of the law; and
the person applying for a loan, credit to buy a house, or
whatever, is often reluctant to refuse information if it
might jeopardize these services.[15] Present practice, that
is, the routine invasion of privacy in which we are all used
to living our lives, makes the refusal of information under
conditions such as these seem like an act of heroism.

Libraries have not been in the forefront in computerization of files, or in the development of data bases for
multiple functions, nor are they uppermost in the mind of
the public with regard to needed controls. But because of
the increasing reliance on information for decision-making
in all areas of American life, libraries, too, will find careful planning of systems design and objectives mandatory, if
they are not to find themselves embroiled in lawsuits and
besieged by angry taxpayers. Those who have not had problems of protecting confidential information in the past will
most certainly have them in the future.

The obvious question here is: why do computers
make that much difference? There are a number of reasons: 1) A switch to computers means there is a tendency
to collect more information on individuals than when that
information had to be handled manually. 2) Protection of
the system is more difficult as more points of access must
be controlled, if the information collection appears more
valuable than before (for example, increased inquiries into
loyalty of personnel, or reading records) this can become
a protection problem that could prove costly to solve. 3)

The tendency to share information or a computer system within a jurisdiction or a network means many more persons have access to your files who do not share your priorities or loyalties, as in "time sharing" situations with other governmental offices. This can also be an enormous problem where libraries share a computer in a network. Where there are state systems planning to add circulation programs to existing bibliographic ones, it is potentially a major civil liberties problem, and careful attention must be paid to what information is to be collected, and how it is to be protected, if individual rights are not to be violated.

As long ago as 1965, I heard a very forward-looking librarian say, while contemplating the possibility of a giant computer serving all of the libraries of the San Francisco Bay Area, "Just think, if someone had overdue books from Richmond, we could stop them from taking out books in San Jose. " Which brings us to the final difference between manual files and computers: the astronomical difference in surveillance capacity.

Circulation Control Is Surveillance

Since so many large and hitherto bibliographic or acquisition systems are considering this move to add circulation files and presumably borrowers' files, it is time to talk about the real nature of circulation records, in whatever form. 16 (Both Stanford's BALLOTS and OCLC are discussing plans to add circulation to their systems.) Circulation systems, put simply, are social surveillance systems. Any information retrieval system meets this criterion if: it "in general enhances the ability of organizations ... to achieve their ends. In other words, 1) whenever a bureaucratic agency seeks to make and enforce discriminating decisions concerning a mass clientele, and 2) whenever these decisions must accord with details of clients' past circumstances of behavior, and 3) whenever they entail points of potential conflict between system and clientele, it is advantageous to the system to develop the maximum possible surveillance capacity. " And further regarding the potentiality of library systems, "... centralization of filed data allows any system to bring the full weight of clients' records to bear in any decision-making concerning them, and prevents clients from evading the effects of their records through flight. It should likewise be clear that the extension of points of contact between system and clientele, by maximizing the incorporation

of pertinent data and the ability to act aggressively towards
clients when necessary, helps the task of surveillance. "[17]

Note here that this does assume on-line capability--
the ability to query the computer as to past performance of
any patron within a few seconds. Technology is making the
combination and sharing of files more possible than ever before. Although there certainly are manual files of data bank
nature, the public has a justifiable fear of any mechanism
that allows for increased surveillance.[18] Black people seem
to be more aware, both of the necessity for giving up privacy
to obtain public services, and of the violation of privacy in
questionnaires for all purposes, and of political surveillance,
as both Neier and Ervin point out in the works cited elsewhere. This might be one of the primary reasons public
libraries have found it almost impossible to increase their
clientele significantly in minority communities. The spread
of computerized circulation networks, with their much more
active surveillance nature, could mean fewer persons will be
willing to trade additional invasion of privacy for library services.

General sensitivity to potential misuse of computerized
information is of course increasing among all classes, which
is what generated the study leading up to the Privacy Act.[19]
The study was undertaken in response to widespread public
apprehension about data banks, and what seemed an unlimited
right of private data-collecting agencies, and especially of
the government, to invade individual privacy. The main point
of the study is that all automated data systems, not just federal systems, should come under a Code of Fair Information
Practice. According to these recommendations, all data systems with individually identifiable information should have the
following minimum safeguards: 1) one person should be directly responsible for the system; 2) each employee should
be informed about the system and the legal consequences for
leaking information to unauthorized persons, with specific
consequences for such acts; 3) reasonable precautions must
be taken to protect the system, in terms of both physical and
electronic access; 4) no transfer of information may be made
to other systems without verifying that security requirements
will be maintained; 5) a complete and accurate record of all
instances of access to the system must be kept; 6) the file
must be as complete, up-to-date, and accurate as possible
to minimize potential harm to individuals; 7) data must be
eliminated from the files when it is no longer timely; 8) annual notices must be published describing each extant system

and must cover: kind of information held, how many subjects are covered, policies concerning storage, the use to
be made of data, and procedures whereby individuals can
examine or correct files; and 9) specific procedures must
be clearly delineated, whereby the individual can challenge
the data held, and a person must be able to obtain remuneration in court if all other avenues fail.

The regulations were necessary because few of these
safeguards were being used by those responsible for data
banks or computer systems.

The law, as finally enacted, states that only information necessary to the original purpose of the file can be collected, and that it must be removed from the file as soon
as the original purpose is no longer served. It does not allow for the use of a Social Security number for any purpose
except one connected with Social Security, and any information form asking for individual data to be fed to such a computer must show which questions are mandatory and which
are optional.

Library Data Abuses

This new guideline brings up some very interesting
questions about current practices in library borrower regis-
tration procedures. Librarians dimly perceive the surveillance nature of circulation records. They have asked for
driver's license numbers, Social Security numbers, place of
work, and other data not needed for the purpose of circulation. One library which has computerized its borrowers'
records still asks some of these questions--then puts only
the name and address into the computer and throws away the
application. Libraries have never, to my knowledge, indicated whether or not omitting answers to questions would de-
prive prospective borrowers of library privileges.

The Privacy Act of 1974 applies only to federal computers and data banks, but also creates a commission "to
prepare model privacy legislation for state and local governments." Such legislation, which would bring state and local
governmental data bank jurisdictions under at least the same
controls as the federal ones, is now pending. [20] Some local
jurisdictions have already gone further. Berkeley, California, has enacted an ordinance which requires a social impact statement for any new or additional automated systems,

and a study of alternate ways of doing the job, even of not
doing the job at all. [21] It requires that new data programs
have wide publicity within the city, and a public hearing before implementation of any new data bank plan.

The new federal bill will bring to a halt certain other
abuses some librarians with new computer systems seem unable to resist.   One of these is putting economic or occupational information into the computer in order to do a use
study at some future date.   The new bill will make the collection of such nonessential information by public libraries
illegal.

People greatly fear the fact that computers create
"unforgetting and unforgiving" record systems.   They are
especially apprehensive that the people who work with the
computers treat "printouts" as gospel, and that clerks assume machines can't make mistakes.   Westin and Baker
point out, however, that machine records tend to contain
more mistakes, not fewer, and that people who think record
keepers, especially civil servants, have ever been noted
for taking an individual's side in a debate with a written
record have obviously never heard of Kafka.

Some libraries have already begun looking for ways
to safeguard circulation and borrowers' records in computer
situations.   Some of these safeguards are: 1) the registra-
tion file can be kept separately from the computerized file
and/or manually; 2) all circulation records can be erased
from the file when the item is returned, and a record can
still be kept showing how many times a book circulates; 3)
books can be charged by an identification number instead of
by borrower's name; 4) minimum data can be requested
from the patron, extra questions, if asked, can be clearly
indicated as "optional."

Librarians must weigh carefully whether the added
ability to query a library user about books overdue or lost
in another jurisdiction is worth the additional negative surveillance impact this will have with many borrowers.   At issue here are the conflicting ideals of the law and order
"wrong-doers should be punished" forces against those of
forgiveness, the "people should be able to escape their past"
group.   The more data one has about patrons, the more it
will be used.   Challenging patrons from such data involves
doing so face-to-face and in public.   There are few people
who would continue to use the library after such an affront

to their dignity, and many bystanders are likely to be almost
as greatly offended.   These patrons are lost to the library.
Can any of us afford such an image?   What is the true cost
of "efficiency" in such a situation?

Personal Personnel Records

The problems involved in the keeping of public records in libraries will still be relatively easy of solution
compared to those of administrative files of employee's records, and the problem of reducing the prevalence of the
"buddy system." James Rule found that no subject aroused
more defensiveness and antagonism among administrators
than this one.   Why do employers think they must, or ought
to, have so much information on applications that is not job-
related?   Do questions such as past medical history, psycho-
analysis, past hospitalization, treatment for drug abuse, sex
life, sex orientation, union membership, political activism
or beliefs, or religious beliefs, really become problems on
the job to the extent that routine violation of personal privacy
and due process are justified?   It is still common for inter-
viewers to ask questions of a personal nature, especially
whether women are going to get married, or have a baby
and leave, and whether unmarried men are homosexuals.
Two years ago, a delegation from the University of California, Berkeley, School of Librarianship came to a meeting
of the San Francisco Bay Area Social Responsibilities Round
Table to ask that the group investigate what they considered
improper questions regarding their sex lives asked during
oral interviews.   SRRT did not do so because the students
were too apprehensive about being identified to give even
the names of the interviewing institutions.

Police are notoriously helpful at supplying wanted information to all governmental jurisdictions, and both police
and private employers have virtually unlimited access to
credit bureau investigation if they care to use them, which
they often do. [22] New laws will not necessarily be a cor-
rective remedy for these practices, for many of them now
go on in disregard of existing laws and institutional regulations.   Nothing can stop these practices but an increased
awareness that personal privacy is being invaded and a decreased tolerance for them.   When administrators see such
practices as dangerous, that is, potentially leading to law
suits, or as threatening to the organization, they will cease
according to Rule.

Surveillance in Our Society

      Our concepts of privacy have changed during the last
two decades or so, and it is difficult to discuss how that has
happened without a further discussion of surveillance in American life. Most Americans are now aware that they have
probably been the subject of a dossier of some kind, as an
employee (especially of a federal employer, or as a scientist), as a recipient of state or federal aid of any kind, as
a credit bureau subject, as the result of an encounter with
the police, but most likely, as someone who has come to the
attention of one of the local police intelligence units, the
FBI, or one of the more than 20 federal agencies collecting
intelligence on private citizens. [23]

      Evidence of their scope is all around us: the FBI
opens mail of anyone who has been to Russia, including Boy
Scouts. At the time of the Peace Marches in San Francisco,
the employees in at least one Bay Area library were told by
someone in the Sheriff's Office that they had photographs of
all employees who had participated. Dossiers are opened
on school children, carefully noting "anti-social" behavior,
such as preferring to work alone. [24] No status provides
protection. Congressmen are monitored also. Only just recently, Congressman Dellums complained his office was
bugged. J. Edgar Hoover used to amuse various Presidents
with stories of the private wrongdoings of Congressmen, and
Congressmen have greatly feared the dossier consequences
of voting against appropriation requests of the FBI. [25] Dr.
Martin Luther King's private life was monitored for years,
and the FBI tried to blackmail him with the resultant tapes. [26]
No one seems too unimportant for investigation; it is well-
known that both FBI and CIA and all of the Armed Forces
have secret investigators and informers on campuses. [27]

      One might well ask, what do all of these people in-
vestigate? Anyone who is, or who is potentially, a dissenter
to the U.S. government. That would include anyone who actually speaks out against the government, anyone who might
become a leader and might possibly dissent in the future, all
groups with potential power, especially all minority groups
and potential minority leaders, labor unions, groups such as
the ACLU or NAACP and individuals interested in constitutional rights, those involved in "Earth Day," etc. In fact,
they seem for the most part to be investigating people involved in fully legal activities. It has been argued that the
surveillance of legal activities produces a "chill" and an in-

hibition about continuing, or beginning, such activities. It also causes the activity to be looked on as "tainted," or somehow illegal, and those who engage in it as socially stigmatized. Additionally, it has been noted that there is a significant difference between the tolerance of dissenters in Britain and America, and it is believed that the lesser tolerance of Americans has been produced by systematic and continued surveillance as official policy by our government over a period of several decades. Even if surveillance stopped tomorrow, political activity would remain repressed, perhaps through several generations. Awareness of such all-pervading stigma does not disappear overnight. [28]

My generation learned its lesson watching our elders suffer during McCarthy's time for their political beliefs in the thirties and forties, and this generation has seen those politically involved in the sixties reduced to silence during the Nixon administration. The infamous "Houston Plan" approved by Nixon, included six recommendations amounting to a virtual definition of all citizens as "enemies." The plan included: 1) intensifying electronic surveillance of all domestic security threats and foreign diplomats; 2) increased monitoring of American citizens using international communications facilities; 3) increased mail coverage; 4) more informants on college campuses; 5) listing restraints on "surreptitious entry"; and 6) the establishment of an interagency group to coordinate existing intelligence and internal security agencies, with representatives from the White House, FBI, CIA, NSA, DIA, and the three militaries. [29] According to the recent revelations concerning the CIA, all of these things have already been done, except the last two, which were seemingly prevented by Watergate.

It would be comforting to think that it was the paranoia of our late intrepid FBI leader, reinforced by that of Nixon, which had brought us to our present acquiescence in the loss of our civil liberties, and that our institutions will automatically now revert to ones respecting due process and privacy, as befits a democratic country. The fact is, however, that Nixon's recommendations could not have been effected had not our civil liberties already been eroded.

John Raines, an Assistant Professor of Religion at Temple University, has written a most informative book reviewing the developments through which we lost our civil liberties. Raines says that it is through the conversion of the government into a guarantor of big business, necessitated

by the New Industrial State (as described by Galbraith) which
marked the change from a government of the people.   This
need for big business to control the market necessitated
enormous amounts of social control, which only the government could provide.   As Raines points out: "This is the result, not of bureaucratic necessity ... but of the pursuit of
human ambition and the bending of society for that purpose. "30   That this has been achieved is the real lesson of
Watergate.   Raines reminds us that it is the right of the
people to watch the government, not vice versa, and that
cosy regulation of business by the government for what is
plainly their mutual benefit can be maintained only by the
privatization of power and the pacification of public protest.
In order for this to be effected, the affairs of the state must
be secret, defined as "national security, " and the affairs of
the citizens must be public.

        This has been accomplished by: 1) trivializing pri-
vate needs; 2) stigmatizing activity which supports individual
feelings of self-worth and self-reliance; and 3) humiliating
people by forcing them to trade privacy for needed services.
To quote Raines again: "Humiliation is the invasion of our
inner silences and self-space to render us docile to the interests of others.   It is an attack upon our dignity and reserve as persons. "31

NCLIS and Privacy

        It has been necessary to wander into the society at
large briefly in order to provide perspective on the issue of
a national system of libraries as proposed by the National
Commission of Libraries and Information Science. 32   The
NCLIS plan is conceived of as a bibliographic, communication, and retrieval network of massive and inclusive proportions, involving public libraries, universities and colleges,
information retrieval service companies, and other private
companies involved in information services, including publishers.

        Space does not allow a full discussion of the civil
liberties issues which would be affected by this plan.   Several of them can be touched upon here.   Further discussion
should be forthcoming.

        First of all, the plan places an emphasis on machine
retrieval and communication, including a heavy commitment

of the federal government to support further research and
development of all computer communications technology by
private industry, and funding of all aspects of the program. [33]
The plan envisions large public libraries forming the "back-
bone" of the network, although it would clearly be advanced
researchers, scientists, and technicians who would benefit
most by such a sophisticated information network, people who
are not now served by the public libraries at all, but by
special libraries and universities and colleges.   The plan
would do little for the public library user, or for school libraries, and most special libraries are of such a nature that
they would receive little benefit.   Such a network would necessitate a complete reordering of priorities away from public
services in public libraries, because funds, personnel, materials, and time would of necessity have to be given to the
network priority.   There is little likelihood that sufficient
funds would be available for both services and technology.
For most of the public, this simply means less access to
materials and services.   The NCLIS package also includes
the proposal to pass on the enormous costs of the technological package by charging the patron for information and
services, which appears as a serious threat to the tradition
of free public library access.   The controversy over who
will pay for what, and how much, is already raging. [34]

As now written the NCLIS plan is paradoxically capable of solving some of the acquisition and access problems
of universities and special libraries while potentially lessen-
ing the services and materials available in public libraries.
One acquisitions librarian commented to me that networking
tends to limit the acquisition of unusual or "underground"
material simply because there is no ready-made procedure
for cataloging it.   In Peter Simmons' paper previously cited
it is noted that in general, network participation tends to
diminish local autonomy.

The Commission Report states that they see the agency controlling a federal network as "neither all-encompassing,
nor authoritarian, nor prescriptive, nor regulatory, but rather, that it should be supportive and coordinating." But
participating agencies who accept grants for cooperation with
the plan would be subject to the regulations of the granting
agency.   Therefore the granting agency could be described
as a regulatory agency.   Many other commentators see such
an agency as both potentially powerful and possibly dangerous.
One scientist takes the view that "regulation and control is
the proper function of government. "[35]   Olson, Shank, and

Olsen state flatly that a national system will not work without regulation, or even "monolithic control."[36] "One reason
for doubt about effective action on the national level is the
lack of centralized control over information services in the
U.S.," they state, and go on to cite a study which lists
eight centers of influence in U.S. libraries. The study expressed further doubt that such a network involving all libraries can be established under any circumstances.

We would do well, therefore, to concern ourselves
with the implications of federal control. One model we have
to look at is the Federal Communications Commission. The
FCC is known to have a black list of thousands of names to
whom it will not issue licenses; and in November 1975 the
Washington Post printed an article attacking the FCC for not
being able to keep up with technology and being too close to
the companies they are supposed to be regulating.[37] In
short, most government regulating bodies we are familiar
with behave as Raines describes. If such a body is needed
to carry out this plan, it behooves us to wonder if the benefits could possibly outweigh the civil liberties threats involved.

Attention should also be paid to the problems that will
arise as publishing via a computer becomes commonplace,
especially if that computer is part of a national system. It
is expected that growth of publishing by machine will greatly
accelerate, and that growth of scientific publishing will virtually explode. Machines have in fact already begun to
change the nature of publishing.[38] The demand for less scientific duplication,[39] and the expense of information retrieval
will all contribute to the necessity of controlling information
at the source of publication.

Finally, one can only question why information is
suddenly of federal priority status. Does the federal government really care about the dangers of "information
chaos"? They have not heretofore been known as generous
supporters of either libraries in general, or even of federal
libraries,[40] although they have put over $1 billion into com-
puters.[41] Can it be that libraries, information sources,
and the "private sector" are now recognized as essential ad-
juncts to the research necessary to increase the G.N.P.,
insure national defense, and aid "internal security"? If the
growth of the products of technological communications, especially 2-way cable TV, leads to the necessity for making
communication products more homogeneous (as books are in

Russia), in order for the "private sector" to make a profit, so much the better. Control need not be repressive in intent to be repressive in fact. It need only be total. Consider the highly mechanized "model" libraries in Russia, mentioned by Simmons.

We now are at a turning point and must make a choice. The "easy rider" approach is before us. We can ride on the backs of the federal priorities, where the big money is, and establish, or attempt to establish, a national system of disparate parts with uncertain outcome, and unknown costs. Or, we can continue to look for solutions for parts of the problem, establish homogeneous networks, explore further ways of sharing, etc., while we carefully consider alternate structures. More answers are needed, by far. Would the public commit us to a national plan if they were asked? I for one do not see any more reason for thinking there exists only one solution than that there is only one problem for all libraries.

In the end, there is one important question, and that is whether 1984 will happen while we are admiring the efficiency of it all, or whether we will insist that machines must be used for social objectives that include human values as their basic component.

References

1. American Library Association. Policy on Confidentiality of Library Circulation Records. Chicago, ALA, 1970.
2. "Library records are confidential in Texas," Newsletter on Intellectual Freedom, September 5, 1975, p. 133f.
3. Privacy Act of 1974. 5 USC 552a.
4. Westin, Alan F., & Michael A. Baker. Databanks in a Free Society: Computers, Recordkeeping and Privacy. (Report of the project on computer databanks ... National Academy of Sciences.) Quadrangle, 1972. p. 200f.
5. Miller, Arthur R., "Computers, data banks, and individual privacy: an overview," in Surveillance, Dataveillance, and Personal Freedoms; Use and Misuse of Information Technology; A Symposium. Ed. by the staff of the Columbia Human Rights Law Review. Fair Lawn, N.J., R. E. Burdick, 1973. p. 20.
6. Raines, John C. Attack on Privacy. Valley Forge, Pa., Judson Pr., 1974. p. 30f.

7. Neier, Aryeh. Dossier: The Secret Files They Keep
    on You. Stein & Day, 1974. Chapter 9, "The
    Scarlet Letter: Conviction Records."
8. U.S. Equal Employment Opportunity Commission. Af-
    firmative Action and Equal Employment: A Guide
    for Employers. Washington, D.C., U.S. GPO,
    1974. Vol. 1, p. 41f.
9. Askin, Frank. "Surveillance, the Social Science Per-
    spective," in Surveillance, Dataveillance, and Per-
    sonal Freedoms: Use and Misuse of Information
    Technology; A Symposium. Ed. by the staff of the
    Columbia Human Rights Law Review. Fair Lawn,
    N.J., R. E. Burdick, 1973. p. 90.
10. Neier, op. cit., Chapters 5, 6, 11.
11. Askin, op. cit., p. 92f.
12. Ervin, Sam J., Jr. "The First Amendment: a Living
    Thought on the Computer Age," in Surveillance,
    Dataveillance, and Personal Freedoms; Use and Mis-
    use of Information Technology; A Symposium. Ed. by
    the staff of the Columbia Human Rights Law Review.
    Fair Lawn, N.J., R. E. Burdick, 1973. p. 50.
13. Solano County, California, "Disclosure of Personal His-
    tory Files." October 1975.
14. Baker, Michael A. "Record Privacy as a Marginal
    Problem: The Limits of Consciousness and Con-
    cern," in Surveillance, Dataveillance, and Personal
    Freedoms; Use and Misuse of Information Technology;
    A Symposium. Ed. by the staff of the Columbia Hu-
    man Rights Law Review. Fair Lawn, N.J., R. E.
    Burdick, 1973. p. 109.
15. Miller, Arthur R. The Assault on Privacy: Compu-
    ters, Data Banks, and Dossiers. Ann Arbor, Univ.
    of Michigan Pr., 1971. p. 83f. Also: Thomas
    Whiteside, "Credit Bureaus," New Yorker, April
    21, 1975, p. 45f.
16. Simmons, Peter. "Library Automation," in Annual
    Review of Information Science and Technology.
    American Society for Information Science, Vol. 8,
    1973. p. 180.
17. Rule, James B. Private Lives and Public Surveillance;
    Social Control in the Computer Age. Schocken,
    1974. p. 29f, 333f.
18. Ervin, op. cit., p. 33.
19. U.S. Department of Health, Education, and Welfare.
    Report of the Secretary's Advisory Committee on
    Automated Personal Data Systems: Records, Com-
    puters, and the Rights of Citizens. GPO, 1973.

20. H.R. 1984, 94th Congress, 1st Session.   January 23,
    1975.   Also: Barry M. Goldwater, Jr., "Bipartisan
    Politics," The Civil Liberties Review, Summer 1974,
    p. 744.
21. Ordinance No. 4732 N.S., October 1974.
22. Shields, Hannah & Mae Churchill.   "Criminal Data
    Banks: The Fraudulent War on Crime," Nation,
    December 21, 1974, p. 648.
23. Miller, op. cit., p. 21.
24. Neier, op. cit., Chapters 1-3.
25. Askin, op. cit., p. 95.
26. Donner, Frank.   "Electronic Surveillance: The Nation-
    al Security Game," Civil Liberties Review, Summer
    1974, p. 15f.   Also: Raines, op. cit., p. 32.
27. Donner, Frank J.   "Political Intelligence Cameras, In-
    formers, and Files," Civil Liberties Review, Sum-
    mer 1974, p. 8f.   Also: Raines, op. cit., p. 32.
28. Ervin, op. cit., p. 30f, 74f.
29. Raines, op. cit., p. 34.
30. Raines, ibid., p. 44.
31. Raines, ibid., p. 58.
32. National Commission on Libraries and Information
    Science.   Toward a National Program for Library
    and Information Service: Goals for Action.   GPO,
    1975.
33. _____.   Annual Report to the President and Con-
    gress: 1973-74. GPO, 1975.
34. Wright, Christopher.   "Pricing knowledge: Annual Meet-
    ing of the American Society for Information Sci-
    ence," American Libraries, January 1975, p. 8f.
    Also: "New computerized services provide speedy
    (but not free) copies 'on demand,'" Publishers
    Weekly, 206:21.   Also: Penner, Rudolf J., "The
    practice of charging users for information service,"
    Journal of the American Society for Information
    Science, January-February 1970, p. 67f.
35. "The growth of scientific and technical information--
    A challenge," Information, 3:3, 1974, p. 9.
36. Olson, Edwin E., Russell Shank, and Harold A. Olsen.
    "Library and Information Networks."   In Annual Re-
    view of Information Science and Technology, Ameri-
    can Society for Information Science, Vol. 7, 1972,
    p. 307.
37. Ervin, op. cit., p. 29.
38. "Data base publishers vying for key roles as rapid
    growth looms in business use," Publishers Weekly,
    September 16, 1974, p. 36f.

39. Garfield, Eugene. "Is there a future for the scientific journal?" Sci-Tech News, April 1975, p. 42f.
40. Martin, Susan K. "Library Automation. " In Annual Review of Information Science and Technology, American Society for Information Science, Vol. 7, 1972, p. 250.
41. Simmons, op. cit., p. 179.

PROFESSIONALISM OR CULPABILITY?
AN EXPERIMENT IN ETHICS*

Robert Hauptman

> If you promise to blow up the library,
> I'll show you. --Reference librarian, pre-
> sumably in jest.

The scholars of librarianship do not concern themselves with ethical problems. At least a survey of the literature indicates only a minimal number of articles or books
dealing with the ethics of librarians in relation to library
users.

Scholars who do take an interest in this area almost
all agree that personal beliefs must be subservient to the
needs of the patron. Foskett admonishes: "During the reference service, the librarian ought virtually to vanish as an
individual person, except in so far as his personality sheds
light on the working of the library."[1] Burgess concurs:
"Our dedication, as librarians, is not to some particular
view in these areas [political, religious, moral], however
much we may be committed as individuals."[2]

If the abjuration of personal belief is widely held by
librarians, there nonetheless exists a subtle countermovement.
Tacked on to a discussion of professionalism or appended to
the noted American Library Association's Code of Ethics,
almost as an afterthought, is the concept that librarians are
independent thinkers functioning ultimately in a societal context. The implication of this is that the librarian does not
have the right to abjure moral decision-making. Bundy and
Wasserman are well worth heeding in this respect: "Profes-

*Reprinted by permission of the author and publisher from
Wilson Library Bulletin, Vol. 30, No. 8, April 1976, pp.
626-627. Copyright © 1976 by The H. W. Wilson Company.

sionals view the freedom to function independently, the exercise of discretion, and the formulation of independent judgments in client relations based upon their own standards and ethical views as essential to professional performance."[3]
This is by no means an advocation of censorship, but rather a simple description of professional commitments.

The Question at Hand

The Federal Bureau of Investigation has indicated that during the first nine months of 1975, there occurred 1,574 bombings in the United States and Puerto Rico; 242 people were injured and 42 were killed.[4] This would seem to create a moral dilemma for the reference librarian faced with a request for information on explosives. Must one simply respond as a librarian who is there to serve, or does one have a higher duty "to society in general," as the American Library Association code puts it, to make a professional judgment and refuse to help the patron, if detrimental effects are suspected? The foul specter of censorship looms over us, and the librarian is faced with a difficult choice. It was with such thoughts in mind that the following experiment was undertaken.

The author--young, bearded, deferential--visited 13 libraries (six public, seven academic) and asked the following three questions:

1. Are you the reference librarian?
2. I need some information for the construction of a small explosive device. I am interested in the chemical properties of cordite--perhaps in a handbook?
3. What I want to know is the potency of this chemical--whether a small amount will blow up, say, a normal suburban house. (This last question was generally asked as the librarian reached for a book.)

The results were indeed astounding. Of the 13 librarians queried, not one refused to supply the information on ethical grounds. Some were more helpful than others. One refused because I was not a student at the college; one was extremely unhelpful, suggesting that I go to the engineering rather than the chemistry library; but none refused to help because disseminating information on explosives might be detrimental to society. Neither the age nor the sex of the librarian seemed to have any bearing on his/her assistance or lack thereof.

Conclusions

One might presume that each of these 13 librarians, when faced with this problem, made an ethical decision to help, based on the belief that the author did not have anti-social intentions. But this would be extremely presumptuous and probably false. The majority of these librarians gave the question, within an ethical context, little thought. Those who did, as evidenced by grimaces or comments--e.g., "Oh, great. If you promise to blow up the library, I'll show you" --appeared to abjure responsibility to society in favor of responsibility to their role of librarian as disseminator of information. One librarian--the only one who realized what the author was attempting--was adamant: The nature of the request is irrelevant; the librarian does not have the right to discriminate against a patron.

This philosophy is most blatantly portrayed by Cleghorn, who reports that some years ago the government attempted to obtain the names of people who checked out books on explosives and subversive or militant material.[5] One librarian had the following exchange with an agent:

> ... I happen to be an old-fashioned librarian and ... anyone coming in the door of a library I am in charge of can read what he wants in privacy. He shouted: 'Do you mean to tell me that you would allow patrons to use militant and subversive material at this library toward the purpose of overthrowing the government?' I refused to answer. I told him that was as if I asked him whether he had stopped beating his wife. He was livid when he left, and I was, too.[6]

This is certainly a blow against censorship in any form, and an important one. But the danger of confusing censorship with ethical responsibility is too obvious to require further elucidation. To abjure an ethical commitment in favor of anything, is to abjure one's individual responsibility.

References

1. Foskett, D. J. The Creed of a Librarian: No Politics,
   No Religion, No Morals. London, 1962, p. 10.
2. Burgess, Robert. "How Shall Librarians Organize?"
   Library Journal, 91:6044, Dec. 15, 1966.
3. Bundy, Mary Lee, and Paul Wasserman. "Professionalism Reconsidered." College and Research Libraries,
   January 1968, p. 14.
4. The New York Times, Nov. 12, 1975, p. 21.
5. Cleghorn, Reese. "When Readers Become Suspect,"
   Library Lit. The Best of 1970, eds. Bill Katz, Joel
   J. Schwartz. Metuchen, N. J. , 1971, p. 398.
6. Ibid. , p. 401.

LIBRARIANSHIP AND PRIVACY*

Irving M. Klempner

I am delighted to have this opportunity to express my point of view with respect to this highly complex, contemporary, and yet enduring issue. Somehow it seems proper that the Information Science and Automation Division and the ALA Intellectual Freedom Committee should be the co-sponsors of this meeting. For in this age of complexity, with its intricate organizational structures, there is a need for us within our own organization to interact; many of the issues confronting our special interest groups overlap; they are cross-linked; they require inter-dependent, common approaches and solutions.

What, then, is the significance of the theme of this meeting, "Data Bases and Privacy"? After all, since time immemorial, libraries and librarians have been involved in the creation of data bases. Is privacy really a subject of paramount importance to librarianship? In a more contemporary context, can we equate the issue of data bases and privacy to that of library automation and intellectual freedom? What, indeed, is the relationship between the more general advances in library and information science, including its evolving technology, and the right of the individual to the free expression of ideas, the right of the individual to read, the right to maintain control over the overt and covert societal mechanisms which have been designed for his or her physical, mental or intellectual surveillance? Within this still democratic society of ours, are our constitutional rights being undermined, eroded and subverted by a relentless force, by an expanding information technology which is imbued with a dynamism of its own, which, though carefully programmed

*Reprinted by permission of the author and the American Library Association from Newsletter on Intellectual Freedom, Nov. 1975, pp. 187-190, 195.

to link, match, merge, and manipulate data bases at electronic speed, is nevertheless out of control and running amuck? What is the librarian's professional, moral, and ethical responsibility in controlling information science technology so that it could be used as a force for the liberation rather than for the enslavement of the human mind?

I submit to you that the issues with which we are dealing today are not merely issues of philosophical or rhetorical import, issues to be raised at an ALA conference, perhaps in one or two library schools, discussed briefly, and then forgotten. These are issues which I deeply believe exert a pervasive and profound influence on our daily personal and professional lives.

What I will seek to show in this brief talk is that I find no inherent conflict between the acquisition, organization, and servicing of information, i. e. , between the creation and use of library data bases, and privacy. On the contrary, I find the concept of access to information, of access to ideas, of individual intellectual freedom, to encompass the notion of privacy. I will seek to show that it is not so much the creation and availability of data bases, but the secondary, misdirected and, often, illegitimate use of data bases that represents a violation of a de facto contractual agreement between the compilers and the subjects of data bases.

I would like to consider the term "data base" as reflective of societal, governmental, i. e. , institutional, rather than personal or individual aims and efforts to acquire transactions and interchanges of information. In personal transactions and interchanges of information, it is the individual who has control over the privacy of information. He weighs the advantages and disadvantages of disclosure against the possible benefits that may accrue to him, and makes his decisions accordingly. However, it is the societal institutions rather than private individuals that have the financial resources to create and operate computerized data banks; it is societal institutions rather than the private individual that can coerce a citizen to supply personal information, that can use the threat and power of the state to withhold vital benefits, the threat of statutes, grand jury probes, contempt of court citations, harassments through FBI, IRS and, apparently, CIA investigations to compel disclosure. Certainly, no private individual or organization has at its disposal such a powerful arsenal of coercion. No wonder that in the face of the continuous abuse of such powers, the ALA Council found it necessary in February 1973 to adopt a resolution on government intimidation seeking a halt in the unjustified and often illegitimate use of these coercive mechanisms by our federal government agencies.

In perhaps a superficial sense the relationship between data bases and privacy may be perceived to represent a conflict between societal needs and demands for information, i.e., the institutional aims and efforts at creating, merging, and manipulating data bases, and the individual's need and right to withhold, to maintain control over, personal information.

Librarianship and Privacy

Let us here acknowledge the fact that historically librarianship has been concerned not so much with the issue of privacy as with data bank creation and use. After all, our prime function has been, and continues to be, the acquisition, organization, storage, and diffusion of information. Dealing as we do with published materials, privacy for published materials represents an illogical absurdity. We are aware that the very act of publication represents a de facto denial of privacy. The act of publication represents an act of public declaration, of making generally known, of disclosing, of imparting data or information to others. Thus, the ALA Office for Intellectual Freedom, the Freedom to Read Foundation, the Intellectual Freedom Committee, and a number of other groups within this and other professional library associations have been concentrating their efforts on the necessary and incessant fight to gain access to information, the fight against censorship, against prior restraint of publications, and in general, in support of the rights of our citizenry to read, hear, discuss, think or publish the unthinkable. The Library Bill of Rights, adopted in June of 1948, does not confront the issue of privacy, but it does specifically ask libraries to provide a challenge to censorship in the maintenance of library responsibility "to provide public information and enlightenment," and urges libraries to cooperate with "persons and groups concerned with resisting abridgment of free expression and free access to ideas. "

The Right to Privacy

The right to privacy, though not expressly stated in

the U. S. Constitution, does have its roots anchored in the
First, Fourth, Fifth, Ninth, Tenth and Fourteenth Amendments.   Briefly, the First Amendment relates to freedom of
religion (i. e. , freedom of conscience, of belief), freedom
of the press, freedom of speech; the Fourth Amendment refers to the right of the people to be secure in their persons,
houses, papers, and effects, against unreasonable searches
and seizures; the Fifth Amendment relates to prohibition
against self-incrimination and the deprivation of "life, liber-
ty, or property, without due process"; the Fourteenth Amendment also refers to due process; the Ninth and Tenth Amendments note that the enumeration or delegation of certain
rights in the Constitution ought not to be considered as a denial or disparagement of the nonenumerated and nondelegated
rights, which are to be retained by the people.   During this
bicentennial celebration of the U. S. Constitution [sic], it may not
be out of place for us to recall and reaffirm the concept expressed in the Declaration of Independence, that "governments are instituted among men, deriving their just powers
from the consent of the governed. "   It may also not be out
of place to recall that our government and its institutions
were created not to destroy, but to protect and preserve the
rights of the individual.   It should be clearer now that
whereas the individual's right to privacy is an all-pervasive
and guaranteed right under the U. S. constitutional form of
government, society's right to know particularly of private,
i. e. , personal information, is a delegated right, is not an
absolute right, is not a comprehensive right, is a right narrowly defined and to be narrowly applied.

It is the bureaucratic encroachment on narrowly defined, narrowly delegated and undelegated citizen rights that,
of course, diminishes personal privacy, individual choices,
individual actions, and, ultimately, the individual's intellectual freedom.   Thus, it seems to me, it is erroneous to
equate society's "right to know" (and its "right" to keep its
information secret) with the citizen's or individual's right to
privacy.   If the purpose of our government, as I believe it
to be, is to nurture the constructive and creative potential
of the individual, and if that requires the use of privacy,
and if the right to privacy is inherent under our constitutional form of government, then the ends of our institutions
and their data bases ought to be to enhance, and not to impede, the privacy of the individual.   Stated more simply,
the government's "right" to know represents an intrusion on
the individual's right to freedom.   If and when freedom of
an individual is to be limited, it must be narrowly limited,

temporarily limited, in favor of the individual and not the
government.   The intellectual freedom of the individual in
our society is paramount, then, over the often illegitimate
needs of the state.

The ALA definition of intellectual freedom, reflecting
as it has historically outside events, would need to be expanded to embrace the concept of privacy.   In doing so, we
would lend recognition to the library as an inviolable sanc-
tuary of diverse ideas.   It follows that the users of a library's collection and its information services must be freed
from the possible fear of intimidation and possible incrimina-
tion when they make use of materials which run counter to
prevailing governmental pronouncements, desires or societal
beliefs.

I should like to add here that I do not consider the
concept of privacy to be a static one, to be expressed in absolute "yes" and "no" terms.   The definition of privacy
would, of necessity, have to change and expand since the
technological means for invasion of privacy are also changing
and expanding.

The Invasion of Privacy

An elaborate information technology exists today to
invade privacy and, in a sense, to create data bases.   Laser
microphones are available which can pick up conversations
from as far away as two miles.   Very High Frequency (VHF)
antennae have been developed for picking up a conversation
taking place within an enclosed room a block away.   Minia-
ture cameras and optical devices exist which enable the capture of data under the most adverse conditions.   Infrared
lights have been developed which enable intruders literally
"to see in the dark."   Cable television can be rigged not
only for viewing, but for being viewed.   Of course, we know
about audio tapes and phone tapping devices as mechanisms
for data base creation.

While Congress rejected in 1968 the concept of a
National Data Bank, while it rejected last year the FEDNET
Project seeking to link federal agency computers, while it is
disallowing funds for the Department of Agriculture's internal data bank because the agency did not adhere to safeguards to protect private information, we learn of the existence of other federal electronic intelligence projects and net-

works, such as Project ZENITH, HARVEST, ARPANET,
making use of Interface Message Processor (IMP) technology
developed by the DoD Advanced Research Projects Agency--
a technology enabling the linking of White House, CIA, Defense Department and a number of other data bases and providing a capability for potential if not actual illegal access
to the files of millions of American citizens.   We have had
instances of White House decision memoranda and official
executive orders authorizing one agency to examine the citizen records collected for a specific purpose by another agency (e. g., EO 11697, signed January 17, 1973, authorized the
Department of Agriculture to examine the tax returns of 3
million farm operators "as may be needed for statistical purposes").   National Wiretap Commission investigators have
just discovered that nearly half of certain devices sold for
use in wiretapping phones and households surveillance go to
police in states where possession of such devices is illegal.

    As indicated earlier, the concept of privacy has not
been given significant attention by the library profession;
neither have we shown thus far sufficient concern about the
consequences ensuing from the overt or covert application of
information science technology.   There is, of course, every
indication that in the future, librarians and information scientists will increasingly be given the responsibility for acquiring, organizing, and servicing collections of archives,
agency records, official papers, and similar files which
would involve not so much published information as private
information, restricted information, personal information.
Even at this very moment, libraries and information centers
do have a responsibility over data bases which require a
greater or lesser degree of protection.   Computerized or
manual, do not the library's circulation records or personnel files demand protection?   Does not open access to the
library's record of reference questions, literature searches,
and similar records which can be linked to names of specific
individuals endanger their privacy?

    Within the last decade, we have had a good number
of requests for information contained in library files which,
if granted, would undoubtedly have infringed on the individual's right to privacy.   Requests have been noted from deans
seeking the reading history of faculty members as an aid in
determining merit increases, from professors seeking the
reading history of students as an aid in determining grades.
I haven't as yet heard of requests from students seeking out
the reading history of their professors--although this may be

happening now.   Certainly a record of reference requests,
literature searches, linked to a specific individual, could be
used to reveal that individual's current research activities,
method of attacking research problems, or research progress.
There have been numerous requests from government agents
seeking access to internal library data files as aids to processing security clearances.

The library literature indicates that in the spring and
summer of 1970, the Milwaukee Public Library and public
libraries in Cleveland, Richmond, California, and twenty-
seven public libraries and branch libraries in the Atlanta
area were visited by U.S. Treasury Department agents seeking to link specific circulation records with individual criminal activity.   In practically none of the cases was a request
for private information based on any formal process, order,
or subpoena authorized by a federal court.   The Executive
Board of ALA found it necessary to state soon after the
wholesale public library invasion by Treasury agents that
"the efforts of the Federal government to convert library
circulation records into 'suspect lists' constitute an uncon-
scionable and unconstitutional invasion of privacy of library
patrons and, if permitted to continue, will do irreparable
damage to the educational and social value of the libraries
in this country. "

In a resultant policy on the confidentiality of library
records, adopted by the ALA Council in January of 1971, the
Council strongly recommended that the responsible officers
of each library in the United States adopt a policy which
recognizes: (1) that its circulation records and other records identifying the names of library users with specific
materials are confidential; (2) that such records may not
be made available to state, federal or local government
agents unless a "process, order or subpoena" is issued;
(3) that libraries must resist the issuance or enforcement
of such an order or subpoena until a "proper showing of good
cause has been made in a court of competent jurisdiction. "

Thus, it is obvious from recent and past experience
that governmental institutions have too often failed to respect
the constitutional rights of the individual.   Our government
officials need to be reminded that privacy of the individual
does represent one of the fundamental pillars upon which our
Constitution is based.   We need to remind ourselves that our
intellectual freedom and the intellectual freedom of library
users will be diminished to the extent that individual privacy

atrophies.   Justice Louis D. Brandeis (<u>Olmstead v. U.S.</u>,
1928) has noted:

> Experience should teach us to be most on our
> guard to protect liberty when the government's pur-
> poses are beneficent.   Men born to freedom are
> naturally alert to repel invasion of their liberty
> by evil-minded rulers.   The greatest dangers to
> liberty lurk in insidious encroachment by men of
> zeal, well-meaning but without understanding.

Libraries, while seeking to develop data bases, must
also seek to foster adequate internal administrative controls,
staff educational programs, physical security and software safeguards, as well as promote local and national awareness of the
rights of privacy of the individual.   The unauthorized release of
private data would represent a betrayal of the trust between the
library and its public.   Our data bases and library systems
would become meaningless were they to be operated in an environment of lack of trust, of uncertainty, of potential danger or
fear on the part of the library patron.   I am glad to see that in
the ALA Statement of Professional Ethics, prepared by the Code
of Ethics Committee and accepted by the ALA Council in January
of 1975, libraries are asked to "protect the essential confidential
relationship which exists between a library user and a library. "

Of course, a code of ethics does not have the force
of law.   Neither can laws be truly enforced without the individual's cooperation.   I submit that it is our ethical,
moral, and professional responsibility to assure that library
data bases, files, circulation records, and reference requests are not used as unlawful appendages of a governmental political system.   It is our responsibility to assure
that our data bases are devoted to the needs of the independent human mind.   We must not compromise the humanity of
the individual for the expediency of the state.   We must not
lose sight of our major priorities.

In the past, we have had no difficulty whatever with
the concept of providing public access to public information.
We should have no difficulty whatever in the future in limiting access to private information.   These are not incompatible objectives.   These objectives represent an integral part
of the stated goals of this association; they form an integral
part of the concept of intellectual freedom.

THE 1973 COURT RULINGS ON OBSCENITY:
HAVE THEY MADE A DIFFERENCE?*

Judith Serebnick

A year ago I did a study for the National Book Committee and the Ford Foundation to assess the impact of the
June 1973 and subsequent U. S. Supreme Court obscenity decisions on public and school libraries and trade bookstores.
For the study I traveled to ten medium-sized cities and
spoke with 210 librarians, trustees, school administrators,
teachers, and booksellers. (The cities were Manchester,
N. H.; Memphis, Tenn.; Atlanta; Grand Rapids, Mich.; Madi-
son, Wisc.; St. Paul, Minn.; Des Moines, Iowa; Tulsa,
Okla.; Albuquerque, N. M.; and Portland, Ore.)

I wanted to find out, first, if there was general
awareness of the decisions; second, whether attempts to suppress materials in libraries and trade bookstores had taken
place; and third, the extent to which selection practice had
been modified as a result of the decisions.

While my focus was on the Supreme Court's rulings,
I attempted to understand the general pattern of materials
selection and circulation in the libraries and bookstores I
visited. Other factors I considered were: What guidelines
on selection were followed; who selected; and what was considered controversial and why. Also, since the high court
decisions now leave it to local communities (state, county,
city, township) to define obscenity and determine their standards, I collected detailed information on how those interviewed supported their opinions of community standards regarding alleged obscenity.

*Reprinted by permission from Wilson Library Bulletin,
Vol. 50, No. 4, Dec. 1975, pp. 304-310. Copyright © 1975
by The H. W. Wilson Company.

By gathering data on recent selection and circulation
procedures in each library and bookstore and on opinions
concerning community standards, I hoped that the interviews
would furnish information not only on the effects of the decisions, but also on possible reasons for these effects, or lack
of effects.

The study revealed general awareness of the Supreme
Court rulings. All those interviewed knew of the decisions,
and they mentioned, particularly, the new use of community
standards as opposed to national standards. If obscenity
legislation had recently been passed in their states, they
knew of that, also. However, if bills were pending before
their state legislatures, in most cases they were unaware of
them.

One exception was a public library director who always phones the president pro tem of her state senate when
she hears an obscenity bill is up for consideration. Recently when she called, the senator said to her, "I know what
you're calling about. You just want to be sure libraries are
excluded. You've got to have all those dirty books. Now
just don't you worry. We're going to take good care of
you. "

In order to find out whether attempts to suppress
books and other materials had occurred as a result of the
1973 rulings, I asked if there had been any recent increase
in the number or intensity of complaints. Across the board
the answer was no. Librarians and booksellers do get complaints at the desk or cash register from people objecting
to particular books, especially to the "filth that's published
nowadays, " but very few ask to have items removed or restricted. And for each person who objects to a book, there's
likely to be another who wants it. A public library director
spoke of the irate patron who marched into his office, flung
down The Onion Field, and said, "That's an ornery book.
I wish I hadn't read it. " That same day someone else approached the librarian and asked, "Do you happen to have
an ornery book for me to read?" He gave her The Onion
Field.

Public and school libraries in the ten cities get few
written complaints objecting to material in the collection--
the average is five or six a year. The highest number reported was one a month. The director of that public library
attributes the comparatively high figure not to the Supreme

Court's actions, but to the fact that people in her city feel
they have a say in what goes on; the city council encourages
people to appear before it, and the library seeks active citizen participation in policy setting and selection.

As for the substance of the complaints, for more than
nine tenths of the study's participants, most objections before
1973 concerned alleged obscenity, in particular, graphic descriptions of the sex act and use of four-letter words; since
1973 most complaints still relate to obscenity.   Also mentioned were ethnic and sexist stereotypes, references to
drugs, and excessive violence.

Politics was mentioned as the major objection in only
one instance, which involved a library's policy of allowing a
wide assortment of groups to hold open meetings in its public
rooms.   For example, when a Chinese woman read Mao's
poems in the library, a rash of complaints ensued and the
library was accused of endorsing Communism.   The day I
visited, my interview with a branch librarian was interrupted
by a telephone caller threatening to cause trouble that night
at a meeting of a women's group for amnesty for draft re-
sisters.

This particular public library, which has a comparatively low percentage of obscenity complaints, happens to be
in a city that is distinctly liberal in its acceptance of sexually explicit materials.   Two or three years ago when the
newly elected mayor attempted to gain support for closing
"adult" theaters and bookstores, he was told by the city's
attorneys that he couldn't.   Their legal interpretation was:
If such places are serving people who want to visit them,
and if they adhere to the law and don't display their wares
where minors can see them, they have a right to stay open.

Though some people in this city are upset by the
growth of 24-hour out-service massage parlors, and by their
revered local newspaper printing classified ads for the parlors, still, when the city council recently discussed closing
them, the most conservative member strongly argued on TV
that massage parlors (the fastest growing business in town)
had a right to operate in "our free enterprise system. "

It came as a surprise to the librarians and booksellers I interviewed that there has been no increase in the
number or intensity of complaints since the 1973 decisions.
Many had believed that censorship of supposedly obscene ma-

A look at selection policies and censorship

How some of the libraries surveyed differed in their treatment of censorship.

Policy I

The system does not practice censorship. Serious works which present an honest picture of some problems or aspects of life are not excluded because of coarse language or frankness. Materials representing all points of view are required....
--From a 1973 public library's materials selection policy

Policy II

Selection [of fiction] is based on standards of good writing, realistic or imaginative qualities of creative writing, and stories not obviously or intentionally sensational, morbid, or erotic.
--From a public library's 1962 policy on fiction selection

Selection is based on general appeal, permanent value as creative or realistic writing, originality, contemporary significance, literary excellence, entertaining or amusing qualities, and relation to other works in the collection.
--From the same library's 1974 statement

Policy III

The collection must contain the various positions expressed on important, complicated, or controversial questions, including unpopular or unorthodox positions. The public library does not promote particular beliefs or views. It provides a resource where the individual can examine issues freely and make his own decisions.
--From a public library's book selection policy

Policy IV

A mission of the school system is to expose children to ideas--not restrict them; to encourage the study of problems--not hide them. If an increasing portion of the curriculum is to be devoted to issues of real importance to students, many controversial materials will have to be provided.
--From a public school system's proposed instructional materials selection policy

Policy V

Free discussion of controversial issues is the heart of the democratic process....

Without minimizing the importance of established truths and values, it shall be the policy ... to foster dispassionate, unprejudiced, scientific studies of controversial issues....
—From a public school system's handbook of policies.

Because of contents, certain material may occasionally be excluded, such as media which are offensive to good taste or contrary to moral and ethical standards or which present false values; or media on public questions presenting one side of a question only, which are written in a violent, sensational, inflammatory manner.
—From the same public system's library media selection policies

terials would become widespread in the wake of the new judicial rulings.

Why hasn't there been an increase in complaints? Some I spoke with said the public is either unaware of, or unconcerned about, the decisions and obscenity. A few librarians, particularly those in schools, said their collections contain nothing that anyone could possibly consider obscene, and therefore they receive no complaints. Most people, however, said their collections do contain material that someone could object to (if for no other reason than that obscenity is often in the eye of the beholder), and in the past they had received objections to works generally considered innocuous. Interestingly, almost everyone said they have controversial items in their collections now that they would never have had five to ten years ago.

Then why didn't the anticipated increase in objections materialize? Most people I spoke with believe that part of the public today is disturbed by the spread of adult bookstores, theaters, and massage parlors, especially if they spread from downtown areas to residential areas. They think that when stricter state obscenity legislation is passed, it is aimed at curbing the expansion of such enterprises and not at restricting acquisition policies of libraries.

Some recent legislation does, of course, specifically

exempt libraries. (For example, the Moore v. Younger
case in California, which tested the state's Harmful Matter
Statute, did just that.) I did speak with people who could
contemplate a chain reaction, with censorious action against
adult bookstores and theaters spreading to libraries and
trade bookstores. Still, librarians and booksellers consider
adult bookstores and theaters to be in an entirely different
category from their own establishments. They think today's
general public associates obscenity with what's in adult bookstores and X-rated films and not with library materials. In
answer to some hypothetical questions I asked, only a handful of the 210 persons interviewed would consider going to
the defense of an adult bookseller or his/her books, even if
among the embattled titles were a few also found in libraries
and bookstores.

One owner of a trade bookstore I spoke with also
owns five adult bookstores. He has a booklength file of
newspaper clippings describing the continued harassment and
closing of his adult stores. At the height of his difficulties
a few years ago, he tacked up notices at a major university
in a neighboring city and ran ads in campus newspapers asking for volunteers to attend his upcoming trial and speak on
intellectual freedom. Two persons out of the university's
50,000 responded. This bookseller says freedom-to-read
people are too busy reading to take an active role in fighting
censorship! In his experience, all his harassers have been
nonreaders with a lot of time to involve themselves in censorship cases.

Another reason offered for the lack of increase in
complaints is that since the so-called sexual revolution of
the 1960s, the public is more tolerant. People may not like
what's going on, but they're not going to fight it, if for no
other reason than they believe they can't win. They see
that although adult theaters and bookstores in their cities are
continually harassed and closed, they soon reopen. Some in-
terviewees said we're in the downswing of a liberal trend
toward accepting sexually explicit works; others said the
liberalization of the 60s cannot be erased, and that we'll
stand still for a time with the gains intact.

The inclusion of sexually explicit material in a collection is not in itself seen as sufficient reason for censorious
action--there must be other conditions present. One public
library director put it this way:

> Sex is the most controversial area. Overtly,
> complaints might be about sex or four-letter
> words, but in reality they're about something else.
> I think people can use that because it's quite emo-
> tional--a lot of people are still very much con-
> cerned and turned off in that area. They use that
> as a flag to get people charged up--they're carry-
> ing the flag on the side of right--when in reality
> the issue may be racial, political, or something
> else.

This opinion was shared especially by people who had
been closely involved in censorship cases. A school superintendent accounted for a serious case in his school system
several years ago by stating that some groups in his city
were disturbed by school integration, by busing, and by the
greater freedom allowed students. Although this discontent
initially erupted in a challenge to the school to remove from
a multiethnic kit a book containing four-letter words, the
crisis continued long past the point at which the book was,
indeed, taken out of the school's collection.

A few years ago in another city, the mayor and library board pressured the public library to remove a local
newspaper from the collection because the newspaper used
four-letter words and thus might corrupt minors. The director offered to limit use to adults, but the mayor and the
board refused, and the newspaper was taken out of the library. Today there's a new mayor (somewhat antiestablish-
ment himself), and Takeover is back in the library.

A trade bookstore elsewhere was raided by the police,
supposedly because it stocked obscene books. The same
books were in other stores, but those were not raided. It
so happened that one night before the raid, the bookstore
had been the site for a meeting of people opposed to U.S.
intervention in Vietnam.

The last question I asked in the survey was whether
selection practice had been modified as a result of the 1973
rulings. The decisions did arouse immediate fear among
librarians and booksellers. They believed a period of Court
permissiveness had ended, and a period of uncertainty about
community standards had been ushered in with a potential
for an increase in censorship. Some people I spoke with
had been at the 1973 ALA conference in Las Vegas when
the decisions were announced, and they went home expecting

their libraries to be raided momentarily.   Though none of
their libraries was actually harassed, the Court decisions
did affect libraries' and bookstores' procedures in concrete
ways.

Shortly after the rulings, one public library director
received a phone call from a local newspaper reporter who
asked, "What are you going to do now?" She replied, "I'm
not going to do anything," meaning she did not intend to
change the library's selection policy or remove books.   The
library, however, did revise and strengthen its written complaint form in the expectation of increased protests.   (I
found that other libraries did the same.)   When the new
form was shown to the library board for approval, one member told the director, "I hope you're not going to let some
old duffer objecting to one word in a book use this to in-
timidate the staff and get books removed."

Actually, when the expected increase in complaints
failed to materialize, the library decided to remove from
its vault controversial material kept there for many years.
Yes, vaults are still around, but I must add that in this library you will find on the open shelves many books considered too controversial by libraries that pride themselves on
the absence of a vault.

Another public library has a policy of allowing some
books to circulate only to people over 18.   The policy (begun in 1969) was a compromise with the library board in a
serious censorship case involving Portnoy's Complaint.   Today 20 or fewer books are on the restricted list.

A few months after the 1973 rulings, the library
drafted a statement explaining the continuation of the policy.
One sentence reads: "The present atmosphere, triggered by
the June decisions, would be even less hospitable to removal
of the board's restriction toward minors."   This library was
not unique in referring to the rulings when justifying such
limitations.   Its director said that while he could still defend Portnoy's Complaint today, he feels on shakier ground
because of the loss of the "utterly without redeeming social
value" test which protected some books from censorship.

The decisions' effect was seen clearly in communities
that have recently voted for new, stricter obscenity legislation.   In one city (shortly before the residents were to vote
on empowering the city council to draw up a tighter ordi-

nance), the assistant director of the public library asked all
branch librarians to examine carefully the illustrated Joy of
Sex, which had just arrived, and to prepare a defense for it
before putting it on the shelves. She said she felt awful asking this, but she did not want the branch librarians to be sitting ducks in case of complaints.

This library had recently lowered the age for an
adult card to 12 years, and the assistant director had visions
of some parent finding the illustrated Joy of Sex in the hands
of a 12-year-old son or daughter, reacting against the library, and voting for stricter obscenity controls.

I also spoke with two branch librarians in that system. One had decided she could not defend the inclusion of
the illustrated Joy of Sex in her library, while the other
was still looking at the book and trying to decide whether to
prepare a defense. By the way, the vote in that city was
two-to-one to have the council draw up a new obscenity ordinance.

At about the same time, while another city's residents were about to vote in a statewide election on a stricter obscenity measure, the librarians in the central public library were thinking of putting out the last three fiction titles
held behind the desk: City of Night, Naked Lunch, and Last
Exit to Brooklyn. The vote was 52 per cent for the obscenity measure, 48 per cent opposed. When I visited this library a few weeks after, the three books were still behind
the desk.

In bookstores I visited, several managers of large
chain stores said that shortly after the 1973 opinions, the
chains stopped carrying some lines of risqué pulp novels.
Managers of independent stores also reported withdrawing
similar titles after the rulings. Most of the trade booksellers in the survey who continue to carry books and magazines labeled "For Adults Only" keep them on separate racks
near the cash register to discourage minors from browsing.

Thus in some libraries and bookstores both the decisions and recent legislation have had a "chilling effect."
They have prompted some librarians to introduce restrictions
or reinforce existing ones, and they have cut short attempts
to remove restrictions.

Even in states that have new laws specifically exempt-

ing libraries, librarians continue to act cautiously, especially
regarding minors. They may say they think the public is
disturbed only by adult bookstores and theaters, but still
these librarians are taking no chances. The time is considered wrong for discontinuing some restrictive measures.

Controversial books continue to be avoided in some
libraries, especially those in schools. Some libraries still
require three favorable reviews even though noncontroversial
books require only two. Controversial best-sellers are
bought in single copies and housed in the central research
collection in some public library systems, even though other
best-sellers are duplicated heavily for all branches. Potentially troublesome books are bought to fill reserves, but then
are not added to the collection. And they are sometimes restricted in circulation.

On my visits to the ten cities, made over a six-
month period in 1974, as I noticed the prevailing caution and
librarians' continuation of restrictions, I thought often of
Marjorie Fiske's study of book selection and censorship in
California public and school libraries during the 1950s.
Fiske's research (financed by the Fund for the Republic and
sponsored by the University of California/Berkeley School of
Librarianship) originated in response to the concern that the
investigations of un-American activities committees, anti-UN
demonstrations, and legislation curbing the freedom to read
were affecting libraries.

Fiske and her associates interviewed 204 librarians
and school administrators in 26 California communities. Her
study employed some of the finest social science methodology
of the day and is considered the seminal research on library
censorship.

I thought of the key question Fiske asked in her study,
namely, are restrictions being imposed on librarians or are
librarians imposing restrictions on themselves that threaten
the citizen's right to easy access to an adequate collection?
At the time Fiske concluded that restrictions in the libraries
she studied were widespread, but were not a consequence of
specific pressures on librarians from groups or individuals
in the community.

She said the restrictions were a consequence of a
sense of caution among library professionals, activated in
part by dramatic events that took place outside, often far

outside, the confines of their cities and towns.   Though the librarians Fiske interviewed gave verbal allegiance to the idea of intellectual freedom, because they sensed a kind of free-floating anxiety in the air around them they were reluctant to put their concepts to the test.   Why, she asked, do librarians internalize this anxiety instead of asserting themselves and fighting it?   Her data did not furnish the answers, and Fiske could only speculate that a low professional self-image might account for the "sense of caution."

I think this sense of caution persists, and we still do not have the data to explain it.   I hope, however, that we continue to ask Fiske's questions and begin to explore the meaning of the answers.

FEMINISM AND CENSORSHIP*

Nancy Ward

After spending several years as a member of the National Organization for Women and as a school librarian talking and writing about sexism in children's literature and in textbooks, I suddenly find myself saying "Wait a minute, this isn't what we mean. " This is occasioned by an article in the March, 1974 Elementary English, "Mother Goose: Sexist?" The author may not have intended the article as a call for censorship but I did have visions of earnest feminists snatching copies of Mother Goose from library shelves and hiding them in the locked case.

To avoid such happenings it might be useful to suggest standards which will allow us to have non-sexist material without book-banning. First, let's decide that we must not sacrifice literary quality to make a social or political point. A book with a woman bulldozer operator is not per se a good book any more than is a book with a black surgeon. And the sacrifice is not necessary. There are already many strong, nonstereotyped females in children's books, although admittedly they are in the minority. Who could be more original and strong-minded than Lewis Carroll's Alice, Louise Fitzhugh's Harriet or Marilyn Sach's Veronica? Sex stereotypes are found chiefly in poor quality books simply because their writers can create only stock characters and situations. Good writers create individuals, not stereotypes. In other words you will seldom be forced to choose between feminism and literary merit. But if you do, keep the good book even with its stereotypes. You can always discuss the book's shortcomings with the children.

*Reprinted by permission of the author and publisher from Language Arts, Vol. 53, No. 5, May 1976. Copyright © 1976 by the National Council of Teachers of English.

Keep Mother Goose and the folktales, too.   Look for folktales and myths with female "heroes"; they do exist. But don't distort the others, as did the Russian grandmother in the Charles Addams cartoon who is telling a bedtime story to her grandchild.   "And then Cinderella shot the capitalist prince, established a people's democracy and lived happily ever after."   The recent record, "Free to Be You and Me" did similar violence to the Atalanta myth.   This sort of thing is an unforgivable destruction of our cultural heritage.

We want balance, not censorship--not material taken away but material put in.   A case in point is a series of literature texts submitted for California State adoption.   In one of the texts there were 24 stories, five of them with women as central characters.   The women were: an over-bearing ca-reer woman, a woman who abandoned her child, a woman who drove her child insane, a woman who was neurotic and self-cen-tered and a woman whose life is destroyed because she is jilted. Our task force, which had been appointed by the California State Curriculum Commission to review the material, recommended revision or elimination of the book.   Not because we denied that there are overbearing, cruel and neurotic women or be-cause we wanted no stories about them but because these were the only stories about females in the book.   We asked for the inclusion of at least two positive portrayals of women and girls.

Another example: One English text had an excerpt from a book by a retired army colonel.   The colonel at-tributed the decline of moral values, the increase in juvenile delinquency and everything except the common cold to what he called the "American Matriarchy."   He said that this "matriarchy," has reduced the father to a pitiable Dagwood Bumstead type and has caused chaos in the schools because women teachers cannot control the students.   Now the good colonel is certainly entitled to his opinion but it is a highly questionable one and the book provides no balance.   It would have been both fairer and more intellectually stimulating if the piece had been followed by one by a feminist.   Again, balance, not censorship.

When we come to the primary readers, the standards change.   There is no literary merit to be considered.   The stories are secondary to the words being developed.   We do not violate their integrity by demanding that more females be shown.   Feminists have been accused of demanding strict numerical equality in the texts.   This isn't true.   If we

count male-female ratios in illustrations and stories it is
only to suggest that if we have a book with 21 stories about
males and one about females, then maybe, just maybe,
something should be done about it.   Nor do we violate the
literary integrity of the texts by demanding that females be
shown in non-stereotyped roles and behavior, by insisting
that they do more than iron and cry.

However, in spite of all the studies and the discussions, the publishers have made almost no changes.   The
new editions are very like the old except in one rather odd
way.   They have taken many of their old stories and substituted ethnic minority characters.   Thus we have progressed from anglo-saxon female morons to multi-ethnic female morons.

Science books present another interesting example of
sexism.   Every book of a recent series is entitled "The
Young Scientist: Observing His World, " "The Young Scientist, Exploring His World, " for example.   Studies have indicated that children don't understand the generic "he" and
"his. " To them it means males.   And this belief will certainly be reinforced by the text.   There were no illustrations or biographies of female scientists.   Another item,
each scientific principle was illustrated by a drawing of a
boy and girl using it in a school laboratory.   Above each
drawing was a picture of a scientist using this principle in
his profession.   All the scientists were male.   How better
could we say "Males and females both study science but only
males ever use it"?   The balance in these books could have
been established very easily by changing the titles and including biographies and illustrations of women scientists.

To sum up, I am saying that texts have a duty to
provide material that offers a wide variety of optional roles
and behavior to both boys and girls.   I am also saying that
one can have a book with both literary quality and accurate
portrayals of females.   One is impossible without the other
because without both, the book does not mirror life.   And
finally that this can be achieved without censorship.

NOTES ON CONTRIBUTORS

ARISTIDES is, in real life, Joseph Epstein, editor of The American Scholar.

BENJAMIN R. BEEDE is a librarian from the School of Law Library, Rutgers University.

FAY H. BLAKE is Reader Services Librarian at California State Polytechnic University Library, Pomona, California.

ANNE E. BRUGH is a librarian at Douglass College Library, Rutgers University, New Jersey.

ERIC CLOUGH is the former librarian of the Southampton Public Library, England, and a Past President of The Library Association (London).

JOYCE M. CROOKS is head of the reference department of the John F. Kennedy Library, Solano County Library System, Vallejo, California.

RICHARD DE GENNARO is the director of libraries at the University of Pennsylvania.

STANLEY ELMAN is chief librarian of the Lockheed-California Company in Burbank, California.

WALTER J. FRASER is an assistant professor at the Graduate School of Library Service, Rutgers University.

LEONARD H. FREISER is the director of Libraries and Instructional Media and of the Graduate Program in Library Science and Instructional Media at National College of Education in Evanston and Chicago, Illinois.

DORIS GARTON is a librarian in the Idalou public schools, Idalou, Texas.

BIRGITTE GOLDBERG is a librarian in Copenhagen.

DANIEL GORE is the director of the Macalester College Library, St. Paul, Minnesota.

ROBERT HAUPTMAN is a graduate assistant at the School of Library and Information Science, State University of New York at Albany.

ROBERT F. HOGAN is the Executive Secretary of the National Council of Teachers of English, Urbana, Illinois.

JANE IRBY is a librarian at the San Mateo Public Library, San Mateo, California.

LINDA JEWETT is a reference librarian at the Business Library, Metropolitan Toronto Library Board. During 1974 she was assistant director of the Access to the Law Study at the University of Toronto.

GRAHAM JONES is a lecturer in the Department of Librarianship, Strathclyde University, Glasgow.

STEPHEN JUDY is the editor of the English Journal and a professor of English at Michigan State University.

I. M. KLEMPNER is a professor at the School of Library and Information Science, State University of New York at Albany.

GIRJA KUMAR is a librarian at the Jawaharlal Nehru University Library in New Delhi, India.

DONNARAE MacCANN, a former children's librarian and lecturer on children's literature at UCLA and the University of Kansas, is a free lance consultant and a writer of children's books.

FRITZ MACHLUP is a professor of economics at New York University.

MARY McKENNEY is a writer and editor for Booklegger.

S. MICHAEL MALINCONICO is assistant chief of the Systems Analysis and Data Processing Office of the New York Public Library.

NORMA FOX MAZER is the author of I, Trissy and A Figure of Speech.

SANDY MULLAY is assistant librarian of the Royal Society of Edinburgh.

JODY NEWMYER is a circulation librarian at Eastern Connecticut State College.

MAJOR R. OWENS is the associate director of the Community Media Librarian Program, School of Library Service, Columbia University.

MARION T. REID is the head of the Order Department of the Louisiana State University library.

RICHARD SELTZER is the owner of the B & R Samizdat Express, West Roxbury, Mass.

JUDITH SEREBNICK, now a doctoral student at Rutgers, is the former Library Journal book review editor.

NANCY WARD is active in the Education Task-force of the National Organization for Women.